THE
SHORT STORY
CYCLE

THE SHORT STORY CYCLE

A Genre Companion and Reference Guide

Susan Garland Mann

GREENWOOD PRESS

New York • Westport, Connecticut • London

Library of Congress Cataloging-in-Publication Data

Mann, Susan Garland.
    The short story cycle : a genre companion and reference guide /
Susan Garland Mann.
        p.   cm.
    Bibliography: p.
    Includes index.
    ISBN 0–313–25081–2 (lib. bdg. : alk. paper)
    1. Short stories, American—History and criticism.   2. American
fiction—20th century—History and criticism.   3. Cycles
(Literature).   4. Cycles (Literature)—Bibliography.   5. Short
story—Bibliography.   I. Title.
PS374.S5M36   1989
813'.01'09—dc 19   88–18685

British Library Cataloguing in Publication Data is available.

Library of Congress Catalog Card Number: 88–18685
ISBN: 0–313–25081–2

First published in 1989

Greenwood Press, Inc.
88 Post Road West, Westport, Connecticut 06881

Printed in the United States of America

The paper used in this book complies with the
Permanent Paper Standard issued by the National
Information Standards Organization (Z39.48-1984).

10   9   8   7   6   5   4   3   2   1

Contents

Preface   ix

Introduction: The Development of a Genre and Its Characteristics   1

Part I: The Representative Cycles   **23**

    1.   James Joyce's *Dubliners*   25

    2.   Sherwood Anderson's *Winesburg, Ohio*   49

    3.   Ernest Hemingway's *In Our Time*   71

    4.   John Steinbeck's *The Pastures of Heaven*   93

    5.   William Faulkner's *The Unvanquished*   107

    6.   William Faulkner's *Go Down, Moses*   121

    7.   Eudora Welty's *The Golden Apples*   141

    8.   Flannery O'Connor's *Everything That Rises Must
        Converge*   155

    9.   John Updike's *Too Far to Go: The Maples Stories*   173

**Part II: The Twentieth-Century Short Story Cycle: An
       Annotated Listing**   **185**

Twentieth-Century Short Story Cycles   187

Index   209

Preface

RATIONALE, SCOPE, AND ORGANIZATION

When Ernest Hemingway's *In Our Time* was first reviewed (1924–27), many critics recognized that the book was unusual. It was somehow different from a novel and from most other short story collections. Edmund Wilson, especially impressed by the interchapters, insisted that ''in the dry compressed little vignettes of *In Our Time* [Hemingway] has almost invented a form of his own.'' A reviewer for the *Times Literary Supplement* announced that ''the short stories in the volume . . . achieve their effect by novel and rather puzzling means.'' And D. H. Lawrence, reviewing for *Calendar of Modern Letters*, argues that ''*In Our Time* calls itself a book of stories, but it isn't that. It is a series of successive sketches from a man's life, and makes a fragmentary novel.''

Critical studies through the thirties, forties, and fifties made it increasingly clear that books such as James Joyce's *Dubliners*, Sherwood Anderson's *Winesburg, Ohio*, and *In Our Time* are intricately and powerfully unified. As a result of this recognition, critics became more concerned with generic labels. This is especially true because the first book-length critical studies devoted to these authors were published during this period and established comparisons between these works and the rest of the author's canon. Critics often found it convenient to discuss unified short story collections as ''episodic'' or ''apprenticeship'' or ''fragmentary'' novels, labels which helped them trace the development of the novelist but which clearly condemned books like *Dubliners* or *In Our Time* to a probationary status.

During the thirties through the fifties, some critics suggested that books such as *Dubliners* or *In Our Time* were neither novels nor short story miscellanies. These comments were never developed. For example, Malcolm Cowley noted in a 1949 review of Faulkner's *Knight's Gambit* that it is ''something more than a mere collection. It belongs to a genre that Faulkner has made peculiarly his

own by the artistic success of such earlier volumes as *The Unvanquished* and
Go Down, Moses.'' It was not until the seventies that critics began to offer
systematic descriptions of this distinct genre, defined as different from both the
short story and the novel but taking advantage of the conventions associated
with each. Two studies were influential: Forrest L. Ingram's *Representative Short
Story Cycles of the Twentieth Century: Studies in a Literary Genre* (1971) and
Joanne V. Creighton's *William Faulkner's Craft of Revision* (1977), developed
from her dissertation, ''*Dubliners* and *Go Down, Moses*: The Short Story Composite.''

The books by Ingram and Creighton have encouraged further work. Although
much of it remains inaccessible in unpublished dissertations, there are exceptions.[1] There have been at least twenty source studies trying to establish the
extent to which one cycle has influenced another; and some of these—for example, Martha Mulroy Curry's work on *Winesburg, Ohio* and *Dubliners*—take
advantage of Ingram's distinctions.[2] Numerous other critics have found that
Ingram's terminology and incipient genre theory help them describe individual
cycles. For example, Warren French's revised edition of *John Steinbeck*
(Twayne) demonstrates Ingram's influence: in the chapter ''Naturalism—The
Story Cycles,'' French emphasizes that the form of *The Pastures of Heaven*
underlines its experimental quality as Steinbeck's first naturalistic work. Ingram
has influenced other critics, among them Joseph Fontenrose, in his book-length
study of *The Pastures of Heaven*; Gerald Gillespie, in his ''Barth's 'Lost in the
Funhouse': Short Story Text in Its Cyclical Context''; and Craig Hansen Werner,
in his analysis of post-*Dubliners* cycles. This is not to mention the recent inclusion
of the term ''short story cycle'' in several handbooks to literature. For example,
Ian Reid's *The Short Story* (in Methuen's Critical Idiom series) devotes a brief
chapter to the short story cycle, stressing that it is a distinct genre.

For the last ten to fifteen years, book reviewers have started to demonstrate
some familiarity with the concept of the unified short story collection. Perhaps
this is because so many contemporary fiction writers have experimented with
the form, including major figures such as John Barth, Robert Coover, Mavis
Gallant, William H. Gass, Bernard Malamud, Joyce Carol Oates, and John
Updike. Even if reviewers do not always use the term ''short story cycle,'' they
are often quick to notice and evaluate the kinds of reverberations that connect
the stories. Recent comments in the *New York Times Book Review* illustrate the
point. Tom LeClair, reviewing a book by Steve Barthelme, notes: ''With its
unity of situation, *And He Tells the Little Horse the Whole Story* is more than
the usual collection. . . . Small in themselves (the longest is fourteen pages), the
stories grow in reference and resonance through Mr. Barthelme's considered
arrangement.'' Robert Atwan speaks with confidence about unifying theme in
Nancy Potter's *Legacies*, a collection of fourteen stories. Recent reviews of
books by Joyce Carol Oates (*Last Days: Stories*), Jessica Anderson (*Stories from
the Warm Zone and Sydney Stories*), and Elizabeth Tallent (*Time with Children*)
emphasize that the volumes are subdivided into a series of stories devoted to

related topics or characters. Even criticisms are often based on the extent to which the volume is or is not successfully unified. In her review of *Come to Africa and Save Your Marriage*, Barbara Thompson faults the conclusion as "oddly positive" given the attention the stories pay to "the loss of contact with our own souls, which for Maria Thomas is exemplified by the loss of the bone-deep unifying wisdoms of the traditional African culture."[3]

In spite of the fact that many readers are becoming increasingly familiar with the form of the short story cycle, no theoretical work has been done on the genre in the past ten years. This book extends earlier comments by Ingram and Creighton, among others, and attempts to encourage further discussion. While it is not the comprehensive theoretical study of the genre that deserves to be written, this study breaks ground for such work, primarily by providing detailed analyses of unifying forms in nine "representative" short story cycles and by including an annotated listing of over one hundred and twenty cycles, many of them by contemporary authors. In addition, the Introduction includes a brief history of the genre and its related forms as well as a discussion of conventions associated with the short story cycle.

The Representative Cycles: Selection Principle

The chapters that follow are devoted to short story cycles by James Joyce, Sherwood Anderson, Ernest Hemingway, John Steinbeck, William Faulkner, Flannery O'Connor, Eudora Welty, and John Updike. These were chosen because they are generally well known to a diverse audience. They also represent the variety that exists among cycles: some are more obviously or explicitly unified than others. To explain, I will borrow Ingram's concept of the short story cycle "spectrum." According to his metaphor, Faulkner's *The Unvanquished* and Updike's *Too Far To Go* are characteristic of books at one end of the spectrum, containing stories explicitly unified by chronology, plot, and character and, at least in some ways, closely resembling a novel. Joyce's *Dubliners*, Faulkner's *Go Down, Moses*, and O'Connor's *Everything That Rises Must Converge* represent books found at the other end of the spectrum; implicitly unified, they may initially be mistaken for short story miscellanies. The other books, Steinbeck's *The Pastures of Heaven*, Anderson's *Winesburg, Ohio*, Hemingway's *In Our Time*, and Welty's *The Golden Apples*, typify works found more or less in the center: they contain enough explicit connections (such as continuing characters) so that they are seldom labeled miscellanies, but lack the unity of action generally associated with the novel.

The Chapters on the Representative Cycles

The chapters on the representative cycles describe the composition process—for example, the order in which the stories were written and the extent to which they were revised—as well as the ways in which the stories work together to form a larger whole. I will preview here only what is accomplished in the second or more important division, the analysis of unifying patterns.

The unifying patterns that critics emphasize while discussing these short story cycles are generally similar to those found in other kinds of fiction—the novel, novella, and short story: repeated and developed characters, themes or ideas, imagery, myth, setting, plot or chronological order, and point of view. Some differences, however, are noteworthy. As far as character is concerned, there is much less emphasis on a protagonist in the short story cycle than is generally the case in other fiction. Bert Munroe could certainly not be described as the protagonist in *The Pastures of Heaven* even though he appears in more stories than anyone else; neither could any of the MacLains or Raineys in *The Golden Apples*. Furthermore, there are critics who doubt that Nick Adams (*In Our Time*), George Willard (*Winesburg, Ohio*), and Isaac McCaslin (*Go Down, Moses*) function as protagonists in their respective books. While there are cycles unified by a single protagonist, there are just as many—and probably more—that contain a series of different protagonists or an evolving prototype (for example, a prototypical Dubliner or Southerner).

Another difference is that there is considerably less emphasis in unified short story collections on plot or chronology, at least as these terms are usually defined. While the traditional novel contains action that continues from chapter to chapter—"the continuous, multiple 'action' which is the novel" (Ingram 131)— this is less true of unified short story collections. In *Dubliners*, for example, there is a kind of chronology, as the protagonists in each of the four divisions of the book are generally older than those features in the previous group of stories, but there is no continuing action that connects any of the stories. There is also no continuing plot connecting most of the stories in *Winesburg, Ohio*, *In Our Time*, *The Pastures of Heaven*, *Go Down, Moses*, *Everything That Rises Must Converge*, and *The Golden Apples*.

Further differences exist between these works and other kinds of fiction— differences in their forms, in the ways in which they are unified, and in the ways they generate meaning. These are described further in the Introduction.

The Bibliographies

Different from author bibliographies currently available (although frequently out-of-date), the bibliographies appended to the chapters generally omit explications of single stories. They are limited to those secondary materials (ordinarily criticism) that discuss how the stories are interconnected or that attempt to deal with the question of genre.

About the kinds of materials included, several additional points need to be made. Because it is extremely important to try to reconstruct the author's intentions and the composition process, biographical and autobiographical materials are included in the bibliographies and often discussed in the chapters. In addition, since a significant part of the work done on these cycles is found in unpublished dissertations, I have made an effort to read many of these dissertations and provide annotations for them, realizing how few people have access to them. Some of the foreign language criticism is also annotated.

There are only a few things that someone using the bibliographies would need to know from the outset. To begin with, the cutoff date for all the bibliographies is 1987, although a few items from 1988 are added. Some major items (such as Phillip Herring's *Joyce's Uncertainty Principle*) were obtained too late to incorporate into the chapters, even though they were added to the bibliographies.

In bibliographies and in chapter notes, I have followed the format in *The MLA Style Manual* (New York: MLA, 1985). Abbreviations for periodicals are based on the acronyms currently used by the MLA. If a dissertation has been published, there is no separate entry for the dissertation.

The Annotated Listing of Twentieth-Century Short Story Cycles

As mentioned earlier, the story cycle listing contains over one hundred and twenty entries. The annotation for each entry describes the ways in which the stories are connected. While many other works could have been included in the listing, these examples have been more than sufficient to help me define the field, at least so far as English-language cycles in the twentieth century are concerned. Although most are American, there are also some British, Canadian, and Australian cycles, as well as important examples (generally available in translation) from Italy, France, Germany, the Soviet Union, Poland, and South America.

ACKNOWLEDGMENTS

Completion of this book would not have been possible without the help of others. I am indebted to Sterling Library at Yale and the Humanities Research Center at the University of Texas at Austin for allowing me to examine book and manuscript materials. While living in Luxembourg (1985–1987) I very much appreciated the full access I was given to libraries at the University of London and Cambridge University. Miami University's Interlibrary Loan Department, headed by Sarah Barr, provided additional materials.

At Greenwood Press, I have been blessed with perceptive and patient editors, including Marilyn Brownstein (humanities editor), Barbara Goodhouse (copy editor), and David L. Young (production editor).

I have also benefitted, as the following pages demonstrate, by the work others have done on the short story and the short story cycle. Joanne V. Creighton, Forrest L. Ingram, Susan Lohafer, Charles E. May, and Ian Reid stand out as the most enduring influences.

I am most grateful to those people who encouraged my work in various ways, especially Alice Fox, Judith Fryer, Charles W. Garland, Mary M. Garland,

William J. Gracie, Jr., Robert C. Johnson, and Stanford L. Luce. To the late Richard S. Donnell, Jr., who read the first five chapters and made numerous excellent suggestions, I am more indebted than I can express.

Perhaps my husband, David D. Mann, already understands the extent to which I appreciate his encouragement and help. In addition to proofreading the entire manuscript, he also compiled the index. Even more useful, he has encouraged me to concentrate on important things when the insignificant threatened to overwhelm. For these reasons and still others, this book is dedicated to David.

NOTES

1. For example, Raymond Joel Silverman and Harlan Harbour Winn III both wrote dissertations that attempt to pick up where Creighton's and Ingram's work left off and succeed in doing so, at least so far as describing unifying patterns. For other dissertations dealing with short story cycles or framed cycles, see Dallas Marion Lemmon and Stephen L. Sniderman in the Works Cited section of the Preface; also see Keith Carabine and Pleasant Larus Reed III (as well as Silverman) in the Works Cited section of the Introduction.

2. For instance, there are at least seven essays on the influence of George Moore's *Untilled Field* on Joyce's *Dubliners* (in the *Dubliners* bibliography, see Beckson, Carens, Gandolfo, John Raymond Hart, Kennedy, Marcus, and West).

3. The review of Barthelme's *And He Tells the Little Horse* appeared in the *NYTBR* 20 Dec. 1987: 8; the review of Maria Thomas's *Come to Africa* appeared 11 Oct. 1987: 11–12. With the exception of Oates's *Last Days* (*NYTBR* 5 Aug. 1984), the other books were reviewed in the *NYTBR* between July 1987 and February 1988.

WORKS CITED

Cowley, Malcolm. "Faulkner Stories, in Amiable Mood." Rev. of *Knight's Gambit*, by William Faulkner. *New York Herald Tribune Books* 6 Nov. 1949: 7.

Creighton, Joanne V. "*Dubliners* and *Go Down, Moses*: The Short Story Composite." Diss. U of Michigan, 1969. *DAI* 31 (1970): 1792A–93A.

———. *William Faulkner's Craft of Revision: The Snopes Trilogy, "The Unvanquished," and "Go Down, Moses."* Detroit: Wayne State UP, 1977.

Curry, Martha Mulroy. "Anderson and Joyce: *Winesburg, Ohio* and *Dubliners*." *AL* 52 (May 1980): 236–49.

Fontenrose, Joseph. *Steinbeck's Unhappy Valley: A Study of* The Pastures of Heaven. Berkeley, CA: Albany, 1981.

French, Warren. "Naturalism—The Story Cycles." *John Steinbeck*. 2nd ed. Boston: Twayne, 1975. 54–75.

Gillespie, Gerald. "Barth's 'Lost in the Funhouse': Short Story Text in Its Cyclic Context." *SSF* 12 (Summer 1975): 223–30.

Ingram, Forrest L. *Representative Short Story Cycles of the Twentieth Century: Studies in a Literary Genre*. The Hague: Mouton, 1971.

Lawrence D. H. Rev. of *In Our Time*, by Ernest Hemingway. *Calendar of Modern Letters* 4 (Apr. 1927): 72–73. Rpt. in *Phoenix: The Posthumous Papers of D. H. Lawrence*. Ed. Edward D. McDonald. London: Heinemann, 1936. 365; and in

Hemingway: A Collection of Critical Essays. Ed. Robert P. Weeks. Englewood Cliffs, NJ: Prentice, 1962. 93–94.

Lemmon, Dallas Marion, Jr. "The Rovelle, or the Novel of Interrelated Stories: M. Lermontov, G. Keller, S. Anderson." Diss. Indiana U, 1970. *DAI* 31 (1971): 3510A.

As defined by Lemmon, the rovelle is "a novel or near-novel composed of short tales or stories—a series of stories so interrelated and intertwined that their cumulative effects are novelistic" (1). The term "rovelle" is coined from *roman*, or novel, and from the Italian *novelle*, the plural of *novella* or short story or tale. Its only defining characteristics are that the parts are both self-sufficient and interdependent and that each part contributes to the whole.

Reid, Ian. *The Short Story*. The Critical Idiom 37. London: Methuen, 1977.

Rev. of *In Our Time*, by Ernest Hemingway. *TLS* 4 Nov. 1926: 766.

Sniderman, Stephen Lee. "The 'Composite' in Twentieth-Century American Literature." Diss. U of Wisconsin, 1970. *DAI* 31 (1970): 403A.

The composite, as it is defined by Sniderman, has three major characteristics: (1) it contains parts that can be read and understood separately; (2) it includes at least one character who is explicitly mentioned in two or more of the parts; and (3) when the parts are read together, it creates a new context, forcing the reader to reevaluate his original response to the isolated parts. In addition, there are two kinds of composites, ones that focus on the individual and ones that focus primarily on time and place.

Werner, Craig Hansen. "Dublin(er)'s Joyce: Ernest Gaines, Flannery O'Connor, Russell Banks." *Paradoxical Resolutions: American Fiction since James Joyce*. Urbana: U of Illinois P, 1982. 34–50.

Wilson, Edmund. "Mr. Hemingway's Dry-Points." Rev. of *Three Stories and Ten Poems* and *In Our Time*, by Ernest Hemingway. *The Dial* 77 (Oct. 1924): 340–41. Rpt. in *Hemingway and His Critics: An International Anthology*. Ed. Carlos Baker. New York: Hill and Wang, 1961. 55–60; and in *Ernest Hemingway: Five Decades of Criticism*. Ed. Linda Welshimer Wagner. East Lansing: Michigan State UP, 1974. 222–23.

Winn, Harlan Harbour, III. "Short Story Cycles of Hemingway, Steinbeck, Faulkner, and O'Connor." Diss. U of Oregon, 1975. *DAI* 36 (1976): 4500A.

Winn uses the theory and terminology Forrest Ingram develops in *Representative Short Story Cycles* (see above). He also explains in some detail why he prefers the label "short story cycle" to "rovelle," "short-story compound," or "short story composite."

THE
SHORT STORY
CYCLE

Introduction: The Development of a Genre and Its Characteristics

A BRIEF HISTORY OF THE SHORT STORY CYCLE AND RELATED FORMS

As long as stories have been told, there have been storytellers who combined tales to create larger effects. As Ian Reid, in his book on the short story, argues, "Probably the impulse to combine individual tales into larger wholes has its origin in the very nature of imagination itself, a 'coadunating' power as Coleridge described it. Certainly many old story-clusters show that the impulse goes far back into oral tradition . . . '' (46). *The Odyssey* and *The Iliad*, for example, were originally composed of individual stories sung by different bards and passed on orally from one generation to another.

Throughout the history of literature there are cycles or sequences of tales, stories, novellas, lyric poems, plays, and even novels. It is only human nature for writers (and readers) to want to perpetuate the single work and to resist its completion. In any historical period, many examples of different kinds of cycles coexist. Why a writer chooses one cyclical form over another—sonnet sequence, for example, instead of short story cycle—is no doubt a complex matter. Certain subjects require or take advantage of certain forms. Furthermore, historical periods provide different options for writers: for example, the short story and, consequently, the short story cycle did not develop until the nineteenth century. Finally, an individual writer's abilities, preferences, and past performances influence his or her generic choices.

No one has attempted a history of the short story cycle. While I am not attempting to provide a detailed account here, certain observations can be made about the genre's development, especially its relation to other similar forms, such as framed tales or sonnet sequences.[1] To begin with, since all genres undergo transformations, and "fixed genres" exist only in the imaginations of some critics, it is useful to speculate about the forms (such as framed tales) out of which the short story cycle has evolved. In addition, although the short story cycle has existed only since the nineteenth century, it is important to note some of the directions that the genre has taken in the twentieth century. In order to illustrate its vitality and range—specifically the ways in which its particular form generates meaning—I describe briefly several types or subgenres of the twentieth-century cycles.

To develop these points, I offer a brief historical overview. It is necessarily superficial, given its length, but it is my hope that it will encourage more rigorous accounts.

Fifteenth- through Eighteenth-Century Literature

Middle English

In Middle-English literature, several forms prefigure the development of the short story cycle. Although framed tales date back at least as far as the *Panchatantra* (compiled before A.D. 500) and Ovid's *Metamorphoses*,[2] the first framed tales that had a decided effect on English literature occurred in the Middle Ages. Boccaccio's *The Decameron*, which "dwarfed all previous efforts in the idiom" (Clements and Gibaldi 40), influenced countless subsequent works, including Chaucer's *The Canterbury Tales*. These books are generally labeled "framed tales" or "framed miscellany" or *Rahmenerzahlung*. In most of them, the prologue brings a variety of characters (for example, pilgrims or people escaping the plague) together, and the reader is informed that these people will tell one another tales in order to pass the time. (A variation, of course, is the *Thousand and One Nights* situation, where Scheherazade tells a series of tales in order to save her life.) In every case, however, it is the framing device (the prologue, epilogue, or transitional paragraphs between stories) that is primarily responsible for the book's unity. In exceptional cases, such as with *The Decameron* and *The Canterbury Tales*, the stories may be connected by more than the frame, but this is not generally the situation.[3] Usually there is no connection between the people introduced at the beginning of the book and the tales that follow. Therefore, the frame serves to connect otherwise unrelated tales, much as introductions are used in some contemporary short fiction anthologies to justify the publications of obviously diverse material such as "stories of the sixties" or "stories of the American Southwest."

The epic cycle is another Middle-English genre that attempts to connect self-contained tales. Sir Thomas Malory's *Le Morte D'Arthur* is probably the best example. Unified principally by Arthurian myth, *Le Morte D'Arthur* is divided into eight distinct books. With the exception of the section on the Holy Grail, each of the books is devoted to the adventure of a particular knight ("A Noble Tale of Sir Launcelot du Lake" or "The Most Piteous Tale of the Morte Arthur Saunz Guerdon"). As is the case with *The Decameron* and *The Canterbury Tales*, the parts of *Le Morte D'Arthur* are based on various sources (generally, the thirteenth-century French romances) that have been reworked so extensively that a new creation results. The chief difference between Malory's *Le Morte* and his sources, Eugène Vinaver explains, is the extent to which Malory establishes the parts of the Arthurian myth as independent narratives:

Malory's adaptation . . . was far from possessing or even attempting the unity which is claimed for it by the critics. He never tried to reduce his French romances to 'one story'; the method he used was both more subtle and more drastic. With great consistency, though with varying degrees of success, he endeavoured to break up the complex structure of his sources and replace their slowly unfolding canvas of recurrent themes by a series of self-contained stories. (vii–viii)

The Mystery plays, popular from the thirteenth to the sixteenth century, initiated cyclical drama in England. Many of them were lost, but the Corpus Christi plays that survived (the York, Wakefield, Coventry, and Chester cycles) demonstrate the manner in which these cycles enacted key events from the Bible. Their unity, then, follows the plan of the Bible: the separate episodes are linked through divine intention.

Renaissance

During the Renaissance, Boccaccio's *The Decameron* influenced writers in many countries. Although framed tales were more popular in other parts of Europe, examples can be cited in England. Robert Greene, for instance, enframed three tales devoted to the sins of pride, lust, and gluttony in his *Farewell to Folly* (1591). Of those forms related to the short story cycle, the sonnet cycle or sequence was most important in England during the Renaissance, especially during the last decades of the sixteenth century and the first of the seventeenth. These sequences are connected by subject—generally, the progress of a courtship—and often also by action, character, imagery, and tone. Major examples include Sir Philip Sidney's *Astrophel and Stella* (1591), Samuel Daniel's *Delia* (1592), Edmund Spenser's *Amoretti* (1595), William Shakespeare's *Sonnets* (1609), and Michael Drayton's *Idea* (1619). Given the size of its parts, the sonnet cycle allows subtle and extremely detailed connections that may involve a single word or sound.

Popular also at approximately the same time were historical or chronicle plays, often including events from a single king's reign. As is the case with the Mystery plays, the chronicle's scope often necessitated a series of linked plays, such as Shakespeare's three parts of *Henry the Sixth* or his two parts of *Henry IV* and *Henry V*. Although consisting of independent and connected works, these plays differ from sonnet cycles in a fairly obvious way: the connections among such large works (entire plays) must be broader given the amount of reading (or viewing) time demanded for each work. Furthermore, except in unusual cases, they are not generally read or performed one after the other.

Restoration and Eighteenth Century

While there were fewer examples of cyclical literature in England during this period, there were novelists and dramatists who created sequels. For example, John Dryden's *Conquest of Granada* (produced 1670, 1671) has two parts, as does Aphra Behn's *The Rover* (produced 1677, 1681). Perhaps because of the period's imitative as well as argumentative nature, there were also numerous attempts to rewrite someone else's work or to pen an unauthorized sequel. Some of the characters in Colley Cibber's *Love's Last Shift* (produced 1696) are brought to life again by Sir John Vanbrugh in his *The Relapse; or, Virtue in Danger* (produced 1696). Similarly, Henry Fielding expresses his contempt for Samuel Richardson's *Pamela* (November 1740) by satirizing it in *An Apology for the Life of Mrs. Shamela Andrews* (April 1741). In fact, it is largely because of imitations and purported sequels that Richardson published *Pamela II* in December 1741. Fielding, in his first full-length novel, *Joseph Andrews* (February 1742), includes and extends several characters found in *Pamela* and *Shamela*.

There are other forms popular during the eighteenth century that are more relevant to the development of the short story cycle. Epic-length poems were often subdivided into more or less independent parts. In James Thomson's *The Seasons* (1726–1730), each of the four parts was originally published separately. William Cowper's *The Task* (1785) is divided into six books, each a meditation that evolves around a common object or event such as "The Sofa" and "The Winter Morning Walk." Joseph Addison and Richard Steele are among the few writers who produced a work prefiguring the story cycle. Although their essays in *The Spectator* (1711–1712) are only loosely connected and numerous enough to produce five volumes, they do contain a continuing cast of characters (Mr. Spectator, Sir Roger de Coverley, Sir Andrew Freeport, and so forth) and a consistent moral, social, and aesthetic perspective.

Nineteenth-Century Literature

England and Continental Europe

In nineteenth-century England, lyric and epic cycles were important, as the work of virtually any major poet demonstrates. Among them, to give just a few examples, are George Crabbe's *The Borough* (an epic consisting of twenty-four "letter" poems, 1810), Elizabeth Barrett Browning's *Sonnets from the Portuguese* (1850), George Meredith's *Modern Love* (cycle of sixteen-line poems, 1862), Robert Browning's *The Ring and the Book* (epic cycle, 1868–1869), and D. G. Rossetti's *The House of Life* (sonnet cycle, 1871–1881). The general preoccupation with poetry and longer fiction in England at this time discouraged the development of the short story. Although there are few early examples of the short story cycle in nineteenth-century England, one can point to George Eliot's *Scenes of Clerical Life* (serialized in *Blackwood's Magazine*, 1857), which contains three stories realistically depicting the lives of the clergy. The first two stories feature the parish at Shepperton, and the third continues imagery patterns (light and dark, day and night) started in the second, as David Lodge's "Introduction" to the Penguin edition notes (27–28). The Sherlock Holmes stories (serialized in *The Strand Magazine* and published as *The Adventures of Sherlock Holmes* in 1892) by Arthur Conan Doyle also are loosely connected by character, recurring plots, setting, and theme.

On the continent, there was greater enthusiasm about short fiction. In Germany during the Romantic period, there was interest in the *novelle* (short fiction) and *kunstmarchen* ("art" tales about the supernatural, which were often published together). Collections of supernatural tales written during this time are generally unified by a framing device that introduces or justifies the fantastic material that follows. In E.T.A. Hoffmann's *Die Serapionsbrüder* (1819–1821), for instance, the framing device explains that the narratives that follow are highly imaginative private visions.[4] In France, "the art of the short story was firmly established in 1829–1831, with the magazine publication of a dozen *contes* by Mérimée, Balzac, and Gautier . . . " (Reid 23–24). An early French short story cycle, Alphonse Daudet's *Lettres de Mon Moulin* (1869), uses a framing device ("Foreword" and the first story) as well as internal cross-references to connect his reflections about life in Provence.

One should not forget the crucially important developments in the short story in Russia at this time. Writers such as Alexander Pushkin and Nikolai Vasilevich Gogol produced not only masterpieces of short fiction, but also story cycles, some of which would become well known and respected among English-language readers. Ivan Turgenev's short story cycle, *A Sportsman's Sketches* or *Annals of a Sportsman* (1847–1851), for example, influenced some of the most important cycles written during the beginning of the twentieth century, including George Moore's *The Untilled Field* (1903), Sherwood Anderson's *Winesburg, Ohio* (1919), and Hemingway's *In Our Time* (1925). Other major nineteenth-century Russian cycles include Pushkin's *The Tales of Belkin* (1831), Gogol's *Evenings on a Farm near Dikanka* (1831–32), and Mikhail Yurevich Lermontov's *A Hero of Our Time* (1840). All include a "frame provided by a character who claims to be the author" (Carabine 245).

United States

Whether in Europe, Russia, or the United States, the nineteenth-century development of the short story cycle represents what Alastair Fowler identifies as "the first phase" of several that genres may undergo.

It turns out that genre proper develops through at least three principal phases. These are organic and invariable in sequence, though development need not go beyond the first or second. During the first phase, the genre-complex assembles, until a formal type emerges. ("Life and Death" 212)

Our ability to understand this first phase of the cycle is obviously complicated by the fact that the short story itself is establishing its own generic identity at approximately the same time. In fact, some critics are reluctant to identify any of the short fiction written during the first half of the nineteenth century as "short stories."[5]

Perhaps, however, given the transformations that occur in subsequent generations of the short story—described, for example, as the local color story, the lyric story, the initiation story, the satiric story—critics should be exceedingly flexible in their definitions of the term "short story." Although the term is described in more detail in the second half of the Introduction, I should emphasize here that I consider many works of short fiction written during the first half of the nineteenth century as "short stories." While they may differ substantially from subsequent generations of the genre, I identify them as "short stories" if they are an appropriate size (shorter than novels and generally longer than a few pages), if they contain some kind of development (physical or psychological) or revelation, and if they create a sense of closure.

Given this description of the genre, it is impossible not to label most of the short fiction by Washington Irving, Edgar Allan Poe, Nathaniel Hawthorne, and Herman Melville as early "short stories," even though the term was not introduced until the 1880s. As was the case in England and in Europe, the development of the short story and story cycles in nineteenth-century America is closely linked to the increasing popularity of periodicals featuring short fiction. Although publishers were not generally interested in a volume of stories by a single author, periodicals or gift books would often introduce the general public to a variety of stories written by one person.[6]

When writers were fortunate enough to have a book of their stories published, their organizational plans were often disregarded by editors. According to Pleasant Larus Reed III, Poe's *Tales* of 1845 does not faithfully represent the author's intentions, since the stories selected were chosen by an editor. Similarly, although he designed three "coherent sequences" of stories, the only cycle that Hawthorne succeeded in publishing was the framed "Legends of the Province House"; and this was not published separately, as he had intended, but placed at the end of the expanded *Twice-Told Tales* of 1842 (11–16).

In spite of publishing difficulties, short story cycles were written by many mid-nineteenth-century American writers. As was the case in Europe and Russia, early examples of the genre in the United States demonstrate the influence of framed tales. One could, with historical accuracy, describe them as a generic mixture or hybrid of framed tales and short stories. Framing devices are used in Poe's *Tales of the Grotesque and Arabesque* (1840), Hawthorne's "Legends of the Province House," and Melville's *Piazza Tales* (1856); and, in all of them, the frames attempt to transport the reader from the present ("real world") to the past (fiction).

As one moves through the second half of the century, especially during the last two decades, the framing device grows less important. Writers appear more self-confident about the validity of the genre, thus eliminating the necessity of an explanatory preface, one of the chief functions of the frame. Furthermore, writers apparently feel less need to transport the reader from the "real world" to a fictional one. Contrasting Hamlin Garland's *Main-Travelled Roads* (1891) and Stephen Crane's *Whilomville Stories* (1900) with cycles by Poe, Hawthorne, and Melville, Reed emphasizes that

[Garland's and Crane's books] are notably different in form from the previously discussed integrated sequences. The designated *place*, as fact and metaphor, of both titles points to what was apparently the generating power for the writing of the collections' stories *and* a resulting integrative framework for those stories. There is no framing sketch or tale, no preface for "artistic justification" in either Garland or Crane. (34)

Another story cycle connected primarily by setting is Sarah Orne Jewett's *The Country of the Pointed Firs* (1896), taking place in a Maine seaport town during its declining years. In addition to setting, the use of a continuing character or protagonist made a frame less necessary. Jewett's stories introduce a narrator, and her perceptions of the town provide the book's central focus. Similarly, Crane's *Whilomville* features a protagonist (Jimmie Trescott) who is transformed in the chronological sequence of stories, covering roughly a two-year period.

Twentieth-Century Literature

Although Sherwood Anderson believed that he invented the "Winesburg form" ("It is a form in which I feel at ease. I invented it. It was mine."), he is in fact only one of several writers who made it popular in the United States during the first decades of the twentieth century.[7] Many writers were working with the genre at the beginning of this century, as illustrated by George Moore's *Untilled Fields*, Willa Cather's *The Troll Garden* (1905), Gertrude Stein's *Three Lives* (1909), Henry James's *The Finer Grain* (1910), Edith Wharton's *Tales of Men and Ghosts* (1910), and Joyce's *Dubliners* (written earlier but published in 1914). Also, in the 1920s Jean Toomer published *Cane* (1923); Hemingway, *In Our Time* (1925); and Thornton Wilder, *The Bridge of San Luis Rey* (1927). Although these writers were doubtless influenced by a variety of genres (serial novels, local color stories and novels, imagistic poetry) and even art forms (such as Cubism in painting), many of them were also working within the tradition of the short story cycle. Sherwood Anderson read Turgenev in 1911 and emphasized that he "felt a brotherhood . . . in particular with Turgenev in his *Annals of a Sportsman*" (Carabine ix). Hemingway's admiration for Turgenev is well known and, according to F. Scott Fitzgerald, Hemingway claimed that *Winesburg, Ohio* was his "first pattern."[8] Jean Toomer corresponded with Anderson in 1922 and later claimed that he "could not have matured as an artist without having read *Winesburg, Ohio*."[9] As Fowler defines the second phase of any genre, this is a time of "sophisticated imitation, in the Renaissance sense, varying its themes and motifs, perhaps adapting it to slightly different purposes, but retaining all its main features, including those of formal structure'' (''Life and Death'' 212).

Magazines such as *McClure's*, *Scribner's*, *Ladies' Home Journal*, *Smart Set*, *Collier's*, *Harper's*, *The Dial*, *The Masses*, and *The Saturday Evening Post* encouraged the popularity of stories and story cycles in the first half of this century. Many of the stories in *Winesburg, Ohio* and *In Our Time* as well as Faulkner's *The Unvanquished* and *Go Down, Moses* were first published in such magazines. Periodicals were also frequently interested in stories by the same author dealing with a single character (or group of characters), setting, or topic. As Forrest Ingram summarizes Malcolm Cowley's assessment of the situation: ''Writers of genius . . . realized the fuller possibilities of the cycle form and began conceiving their narratives to fit such a pattern. In other words, the existence of popular story-series tended to encourage in writers like Faulkner and Steinbeck that 'cyclical habit of mind' . . . '' (25).

The development of the short story cycle in the twentieth century can be outlined only briefly here, but the chapters and annotated listing that follow provide more than one hundred and twenty examples. Perhaps the best intro-duction to the genre during this period would be examples of different types or subgenres of short story cycles that are fairly common. Through these illustra-tions, I can also suggest ways in which cycles generate meaning and ways in which their form and content are interdependent.

The subgenres of the twentieth-century cycle that I identify are based on recurrent topics.[10] Although it is doubtful that there are subjects or themes or plot patterns that are better suited for the cycle than, for example, the novel, there are significant differences between the ways both genres evoke or develop meaning. Therefore, although certain kinds of material may be accommodated by a number of different forms, there are no doubt distinct advantages for using one form over another. Otherwise, why would literature offer such a wide assortment of possibilities.

With genres and subgenres, overlapping is unavoidable. Framed stories, for instance, are not distinguishable from short story cycles if the framed stories are well connected through internal means such as recurring plots, characters, and imagery. Neither are the various subgenres—say, the types of Elizabethan love sonnets—always distinct. Literary works contain many different kinds of codes, and among the most important of them are at least several different sets that are generically based. Therefore, as I discuss cycles that are predominantly about the maturation of a single protagonist, I do not exclude the possibility that a book such as Anderson's *Winesburg, Ohio* could not also be about human isolation. Some cycles clearly represent only one of these types, but this is not always the case. Furthermore, I am also not suggesting that the types that I have chosen fully describe the development of the cycle in the twentieth century. These are simply examples of the appropriateness of the short story cycle's form.

Character: Stories about the Maturation of a Protagonist

Many short story cycles seem character-dominated. Some are unified by a single protagonist, while others compare different protagonists (or an entirely different cast) as the reader moves from story to story. One of the most important subgenres involving these cycles is based on the *bildungsroman*: stories joined together to describe the development of a young person, generally from adolescence to maturity. Sherwood Anderson's *Winesburg, Ohio* is probably the most influential early example. Others include Fitzgerald's *The Basil and Josephine Stories* (written 1928–1929), featuring both a male and female protagonist and a group of stories devoted to each; Faulkner's *The Unvanquished* (1938); Steinbeck's *The Red Pony* (1945); Donald Windham's *Emblems of Conduct* (1963); Frederick Busch's *Domestic Particulars: A Family Chronicle* (1976), and Isabel Huggan's *The Elizabeth Stories* (1987).

These stories employ many but not necessarily all of the conventions associated with the *bildungsroman*. The protagonist begins as a child, and his or her development is traced to adulthood; a series of potential father or mother surrogates is presented; a series of tests and initiations is featured; romantic and sexual relations are frequently considered necessary for development but are presented as potentially damaging if they limit the protagonist's development in other areas; and a restrictive and provincial town is abandoned for a larger world. The form of the cycle is especially well suited to describe the maturation process, since it allows the writer to focus on only those people and incidents that are essential to character development. Frequently with these cycles, subordinate characters surface for only a story or two and then disappear entirely with no explanation being necessary.

When the cycle is about the maturation of an artist (*künstlerroman*), as is the case with *Winesburg, Ohio*, additional conventions are involved. There must be some indication that the protagonist possesses exceptional ability (for example, sensitivity to language) and is attempting to develop this potential. Generally there is also some adult figure (perhaps also a parent surrogate) who encourages the young artist's confidence. George Willard has his teacher, Kate Swift, who "recognized [in him] the spark of genius and wanted to blow on the spark" (*Winesburg, Ohio* 163).

In addition, those short story cycles describing the development of women may establish different priorities. In *Lives of Girls and Women* (1984) and *The Beggar Maid* (1979), for example, Alice Munro features two female protagonists: Rose (*Beggar Maid*), who is becoming an artist, and Del (*Lives*), who reveals an artistic potential. Each woman's awareness of her potential develops gradually, and it is only in the final stories of each cycle that the reader is encouraged to take this potential or demonstrated ability seriously. Much time is spent describing relationships that may encourage (or subvert) artistic ability, but the significance of these relationships is not limited to the development of the artist as a young woman. Munro's books should not be used as a model for the way women handle the *künstlerroman*, but they do underline one characteristic that such books generally share. Whether expressed in the form of the novel or the story cycle, *künstlerroman* written by women (about women) take relationships (parents, children, siblings, friends, lovers, spouses) more seriously than the more introspective versions generally written by men.

There are several other types that represent variations on the *bildungsroman*. As developed at greater length in Chapter 3, some cycles are devoted to the maturation of a "composite personality." In Hemingway's *In Our Time*, for instance, Nick Adams appears in the first five stories and irregularly after this. His presence is felt nonetheless, because other protagonists (such as Harold Krebs in "Soldier's Home") bear a close family resemblance to him. The stories are arranged so that the composite protagonist gradually grows older. This group of cycles displays the same characteristics exhibited by the first one, those describing the maturation of a single protagonist. The major difference between the two groups is that those with a composite protagonist are in a better position to generalize: as Joseph DeFalco stresses, Nick Adams "typifies his genera-tion."[11] Joanne V. Creighton makes much the same point discussing *Dubliners* and *Go Down, Moses*:

The composite [or cycle] lends itself to an exploration of the unique cultural identity shared by a group of people, whereas the novel is suited to an intensive study of an individual or a few individuals. The composite, in other words, offers a panoramic view of a setting and its people, whereas the novel's form demands limitation of focus to individuals. (154)

Other cycles unified by "composite" protagonists include James Baldwin's *Going to Meet the Man* (1965), John Updike's *Olinger Stories: A Selection* (1964), Andre Dubus's *Adultery and Other Choices* (1977), Mavis Gallant's *Home Truths: Selected Canadian Stories* (1981), and Russell Banks's *Success Stories* (1986). Brief descriptions of a few should suffice. Baldwin's stories are about what it is like to be a black person in the United States in the mid–1950s to mid–1960s. The book begins with two stories about the same young male protagonist, his family, and school; after this, various protagonists are featured, confronting the same injustices again and again. The protagonists also appear to age: while the first stories feature children, the last ones are about adults. Updike's *Olinger Stories* is tightly unified by the rural Pennsylvania setting and by striking similarities among the protagonists. As Updike explains in the book's foreword, "[The stories] have been arranged here in the order of the hero's age; in the beginning he is ten, in the middle stories he is an adolescent, in the end he has reached manhood. He wears different names and his circumstances vary, but he is at bottom the same boy, the local boy . . . " (v). In Mavis Gallant's *Home Truths*, the same female protagonist (Linnet Muir) is featured in the last six stories; although not arranged in chronological order, they trace her devel-opment from childhood to young adulthood. Some of the children and adolescents in the first stories ("At Home") also resemble Linnet. The middle stories feature Canadians who are often living abroad for the first time, and they are used to generalize what Gallant has said about Linnet and her look-alikes.

Theme: The Theme of Isolation or Fragmentation

Because cycles consist of discrete, self-sufficient stories, they are especially well suited to handle certain subjects, including the sense of isolation or fragmentation or indeterminacy that many twentieth-century characters experience.

As far as the subject of isolation is concerned, Sherwood Anderson was correct when he indicated that the form of *Winesburg, Ohio* reinforces the characters' overwhelming sense that they are estranged from one another and that meaningful contact is impossible. Describing his difficulty writing *Men and Their Women*, he says:

My theme is American men in relation to their women. . . . In getting at this theme I have decided to return to a form I used in *Winesburg, Ohio*; that is to say, taking a related group of people, their lives touching, never quite touching. . . . I find myself curiously at ease in the form. It seems to relate itself to life as I feel it.[12]

Unlike the novel, where a protagonist generally assumes the center of the stage through most of the book, there is often no protagonist in a cycle or, if there is one, his or her importance is usually restricted to a limited number of stories, as is the case with George Willard and Nick Adams. In cycles where there is a new protagonist in virtually every story and where few of them appear in more than one story—*Dubliners* and *Everything That Rises Must Converge* would be good examples—characters are physically separated from one another by the boundaries of the short story. As Silverman puts it, also describing *Winesburg, Ohio*: "In story after story, the theme of loneliness, the motif of walls between people, the lack of communication, all demand a structure which will intensify the feeling of the tremendous gulf between people. Thus, as one story ends, it stays ended" (229). Because characters such as Maria (Joyce's "Clay"), Wing Biddlebaum (Anderson's "Hands"), and Junius Maltby (Steinbeck's story VI in *The Pastures of Heaven*) exist only in the restricted world of a single story, their respective authors are able to use the form of the short story to emphasize the characters' solipsistic and isolated lives.

Among more recent story cycles, the inability of characters to connect is similarly emphasized. Some chronicle the failure of marriage from the male point of view. Reynolds Price focuses on a series of dishonest and cruel male-female relationships in *Permanent Errors* (1970). As is the case with Sherwood Anderson's *Death in the Woods* (1933), Price's stories inextricably connect the subject of love between the sexes with death. In contrast, Updike describes the twenty-year breakdown of the Maples' marriage in *Too Far to Go* (1979), but he does so ultimately to pay tribute to a relationship that continues even as a marriage is terminated. Many cycles written by women, especially in recent years, depict unsatisfactory love relationships and families. Simone de Beauvoir in *The Woman Destroyed* (trans. 1969) describes three aging women as they cope with disintegrating marriages and families. In *The Bloody Chamber* (1979) and *Black Venus* (1985), Angela Carter imaginatively retells fairy tales and creates stories about historical, legendary, and literary characters, presenting a series of sadomasochistic relations. Finally, Joyce Carol Oates dramatizes the deterioration of the family—a problem that jeopardizes even the physical safety and sanity of children (the first half of *Last Days [1984]*)—and the inability of women to deal in positive ways with their own sexuality (*The Goddess and Other Women* [1974]).[13]

Along with this sense of isolation, the lack of continuity (or the gaps that exist between stories in cycles) is used by some writers to emphasize the fragmentary nature of life, especially in the twentieth century. For instance, Philip Stevick uses *In Our Time* as an extreme example of fiction which subverts conventions associated with the novel by refusing to provide transitions between chapters:

Explicitly developed progressions between narrative units imply a great deal, one hardly realizes how much until one notes their absence: they imply a coherence within the fictive world that is physical, epistemological, and moral. Most of the coherences Hemingway did not believe in and would not counterfeit. The interchapters of *In Our Time*, in their relation to the stories that occur between them, are examples of a lack of faith in coherence made into a structural principle. (127)

Similarly, John T. Matthews argues that in *Go Down, Moses* "the degree of narrative fragmentation, the extent of the falling away of novelistic wholeness, is itself a dramatization of the fracturing power of time. Faulkner's view of history includes the momentum toward disintegration."[14] Although novels do frequently contain abrupt transitions between chapters—moving suddenly to a different point of view, time, or location—seldom if ever are the transitions between chapters in novels as demanding as those between stories in cycles. After all, the cycle's reader must leave behind the self-contained and completed world of one story before entering the next independent story.

Finally, as developed further in Chapter 6, the simultaneous independence and interdependence of the stories can contribute to the cycle's ability to maintain apparently contradictory themes or philosophies. This is because the parts of the cycle remain as important as the book's overall effect, unlike the novel, where the importance of the parts is necessarily subordinated to the whole. *Go Down, Moses*, for example, depicts multiple perspectives, comparing the myths or philosophies that enable the characters to organize their experiences but refusing to endorse one myth over the other. Ike McCaslin's asceticism is contrasted to Cass Edmonds's materialism, and Ike McCaslin's Christianity is compared to Sam Fathers's totemism. The separate stories offer the reader more than one way of perceiving reality and thereby enable the reader to experience the difficulty Ike encounters in choosing among these alternatives.

Other Types of Twentieth-Century Short Story Cycles

As emphasized above, this is only a sampling of twentieth-century short story cycles. One could go further and mention the large number of recent cycles devoted to statements about art in general, especially the difficulty of being an artist: for example, William Gass's *In the Heart of the Heart of the Country* (1968), John Barth's *Lost in the Funhouse* (1968) and *Chimera* (1972), Updike's *Bech: A Book* (1970) and *Bech is Back* (1982), Joyce Carol Oates's *The Poisoned Kiss and Other Stories from the Portuguese* (1975), Italo Calvino's *The Castle of Crossed Destinies* (trans. 1976), E. L. Doctorow's *Lives of the Poets* (1984), Angela Carter's *Black Venus* (also called *Saints and Strangers* [1985, 1986]), Primo Levi's *The Monkey's Wrench* (trans. 1986), Gordon Weaver's *The World Quite Round* (1986), and Robert Coover's *A Night at the Movies* (1987). Given the extent to which the framed tale has influenced the development of the cycle, it is not surprising that about half of these books include brief prefaces. A few of the cycles, including *Bech: A Book* and *The Poisoned Kiss*, use a preface that argues (tongue in cheek) for the historical authenticity of the work that follows. Only Calvino's *The Castle of Crossed Destinies* contains framing stories ("The Castle" and "The Tavern") that attempt to unify the tales that follow, both establishing the dramatic situation and transporting the reader from the "real" world to a fictional one. This is because Calvino wants to establish a dramatic contrast between his contemporary ideas and his archaic form and medieval setting.

Instead of examining the role of art or the artist, many cycles concentrate on a particular setting or community. As indicated earlier, cycles are often more concerned with a group than with one or two people. When the stories are also unified by a limited period of time, cycles can be devoted to evoking a historical epoch: Isaac Babel's *Red Calvary* (orig. pub. 1926; trans. 1955) describes the Polish front in 1920; John Dos Passos's *U.S.A.* (1938), 1900–early 1930s in the United States; Richard Wright's *Uncle Tom's Children* (1938), the situation of blacks in the United States before World War II; James Michener's *Tales of the South Pacific* (1947), the campaign in the Pacific; Primo Levi's *The Periodic Table* (trans. 1986) and *Moments of Reprieve* (trans. 1987), the experience of German concentration camps; and Kay Boyle's *The Smoking Mountain* (1951) as well as Mavis Gallant's *The Pegnitz Junction* (1984), Germany after the war.

Other cycles are devoted to a particular place which has mythic rather than historic importance. Often there is a sense of timelessness about such books. More than anyone else, Forrest Ingram has emphasized the symbolic use of setting in twentieth-century cycles:

The writers of today often seem intent on building mythic kingdoms of some sort. Faulkner has his Yoknapatawpha County, Steinbeck his Pastures of Heaven, Camus his kingdom of solidarity, Joyce his city of paralysis, and Anderson his Winesburg. Heroes, usually diminished in stature, roam the imaginary streets and plains of these kingdoms.(25)

Although there is no limit to the kinds of subjects or themes that are found in cycles, one repeatedly discovers that twentieth-century cycles are preoccupied with certain themes, including isolation, disintegration, indeterminacy, the role of the artist, and the maturation process. One also finds that they tend to be dominated by one particular element of fiction, whether it is character, plot, or setting. While this overview neglects to mention many cycles and to take others fully enough into account, it does suggest the kind of variety and vitality one can expect from the short story cycle.

CONVENTIONS ASSOCIATED WITH THE SHORT STORY CYCLE

Generic Signals

The first generic signal that the reader receives is a work's title. In the case of the short story cycle, the title is used to emphasize that a book is not a miscellany or a "mere" collection. It underscores a major form of unity in the book: perhaps setting, as is the case in *Winesburg, Ohio, Georgia Boy, Tales of the South Pacific*, or the *Olinger Stories*; protagonist or a group of people, as with *The Pat Hobby Stories, Mrs. Bridge*, or *Domestic Particulars: A Family Chronicle*; or an idea or thematic plot, as with *Knight's Gambit, Going to Meet the Man, Everything That Rises Must Converge, Searching for Survivors*, or *Success Stories*. Although the practice is becoming less common, collections that are not cycles have traditionally been named after a single story to which the phrase "and other stories" is appended: for example, Isaac Bashevis Singer's *Passions and Other Stories*. Generally placed first or last in the volume, the title story represents what the author feels is the best work or, in some cases, the best-known work. Titles of collections containing the words "and other stories" obviously make no claims for unity among the stories. The importance of the title as a means of communicating generic expectations is so important that William Faulkner became furious when Random House took the initiative to change the title of *Go Down, Moses* to *Go Down, Moses And Other Stories*. When the book was reissued in 1949, Faulkner made sure that the subtitle ("And Other Stories") was permanently deleted.[15]

In addition to the title, other material may immediately influence a reader's expectations. Often the blurb on the dust jacket encourages the reader to expect connected stories. For example, the inside cover of Updike's *Trust Me* (1987) begins with this sentence: "The theme of trust, betrayed or fulfilled, runs through Mr. Updike's new collection of short stories. . . ."[16] At times, the author (or editor) may include a note or preface at the beginning of the book, informing the reader that the stories work together: "This book differs . . . from most volumes of short fiction. . . . it's neither a collection nor a selection, but a series; though several of its items have appeared separately in periodicals, the series will be seen to have been meant to be received 'all at once' and as here arranged" (Barth's *Lost in the Funhouse*: ix).

Often it is the table of contents that does the most to establish generic expectations. Most cycles distinguish themselves from modern novels by listing the names of the stories in the tables of contents. Only in very rare cases, such as with Steinbeck's *The Pastures of Heaven*, are the stories unnamed but numbered. In the table of contents, subdivisions are also occasionally used to emphasize thematic groupings: for example, the world of Italo Calvino's *Mr. Palomar* is divided into categories such as "Palomar on the beach" and "Palomar does the shopping," and three stories are included in each of these groups. At times, other prefatory matter is included to stress organizational plans. In Eudora Welty's *The Golden Apples* the major families in Morgana are listed, and in *Winesburg, Ohio* a much simplified map of the town precedes the first story. Also, epigraphs or brief quotations frequently appear at the beginning of the cycle to emphasize key ideas. For instance, Gordon Weaver (*A World Quite Round*) uses lines from Wallace Stevens; Primo Levi (*The Periodic Table*), a Yiddish proverb; and Bernard Malamud (*Pictures of Fidelman*), brief passages from Rilke and Yeats as well as a quotation from the book's protagonist, A. Fidelman, correcting Yeats's assumption that we must choose between the "Perfection of the life, or of the work."

Essential Characteristic: Simultaneous Self-Sufficiency and Interdependence

While there are various conventions associated with the genre, including those formal features just described, there is only one essential characteristic of the short story cycle: the stories are both self-sufficient and interrelated. On the one hand, the stories work independently of one another: the reader is capable of understanding each of them without going beyond the limits of the individual story. On the other hand, however, the stories work together, creating something that could not be achieved in a single story. For example, the pervasive and overwhelming sense of paralysis in *Dubliners* is established only by the series of different examples, including characters such as Eveline in the story by the same name, Mr. Doran in "The Boarding House," Little Chandler in "A Little Cloud," Maria in "Clay," and Mr. Duffy in "A Painful Case." The ability of the story cycle to extend discussions—to work on a larger scale—resembles what is accomplished in the novel. But the forms of the cycle and novel are significantly different: only the first is constructed from independent stories.

Anyone familiar with cycles such as *Dubliners* or *Winesburg, Ohio* should have an idea of what I am talking about, but the concept of simultaneous self-sufficiency and interdependence is abstract enough to warrant further discussion.

Interdependence of the Stories

Although there are always similarities among stories written by the same author, not every collection of stories is a cycle. This in no way reduces the significance of such collections: they are simply not cycles. The collected short stories of any writer would not ordinarily be a cycle.[17] Neither would the anthology of short stories written in the sixties, or written by women in the 1980s, or written by French Canadians. The connections among the stories would not be sufficiently specific or pronounced. In most cases, cycles are written by a single person.[18] Furthermore, while there are "arranged" cycles—that is, cycles designed by an author or editor only after all of the stories have been written— most cycles are either "composed" or "completed."[19] That means that writers frequently commit themselves to cycles (or some larger effort involving blocks of interrelated material) early in the composition process, often after writing only one or two stories. As the following chapters illustrate, the extent to which an author revises—or even the point at which the author becomes aware that stories might be combined to form a cycle—differs from writer to writer and book to book. The important point is that there is generally some conscious effort on the part of the writer to make the stories work together.

A cycle can be unified to varying degrees and through various means, but the reverberations must involve more than the connections that link any writer's work: that is, the places the author knows, or the historical period in which the author lives, including certain social, economic, or political realities. It is not enough—as is the case with most of John Cheever's and Ann Beattie's collections—simply to depict a particular class of people at a particular time and in a particular geographic setting. The book must achieve greater coherence than this. Mavis Gallant's recent *Overhead in a Balloon: Twelve Stories of Paris* (1987), for example, is not as tightly unified as many cycles, but it illustrates the extensive connections that all cycles possess. One of several cycles she has written, *Overhead in a Balloon* is connected by more than the setting in Paris during the last ten years, or by the tendency of the characters to live on the fringes of the art world and the upper class. Collectively, the stories demonstrate that people are isolated from one another by their need to tell the truth but their inability to do so. Because of the distances that people maintain from one another, especially in families or groups resembling families, characters live on their own imaginative reconstructions of themselves and other people.

The chapters that follow describe in greater detail the subtlety with which cycles are unified. Perhaps it will suffice for now to say that short story cycles contain unifying devices and patterns that are just as varied and complex as those found in other forms of extended fiction.

Self-Sufficiency

Almost anyone can perceive at least some ways in which the stories in cycles are unified. However, readers may well question the self-sufficiency of some of the stories in the cycles. For example, are the brief "The Revolutionist" and "A Very Short Story" in *In Our Time* stories or sketches?[20] Ian Reid uses "A Very Short Story" as an example of an outline for a story rather than a story itself. Furthermore, does the sequence of "inter-chapters," placed between the short stories in *In Our Time*, consist of stories? If so, then there are two—not one—short story cycles operating in this Hemingway volume, and the book is much more complex structurally than is generally acknowledged. Finally, what about the brief prologues or epilogues in cycles such as *In Our Time* or *The Pastures of Heaven* or *Bech: A Book*? In many cases they lack the development to be short stories and are not self-sufficient, concerned as they are with setting the stage for what will follow or commenting on what has been already accomplished in the book.

Although short story cycles generally consist of ''short stories,'' one has to acknowledge that there are exceptions. Without such flexibility, one is unable to emphasize the adaptability of the genre. Although it is unusual, some cycles even include lyrics between the stories to introduce or reiterate what is said in the stories. Jean Toomer's *Cane* is probably the best-known example, since the lyrics are so well integrated, but the practice goes back to the nineteenth century, as Rudyard Kipling's stories about Mowgli in *The Jungle Books* (1894–1895) illustrate.

In addition to acknowledging these exceptions, one must be inclusive rather than exclusive when describing what ''short stories'' are and what they can do. While it is doubtful that this—or any other genre—can be fully defined, one can describe it in ways that are useful. When I employ the term ''short story,'' I am referring to something that is shorter than a novel and generally longer than two pages; as far as size is concerned, it would be impossible to be more specific than this. I am also referring to a narrative that contains some kind of development, although the development will take more forms than I can suggest here. It might involve completed physical action, although the movement may be nothing more dramatic than walking inside (or outside) of a house, as is the case in Hemingway's ''The Doctor and the Doctor's Wife.'' It might also involve the reversal of the story's original situation or the character's original psychological state. For example, at the end of Joyce's ''Araby,'' the young protagonist recognizes his own vanity: ''I saw myself as a creature driven and derided by vanity'' (*Dubliners* 35). It might simply involve a discovery on the part of the protagonist, another character, or the reader. The reader may recognize why a character acts as she does or why a situation is the way it is. There would be no reversal involved in these stories—just the movement toward enlightenment. As is probably clear by now, in most stories there are multiple forms of development: the initiation story, for instance, will typically involve completed physical action, character revelation or development, and the reversal of the original situation or psychological state of the protagonist.

As the previous paragraph suggests, the end of the short story must also create a sense of finality or closure. ''Short fiction . . . is the most 'end-conscious' of forms. Readers of short fiction are the most end-conscious of readers. Perhaps the reason is that the end is generally not given before they have had time to be curious about it, nor is it then withheld for very long'' (Lohafer 94). But, as indicated, the methods by which this sense of closure is achieved differ greatly depending on the work, the writer, and the historical period. Some contemporary writers try to create ''anti-stories'' by refusing to allow their stories to end or by creating a choice of different possible endings. These stories, perhaps contrary to their author's intentions, are often among those that make readers most aware of the need for closure. Other writers may resist the kind of ending that readers have come to expect in order to criticize the assumptions that support such conclusions.

Nevertheless, even in "open-ended" stories—those that are most resistant to closure or that conclude by looking forward to new beginnings—the sense of closure is still more definite than the end of chapters in contemporary novels.[21] In fact, the chapter does not have to end with closure, and when it does, it requires a less absolute sense of ending. As Philip Stevick discusses at length in *The Chapter in Fiction*, the novelist must make it very clear to the reader that any sense of closure achieved at the end of a chapter is tenuous, offering "minor, secondary conclusions" (40). The world of the novel continues as soon as the reader turns to the next chapter, unlike the world of the short story, which no longer exists after the last sentence. Some of the devices used to achieve a sense of finality at the end of a chapter might also be used at the end of a short story: the difference is that the short story writer must make a larger effort, gathering together or resolving a larger part of the discourse.

Tension between the Separateness and Interdependence
of the Stories

Although cycles may occasionally contain prefaces, sketches, or lyric poems, they generally consist of short stories, which are at the same time free-standing and inexorably linked. Because the stories are both separate and interdependent, there is necessarily a tension in the work between "the individuality of each of the stories and the necessities of the larger unit" (15). As Forrest Ingram further explains:

Central to the dynamics of the short story cycle is the tension between the one and the many. When do the many cease being merely many and congeal into one? Conversely, when does a "one" become so discrete and differentiated that it dissolves into a "many"? Every story cycle displays a double tendency of asserting the individuality of its components on the one hand and of highlighting, on the other, the bonds of unity which make the many into a single whole. (19)[22]

This tension is revealed in the way people read cycles. The reader continually has the choice of reading a story like "Araby" (*Dubliners*) by itself, attempting to ignore its context in the book as a whole, or of reading primarily to see what the story contributes to the rest of the work, perhaps the enveloping sense of dreariness, inaction, and betrayal. Generally, however, the process is more complex than the last sentence suggests, for one may read a sentence, thinking mostly about the individual story, and suddenly, in the next sentence, be forced to remember a similar incident or image in the previous story.

Anyone familiar with a few cycles can appreciate the difficulty that critics experience when trying to describe this tension between the parts and the whole.

As with any reading experience, many variables need to be taken into consideration. For example, a reader would probably focus more exclusively on the individual stories during an initial reading, especially with the first stories. The reasons for this are obvious: the reader would have less opportunity to establish a larger context in which the stories could be placed. (It is likely, however, that a reader alert to early generic signals would be encouraged from the beginning to emphasize connections among the stories.) After reading the entire book several times, it would be difficult for the reader to respond to one of the stories in the book without repeatedly considering its relation to the entire book. Nevertheless, even as they grow increasingly familiar with a cycle, readers would always respond on some levels to the stories as discrete entities. The stories would retain their dual nature as both independent and interdependent.

While difficult to describe, this tension between the separateness and interdependence of stories is one of the chief pleasures that readers of cycles experience. They enjoy experiencing the worlds of the short story and the novel simultaneously. Despite their familiarity with the books, readers continue to appreciate the fact that Ike McCaslin exists beyond the boundaries of "The Bear," that Virgie returns revitalized in the final story in *The Golden Apples*, and that Joyce allows imagery to develop, often ironically, through the apparently separate lives of characters as diverse as Eveline, Lenehan, and Gabriel Conroy. I do not think the case is overstated if I say that readers enjoy reveling in the necessarily restricted form of a single story and then discovering that they can, as they continue to read, transcend these boundaries.

NOTES

1. The *Princeton Encyclopedia of Poetry and Poetics* emphasizes that the term "form" is used in a variety of ways, some even contradictory. Among the definitions that are given, two are pertinent to this study: "In this sense form is the structure, tight or loose, supple or flaccid, of the whole composition. . . . This brings us to another widely accepted meaning of form, viz. genre or kind of composition. The epic, the lyric, the drama, with all their subdivisions, are said to be the forms of poetry" (286). (Orsini, *Princeton Encyclopedia of Poetry and Poetics*. Ed. Alex Preminger. Princeton: Princeton UP, 1974.) When I use the term "form," I am referring to a work's overall structure or, more specifically, that part of its structure predetermined by genre.

2. Clements and Gibaldi note that "within the literature of classical antiquity perhaps the closest analogue to the novella frame-tale is that extended passage in Book IV of Ovid's *Metamorphoses* in which the daughters of Minyas decide to lighten their household tasks by each in turn telling a short tale . . . " (37).

3. In the case of framed collections that are well unified, the distinction between the terms "short story cycle" and "framed stories" blurs.

4. Clements and Gibaldi note other nineteenth-century German *novellen* that are bound together with framing tales: Goethe's *Unterhaltungen deutscher Ausgewanderten* (1795), Wieland's *Das Hexameron von Rosenhain* (1805), Jeremias Gotthelf's *Die schwarze Spinne* (1842), and Gottfried Keller's *Das Sinngedicht* (1850–51). (Lemmon's

dissertation has a chapter devoted to *Das Sinngedicht*. See Works Cited section in the Preface.)

5. See Robert F. Marler's "From Tale to Short Story: The Emergence of a New Genre in the 1850's." *AL* 46 (May 1974): 153–69.

6. The following discussion of nineteenth-century American cycles is influenced heavily by Reed's "The Integrated Short-Story Collection."

7. Sutton's *The Road To Winesburg*: 434. See the *Winesburg, Ohio* bibliography.

8. Fenton's *Apprenticeship*: 149. See the *In Our Time* bibliography.

9. This is Kim Townsend's paraphrase of a letter at the Newberry Library. See his *Sherwood Anderson* (226) in the *Winesburg* bibliography.

10. As Alastair Fowler acknowledges in his chapter "Mode and Subgenre" in *Kinds of Literature*, the "division of kinds into subgenres normally goes by subject matter or motifs" (112).

11. *The Hero in Hemingway's Short Stories* 26–27. See *In Our Time* bibliography.

12. *The Letters of Sherwood Anderson* 410. See the *Winesburg* bibliography.

13. Other cycles discussing the inadequacy of family or domestic life include Camus, *Exile and the Kingdom* (trans. 1958); Mavis Gallant, *Home Truths* (1981) and *Overhead in a Balloon* (1987); Gail Godwin, *Dream Children* (1976); Nancy Potter, *Legacies* (1987); Gertrude Stein, *Three Lives* (1909); Peter Taylor, *Widows of Thornton* (1954); Welty, *The Golden Apples* (1949); and Wilder, *The Bridge of San Luis Rey* (1927).

14. Matthews's "Creative Responses": 219. Grimwood ("Pastoral and Parody"), Harter ("Diaphoric Structure"), Kinney (*Narrative Poetics*), and Morris make similar points. See the *Go Down, Moses* bibliography.

15. Faulkner's *Selected Letters*: 284–85. See the *Go Down, Moses* bibliography.

16. In the case of *Trust Me*, however, the advertising is not wholly trustworthy, since only the first half of the book is unified by the subject. Publishers have learned that cycles often sell better than selected stories or miscellanies.

17. There are exceptions, such as Faulkner's *Collected Stories* (1950). In his 1970 Johns Hopkins dissertation, Philip Momberger describes the book's six-part structure, concluding that it is organized by a "contrast between communal order and anarchic violence" (*DAI* 33 [1972]: 2386A).

18. This does not mean that a cycle cannot be written by different people: Forrest Ingram mentions Zola's *Les Soirées de Médan* (1880) and *The New Decameron* (1919–25) as two such examples. But in both of these cases, the stories were written expressly for publication together and represent a rare exception.

19. Forrest Ingram introduces terminology that may help some readers distinguish among cycles on the basis of the method of composition and the author's intentions:

—*the composed cycle*, conceived of as a cycle from the time the first story was written, and as a result, generally tightly organized.

—*the completed cycle*, generally less unified, conceived of only after some of the stories have been written.

—*the arranged cycle*, the most loosely structured, conceived of by the author and/or the editor only after all of the stories have been written. (17–18).

Please note that these categories introduce at least one problem. Completed cycles are frequently as well unified as composed ones, especially if revision is involved.

20. As Reid distinguishes between "sketches" and "short stories," "there is a broad initial distinction between writing about *conditions* and writing about *events*. On the one

hand primary emphasis falls on what some thing, place or person is like; on the other, it falls on what happens. The former, then, is predominantly descriptive, while the latter follows a line of action'' (30).

21. In her discussion of the short story, Susan Lohafer does an excellent job of describing how contemporary short fiction often ends. Extending work done on the novel by Alan Friedman, Lohafer argues that closure in the short story involves either a sense of "coming home" or a "leaving home":

If we interpret "home" in the broadest sense, as the place where our reality is so comfortable and well known . . . that we can manage in the dark, then perhaps we can say that every story shows us someone either coming home or leaving home. Though there is nothing fixed about these directions, many stories give us a character moving toward knowledge of his past, his true self, his real fate. These movements might be called homecomings. Movements into the future, the unknown, some other, as yet undefined self—these might well be home-leavings. (95–96)

22. I do not think it is useful to argue, as some do, that short story cycles must "maintain a *balance* between the individuality of each of the stories and the necessities of the larger unit" (Ingram 15; my emphasis). Both Ingram and Harlan Harbour Winn (see Works Cited section in the Preface) claim that this "balance" is an essential characteristic of the genre. Apart from the fact that "balance" is a quantitative term applied to something that cannot be quantified, the concept is problematic because those who use it do not address the variables involved in the reading process. Moreover, the term introduces a method of evaluating short story cycles that is suspect.

WORKS CITED

Carabine, Keith. " 'A Pretty Good Unity': A Study of Sherwood Anderson's *Winesburg, Ohio* and Ernest Hemingway's *In Our Time*." Diss. Yale U, 1978. *DAI* 39 (1978): 2936A–37A.

   Although he deals only briefly with the question of genre in the body of the dissertation, two appendices contain relevant material: Appendix C, "Factors which Might Point to a New Literary Genre"; and Appendix D, "Russian Precursors of 'The Hybrid Novel' or the Short Story Cycle."

Clements, Robert J., and Joseph Gibaldi. *Anatomy of the Novella: The European Tale Collection from Boccaccio and Chaucer to Cervantes*. New York: New York UP, 1977.

Creighton, Joanne V. "*Dubliners* and *Go Down, Moses*: The Short Story Composite." Diss. U of Michigan, 1969. *DAI* 31 (1970): 1792A–93A.

   The short story composite is defined as a collection in which "the stories are autonomous units governed by their own principles while they are at the same time integral parts of a larger whole" (86). In the fourth chapter, devoted to the question of genre, Creighton argues that the composite is distinct from the novel in two ways: (1) "The composite retains a dual identity as a collection of short stories and as a larger whole, whereas the novel is a single entity . . . " (153–54), and (2) "The composite lends itself to an exploration of the unique cultural identity shared by a group of people, whereas the novel is suited to an intensive study of an individual or a few individuals" (154). (See Works Cited section in Preface for Creighton's *William Faulkner's Craft of Revision*.)

Fowler, Alastair. *Kinds of Literature: An Introduction to the Theory of Genres and Modes*. Oxford: Oxford UP, 1982.

————. "The Life and Death of Literary Forms." *NLH* 2.2 (Winter 1971): 199–216. Rpt. in *New Directions in Literary History*. Ed. Ralph Cohen. Baltimore: Johns Hopkins UP, 1974. 77–94.

Ingram, Forrest L. *Representative Short Story Cycles of the Twentieth Century: Studies in a Literary Genre*. The Hague: Mouton, 1971.

Lohafer, Susan. *Coming to Terms with the Short Story*. Baton Rouge: Louisiana UP, 1983.

Reed, Pleasant Larus, III. "The Integrated Short-Story Collection: Studies of a Form of Nineteenth- and Twentieth-Century Fiction." Diss. Indiana U, 1974. *DAI* 35 (1975): 6730A.

    The "integrated short-story collection" is defined as "a sequence in which through arrangement the writer suggests or establishes relationships of plot, character, setting, image, and theme among separate stories to form an integrated whole." Examples of the genre include *Dubliners*, *Winesburg, Ohio*, and *In Our Time*. *The Unvanquished* and *Go Down, Moses* are labeled "story novels" since the stories in them are not actually self-sufficient and they "must be read together for their full effect" (287).

Reid, Ian. *The Short Story*. The Critical Idiom 37. London: Methuen, 1977.

Silverman, Raymond Joel. "The Short Story Composite: Forms, Functions, and Applications." Diss. U of Michigan, 1970. *DAI* 31 (1971): 6633A.

    Silverman's definition of the short story composite is largely based on Joanne V. Creighton's (see above). For a book to be considered a short story composite, all of its stories must be autonomous, all must be unified by a single idea, all must contain a beginning and an end, and all must have a definite place in the book's sequential order. The short story composite differs from the novel primarily because the parts and the whole are coordinate in the composite, while the parts are subordinate to the whole in the novel.

Stevick, Philip. *The Chapter in Fiction: Theories of Narrative Division*. Syracuse: Syracuse UP, 1970.

Vinaver, Eugène. Introduction. *Malory: Works*. By Sir Thomas Malory. 2nd ed. London: Oxford UP, 1971.

PART I
The Representative Cycles

1

James Joyce's *Dubliners*

INTRODUCTION TO THE BOOK

Dubliners consists of fourteen brief short stories, culminating in the considerably longer story "The Dead." Each takes place in Dublin and describes a Dubliner's response to a life that proves tedious, humiliating, suffocating, or in some other way compromised. The protagonists' situations do not generally seem improved by the end of the stories. For example, Eveline is too paralyzed by fear to leave her family responsibilities for another, possibly more carefree, life in Buenos Aires; Bob Doran is vaguely aware that he is "being had" (*Dubliners* 66) but agrees to a marriage that can only prove disastrous; and Little Chandler shouts at his infant son, angry that his life appears so mean in comparison to the one he imagines his friend Gallaher lives in London.

Although external situations do not seem to improve in *Dubliners*, some protagonists develop in the sense that they achieve a degree of self-awareness. The young boy in "An Encounter" and "Araby" realizes that he is disloyal and "a creature driven and derided by vanity" (*Dubliners* 35). Similarly, Mr. Duffy and Gabriel Conroy recognize both their egotism and self-imposed isolation. In several stories, it is not the protagonist but another person who is enlightened: Maria, in "Clay," is not sufficiently perceptive to see herself as Joe sees her when she sings "I Dreamt that I Dwelt" and inadvertently changes the last line.

In some of the stories, it can only be the reader who understands the ironies and full implications of Joyce's criticism of Dublin and specific Dubliners. For example, "After the Race," "Two Gallants," "Ivy Day," and "Grace" do not contain characters with sufficient moral vision or objectivity to provide commentary. Furthermore, because Joyce's criticism of Dublin is communicated by "discourse" (that is, how the story is told) as well as by "story" (that is, what is said), the reader should necessarily be capable of insights denied to the characters.

COMPOSITION AND PUBLICATION OF *DUBLINERS*

Joyce began writing the stories soon after George Russell encouraged him to submit fiction to the *Irish Homestead*.[1] "The Sisters," which would eventually be included as the first story in *Dubliners*, was the first story written, published in the weekly in August 1904. "Eveline" and "After the Race" followed, appearing in the *Irish Homestead* in September and October. It is impossible to identify exactly when Joyce first thought of publishing the stories as a series, but it must have been while he was writing these initial stories. In a letter that appears to have been written after "The Sisters" and before "Eveline," Joyce states that he is writing a book, consisting of ten stories which will be called *Dubliners* "to betray the soul of that hemiplegia or paralysis which may consider a city" (Joyce's *Letters* I: 55).

Although Joyce was busy working on *Stephen Hero*, he submitted an early version of "Clay" (at this point entitled "Christmas Eve") to the *Irish Homestead* in January 1905. The story was rejected, because the *Homestead* readers had complained that Joyce's earlier stories were obscure and blasphemous. Nevertheless, Joyce continued the stories, writing "The Boarding House," "Counterparts," and "A Painful Case" during the first seven months of 1905. He completed "Ivy Day in the Committee Room" by the end of August, and by late September, "An Encounter" and "A Mother."

Thus, by September 1905, though probably earlier, Joyce had decided that he would arrange the stories according to the protagonists' ages and preoccupations. As he explains in a letter to his brother Stanislaus, who had previously helped him organize the sequence of lyrics in *Chamber Music*:

The order of the stories is as follows. *The Sisters, An Encounter*, and another story ["Araby"] which are stories of my childhood: *The Boarding-House, After the Race*, and *Eveline*, which are stories of adolescence: *The Clay, Counterparts*, and *A Painful Case* which are stories of mature life: *Ivy Day in the Committee Room, A Mother* and the last story of the book ["Grace"] which are stories of public life in Dublin. (*Letters* II: 111)

In October Joyce wrote "Araby" and "Grace," filling in the two empty slots in the first and last group of stories, and he submitted the original *Dubliners* to Grant Richards at the beginning of December.

This first submitted version of *Dubliners* is more or less the same as the version Joyce had described to Stanislaus in September 1905. There are only three major changes: (1) "Eveline" and "The Boarding House" have changed places, (2) "Two Gallants" and "A Little Cloud" have been added to the middle group of stories, and (3) "Clay" and "Counterparts" have been reversed. In fact, the only other major change that Joyce would later make in *Dubliners* was to add

"The Dead" in 1907 as the final story. Therefore, after Joyce committed himself to a basic organizational plan—that is, the four divisions devoted to childhood, adolescence, maturity, and public life—he maintained these divisions, simply adding several stories and occasionally rearranging the order of the stories within the sections.

Since the publishing history of *Dubliners* is well known, I will only briefly describe Joyce's difficulties getting the book published. Although Richards signed a contract to publish *Dubliners*, he began to have second thoughts about doing so in the spring of 1906. Richards eventually demanded that Joyce omit "Two Gallants," delete a paragraph in "The Boarding House," and substitute another expression for "bloody" wherever it occurred in the stories. Joyce agreed to these changes, but only after it became clear that the book might not be published at all unless the alterations were made. Repeatedly throughout his correspondence with Richards, Joyce stressed that *Dubliners* would be damaged if these changes were made, especially if "Two Gallants" were omitted.[2]

In spite of Joyce's concessions, Grant Richards finally refused to publish *Dubliners*. When Joyce found another publisher in 1909—George Roberts, managing director of Maunsel & Company—his new publisher also began to have second thoughts soon after signing the contract. Responding to Roberts's insistence that "An Encounter" be omitted, Joyce said that he would not agree to this unless a note were placed at the beginning of the book informing the reader that "this book in this form is incomplete. The scheme of the book, as framed by me includes a story entitled An Encounter which stands between the first and second stories in this edition" (*Letters* II: 309). Joyce was convinced that all the stories in *Dubliners* were essential, and the order in which they were placed was not negotiable.

Ultimately, Roberts backed out of the contract, and Grant Richards, apparently suffering from a guilty conscience, reconsidered and published *Dubliners* in June 1914. This first printing more or less represented Joyce's intentions: it included all of the stories that Joyce had written for *Dubliners* and placed them according to his design.[3]

UNITY IN *DUBLINERS*

Dubliners has, of course, received a great deal of critical attention. The only short story cycle (at least in modern British or American literature) receiving equal attention from critics is Faulkner's *Go Down, Moses*. In addition to Warren Beck's book-length study of *Dubliners*, there are several other books that exclusively analyze Joyce's early work and four anthologies of criticism on *Dubliners* alone (Baker and Staley, Garrett, Clive Hart, Scholes and Litz). In fact, there is even a separate book, a collection of critical essays, on a single story from *Dubliners*, William T. Moynihan's *Joyce's "The Dead."* This large body of criticism provides varied and fairly comprehensive descriptions of unifying patterns in the book.

Because of the amount of criticism devoted to *Dubliners*, it is difficult to summarize critics' descriptions of the ways in which the book is unified. In order to point out various critical trends, I start with critics' attempts to identify a single external pattern, such as *The Odyssey* or *The Inferno*, upon which the sequential ordering of the stories is based. I also emphasize Joyce's own explanation of the key to the book's organization: the arrangement of stories into groups based on the progressive maturation of the protagonists. The largest part of the remainder of this chapter, however, is spent describing how patterns—character, plot, image, theme, and point of view—reverberate through the book, complicating the effect that individual stories have on the reader.

The Single External Pattern as a Unifying Device

In their attempts to explain the overall organization of the stories, especially their sequential ordering, a number of critics argue that the book is patterned after a single external source. Richard Levin and Charles Shattuck suggest *Dubliners* is based on Homer's *The Odyssey*; Warren Carrier, Jackson I. Cope, and Mary T. Reynolds argue that the primary source is Dante's *Inferno*; Brewster Ghiselin identifies the source as the deadly sins and the theological and cardinal virtues of Christianity; and Florence L. Walzl ("Liturgy of the Epiphany Season") cites the liturgical sequence of services in the Epiphany subcycle.

In spite of their detailed comparisons of *Dubliners* to other works, these critics do not convincingly establish that the content or organization of the book reflects a single major influence. No doubt Joyce was influenced by some of these works and philosophies, and perhaps profound correspondences exist between some of them and *Dubliners*, but it is highly unlikely that *Dubliners* was based on any one of these sources to the extent that *Ulysses* was based on *The Odyssey*. The positioning of the stories is not adequately explained by any of these critics.

To illustrate the limitations of arguments claiming that the structure of *Dubliners* is based on a single external source, I would like to discuss two examples briefly: Levin and Shattuck's "First Flight to Ithaca" and Ghiselin's "The Unity of *Dubliners*." Arguing that *Dubliners* is an "analogue" to *The Odyssey*, Levin and Shattuck examine in detail correspondences between the works. According to them, the first three stories ("The Sisters," "An Encounter," and "Araby") are "derived" from the adventures of Telemachus, Books I through IV and part of Book XV in *The Odyssey*; the next four stories ("Eveline" through "The Boarding House") on Odysseus's journey home, Books V through VIII and part of Book XIII; the next four stories ("A Little Cloud" through "A Painful Case") on Odysseus's recapitulation of his wandering, Books IX through XII; and the last three stories ("Ivy Day" through "The Dead") on parts of the second half of *The Odyssey*. While *Dubliners* may well contain allusions to *The Odyssey*, and while there is no doubt that the journey motif is pervasive, they fail to prove their central thesis: "*Dubliners* has an architectural unity in a secret technique—

that like *Ulysses*, only far more obviously and demonstrably . . . *Dubliners* is based upon Homer's *Odyssey*" (76).

To perceive the weakness in Levin and Shattuck's idea of unity in *Dubliners*, one must note how frequently they strain to see correspondences. Are many readers, for example, willing to accept their view that Maria's story ("Clay") parallels and is based on the Hades episode in *The Odyssey*? When Maria goes to Joe's house in the rain, is it a parallel to Odysseus's leaving Aeaea weeping? Do Maria's fears that Joe will be drunk parallel Odysseus's fears concerning the journey to Hell? Do these juxtaposed passages and the others they cite prove that *Dubliners* was consciously modeled, story after story, on *The Odyssey*, or do they merely demonstrate that Levin and Shattuck have worked hard to find similarities in the two books, especially similarities that are fairly common in narratives featuring quests or journeys?

In addition to Levin and Shattuck, there are other critics who describe limited correspondences between *Dubliners* and *The Odyssey*. However, these critics—for example, Robert Boyle and William York Tindall—do not suggest that Joyce consciously structured major portions of *Dubliners* after *The Odyssey*.

I will give only one more example of arguments based on a single external source. In his frequently anthologized "The Unity of *Dubliners*," Ghiselin claims that the stories in *Dubliners* are sequentially ordered so that they depict "a movement of the human soul . . . through various conditions of Christian virtue and stages of deadly sin" (80)—more specifically, through the three theological virtues, the four cardinal virtues, and the seven deadly sins.

Although there are a few exceptions, Ghiselin argues that in general the pattern of virtues and vices appears in the stories in the order commonly expected. In the first three stories, the theological virtues of faith ("The Sisters"), hope ("An Encounter"), and love ("Araby") are depicted as the protagonist in each finds it impossible to practice the specific virtue even though he makes an attempt to do so; in the fourth story, Eveline's inability to demonstrate the cardinal virtue of fortitude is depicted; in the fifth through eleventh stories, the characters are guilty of pride ("After the Race"), covetousness ("Two Gallants"), lust ("The Boarding House"), envy ("Little Cloud"), anger ("Counterparts"), gluttony ("Clay"), and sloth ("A Painful Case"); in the twelfth through fourteenth stories, the characters are unable to practice the cardinal virtues of justice ("Ivy Day"), temperance ("A Mother"), and prudence ("Grace"); and, finally, in the last story, where no single virtue or vice predominates, the disintegration of the soul or death is depicted.

Ghiselin's faith in Joyce's purposeful ordering of stories is impressive, as is his attempt to establish an elaborate framework in which recurring action, imagery, and themes can be seen in perspective. Nevertheless, in spite of the usefulness of his article, especially the accurate and detailed tracing of major recurring action and imagery in *Dubliners*, one cannot ignore the fact that the moral frame he uses in order to interpret the stories appears at times highly arbitrary. As he acknowledges, the traditional order of virtues and vices is sometimes violated by Joyce's ordering of the stories: for example, while it is customary for the sin of gluttony to be listed before anger, the depiction of anger ("Counterparts") appears before the depiction of gluttony ("Clay"). More disturbing that these inconsistencies, however, is Ghiselin's questionable attempt to pair each story with a single virtue or vice. For example, why is faith more important in "The Sisters" than love or charity? Isn't the sin of pride just as important in "An Encounter" as the suppression of hope? Certainly lust is not the predominant sin in "The Boarding House," since most critics agree that the story focuses on Mrs. Mooney's and Polly's unscrupulous behavior and not on the sexual relationship that took place before the story even started. Most difficult of all to believe is that gluttony should be the fatal flaw in "Clay," even if, as Ghiselin explains, in this story the predominant sin involves the supporting cast and not the protagonist.

Although he probably did not organize the stories in *Dubliners* by imitating or parodying the structure of another work, Joyce did consciously order the stories. As mentioned before, he was aware early in the composition process that the stories were divided into four loosely defined groups—childhood, adolescence, maturity, and public life—and most of his last stories were written at least in part to fill in gaps within these divisions. Furthermore, as Joyce's revisions demonstrate, he occasionally rearranged the way the stories were organized within the four major divisions, but he never switched a story from one group to another.

One should not overemphasize the importance of any single unifying pattern—even the one that Joyce himself identified as most important. Although the concept of the chronological development of a protagonist enabled him to define the book's scope and arrange the stories, its influence is less pronounced in the last group of stories ("public life"), and it in no way explains all that needs to be said about the ways in which the stories work together. Nevertheless, if there is one major key to the sequential ordering of the stories in *Dubliners*, then it is the one Joyce stressed in his letters: the gradual aging of the protagonists and the broadening of their perspectives from the subjectivity in "The Sisters" to the more objective and comprehensive point of view revealed in "The Dead."

Other Forms of Unity

Character

Perhaps because of its subtlety, Joyce's use of recurring character as a unifying pattern is often overlooked in spite of the importance critics place on the division of the book into stories based on childhood, adolescence, maturity, and public life. Since there is no protagonist who reappears and develops in the process of the book, critics often fail to notice that the book presents the gradual maturation of what one might consider the archetypal Dubliner. Because the four-part structure progresses from a child's subjectivity to ways of looking at the world that are both more objective and comprehensive, the reader may almost sense that *Dubliners* contains a single protagonist who develops in the process of the book. Even though the same protagonist with the same name does not appear in more than one story, all bear a family resemblance: they are products of middle-class Catholic Ireland and trapped by limitations in the environment and in their own personalities.

In her attempt to see the protagonists in *Dubliners* as "variants of a central everyman figure" ("Book of Signs"), Walzl goes further than most other critics in establishing a central protagonist. Her argument is well developed and solidly based on the large body of *Dubliners* criticism already devoted to Christian themes and imagery, as will become clearer when I focus primarily on imagery instead of character. If one keeps in mind the similarities the characters share, it is much easier to accept Walzl's thesis.[4] It is also easier to accept Ghiselin's claim that in *Dubliners* "the separate histories of its protagonists [compose] one essential history, that of the soul of a people . . . " (318).

A number of critics note that "The Sisters," "An Encounter," and "Araby" feature the same protagonist, because even though he is not given a name, in each story he seems the same kind of person living in the same circumstances: he has no parents (in two stories he is said to reside with an aunt and uncle), he lives north of the Liffey, he is bookish and sensitive to language, and he is extremely self-conscious and remains aloof. Other critics perceive Gabriel Con-roy in "The Dead" as a grownup version of the boy in "The Sisters" (for example, Torchiana's "The Opening of *Dubliners*" and *Backgrounds for Dubliners*, 228) or the boy in all three opening stories (Cronin). However, if one accepts that a family relationship exists among the protagonists, then it is not necessary to argue whether the boy in the first three stories is Gabriel as a child or simply the sort of child that Gabriel might have resembled when he was young.

Plot

Plot is another subtle unifying device frequently overlooked. Since there are no protagonists who appear in more than one story—with the possible exception of the boy in the first three stories—there is no obvious plot or action that continues from story to story in *Dubliners* as the Civil War and Reconstruction unify *The Unvanquished*. Nevertheless, the maturation of the archetypal Dubliner and the similar situations in which characters are placed indicate the importance of plot in *Dubliners*. Because characters are often forced into a position where they must choose to act or be acted upon, many of the plots resemble one another. In fact, many of the stories share the same tripartite structure, the action generally occurring in the middle of the story (Atherton's "Joyce of *Dubliners*," Jedynak's "Epiphany as Structure," Peake, and Senn). Although it is not always the case, very often the stories are divided into three discernible parts, the first serving as an introduction and establishing the story's general tone, the second containing action or a situation in which the character is acted upon, and the third providing comment on the protagonist's world.

Plot similarities are also created by Joyce's handling of the action in the middle and sometimes at the end of the stories. Although the tripartite structure cited above is frequently found in twentieth-century stories,[5] Joyce's use of the divisions is individualistic and consistent with the major preoccupations and imagery in the book. As critics frequently note, when protagonists in the stories move from west to east, it generally underlines their passivity or paralysis. When direction is not this specific there are repeated instances of characters who seek and, at times, embark on adventures, journeys, or pilgrimages in an attempt to escape lives that are dull and constricting.

In the seminal discussion of this unifying pattern, Ghiselin's "The Unity of *Dubliners*," the best examples of recurring symbolic action include (in the order in which they appear in *Dubliners*) the incomplete eastward journey to the Pigeon House in "An Encounter," the eastward pilgrimage to the exotic bazaar in "Araby," the thwarted movement eastward toward the ship in "Eveline," the movement southeastward and then westward in "Two Gallants" as Corley takes advantage of the woman in the story, the movement downstairs toward confinement in "The Boarding House" while Bob Doran dreams of "ascending through the roof" (*Dubliners* 67) and flying to another country, the eastward but circling movement of Farrington in "Counterparts," the movement north and then westward in "Clay," and the movement of Duffy eastward to Phoenix Park when he learns of Mrs. Sinico's death and then westward as he returns homeward to self-imposed solitary confinement.[6]

Imagery

As the previous paragraphs, especially those on symbolic action demonstrate, it is finally impossible to discuss character and action in *Dubliners* without also discussing imagery. The book is so highly symbolic that, even to facilitate the discussion, it is difficult to maintain these categories as mutually exclusive. Therefore, in addition to Joyce's use of an archetypal Dubliner and his repeated use of symbolic action, there are other uses of imagery in *Dubliners* that deserve comment.

To begin with, some other important unifying imagery involves the locations of the stories. As the title of the book emphasizes, all of the stories take place in Dublin; but

Dublin as *place*, as setting in the physical sense, is not of major importance. . . . For the most part, the Dublin of the book might be any large European city: in the cases of many of those poignantly real details of setting throughout the stories we need not be in Dublin at all—the quay, the bridge, the green field, the doorway, the back yard, for instance, might be almost anywhere. (Ostroff 198)

Certainly what unifies the stories (at least for the present-day reader) is not the fidelity with which the stories recreate turn-of-the-century Dublin, but the fact that the action in the stories consistently takes place in dreary, dark or dimly lit, and confined urban spaces. As Joyce himself vividly describes the atmosphere, "the odour of ashpits and old weeds and offal hangs round my stories" (*Letters* I: 64).[7]

Of all the images that echo in readers' minds as they move from one story to another, those that are primarily important as far as setting and tone are concerned include images of light and dark; of colors, especially brown and green; of weather; and of enclosed or confined spaces. The most detailed analyses of light and dark and color imagery are provided by M. W. Murphy in "Darkness in *Dubliners*" and by B. Eliot Wigginton in "*Dubliners* in Order."[8] According to Murphy, "so pervasive is darkness in *Dubliners* that it is difficult to discover one major scene that takes place in bright sunlight in any of the stories. From first to last the usual setting is a dark street or a dark room in Dublin, and the action almost always takes place at night or in early evening after the sun has gone down" (97). In two stories where there are no night scenes, Murphy continues, Joyce dims the light at climactic moments: for example, in "An Encounter," a cloud suddenly appears and blots out the sun, leaving the boys in comparative darkness just as the pervert appears.

Coming to similar conclusions but with a more quantitative approach, Wigginton explains that in thirteen out of fifteen stories the central action takes place in either darkness, overcast weather, or both, most of the sunlight occurring in the first stories, where the protagonist still has hope for the future. Exacerbating the dreariness and the lack of light, unpleasant weather occurs simultaneously with the major action in five stories and accompanies secondary action in at least four others. Wigginton also suggests that even though some brighter colors appear, especially blue, green, and yellow, they are usually associated with unpleasantness in the story and therefore do not function in such a way as to lessen the general gloom.

Ghiselin, who focuses on recurring instances of green and brown in *Dubliners*, suggests that green (most vividly associated with the eyes of the pervert in "An Encounter") symbolizes "degeneracy in Ireland, with crippling spiritual limitations" (87). In addition, Ghiselin finds that brown—the color that Wigginton cites as the fourth most frequent—suggests the stagnation of life in Dublin, but it does so with greater emphasis and finality than is the case when green is used.

The symbolic use of enclosed or confined spaces also contributes to Joyce's depiction of his characters' lives as limited or paralyzed. One of the only critics to comment on this pattern, Ghiselin explains that in many stories "closed or circumscribed areas, such as coffin, confession-box, rooms, buildings, the city and its suburbs become symbolic when they are presented in any way suggesting enclosure . . . " (88).[9] One could add to Ghiselin's list: for example, I discovered a number of instances of blocked off spaces in *Dubliners*: "Araby" begins with a statement that North Richmond Street is a "blind" or dead-end street, and, at the end of the story, the boy is unable to find a sixpenny entrance at the bazaar; at the end of "Counterparts," the boy tries to escape around his father, but Farrington blocks the way and catches his son; and at the end of "A Mother," Mrs. Kearney refuses to allow her daughter on stage until she is paid, attempting to halt an entire concert.

Ghiselin adds that the constricting nature of houses in *Dubliners* is emphasized by Joyce when he describes the brick exteriors as brown in color. Descriptions of the interiors frequently contribute to the effect of stagnation: for example, the musty odor in the houses in "Araby" and "Eveline," the yellowing photograph of the priest that hangs on the wall in "Eveline," the "mean" furniture that Little Chandler's wife has obtained on the "hire system" (*Dubliners* 83), and the uncarpeted, undecorated, and cheerless room that Mr. Duffy rents in "A Painful Case."

Most of the other imagery in *Dubliners* reflects Joyce's Catholic or Christian orientation: water or baptism (Creighton, Ghiselin); food and drink or communion (Adicks, Creighton, Ghiselin, Hayman, Walsh, and Walzl's "Joyce's 'The Sisters' ''); money or simony (Benstock's "Joyce's Rheumatics," Friedrich's "The Gnomonic Clue," Scholes's "Counterparts," Somerville, and Torchiana's "Opening of *Dubliners*''); wind, air, fire, music, tongues, or the Holy Ghost (Benstock's "Joyce's Rheumatics''); Christ and crucifixion (Walzl's "Liturgy of the Epiphany Season," "Gabriel and Michael," and "Book of Signs''); the Virgin Mary (Magalaner's *Joyce: The Man*, and Walzl's "Liturgy of the Epiphany Season" and "Book of Signs''); God the Father (Creighton and Lachtman); and the archangels Michael and Gabriel (Walzl's "Gabriel and Michael'').

While there is not room to discuss all of these patterns, it should be stressed that critics find the presence of communion imagery and representations of the Holy Family especially important. This imagery, like most of the other patterns, is repeated to emphasize the characters' distance from God and the failure of the Church. Two of the most memorable examples of symbols used for this purpose, both taken from "The Sisters," include the priest's dropping and breaking the chalice, signifying his unfitness to serve as intermediary between man and God, and the boy's refusal of cream crackers and sherry at the priest's wake, suggesting his "disillusionment with and the partial repudiation of a clerically dominated society" (Walzl's "Pattern of Paralysis": 224).

Christian imagery is so pervasive throughout *Dubliners* that Walzl suggests that the various protagonists of the stories function as symbols of Christ, the Virgin Mary, and God the Father, emulating or ironically reflecting their conception of the Holy Family. As a result, Walzl ultimately concludes that there is "a composite protagonist" in *Dubliners*: "a composite figure deriving from classical and Christian archetypes" ("Book of Signs" 118).

Although Christian or Catholic imagery generally serves to emphasize inadequacies—even the death—of the Catholic Church in Ireland, its functions on occasion in a secular manner. When Joyce uses this imagery to describe characters who are spiritually paralyzed, their paralysis frequently involves more than (or at times something different from) the absence of God. It involves the longing for closer relations with other human beings, for intellectual or mental vitality, for a secular adventure that transmits one to another place and other people. For example, communion symbolism is used in "Clay," "A Painful Case," and "The Dead" to underline the characters' inability to communicate or to connect with one another; and the use of various imagery—including eye, glass, mirror, and upstairs spaces—symbolizes characters' attempts at understanding or self-knowledge, generally used ironically, since enlightenment is rare in *Dubliners*.

In addition to identifying major image patterns and explaining their significance, several critics examine a single pattern in sufficient detail so that they can describe how it functions from story to story. Among these critics, a few note that some of the symbols change meaning as they are repeated in different parts of the book. In "Gabriel and Michael," Walzl explains that in "The Dead" Joyce once again uses directional or east-west symbolism, but this time he reverses what each direction signifies: in some parts of "The Dead," "the east suggests the old, traditional, and effete; the west, the new, primitive, and vital" (22). Similarly, in "Rhetoric of Spatial Focus," William P. Keen describes the significance of lower or ground-floor perspectives and upper or second-story ones. He concludes that whether a lower (or higher) perspective has a positive or negative value depends on where the image occurs in the book.

While some critics may fault Joyce for using the same symbols in markedly different ways (e.g., Jordan), it seems a testimony to the complexity and vitality of Joyce's treatment of theme that symbols acquire new and, at times, contradictory meanings as they expand.

Theme or Topic

As the discussion of character, plot, and imagery emphasizes, the major unifying subject or theme in *Dubliners* is paralysis. The stories are preoccupied with the subjects of spiritual, physical, and intellectual paralysis, but there is some question about whether the weakness of the individual will or the oppressive environment is the cause of this pervasive paralysis. Those critics who define the thematic unity of *Dubliners* by concentrating on the environment's effect upon the individual find numerous targets for blame: the Church is seen as corrupt and repressive; the city is considered the destroyer of individuality and the rural institutions of the family, Church, and community; and the preoccupation with money or excessive materialism is perceived as the cause of spiritual paralysis. As a result of any or all of these negative influences, not only do the characters have severely limited desires and imaginations, but they appear isolated and estranged from one another—ultimately becoming like the middle-aged celibates Maria in "Clay" and Mr. Duffy in "A Painful Case."

Those critics who instead find fault with the individual will are in the minority, but they convincingly argue that characters such as Eveline, Jimmy ("After the Race"), Little Chandler ("A Little Cloud"), Maria ("Clay"), and Mr. Duffy ("A Painful Case") are defeated because of weakness inherent in their personalities. Edward Brandabur, in *A Scrupulous Meanness*, provides an especially compelling and detailed description of the protagonists' psychological handicaps, specifically their sadomasochism. The question of whether paralysis results from the individual's weakness or society's oppressiveness is one that can only be answered by our recognition that both individual and society are responsible. The weak individual both creates and is the direct result of society's oppressiveness.

While discussing ambiguity in *Dubliners*, especially so far as it concerns the theme of paralysis, one must also, if only briefly, consider the end of the book. Although most critics argue that Gabriel's reflection that "time had come for him to set out on his journey westward" (*Dubliners* 223) is the culmination of his development from "insularity and egotism to humanitarianism and love" (Walzl's "Gabriel and Michael": 21), there are others who instead interpret this statement as an indication that Gabriel, like the paralytics that precede him in the book, is moving toward self-annihilation or death.[10] Which position one takes depends a great deal on how one interprets key symbols like the snow, and whether the story is read as part of *Dubliners* or separately. Written after Joyce had completed the original *Dubliners* and submitted it for publication, "The Dead" reveals a more generous attitude toward Ireland, arrived at only after he had spent several years in exile.

In order to accommodate "The Dead" to the rest of *Dubliners*, Walzl suggests that Joyce created or at least took advantage of various ambiguities in the story:

first, use of ambiguous or ambivalent images that mirror the oscillation in Gabriel's character, and second, by means of a conclusion in which a series of key images, all employed earlier in both the story and the book as a whole, operate to reflect one set of meanings from *Dubliners* as a total entity and a slightly different set from "The Dead" as an individual story. ("Gabriel and Michael" 21)

One of the most convincing and detailed analyses of the book's conclusion, Walzl's article helps explain how Joyce might have taken advantage of the simultaneous independence and interdependence of the stories in order to create an ambiguous or open-ended final story.

Point of View

Point of view has already been noted briefly above when I mentioned that the stories progress from a limited subjective perspective to one that is more objective and comprehensive. It has also been suggested that point of view contributes to the sense of unity achieved in each of the four major divisions in the book. As William V. Davis explains, the first person is used in the opening three stories; the third-person limited point of view is used in the next three ("Eveline" through "Two Gallants"); the third-person omniscient is used in "The Boarding House"; the third-person limited point of view is used in the next four ("A Little Cloud" through "A Painful Case"); and the third-person omniscient point of view is used in the last four ("Ivy Day" through "The Dead").

Another issue that has not been developed adequately in this chapter and that is pertinent to the present discussion is the manner in which Joyce used an increasingly objective point of view in *Dubliners* to facilitate Gabriel Conroy's enlarged vision or perspective at the end of the story. According to Homer Obed Brown in *James Joyce's Early Fiction*, the narrator in "The Dead" is different from the distant or ironic narrators whose presences can be glimpsed in most of the other stories; instead, he

represents something like the spirit of the occasion as experienced by the chief participants. . . . At first the narrator suggests the thoughts of Lily, the maid, but then the voice shifts to the Misses Morkan. . . . The voice is finally indeterminate. It combines the way Lily and the Misses Morkan might think of the occasion with the way they might be seen by someone close to them and familiar with their life over a long period. It fuses a curiously external view with the way they might explain themselves. (89–90).

Therefore, as Gabriel transcends his own limited ego or consciousness, Brown argues that the narrator of "The Dead" does likewise, dropping the distance he has maintained through most of the book between himself and the world he describes.

What has been said earlier in this chapter in no way indicates how detailed some recent analyses of point of view are. In fact, the most impressive recent work is devoted to this area. To take two excellent examples, both L. J. Morrissey ("Joyce's Narrative Strategies") and John Paul Riquelme describe progressive patterns found within the first-person narratives: "The Sisters," "An Encounter," and "Araby." Morrissey's close reading of the second two stories demonstrates that in both stories there is a shift from the third person to the collective "first" person ("we saw," "our house") to the first-person singular ("I saw," "my house"). "Araby" is identified as a crucially important story because it "mediates between those characters who are free of restraints, or who try to free themselves, and those who give up, who succumb to Dublin and Ireland. Until 'Araby,' the children tell their own stories; after 'Araby,' the narrator tells the tales of the lost souls" (47). Morrissey stresses that in these first stories the reader must be especially alert, since it is only in these stories that the author generally refrains from judgment.

Focusing on a progression that occurs as one moves from story to story—as well as the movement within the individual stories—John Paul Riquelme describes how *Dubliners* as a whole "bridges the apparently uncrossable chasm between first- and third-person narration" (130):

Early in *Dubliners* the stories told in first-person reach a point of self-consciousness in style and story that becomes the hinge for a turn toward a third-person narration that can view character from both inside and out. Within broad limits, the stories that follow, up until those of public life, maintain this combination of inner and outer views in a third-person perspective. In those stories, the three following "A Painful Case," the external view predominates. But . . . "The Dead" reestablishes the internal view and its dominance. This complex and powerful story holds a special place in Joyce's early writing . . .

because it repeats and reverses the previous shift from first person to third person. (96)

CONCLUSION

The stories in *Dubliners* interact in extremely complicated and subtle ways, as illustrated by the descriptions provided by H. O. Brown, Morrissey, and Riquelme of the progressive development of point of view in *Dubliners*. Consciously and unconsciously, Joyce introduces various connections among the stories that force the first-time reader to assess each new story in an increasingly wider context. As one example of spiritual, moral, or emotional paralysis is followed by another—and still another—the reader's sense of the Dubliner's plight is much keener than can be explained by any of the stories taken separately. Although with a book containing separate stories readers often expect to discover substantially different worlds as they move from story to story, in *Dubliners* (as in many short story cycles) readers are surprised to discover that entirely different and apparently unconnected people are essentially the same. Certainly in *Dubliners* characters' lives are limited in very similar ways, and they are used collectively to criticize what disturbed Joyce most about life in Ireland. The strong impact of the book is created largely through the cumulative effect of the same basic story—of an individual's attempt to escape from dullness and paralysis—being told again and again with a different cast.

Anyone interested in the short story cycle should spend time with *Dubliners* and the criticism it has generated. The stories are sequentially ordered in the sense that there is an archetypal Dubliner who moves from childhood to adulthood; there are also shifting points of view that evoke this development; and there are images as well as ideas that resurface and are ultimately treated in a much more complex way than one realizes on a first or second reading of the book. Ultimately, one's interpretation of the book depends on the reader's ability to reconcile what the last story, "The Dead," seems to be saying by itself and the position it holds in the book. As with many short story cycles, the book's final meaning is complicated by its last story, which (in this case) is much longer than the other stories. "The Dead"—much as "Big Two-Hearted River" in *In Our Time* or "The Wanderers" in *The Golden Apples*—serves to challenge whatever sense we have made of the book thus far.

Appreciation of the reverberations in *Dubliners* prepares one for the kinds of unifying forms one discovers in other short story cycles. Furthermore, acquaintance with the criticism—which has provided increasingly precise descriptions of these forms—makes one alert to patterns that exist in other cycles which are to be discussed in the following chapters.

NOTES

1. Sources describing the composition process and Joyce's attempts to get the book published include Ellmann's biography of Joyce, Gabler's preface to *Dubliners: A Fac-*

simile of Drafts and Manuscripts, David E. Jones's "Approaches to *Dubliners*," the *Letters of James Joyce*, and the series of textual essays by Scholes in *Studies in Bibliography*.

2. See *Letters* I: 62, and II: 142.

3. As Robert Scholes has explained in detail, the first edition did not entirely honor Joyce's intentions, especially concerning punctuation and the manner in which direct discourse is handled. (See Scholes's brief introduction to *Dubliners* in Joyce, *Dubliners* 5–6, and *James Joyce's* Dubliners: *Text, Criticism, and Notes*, ed. Scholes and Litz, 225–26. For a lengthier discussion, see Scholes's articles in *Studies in Bibliography*.)

4. Florence L. Walzl also describes the family resemblance shared by the women characters in *Dubliners*. See "*Dubliners*: Women in Irish Society."

5. For examples see Sheldon Grebstein's and Chaman Nahal's analyses of tripartite structure in *In Our Time*. (*In Our Time* bibliography.)

6. As Ghiselin collates the instances of each particular movement:

In a sequence of six stories, [there is] an impulse and movement eastward to the outskirts of the city or beyond; in a single story, an impulse to fly away upward out of a confining situation near the center of Dublin; in a sequence of four stories, a gradual replacement of the impulse eastward by an impulse and movement westward; in three stories, a limited activity confined almost wholly within the central area of Dublin; and in the concluding story a movement eastward to the heart of the city . . . then, in vision only, far westward into death" (78).

For other discussions of recurring action—especially the movement from east to west or west to east—see Baker, Bidwell and Heffer, H. O. Brown, Creighton, Joseph K. Davis, Garrett, Ingram, Keen, Litz, and Wight.

7. For another point of view, see Bidwell and Heffer's description of how faithfully turn-of-the-century Dublin is revealed in the stories.

8. Also see Morris Beja's analysis of eye and sight imagery and other related patterns.

9. Keen and Kronegger discuss spatial imagery in detail.

10. This debate involves a number of participants. Those critics who stress an optimistic interpretation of the book include Burke, Daiches, Ellmann, Higgins, Humma, Loomis, Tate, and Torchiana ("The Ending of 'The Dead' "). Brandabur, Ghiselin, and Kenner ("*Dubliners*") instead argue that Gabriel moves toward a spiritual death. In a recent article, Vincent P. Pecora rejects the claims of both groups and argues that no transcendental experience occurs at the end of "The Dead": "What appears to be a great alteration in an individual's perception and understanding of self—a movement from blind egotism to moral selflessness . . . —becomes instead the ideologically supported transformation of one set of illusions into another to enable the individual to cope with a new and threatening social environment" (237).

WORKS CITED AND BIBLIOGRAPHY

Adams, Robert M. "*Dubliners*." *James Joyce: Common Sense and Beyond*. New York: Random, 1966. 63–90.

Adicks, Richard. "The Unconsecrated Eucharist in *Dubliners*." *SSF* 5 (Spring 1968): 295–96.

Anderson, Chester G. *James Joyce and His World*. New York: Scribner's, 1978.

Atherton, James S. "Araby." Clive Hart 39–47.

———. "The Joyce of *Dubliners*." Staley, *James Joyce Today* 28–53.

Baker, James R. "Ibsen, Joyce, and the Living Dead." *A James Joyce Miscellany, Third Series*. Ed. Marvin Magalaner. Carbondale: Southern Illinois UP, 1962. 19–32. Rpt. in Baker and Staley 62–71; and in Moynihan 64–70.

Baker, James R., and Thomas F. Staley, eds. *James Joyce's* Dubliners: *A Critical Handbook*. Belmont, CA: Wadsworth, 1969.

Beck, Warren. *Joyce's* Dubliners: *Substance, Vision, and Art*. Durham: Duke UP, 1969.

Beckson, Karl. "Moore's *The Untilled Field* and Joyce's *Dubliners*: The Short Story's Intricate Maze." *ELT* 15.4 (1972): 291–304.

Beja, Morris, ed. *James Joyce:* Dubliners *and* A Portrait of the Artist as a Young Man: *A Casebook*. London: Macmillan, 1973.

———. "One Good Look at Themselves: Epiphanies in *Dubliners*." Peterson, Cohn, and Epstein 3–14.

Benstock, Bernard, ed. *Critical Essays on James Joyce*. Boston: Hall, 1985.

———. "The Dead." Clive Hart 153–69.

———. "The Dead: A Cold Coming." Benstock, *Critical Essays*, 148–62.

———. "Joyce's Rheumatics: The Holy Ghost in *Dubliners*." *SoR* 14 (Winter 1978): 1–15.

———. "The Road to *Dubliners*." *James Joyce*. New York: Ungar, 1985.

———, ed. *The Seventh of Joyce*. Bloomington: Indiana UP; Brighton, Eng.: Harvester, 1982.

Bidwell, Bruce, and Linda Heffer. *The Joycean Way: A Topographic Guide to* Dubliners *and* A Portrait of the Artist as a Young Man. Baltimore: Johns Hopkins UP, 1982.

Bowen, Zack. "Joyce and the Epiphany Concept: A New Approach." *JML* 9.1 (1981–82): 103–14.

———. "Joyce's Prophylactic Paralysis: Exposure in *Dubliners*." *JJQ* 19.3 (Spring 1982): 257–73.

Bowen, Zack, and James F. Carens, eds. *A Companion to Joyce Studies*. Westport, CT: Greenwood, 1984.

Boyle, Robert. " 'Two Gallants' and 'Ivy Day in the Committee Room.' " *JJQ* 1 (Fall 1963): 3–9. Rpt. in Garrett 100–106.

Brandabur, Edward James. "Arrayed for the Bridal: The Embodied Vision of 'The Dead.' " Moynihan 108–19.

———. *A Scrupulous Meanness: A Study of Joyce's Early Work*. Urbana: U of Illinois P, 1971. The section on "The Sisters" also appears in Scholes and Litz 333–43.

Breman, Brian A. " 'He Was Too Scrupulous Always': A Re-examination of Joyce's 'The Sisters.' " *JJQ* 22.1 (Fall 1984): 55–66.

Brivic, Sheldon. *Joyce between Freud and Jung*. Port Washington, NY: Kennikat, 1980.

Brown, Homer Obed. *James Joyce's Early Fiction: The Biography of a Form*. Cleveland: Case Western Reserve UP, 1972.

Brown, Terence. "The Dublin of *Dubliners*." *James Joyce: An International Perspective*. Ed. Suheil Badi Bushrui and Bernard Benstock. Irish Literature Series 10. Totowa, NJ: Barnes; Gerrards Cross, Eng.: Colin Smythe, 1982. 11–18.

Brugaletta, John J., and Mary H. Hayden. "The Motivation for Anguish in Joyce's 'Araby.' " *SSF* 15 (Winter 1978): 11–17.

Burgess, Anthony. "A Paralysed City." *Re Joyce*. New York: Norton; London: Faber, 1965. 40–56. The book was published in London as *Here Comes Everybody: An Introduction to James Joyce for the Ordinary Reader*.

Burke, Kenneth. "Three Definitions." *KR* 13 (Spring 1951): 173–92. Rpt. as " 'Stages' in 'The Dead' " in Scholes and Litz 410–16.

Carens, James F. "In Quest of a New Impulse: George Moore's *The Untilled Field* and James Joyce's *Dubliners.*" *The Irish Short Story: A Critical History.* Ed. James F. Kilroy. Boston: Twayne, 1984. 45–93.

Carrier, Warren. "*Dubliners*: Joyce's Dantean Vision." *Renascence: Essays on Value in Literature* 17 (Summer 1965): 211–15.

Chambers, Ross. "Gabriel Conroy Sings for His Supper, or Love Refused ('The Dead')." *Story and Situation: Narrative Seduction and the Power of Fiction.* Theory and History of Literature 12. Minneapolis: U of Minnesota P. 1984. 181–204.

Chesnutt, Margaret. "Joyce's *Dubliners*: History, Ideology, and Social Reality." *Éire-Ireland* (St. Paul, MN) 14.2 (1979): 93–105.

Church, Margaret. "*Dubliners* and Vico." *JJQ* 5.2 (Winter 1968): 150–56.

———. "Time as an Organizing Principle in the Fiction of James Joyce." Peterson, Cohn, and Epstein 70–81.

Cixous, Hélène. "Joyce: The (r)use of writing." *Post-Structuralist Joyce: Essays from the French.* Ed. Derek Attridge and Daniel Ferrer. Cambridge, Eng.: Cambridge UP, 1984. 15–30.

Collins, Ben L. "Joyce's 'Araby' and the 'Extended Simile.' " *JJQ* 4 (Winter 1967): 84–90. Rpt. in Garrett 93–99.

Connolly, Thomas E. "A Painful Case." Clive Hart 107–14.

Cooke, M. G. "From Comedy to Terror: On *Dubliners* and the Development of Tone and Structure in the Modern Short Story." *MR* 9 (Spring 1968): 331–43.

Cope, Jackson I. "The Waste Land." *Joyce's Cities: Archaeologies of the Soul.* Baltimore: Johns Hopkins UP, 1981. 1–28. The section on *Dubliners* appeared as "Joyce's Waste Land" in *Genre* 12 (Winter 1979): 505–32.

Corrington, John William. "Isolation as Motif in 'A Painful Case.' " *JJQ* 3 (Spring 1966): 182–91. Rpt. in Baker and Staley 130–39.

———. "The Sisters." Clive Hart 13–25.

Creighton, Joanne V. "*Dubliners* and *Go Down, Moses*: The Short Story Composite." Diss. U of Michigan, 1969. *DAI* 31 (1970): 1792A–93A.

Chapter 1 contains a reading of the first three stories in *Dubliners* for the purpose of demonstrating the extent to which they are open-ended and enriched by their context in *Dubliners*. Chapter 2 analyzes the book's unifying principles through discussion of the remaining stories. Chapter 3 compares the dramatic form of *Go Down, Moses* with the lyrical form of *Dubliners*. Chapter 4 describes Faulkner's and Joyce's fiction in order to differentiate between the short story composite (or cycle) and the novel.

Cronin, Edward J. "James Joyce's Trilogy and Epilogue: 'The Sisters,' 'An Encounter,' 'Araby,' and 'The Dead.' " *Renascence: Essays on Value in Literature* 31 (Summer 1979): 229–48.

Curry, Martha Mulroy. "Sherwood Anderson and James Joyce." *AL* 52 (1980): 236–49.

Daiches, David. "*Dubliners.*" *The Novel and the Modern World.* Chicago: U of Chicago P, 1960. 63–82. Rpt. in Garrett 27–37; in *Modern British Fiction.* Ed. Mark Schorer. Oxford: Oxford UP, 1961. 308–21; and in *Discussions of the Short Story.* Ed. Hollis Summers. Boston: D. C. Heath, 1963. 80–88.

Davis, Joseph K. "The City as Radical Order: James Joyce's *Dubliners.*" *SLitI* 3 (Oct. 1970): 79–96.

Davis, William V. "Point of View in Joyce's *Dubliners.*" *CEA* 31 (Apr. 1969): 6.

Delany, Paul. "Joyce's Political Development and the Aesthetic of *Dubliners.*" *CE* 34 (Nov. 1972): 256–66. Rpt. in *The Artist and Political Vision.* Ed. Benjamin R. Barber and Michael J. McGrath. New Brunswick, NJ: Transaction, 1982. 221–31.

Dilworth, Thomas. "Sex and Politics in 'The Dead.' " *JJQ* 23.2 (Winter 1986): 157–71.

Duffy, Edward. " 'The Sisters' as an Introduction to *Dubliners.*" *PLL* 22.4 (Fall 1986): 417–28.

Duffy, John J. "The Stories of Frederick Wedmore: Some Correspondences with *Dubliners.*" *JJQ* 5 (Winter 1968): 144–49.

Ellmann, Richard. *James Joyce.* Rev. ed. Oxford: Oxford UP, 1982. (Originally pub. by Oxford UP in 1959.) "The Backgrounds of 'The Dead,' " 243–53, also appears in Moynihan 46–57; in Scholes and Litz 388–403; in Beja, *Casebook*, 172–87; in Benstock, *Critical Essays*, 90–101; and in *Joyce: A Collection of Critical Essays.* Ed. William M. Chace. Englewood Cliffs, NJ: Prentice, 1974. 18–28.

Engel, Monroe. "*Dubliners* and Erotic Expectation." *Twentieth-Century Literature in Retrospect.* Harvard English Studies 2. Ed. Reuben A. Brower. Cambridge, MA: Harvard UP, 1971. 3–26.

Fairhall, James. "Joyce's *Dubliners.*" *Expl* 43.2 (Winter 1985): 28–30.

Ferguson, Suzanne. "A Sherlock at *Dubliners*: Structural and Thematic Analogues in Detective Stories and the Modern Short Story." *JJQ* 16 (Winter 1979): 111–21.

Fischer, Therese. "From Reliable to Unreliable Narrator: Rhetorical Changes in Joyce's 'The Sisters.' " *JJQ* 9 (1971): 85–92.

French, Marilyn. "Missing Pieces in Joyce's *Dubliners.*" *TCL* 24 (Winter 1978): 443–72.

Friedrich, Gerhard. "The Gnomonic Clue to James Joyce's *Dubliners.*" *MLN* 62 (June 1957): 421–24.

———. "Joyce's Pattern of Paralysis in *Dubliners.*" *CE* 22 (Apr. 1961): 519–20.

———. "The Perspective of Joyce's *Dubliners.*" *CE* 26 (Mar. 1965): 421–26. Rpt. in Baker and Staley 71–78.

Fuger, Wilhelm. Introduction. *Concordance to James Joyce's* Dubliners. New York: Olms, 1980.

Gabler, Hans Walter. Introduction. Dubliners*: A Facsimile of Drafts and Manuscripts.* Arranged and prefaced by Hans Walter Gabler. New York: Garland, 1978. xxv–xxxi.

   Detailed information about when the draft and manuscript versions of the stories were written and about the changes Joyce made in his ordering of the *Dubliners* stories.

Gajdusek, Robert E. "Dubliners in Michigan: Joyce's Presence in Hemingway's *In Our Time.*" *Hemingway Review* 2.1 (Fall 1982): 48–61.

Gandolfo, Anita. "A Portrait of the Artist as Critic: Joyce, Moore, and the Background of 'The Dead.' " *ELT* 22.4 (1979): 239–50.

Garrett, Peter, ed. *Twentieth Century Interpretations of* Dubliners: *A Collection of Critical Essays.* Englewood Cliffs, NJ: Prentice, 1968.

Garrison, Joseph M. "*Dubliners*: Portraits of the Artist as a Narrator." *Novel: A Forum on Fiction* 8 (1975): 226–40.

Ghiselin, Brewster. "The Unity of *Dubliners*." *Accent* 16 (Spring 1956): 75–88; (Summer 1956): 196–213. Rpt. in Garrett 57–85; in Baker and Staley 35–62; and (only Part I) in Scholes and Litz 316–32.

Gifford, Don. *Joyce Annotated: Notes for* Dubliners *and* A Portrait of the Artist as a Young Man. Berkeley: U of California P, 1982.

Gillespie, Michael Patrick. "Aesthetic Evolution: The Shaping Forces behind *Dubliners*." *Lang&S* 19.2 (Spring 1986): 149–63.

————. *Inverted Volumes Improperly Arranged: James Joyce and His Trieste Library.* Ann Arbor: UMI, 1983.

Givens, Seon, ed. *James Joyce: Two Decades of Criticism.* Rev. ed. New York: Vanguard, 1963.

Goldberg, S. L. "The Development of the Art: *Chamber Music* to *Dubliners*." *James Joyce.* Edinburgh: Oliver and Boyd; New York: Grove, 1962. 29–46. Rpt. as "The Artistry of *Dubliners*" in Garrett 86–92, and as "Virtues and Limitations" in Baker and Staley 29–35.

Goldman, Arnold. "The Early Stories in *Dubliners*." *The Joyce Paradox: Form and Freedom in His Fiction.* Evanston, IL: Northwestern UP; London: Routledge, 1966. 1–21.

Gordon, John. "The Dialogue of *Dubliners*." *James Joyce's Metamorphoses.* Dublin: Gill and Macmillan; Totowa, NJ: Barnes, 1981. 13–27.

Gorman, Herbert. *James Joyce.* Rev. ed. New York: Farrar, 1948.

Gray, Paul Edward. "James Joyce's *Dubliners*: A Study of the Narrator's Role in Modern Fiction." Diss. U of Virginia, 1965. *DA* 26 (1966): 6042.

His goal is to demonstrate that Joyce's handling of the narrator in *Dubliners* anticipates his subsequent use of the narrator. In chapters 3, 4, and 5, he analyzes each story, demonstrating methods by which narrators covertly comment on events. Ultimately, Gray concludes that the narrators in Joyce's fiction resemble one another because they all represent perceiving consciousnesses that are extremely sensitive to language.

Halper, Nathan. "The Boarding House." Clive Hart 72–83.

————. *The Early James Joyce.* Columbia Essays on Modern Writers 68. New York: Columbia UP, 1973.

————. "The Life Chronology of *Dubliners*." *JJQ* 16 (Summer 1979): 473–77.

————. "A Note on Design in *Dubliners*." *Studies in Joyce.* Ann Arbor, MI: UMI, 1983. 123–55.

Hart, Clive, ed. *James Joyce's Dubliners: Critical Essays.* New York: Viking; London: Faber, 1969.

Hart, John Raymond. "Moore on Joyce: The Influence of *The Untilled Field* on *Dubliners*." *Dublin Magazine* 10 (Summer 1973): 61–76.

Hayman, David. "A Mother." Clive Hart 122–33.

Hedberg, Johannes. "Some Notes on Language and Atmosphere in *Dubliners*." *MSpr* 75.2 (1981): 113–32.

Hendry, Irene. "Joyce's Epiphanies." *SR* 54 (Summer 1946): 449–67. Rpt. in Givens 27–46.

Henke, Suzette, and Elaine Unkeless. *Women in Joyce.* Urbana: U of Illinois P. 1982.

Henke, Suzette A. "Through a Cracked Looking-Glass: Sex-Role Stereotypes in *Dub*-

liners." *International Perspectives on James Joyce*. Ed. Gottlieb Gaiser. Troy, NY: Whitston, 1986. 2–31.

Herring, Phillip. *Joyce's Uncertainty Principle*. Princeton, NJ: Princeton UP, 1987.

———. "Structure and Meaning in Joyce's 'The Sisters.' " Benstock, *Seventh of Joyce*, 131–44.

Higgins, Joanna. "A Reading of the Last Sentence of 'The Dead.' " *ELN* 17 (Mar. 1980): 203–7.

Hodgart, Matthew. "*Dubliners*." *James Joyce: A Student's Guide*. London: Routledge, 1978. 44–56.

Humma, John B. "Gabriel and the Bedsheets: Still Another Reading of the Ending of 'The Dead.' " *SSF* 10 (Spring 1973): 207–9.

Ingram, Forrest L. *Representative Short Story Cycles of the Twentieth Century: Studies in a Literary Genre*. The Hague: Mouton, 1971. (See especially 26–34.)

Jedynak, Stanley Louis. "Epiphany and Dantean Correspondences in Joyce's *Dubliners*: A Study in Structure." Diss. Syracuse U. 1962. *DA* 23 (1962): 1018–19.

———. "Epiphany as Structure in *Dubliners*." *Greyfriar: Siena Studies in Literature* 12 (1971): 29–56.

Johnsen, William A. "Joyce's *Dubliners* and the Futility of Modernism." *James Joyce and Modern Literature*. Ed. W. J. McCormack and Alistair Stead. London: Routledge, 1982. 5–21.

Johnson, Greg. "Dreaming Lives: The Inner World of Joyce's *Dubliners*." *BSUF* 20 (Summer 1979): 36–43.

Jones, David E. "Approaches to *Dubliners*: Joyce's." *JJQ* 15 (Winter 1978): 108–17.

Jones, William Powell. "*Dubliners*: or the Moral History of Ireland." *James Joyce and the Common Reader*. Norman: U of Oklahoma P. 1955. 9–23.

Jordan, Richard Douglas. "The Trouble with *Dubliners*." *DUJ* 39.1 (1977–1978): 35–40.

Joyce, James. *Dubliners*. Ed. Robert Scholes and A. Walton Litz. New York: Viking, 1968.

———. Dubliners: *A Facsimile of Drafts and Manuscripts*. Prefaced and arranged by Hans Walter Gabler. New York: Garland. 1978.

———. Dubliners: *A Facsimile of Proofs for the 1910 Edition*. Prefaced and arranged by Michael Groden. New York: Garland, 1977.

———. Dubliners: *A Facsimile of Proofs for the 1914 Edition*. Prefaced and arranged by Michael Groden. New York: Garland, 1977.

———. *Letters of James Joyce*. Ed. Stuart Gilbert and Richard Ellmann. 3 vols. New York: Viking, 1957–1966.

Joyce, Stanislaus. *The Complete Dublin Diary of Stanislaus Joyce*. Ed. George Harris Healey. Ithaca: Cornell UP, 1971.

Keen, William P. "The Rhetoric of Spatial Focus in Joyce's *Dubliners*." *SSF* 16 (Summer 1979): 195–203.

Kennedy, Eileen. "Moore's *Untilled Field* and Joyce's *Dubliners*." *Éire-Ireland* (St. Paul, MN) 5 (Autumn 1970): 81–89.

Kenner, Hugh. "Berlitz Days." *Renascence: Essays on Value in Literature 35.2 (Winter 1983): 69–83.*

———. "*Dubliners*." *Dublin's Joyce*. Bloomington: Indiana UP, 1956. 48–68. Rpt. in Garrett 38–56.

Kronegger, Maria Elisabeth. *James Joyce and Associated Image Makers*. New Haven: College & Univ., 1968.

Lachtman, Howard. "The Magic-Lantern Business: James Joyce's Ecclesiastical Satire in *Dubliners*." *JJQ* 7 (Winter 1969): 82–92.

Laroque, François. "Hallowe'en Customs in 'Clay': A Study of James Joyce's Use of Folklore in *Dubliners*." *Cahiers Victoriens et Edouardiens* 14 (Oct. 1981): 47–56.

Leatherwood, A. M. "Joyce's Mythic Method: Structure and Unity in 'An Encounter.' " *SSF* 13 (Winter 1976): 71–78.

Leigh, James. "The Gnomonic Principle in *Dubliners*." *LJHum* 9.1 (Spring 1983): 35–40.

Levin, Harry. *James Joyce: A Critical Introduction*. 2nd ed. New York: New Directions; London: Faber, 1960.

Levin, Richard, and Charles Shattuck. "First Flight to Ithaca: A New Reading of Joyce's *Dubliners*." *Accent* 4 (Winter 1944): 75–99. Rpt. in Givens 47–94.

Litz, A. Walton. "*Dubliners*." *James Joyce*. Rev. ed. New York: Twayne, 1972. 47–59.

Lohani, Shreedhar Prasad. "The Narrator in Fiction: A Study of the Narrator's Presence in Joyce's *Dubliners* and Hemingway's *In Our Time*." Diss. Southern Illinois U, 1984. *DAI* 45 (1985): 2517A.

Loomis, C. C., Jr. "Structure and Sympathy in Joyce's 'The Dead.' " *PMLA* 75 (1960): 149–51. Rpt. in Garrett 110–14, and in Scholes and Litz 417–22.

Loss, Archie K. *Joyce's Visible Art: The Work of Joyce and the Visual Arts, 1904–1922*. Ann Arbor, MI: UMI, 1984.

Lyons, J. B. "Diseases in *Dubliners*: Tokens of Disaffection." *Irish Renaissance Annual* 2 (1981): 185–203.

MacCabe, Colin. *James Joyce and the Revolution of the Word*. New York: Barnes, 1979.

McGuinness, Arthur E. "The Ambience of Space in Joyce's *Dubliners*." *SSF* 11 (1974): 343–51.

Magalaner, Marvin. "*Dubliners*." *Joyce: The Man, the Work, the Reputation*. Ed. Marvin Magalaner and Richard M. Kain. New York: New York UP, 1956. 53–101. The sections discussing "Clay" and those writers who influenced Joyce are rpt. in Baker and Staley 16–28, 124–30.

———. "The Evolution of *Dubliners*." *Time of Apprenticeship: The Fiction of the Young James Joyce*. New York: Abelard-Schuman, 1959. 72–96.

———. "James Joyce and the Uncommon Reader." *SAQ* 52 (Apr. 1953): 267–76.

———. " 'The Sisters' of James Joyce." *Univ. of Kansas City Review* 18 (Summer 1952): 255–61.

Marcus, Phillip L. "George Moore's Dublin 'Epiphanies' and Joyce." *JJQ* 5 (Winter 1968): 157–61.

Martin, Augustine. "Joyce's Narrative Strategies in the Central Stories of *Dubliners*." *Dolphin* 8 (Oct. 1983): 27–46. Also appears in *Joyce Centenary Offshoots: James Joyce, 1882–1892*. Ed. Karl-Heinz Westarp. Aarhus, Denmark: Seklos, Dept. of English, U of Aarhus, 1983.

Martin, Jacky. " 'Paralysie,' 'Simonie,' 'Gnomon': Les Conditions de représentation du désir dans *Dubliners*." *Cahiers Victoriens et Édouardiens* 14 (Oct. 1981): 29–37.

————. "Pessimisme et fonctionnements textuels dans *Dubliners* de James Joyce." *Cahiers Victoriens et Édouardiens* 15 (Apr. 1982): 87–90.

Meindl, Dieter. "Der Kurzgeschichtenzyklus als modernistisches Genre." *GRM* 33.2 (1983): 216–28.

Montgomery, Judith. "The Artist as Silent Dubliner." *JJQ* 6 (Summer 1969): 306–20.

Morrissey, L. J. "Joyce's Narrative Strategies in 'Araby.' " *MFS* 28 (Spring 1982): 45–52.

————. "Joyce's Revision of 'The Sisters': From Epicleti to Modern Fiction." *JJQ* 24.1 (Fall 1986): 33–54.

Moynihan, William T., ed. *Joyce's "The Dead."* Boston: Allyn, 1965.

Murphy, M. W. "Darkness in *Dubliners*." MFS 15 (Spring 1969): 97–104.

Nilsen, Kenneth. "Irish Language and Mythology in *Dubliners*." *CJIS* 12.1 (June 1986): 23–34.

O'Connor, Frank [Michael O'Donovan]. "Joyce and the Dissociated Metaphor." *The Mirror in the Roadway: A Study of the Modern Novel*. New York: Knopf, 1956. 295–312. Rpt. in Moynihan 89–92.

————. "Work in Progress." *The Lonely Voice: A Study of the Short Story*. Cleveland: World, 1963. 113–27. Rpt. in Garrett 18–26, and in Scholes and Litz 304–15.

Ostroff, Anthony. "The Moral Vision in 'Dubliners.' " *Western Speech* 20 (Fall 1956): 196–209.

Parrinder, Patrick. "*Dubliners*." *James Joyce*. Cambridge, Eng.: Cambridge UP, 1984. 41–70. Rpt. in *James Joyce*. Ed. Harold Bloom. New York: Chelsea, 1986. 245–73.

Peake, C. H. "*Dubliners*." *James Joyce: The Citizen and the Artist*. London: Edward Arnold; Stanford: Stanford UP, 1977. 1–55.

Pecora, Vincent P. " 'The Dead' and the Generosity of the Word." *PMLA* 101.2 (Mar. 1986): 233–45.

Peterson, Richard F. "Joyce's Use of Time in *Dubliners*." *BSUF* 14 (Winter 1973): 43–51.

Peterson, Richard F., Alan M. Cohn, and Edmund L. Epstein, eds. *Work in Progress: Joyce Centenary Essays*. Carbondale: Southern Illinois UP, 1983.

Rabaté, Jean-Michel. "Le Silence dans *Dubliners*." *Cahiers Victoriens et Édouardiens* 14 (Oct. 1981): 13–27. Trans. and rpt. in *James Joyce: New Perspectives*. Ed. Colin MacCabe. Brighton, Eng.: Harvester; Bloomington: Indiana UP, 1982. 45–72.

Reed, Pleasant Larus, III. "The Integrated Short-Story Collection: Studies of a Form of Nineteenth- and Twentieth-Century Fiction." Diss. Indiana U, 1974. *DAI* 35 (1975): 6730A

    Reed unconvincingly argues that Joyce wrote *Dubliners* to try to improve upon George Moore's *Untilled Field*. He also attempts to define how *Dubliners* is unified. The first three stories are unified by character and point of view. "A Little Cloud" and "The Dead" were written specifically to fill gaps in the book. Additionally, "A Little Cloud" is used to begin the mature character section, and "The Dead" reverses the paralysis described in the rest of the book.

Reynolds, Mary T. *Joyce and Dante: The Shaping Imagination*. Princeton: Princeton UP, 1981. The section on *Dubliners* is rpt. in Benstock, *Seventh of Joyce*, 124–30.

Riquelme, John Paul. "Precursors of Portraiture/Preludes for Myth: *Stephen Hero* and

Dubliners." Teller and Tale in Joyce's Fiction: Oscillating Perspectives. Baltimore: Johns Hopkins UP, 1983. 86–130.

Ristkok, Tuuli. "A Study of Joyce's Narrative Technique in *Dubliners.*" Diss. U of Chicago, 1970 (No *DAI* entry)

Robinson, David W. "The Narration of Reading in Joyce's 'The Sisters,' 'An Encounter,' and 'Araby.' " *TSLL* 29.3 (Fall 1987): 377–96.

San Juan, Epifanio, Jr. *James Joyce and the Craft of Fiction: An Interpretation of* Dubliners. Rutherford, NJ: Fairleigh Dickinson UP, 1972.

Schneider, Ulrich. *James Joyce:* Dubliners. Munich: Fink, 1982.

Scholes, Robert. "Counterparts." Scholes and Litz 379–87; and Clive Hart 93–99.

———. "Further Observations on the Text of *Dubliners.*" *SB* 17 (1964): 107–22.

———. "Grant Richards to James Joyce." *SB* 16 (1963): 139–60.

———. "Some Observations on the Text of *Dubliners*: 'The Dead.' " *SB* 15 (1962): 191–205.

Scholes, Robert, and A. Walton Litz, eds. *James Joyce's* Dubliners: *Text, Criticism, and Notes.* New York: Viking, 1969.

Scholes, Robert, and Florence L. Walzl. "Notes, Documents, and Critical Comment: The Epiphanies of Joyce." *PMLA* 82 (Mar. 1967): 152–54.

Scott, Bonnie Kime. *James Joyce.* Atlantic Highlands, NJ: Humanities, 1987.

———. *Joyce and Feminism.* Bloomington: Indiana UP, 1983.

Senn, Fritz. "An Encounter." Clive Hart 26–38.

Shields, David. "A Note on the Conclusion of Joyce's 'The Dead.' " *JJQ* 22.4 (Summer 1985): 427–28.

Shurgot, Michael W. "Windows of Escape and the Death Wish in Man: Joyce's 'The Dead.' " *Éire-Ireland* (St. Paul, MN) 17.4 (Winter 1982): 58–71.

Smith, Paul. "Crossing the Lines in 'A Painful Case.' " *SHR* 17 (Summer 1983): 203–8.

Sniderman, Stephen L. "The 'Composite' in Twentieth-Century American Literature." Diss. U of Wisconsin, 1970. *DAI* 31 (1970): 403A.

    Sniderman notes that unity in some composites (cycles) is maintained even though there are no recurring characters; in *Dubliners*, theme serves to connect stories. Of the two kinds of composites he describes (see Introduction's bibliography), Sniderman sees *Dubliners* as representative of composites concerned with something more than the development of a single character.

Somerville, Jane. "Money in *Dubliners.*" *SSF* 12 (Spring 1975): 109–16.

Staley, Thomas F. "A Beginning: Significance, Story, and Discourse in Joyce's 'The Sisters.' " *Genre* 12 (Winter 1979): 533–49. Rpt. in Benstock, *Critical Essays*, 176–90.

———, ed. *James Joyce Today: Essays on the Major Works.* Bloomington: Indiana UP, 1966.

Stewart, J. I. M. "*Dubliners.*" Beja, *Casebook*, 202–7.

Tate, Allen. " 'The Dead.' " *The House of Fiction.* Ed. Caroline Gordon and Allen Tate. New York: Scribner's, 1950. 279–82. Rpt. in Scholes and Litz 404–9.

Thorn, Eric P. "James Joyce: Early Imitations of Structural Unity." *Costerus* 9 (1973): 229–39.

Tindall, William York. "*Dubliners.*" *A Reader's Guide to James Joyce.* New York: Farrar, 1959. 3–49. Sections on "The Boarding House" and "A Mother" are rpt. in Baker and Staley 106–7, 146–48. The book was rpt. by Octagon in 1971.

Torchiana, Donald T. *Backgrounds for Joyce's* Dubliners. Boston: Allen & Unwin, 1986.
———. "The Ending of 'The Dead': I Follow Saint Patrick." *JJQ* 18.2 (Spring 1981): 123–32.
———. "James Joyce's Method in *Dubliners*." *The Irish Short Story*. Ed. Patrick Rafroidi and Terence Brown. Buckinghamshire: Colin Smythe; Atlantic Highlands, NJ: Humanities, 1979. 128–40.
———. "The Opening of *Dubliners*: A Reconsideration." *Irish University Review* 1 (Spring 1971): 149–60.
Voelker, Joseph C. " 'Chronicles of Disorder': Reading the Margins of James Joyce's *Dubliners*." *Colby Library Quarterly* 18.2 (June 1982): 126–44.
Walsh, Ruth M. "That Pervasive Mass—in *Dubliners* and *A Portrait of the Artist as a Young Man*." *JJQ* 8 (Spring 1971): 205–20.
Walzl, Florence L. "A Book of Signs and Symbols: The Protagonist." Benstock, *Seventh of Joyce*, 117–23.
———. "*Dubliners*." Bowen and Carens 157–228.
———. "*Dubliners*: Women in Irish Society." Henke and Unkeless 31–56.
———. "Gabriel and Michael: The Conclusion of 'The Dead.' " *JJQ* 4 (Fall 1966): 17–31. Rpt. in Scholes and Litz 423–43.
———. "Joyce's 'Clay': Fact and Fiction." *Renascence: Essays on Value in Literature* 35 (Autumn 1983): 119–37.
———. "Joyce's 'The Sisters': A Development." *JJQ* 10 (Summer 1973): 375–421.
———. "The Life Chronology of *Dubliners*." *JJQ* 14 (Summer 1977): 408–15.
———. "The Liturgy of the Epiphany Season and the Epiphanies of Joyce." *PMLA* 80 (Sept. 1965): 436–50. Rpt. in *Twentieth Century Interpretations of* A Portrait of the Artist as a Young Man. Ed. William M. Schutte. Englewood Cliffs, NJ: Prentice, 1968. 115–17.
———. "Pattern of Paralysis in Joyce's *Dubliners*: A Study of the Original Framework." *CE* 22 (Jan. 1961): 221–28.
Werner, Craig Hansen. "Dublin(er)'s Joyce: Ernest Gaines, Flannery O'Connor, Russell Banks." *Paradoxical Resolutions: American Fiction since James Joyce*. Urbana: U of Illinois P, 1982. 34–50.
West, Michael. "George Moore and the Hermeneutics of Joyce's *Dubliners*." *HLB* 26 (Apr. 1978): 212–35.
West, Michael, and William Hendricks. "The Genesis and Significance of Joyce's Irony in 'A Painful Case.' " *ELH* 44 (Winter 1977): 701–27.
Wigginton, B. Eliot. "*Dubliners* in Order." *JJQ* 7 (Summer 1970): 297–314.
Wight, Doris T. "Vladimir Propp and *Dubliners*." *JJQ* 23.4 (Summer 1986): 415–33.
Wright, David G. "*Dubliners*." *Characters of Joyce*. Totowa, NJ: Barnes; Dublin: Gill and Macmillan, 1983. 13–29

2

Sherwood Anderson's
Winesburg, Ohio

INTRODUCTION TO THE BOOK

Much like the characters in *Dubliners*, the protagonists in *Winesburg, Ohio* feel trapped in wasted lives and generally seem incapable of freeing themselves. The second book differs from the first in some important respects, however. While the protagonists in *Dubliners* feel trapped for a variety of reasons, their counterparts in *Winesburg* feel limited largely because of their inability to establish close relations with others. Although the topic of human isolation is important in many of the stories in *Dubliners*—especially "Eveline," "Clay," "A Painful Case," and "The Dead"—it is of overriding importance in every story in *Winesburg*. Jesse Bentley in "Godliness" drives away his grandson, the only person important to him, in his desperation to win God's approval; Alice Hindman in "Adventure" is resigned to loneliness since she can no longer imagine that love is possible for her; Enoch Robinson in "Loneliness" tries to hide from other people because he is overwhelmed by their personalities; Elizabeth Willard in "Death" is eager to die because she thinks that death comes to her as a lover: "She personified the figure of death and made him now a strong black-haired youth running over the hills . . . " (*Winesburg* 228).

Other major differences between *Dubliners* and *Winesburg* are the degree to which protagonists realize the limits of their lives and the extent to which they are able to overcome those limitations. In general, protagonists in Winesburg seem more aware of their situations than those in Dublin, even though the Winesburgers lack the ability to communicate these insights to anyone other than George Willard. Additionally, unlike the cast of *Dubliners*, several characters in *Winesburg* act positively in order to improve their situations. Doctor Reefy, Elizabeth Willard, Reverend Curtis Hartman, George Willard, and Helen White all establish satisfactory if brief contact with another person. Perhaps more driven than Joyce to provide an uplifting conclusion, Anderson also enables George

Willard to leave Winesburg so that he can become a writer and communicate to his readers what the people in Winesburg find impossible to express out loud.

COMPOSITION AND PUBLICATION OF *WINESBURG, OHIO*

When Sherwood Anderson described how he wrote "Hands," the second story in *Winesburg*, he romanticized the experience, as William L. Phillips suggests in his article based on the manuscript at the Newberry Library. Nevertheless, Anderson was probably accurate in some respects, including his insistence that "Hands" and most of the other Winesburg stories were written rapidly, one story leading quickly to another:

["Hands"] was written that night in one sitting. No word of it ever changed. I wrote the story and got up. I walked up and down in that little narrow room. Tears flowed from my eyes.
  "It is solid," I said to myself. "It is like a rock." (*Sherwood Anderson's Memoirs: A Critical Edition*, 1969: 352)

The tales were all written in a few months, one following the other, a kind of joyous time for me, the words and ideas flowing freely. . . . (*Memoirs*, 1969:348)

According to Phillips, the first eighteen stories seem to have been written at approximately the same time, since they are on the backs of twenty numbered tales that Anderson had previously abandoned ("How Anderson Wrote *Winesburg*" 10–11).

The first stories were written in the fall of 1915, and Phillips calculates that they were all finished by early 1916 except for the last four stories—"The Philosopher," "Death," "Sophistication," "Departure"—which were apparently written after the others in order to emphasize George Willard's development and to complete plots pertaining to other major characters (27–29). Between February 1916 and December 1918, ten of the Winesburg stories were published in *The Masses*, *The Little Review*, and *The Seven Arts*, and the book, originally subtitled *A Group of Tales of Ohio Small-Town Life*, was published by B. W. Huebsch in 1919.

In addition to stressing that the *Winesburg* stories came easily, Sherwood Anderson also insisted that they represented a turning point in his career. Once again, describing the composition of "Hands," Anderson says: "I am quite sure that on that night, when it happened in that room, when for the first time I dared whisper to myself, perhaps sobbing, that I had found it, my vocation, I knelt in the darkness and muttered words of gratitude to God" (*Memoirs*, 1969: 353).

While it is difficult to question his recollections of his emotions at the time "Hands" was completed, Anderson is less reliable when he declares that the stories received little or no rewriting. To some his changes may appear minor (primarily revisions in syntax and phrasing), but their cumulative effect is of major significance. "Hands," the story which Phillips describes in greatest detail, is a good example. While Anderson maintained that "no word of it ever changed," Phillips notes that about 200 changes were made, mostly deletions or revitalizations of awkward or lifeless phrasing. These revisions, typical of those made in all of the stories, often enabled Anderson to define more precisely a character's essence: for example, realistic details in the setting of "Hands" (e.g., Wing Biddlebaum's veranda) become metaphors ("the half decayed veranda"). Also, although he retained (in Phillips's words) the "intrusions of the author into this story" (23), Anderson's revisions made his entrances and exits less distracting. Finally, through revisions Anderson introduced many of the stylistic traits critics have praised: the repetition of key words and phrases, especially proper nouns, and the substitution of colloquial expressions for more formal ones (19–24).

If Anderson romanticized the composition process slightly, it is no doubt because the stories did come easily—they were "grasped whole as one would pick an apple" (*Memoirs*, 1942: 341)—and because *Winesburg* was his first noteworthy accomplishment, following the disappointing novels *Windy McPherson's Son* and *Marching Men*. Anderson also recognized that his stories were superior to those that were currently popular: they "broke the O. Henry grip" by de-emphasizing plot in order to focus instead on characterization or psychological realism (*Memoirs*, 1969: 349; Sutton 433–34). Ultimately, Anderson became convinced that in his book about the rural Midwest he had "invented" what he called "the Winesburg form." Although he never precisely defined the word "form," Anderson specified several characteristics of "the Winesburg form," and he found it appropriate for subsequent books:

Out of necessity I am throwing the Mary Cochran book into the Winesburg form, half individual tales, half long novel form. (Sutton 433)

My theme is American men in relation to their women. . . . In getting at this theme I have decided to return to a form I used in *Winesburg, Ohio*; that is to say, taking a related group of people, their lives touching, never quite touching. . . . (*Letters* 410)[1]

Regardless of how he defined "form," it is clear that Anderson consistently maintained that the book was a series of interrelated stories and not a novel. As late as the 1942 edition of his *Memoirs*, Anderson says: "I have even sometimes thought that the novel form does not fit an American writer, that it is a form which had been brought in. What I wanted is a new looseness; and in *Winesburg* I had made my own form" (289).

UNITY IN *WINESBURG, OHIO*

Prologue or Framing Story

Even at the beginning of a first reading of *Winesburg*, it is absolutely clear that the book is not a short story miscellany or anthology. Most obvious is the title, which foreshadows the unity of place that is maintained throughout the book. Also, "The Book of the Grotesque" clearly functions as a prologue.[2] It is the only story that is not set in Winesburg and that does not contain people from Winesburg, featuring instead a writer and an old carpenter supposedly representative of what is "understandable and lovable of all the grotesques in the writer's book" (*Winesburg* 26). Also, considerably more abstract, more concerned with discussion of storytelling than with actual storytelling, "The Book of the Grotesque" serves to introduce the major subjects dramatized in *Winesburg*: the relationship between art and society and the old writer's theory of the grotesque.

Setting

As one reads past the prologue, the Winesburg setting becomes a major unifying device, but it functions in more complex ways than is commonly acknowledged. Although considerable attention is given to realistic details, including the names of buildings, their locations, and the names of streets, one is never able to visualize the town's geography; these specific details evoke small-town life, but there is no attempt to unify the stories through a precisely defined sense of Winesburg geography. In fact, the map of the town that is placed at the beginning of the 1960 edition demonstrates this point. Even though there are over one hundred Winesburgers mentioned in the book, and over forty or fifty houses, offices, banks, stores, farms, and other buildings, the legend of the map identifies only eight places. Many of the most important sites cannot be located: for example, Wing Biddlebaum's house and the Bentley farm on the outskirts of Winesburg, Louise Bentley Hardy's house on Elm Street (a street that doesn't even appear on the map), and Banker White's house.

Some places in Winesburg are mentioned several times—especially the New Willard House, which appears in most stories—and these recurrences help connect the stories. More important than this kind of repetition, however, are the similarities that Forrest L. Ingram and Anita V. R. Yancey note among the diverse settings: in front of Wing Biddlebaum's house, which stands near the edge of a ravine, is a half-decayed veranda; Doctor Reefy's vacant, musty office is no longer used except for his daydreaming; the interior of the New Willard House is so faded and down at the heels that it keeps business away; Doctor Parcival's office is described as dirty and unoccupied, except for Parcival, who is afraid to leave his office; Reverend Hartman's office is a tiny, sparsely furnished room in the bell tower, and, like most of the other characters, he stares out of his window, imagining a relationship with a person he hardly knows. Repeatedly, rooms, offices, or houses are described as run-down and poorly or sparsely furnished, as claustrophobic, as unoccupied except for the protagonist, even as located in a precarious setting (for example, the ravine next to Biddlebaum's house as well as the financially unsuccessful New Willard House or Cowley & Son's store). Although dwellings are described in different ways, reflecting the character's idiosyncrasies or social standing in the community, the setting in each case is used to emphasize the theme of isolation.

Time or Chronology

Chronology is less important in *Winesburg* than unity of setting. Since characters such as Wing Biddlebaum, Elizabeth Willard, Doctor Parcival, Enoch Robinson, Wash Williams, and Alice Hindman remain static and generally unaffected by the passage of time, their stories or the events in their lives do not need to be told chronologically, and inconsistencies in chronology are relatively unimportant. For example, George in "The Thinker" is said to be older than Seth Richmond, who is already eighteen, but in "Death," which supposedly takes place a year later, we are told that George has just become eighteen (Ingram 168–169).

Only insofar as George Willard develops as a character is chronology important. This development is described below.

Character

Similarities among the Characters

Although almost every story features a different protagonist, there are, according to Ingram's count, thirty-three characters who appear in more than one story (151n). This large circulating cast obviously helps unify the Winesburg stories, especially since the characters not only reappear but also closely resemble one another. Convinced that there is a limited number of types or kinds of characters in the book, several critics have attempted to classify them.

Providing a useful scheme, George D. Murphy divides the characters into four groups on the basis of each character's attitude toward sex: (1) those characters such as Wash Williams who are disgusted by sex and avoid it entirely; (2) those characters such as Will Henderson who indulge in sex but expect nothing from it but pleasure; (3) those characters such as Elizabeth Willard who are disappointed by sex because they expect more than sexual pleasure; and (4) those characters such as Doctor Reefy or Kate Swift who "sublimate their desire and, by avoiding the trap of a merely sensual mode of communication, are admitted to a plane of consciousness where communication operates in terms of an imaginative, mystical sympathy" (242).

Another more problematic classification system is provided by Thomas M. Lorch, who suggests that three mythic or archetypal figures predominate: the old guide, the Woman as mother and lover, and the questing hero. Although he accurately describes the significance of the quest and the roles some characters play, Lorch's categories seem ill-conceived. Almost all of the characters fall into the last two classes, and these two classes heavily overlap, since most women in the book are also involved in their own quests.

Not interested in classifying characters, Marilyn Judith Atlas points out similarities shared by the women characters in *Winesburg*, especially Elizabeth Willard, Louise Bentley, Alice Hindman, Kate Swift, and Helen White. In her article, she argues convincingly that while Anderson demonstrates some sensitivity in his depiction of women, he denies them the same needs and opportunities he provides for male characters: "Too often he was comfortable assuming that what women wanted most was to give themselves away to an ideal lover. His belief that women wanted men and men wanted to create is depicted in the love relationships of Winesburg" (253).[3]

George Willard as Protagonist

In addition to these correspondences among the characters, the stories in *Winesburg* are obviously connected by George Willard's presence. Because he appears or is mentioned in almost every story, because he is one of the only characters who develops in the book, and because he resembles the older writer mentioned in the prologue as well as the narrator, George Willard is clearly of major importance. Less clear, however, are the way and the extent to which he unifies the stories.

Since he is present in almost every story as listener or participant, and since the stories in which he plays a major part are ordered in such a way that they emphasize subtle changes in his personality, some critics argue that George Willard is the book's major unifying device. As a result, these critics stress that the other characters—using the narrator's term, the "grotesques"—are primarily important as they contribute to George's education and maturation. For example, according to Edwin Fussell, George's experiences with the grotesques enable him in "Sophistication" and "Departure" to realize that loneliness is inescapable and that "love is essentially the shared acceptance by two people . . . of their final separateness" (114). Similarly, Sylvia A. Holladay emphasizes that through his varied experiences with the grotesques and his interest in their stories, George realizes by the end of the book that "human feelings with responsiveness" (12) are more important than anything else.

Although George Willard does develop over the course of the book and his presence encourages other people to reveal their secrets, one must recognize that certain limitations are placed upon him as a unifying device. To begin with, George's perspective is less sympathetic, comprehensive, and objective than the narrator's. As a young man, often close to the related events, he cannot respond as generously as the narrator does when other characters reveal their weaknesses. Therefore, George lacks the sympathetic vision of Winesburg that the narrator possesses and that provides the sense of community achieved in the stories in spite of the fact that people are largely estranged from one another.

In addition, George's presence in the book does not determine the order in which the majority of the stories are placed. Anderson orders certain stories so that he can introduce George and his background early in the book ("Paper Pills" and "Mother"). Other stories are arranged to trace the development of

George's relations with women ("Nobody Knows," "The Teacher," "An Awakening," and "Sophistication"). Finally, the first and last stories ("Death," "Sophistication," and "Departure") are used to provide the book with a circular ending, returning to the issue of whether or not George will leave Winesburg.

Neither does George Willard's development involve mutually exclusive stages, as some suggest. Walter B. Rideout, for example, identifies "aspects" or stages of George's development, but his related processes occur simultaneously and continue throughout the book: (1) George attempts to resolve the conflict that exists in his mind between the demands made by the practical world of affairs and the world of dreams; (2) George considers becoming a writer; and (3) George recognizes that one must look beyond appearances in order to try to discover the truth ("Simplicity").

Perhaps the most productive approach to *Winesburg* is to think of George Willard as a pivotal character in the cycle. He is an important actor in the lives of other Winesburgers, but not necessarily the most important individual in town. Even though he appears more often than other characters, he may not be as memorable to the reader as Wing Biddlebaum, Doctor Reefy, or Elizabeth Willard. Because he functions primarily as a listener or observer, most of the book's dramatic interest results from the other characters' actions and their nearly strangled dreams and desires.

Plot

While George Willard's development is the plot pattern most commonly cited as a unifying device, there are others that warrant discussion. Less important than those involving George, several other plots connect small groups of stories. For example, "The Strength of God" and "Teacher" involve basically the same events, but the second takes place slightly after the first. (The second also renders Kate Swift's perspective, whereas the first describes Reverend Hartman's). Additionally, the four parts of "Godliness" are unified by Jesse Bentley's religious fanaticism, specifically his desperate attempts to win favor with God and the effect his self-righteousness has on his daughter and grandson.

More important than these two illustrations is the repeated use—in story after story—of a single basic plot pattern. Sometimes called a quest, the plot contains the following ingredients: the longing for connection; the attempt to express love; the sense of rejection and failure that follows when the protagonist cannot express affection or the other person fails to respond satisfactorily; finally, the withdrawal, generally accompanied by either self-delusion or a sense of resignation.[4] This recurring basic plot is most impressively described by Irving Howe, who uses the metaphor of the dance:

It is possible to abstract the choreography of *Winesburg*. Its typical action is a series of dance maneuvers by figures whose sole distinctive characteristic is an extreme deformity of movement or posture. Each of these grotesques dances . . . toward a central figure who seems to them young, fresh, and radiant. For a moment they seem to draw close to him and thereby to abandon their stoops and limps, but this moment quickly dissolves . . . : the central figure cannot be reached. Slowly and painfully, the grotesques withdraw while the young man leaves the stage entirely. (38)

The problem with Howe's description is that it acknowledges George Willard as the only person whom the grotesques approach. While George is sought out more than anyone else, there are several other characters who function in the same way, although they are often figures from the past appearing in the long stories that the grotesques tell. Responding to Howe's argument, Lorch expands Howe's metaphor further. He does this, in part, because he recognizes that George is not the only character pursued by the grotesques, but also because he recognizes that two recurring plot patterns function as subdivisions of Howe's single unifying plot pattern. According to Lorch, a number of the stories involve parents or surrogate parents: Kate Swift or Doctor Reefy, for example, offer advice in an attempt to establish a relationship with a younger person. In the majority of the stories, however, the attempt to connect with another person involves a romantic or sexual relationship. In each case, the plot consists of the same general movement described by Howe's dance metaphor: the attempt to establish contact with another person, the failure to do so, and the retreat or the return to one's original isolated condition.

Critics such as Howe and Lorch succeed in emphasizing that basically the same action is repeated in almost every story and that many characters' functions are determined by the manner in which they participate in this action.

Theme or Topic

In *Winesburg* most of the stories chronicle unsuccessful attempts to establish intimate relationships, but there are some exceptions to the general rule that satisfactory relationships are not possible. Substantial if temporary connections are established in several stories: the relationship between Doctor Reefy and the "quiet, tall, and dark" (35) woman in "Paper Pills"; between the Reverend Curtis Hartman and God in "The Strength of God"; between Elizabeth Willard and Doctor Reefy in "Death"; and between George Willard and Helen White in "Sophistication." Because characters connect so rarely in Winesburg, the exceptional nature or fragility of the relationships is repeatedly underscored.

As critics discuss the ways in which the subject of isolation unifies *Winesburg*, they also attempt to explain why the characters are isolated. According to some (for example, Berland and Ciancio), isolation occurs because, as the old writer explains in "The Book of the Grotesque," characters obsessively attempt to adhere to a single truth or ideal:

It was the truths that made the people grotesques. The old man had quite an elaborate theory concerning the matter. It was his notion that the moment one of the people took one of the truths to himself, called it a truth, and tried to live his life by it, he became a grotesque and the truth he embraced became a falsehood. (*Winesburg* 25–26)

Yancey, arguing that this debilitating dedication to a single truth is the major unifying pattern in *Winesburg*, even attempts to identify the specific truths involved. For example, according to her, Elizabeth Willard, Louise Bentley, Wash Williams, and Alice Hindman are all obsessed with the truth of love; Jesse Bentley, Joe Welling, and Seth Richmond are driven by the truth of ambition for power; and the minister, Curtis Hartman, not unexpectedly, lives according to the truth of religion.

Although some of the protagonists in *Winesburg* have become cripples or grotesques while pursuing single truths, the theory of the grotesques does not adequately describe each character's situation. As Carlos Baker emphasizes, "This theory, such as it is, applies to a bare minimum of the stories that follow" (574). That Anderson expected "The Book of the Grotesque" to provide definitive answers is doubtful. After all, the narrator is frequently ironic when describing the old writer and explaining his theories:

The old writer, like all the people in the world, had got, during his long life, a great many notions in his head. He had once been quite handsome and a number of women had been in love with him. And then, of course, he had known people, many people, known them in a peculiarly intimate way that was different from the way in which you and I know people. At least that is what the writer thought and the thought pleased him. Why quarrel with an old man concerning his thoughts? (*Winesburg* 24)

Because the narrator distances himself from the old writer, undercutting his ideas, it is unlikely that the old writer functions in such a straightforward way as Anderson's mouthpiece.[5]

"The Book of the Grotesque" introduces another important unifying subject: the relationship between the artist and the rest of society. This topic connects subtly with the subject of isolation, and several critics have described themes based on the interaction. Probably most important is Fussell's analysis of the "complementary union" (109) that exists in *Winesburg* between the artist and the ordinary people. What the townspeople of Winesburg give to George Willard is fairly obvious: they provide him with the subject matter that he will later use to write fiction. What George offers to them is more difficult to define; nevertheless, Fussell provides an answer that deserves consideration. George as a developing artist has the ability both to maintain his distance from others and to understand why objectivity or separateness is necessary. Therefore, even though he cannot provide the companionship they desperately seek, George can teach other people to "recognize and respect the essential privacy (or integrity) of human personality": "The loneliness is assuaged—there is no other way— by the realization that loneliness is a universal condition and not a uniquely personal catastrophe . . . " (114). In spite of the fact that the grotesques probably do not benefit from George Willard's example or from the example of art in general, Fussell argues that the subjects of art and the artist are important because they emphasize that one can experience isolation without necessarily becoming a grotesque. The only problem with Fussell's analysis is that he seems at times to confuse George's potential as an artist with George the actual character. As a result, some of the insights he attributes to George are Fussell's own precise restatements of the narrator's observations.[6]

Other subjects or themes are important: for example, Anderson's satiric treatment of small-town life (Burbank) or, for those with a different perspective, his nostalgic treatment of agrarian or turn-of-the-century America (Love). Additionally, Ingram develops the quest myth in the book further by concentrating on four interrelated motifs—departure, adventure, dream, and hungering. But the subject of isolation, including the extent to which art assuages or exacerbates the characters' loneliness, is the thematic idea seen by most critics as central to *Winesburg*.

Imagery

While describing the pervasive sense of isolation and estrangement that exists in *Winesburg*, critics have identified image patterns and symbols that evoke the theme and have even made attempts to describe the cumulative effect of certain repeated patterns. The three patterns that are most important as far as the subject of isolation is concerned are imagery pertaining to the rooms, office spaces, and dwellings, discussed above in the section of setting; eye and hand imagery; light and dark imagery; and imagery based on Christian myth.

Carol J. Maresca, Rideout, and Ingram have all described how gestures made with the hands and eyes are used to reveal a character's psychological state or his awkward attempt to establish contact with another person. The best-known example, of course, is Wing Biddlebaum's fluttering hands: "Biddlebaum talked much with his hands. The slender expressive fingers, forever active, forever striving to conceal themselves in the pockets or behind his back, came forth and became the piston rods of his machinery of expression" (*Winesburg* 28). While tracing the pattern of hand imagery throughout the book, Ingram adds that "the mere act of reaching out to touch another human being achieves, as story builds on story, a mythic dimension quite beyond the reach of a single story (even 'Hands') taken by itself" (189). He also notes that "the intensity of hand-symbolism increases" (191) during the last three stories.

Emphasizing that *Winesburg* is primarily a book about the " 'night world' " of human personality, Rideout explains that the repeated use of dim light and darkness helps unify the stories in the following ways: "The dim light equates with, as well as literally illuminates, the limited glimpse into an individual soul that each crisis scene affords, and the briefness of the insight is emphasized by the shutting down of the dark" ("Simplicity" 24). Similarly, Yancey emphasizes that characters come closer to revealing themselves in the late afternoon or evening, especially when there is a sense of ''dreaminess'' (33) or unreality about the twilight.

In addition to these patterns, other unifying imagery based on Christian mythology—images associated with the Grail, the Garden of Eden, the Tree of Knowledge, the Fall, the Crucifixion, Holy Communion—helps develop the subject of isolation. The function of this imagery is difficult to define precisely, but both Ralph Ciancio an John J. McAleer analyze it in detail. In ''Christ Symbolism in *Winesburg*,'' McAleer argues that the book should be read as a modern, secularized Grail romance:

As the Arthurian knight sought the Holy Grail because it symbolized to him Christ's sacrifice to redeem man, George Willard quests a latter-day Holy Grail, a cup of explanation in which to catch man's spilled blood and endow it with significance, a way of accounting for man's suffering, which, if it cannot bring it to an end, will at least sanctify it. (170–71)

Ciancio agrees with most of the major points made by McAleer. Not only does he argue that Anderson appropriates Christian myth for secular purposes, but Ciancio also emphasizes that the grotesques are self-crucified and that they can be saved only by George Willard's or Doctor Reefy's artistic imagination: ''though they will not be made whole and beautiful, the peculiar value of their twisted state will be recognized'' (1004–5).[7]

Point of View

Although George Willard's function as a unifying figure has received much attention, the role of the narrator is probably more important. This is because, as Ingram emphasizes, it is only in the narrator's storytelling that the people of Winesburg are given full significance and a sense of community: ''They touch one another and hardly touch one another at all. In Winesburg itself, they seem hardly to know one another; in the narrator's mind they are brothers'' (165).

In addition, as both Ingram and John J. Mahoney note, the reader is almost always aware of the narrator's presence. Not only is there relatively little dialogue—Mahoney suggests that ''the voice of the author predominates over the characters' voices in a proportion of about five parts to one'' (246)—but when the characters do speak, because of the highly stylized and poetic language used throughout the book, it is difficult to distinguish their language habits from the narrator's. The narrator's presence is further felt because he is forever influencing the reader's attitude toward the events he describes by his philosophizing and editorializing, by his both objective and compassionate evaluations of his characters, and by his criticism of art and his own ability as a raconteur.

Much of the book's impressive and subtle unity results from the symbolic relationships involving the narrator, the old writer, George Willard, and Sherwood Anderson. As an artist, the narrator is closely linked to George Willard, a young writer who has intimate knowledge of grotesques that may someday be used as material for a book; to the old man in the prologue, who, we are told, has written but never published a book of his own about grotesques; and to the author of *Winesburg* himself, Sherwood Anderson, who shares many opinions and experiences with the narrator.

Perhaps Anderson established this network of relationships to distance himself from his own past. In any case, it enables him to deal with the writer at a number of different stages in the same book. As Ingram suggests:

It is possible, then, that the old writer stands at the head of the work as a later George Willard, a prototype of the George Willard to come. It is possible, too, that the narrator, by summoning to fictional life the figures of the old writer and of George Willard, fictionalized his own initiation into, and projected culmination of his creative career. (156)

Like Ingram, Dallas Marion Lemmon emphasizes that it is impossible to understand *Winesburg* without carefully defining how point of view is handled. Unlike Ingram, however, Lemmon focuses exclusively on the relationship between the narrator and George Willard. According to him, the point of view changes during the book, and the two major perspectives, the narrator's and George Willard's, merge:

The omniscient narrator pervades the early stories with his tone and presence, moves freely from one character's mind to another. . . . But in the later stories, especially the last three, the narrator, without giving up his omniscience, moves closer and closer to a selective omniscience limited to seeing the world not only through George's eyes but also through his opinions and ideals . . . '' (176)

Lemmon's comments underline a shift in point of view that takes place in other short story cycles: the gradual fusing of the narrator with a protagonist's point of view. For example, in the case of *Dubliners*, the narrator becomes increasingly less defensive and ironic in ''The Dead,'' allowing himself to move closer to the world from which he has so carefully distanced himself through the rest of the book. While there is some validity to Lemmon's arguments concerning point of view, the narrator's presence is more pronounced in ''Sophistication'' and ''Departure'' than it is at the end of ''The Dead.'' Perhaps this is simply because George Willard lacks Gabriel Conroy's maturity as well as his skill with language. Even though the narrator of *Winesburg* spends considerable time in the last stories describing George's thoughts and feelings, he still takes pains to distinguish his own sense of experience from George's youthfulness. Frequently the narrator explains things that George does not yet fully understand: ''For some reason [Helen and George] could not have explained they had both got from their silent evening together the thing needed. Man or boy, woman or girl, they had for a moment taken hold of the thing that makes the mature life of men and women in the modern world possible'' (243).

CONCLUSION

Study of *Winesburg* is important because the book demonstrates that the short story cycle is especially well suited to accommodate certain topics or themes. The form of the book—self-sufficient, discrete stories that are loosely connected to one another—well accommodates the subject of isolation, "of lives touching, never quite touching." As Raymond Joel Silverman explains:

No other form could have been more appropriate for Sherwood Anderson than the short story composite. In story after story, the theme of loneliness, the motif of walls between people, the lack of communication, all demand a structure which will intensify the feeling of the tremendous gulf between people. Thus, as one story ends, it stays ended. (229)

Also, as was the case with the theme of paralysis in *Dubliners*, the theme of isolation grows more powerful as we see repeated instances in *Winesburg* of characters who are crippled because they cannot connect with one another. In addition, the cumulative effect of this basic plot pattern and theme—the unsuccessful attempt to connect—is further complicated because of the rare moments when individuals do come together. Although the reader is conditioned by previous stories to expect failure whenever characters move toward someone to try to establish contact, Anderson sometimes reverses the last step in the process, allowing characters to connect momentarily. Because these moments occur so infrequently, the fragility and significance of connections are underscored. As a result, the sense of closure achieved in "Sophistication" and "Departure" is largely the result of Anderson's manipulation of this recurring plot, specifically his inversion of the last step in the pattern. George's closeness to Helen boldly contrasts all the previous failures and seems to complete symbolically those unsuccessful attempts.[8]

Future criticism might also examine in greater detail ways in which the different parts of the book work together. For example, there is still controversy over the extent to which (as well as the manner *in* which) the prologue, "The Book of the Grotesque," helps unify the work. Similarly, there is the question of whether or not the four parts of "Godliness" ("Godliness, I," "Godliness, II," "Surrender," and "Terror") enhance or damage the overall unity of the book. The series of stories is four or five times longer than the other narratives in the book, and George Willard is never even mentioned in it. Does the independence of "Godliness" overwhelm its importance as a part of *Winesburg*? I would say no, since the characters, events, and themes developed here echo what happens in the rest of the book. Regardless of one's response, however, the reader must acknowledge that "Godliness" complicates the tension in the book between the stories' self-sufficiency and interdependence. This is especially true since at least two of its subdivisions—"Surrender" and "Terror"—are independent (and interrelated) short stories. A similar complication of the relationship between parts and wholes occurs in many recent short story cycles that are subdivided into groups of stories containing related themes or characters.[9]

Finally, more precise description of point of view in *Winesburg* would be extremely useful: the role the narrator plays is essential to an understanding of the book. A number of the disagreements concerning the stories result from the fact that too little attention is paid to point of view. One needs to distinguish very carefully between characters' thoughts and the narrator's assessment of situations, and this is especially true when George Willard's development is discussed.

While much critical work has been done on *Winesburg*, more remains to be done. This book was not only a significant breakthrough for Sherwood Anderson: it also serves to introduce countless readers to the form of the short story cycle. While Anderson did not invent the genre, he certainly popularized it and encouraged other writers to experiment with its form. His influence on Hemingway is discussed in the next chapter. Another, perhaps less well known, example is his relationship with Jean Toomer, who published his own cycle, *Cane*, in 1923. In a letter to Anderson, Toomer told him that "he himself could not have matured as an artist without having read *Winesburg, Ohio* and *The Triumph of the Egg*."[10]

NOTES

1. As Curry explains briefly ("Theories on Writing" 99–102), one is not always certain what Anderson means by "form," even though the term appears frequently in his letters, biographical writings, and critical essays. In *A Story Teller's Story*, Anderson suggests that "form" is something "altogether more elusive and difficult" (255) than plot; at another point, he is more specific, explaining that "[form] grew out of the materials of the tale and the teller's reaction to them. It was the tale trying to take form that kicked about inside the tale teller . . . " (261). As he uses the term in the second example, Anderson appears to consider "form" a synonym for what Seymour Chatman later identifies as "discourse," the actual presentation or communication of a narrative as opposed to the narrative's content (*Story and Discourse*. Ithaca: Cornell UP, 1978. 19–27).

2. In some editions and reprintings, its role is made more explicit than in others. For example, in the Modern Library reprint, which is based on the first edition, the prologue is placed before the title of the book; in the Penguin reprint, which is based on the second edition (Viking, 1960), the prologue is placed before the map of Winesburg, which comes at the very beginning of Viking reprints; and in the 1966 Viking Critical Edition (*Winesburg, Ohio: Text and Criticism*), which is based on the second edition, the prologue simply appears as the first story, and its function as prologue is made explicit only in the table of contents.

3. As a contrast, see the article by Nancy Bunge in the same collection.

4. Other critics discussing this plot pattern include Abcarian, David D. Anderson ("Moments of Insight"), Bort, Holladay, Howe, Lorch, McDonald, Picht, Sniderman, and Yancey.

5. Carabine (" 'Pretty Good Unity' ") and Howe both argue that "The Book of the Grotesque" is a confusing introduction to *Winesburg*.

6. Carabine ("'Pretty Good Unity'"), Ciancio, Love ("Rhetoric of Silence"), and McAleer make similar points. Responding to Edwin Fussell's "*Winesburg, Ohio*: Art and Isolation," David Stouck denies that the subjects of art and the artist are introduced "as a means of transcending frustration and failure" (150). Instead, he suggests that the repeated failures of art, depicted throughout the book, are used to underline the characters' inability to communicate.

7. For further discussion of Christian imagery see Gochberg, Picht, Schevill, and Taylor.

8. Subsequent criticism also needs to identify further similarities and differences in the basic plot as it reappears in the book. For example, in how many stories does this particular plot appear more than once? In stories containing two or more instances of the plot, how many embed the second or subsequent instances within the first; in other words, how often does a character attempt to establish contact with someone (generally George Willard) by telling the person a story describing an unsuccessful attempt at communication in the past? What differences occur as the plot is repeated?

9. In the listing of short story cycles at the end of this book, see Jessica Anderson's *Stories from the Warm Zone*, Russell Banks's *Searching for Survivors*, Italo Calvino's *Castle of Crossed Destinies* and *Mr. Palomar*, Andre Dubus's *Adultery and Other Choices*, Mavis Gallant's *Home Truths*, Joyce Carol Oates's *Last Days*, Reynolds Price's *Permanent Errors*, and Elizabeth Tallent's *Time with Children*. In some of these books, the subdivisions suggest that the stories are connected, but very loosely. Obviously, this is not the case with *Winesburg*.

10. This is Townsend's paraphrase of a letter at the Newberry. See his *Sherwood Anderson* 226. Although unable to prove that *Winesburg* influenced *Cane*, Mary Jane Dickerson (see bibliography) demonstrates that this was probably the case. Not only was Toomer familiar with *Winesburg*, but he had a friendship with Waldo Frank, who was a close friend of Anderson's and with whom Anderson had extensively discussed *Winesburg* before its 1919 publication. In addition, Frank accompanied Toomer on a trip to Georgia, an experience that produced *Cane*.

WORKS CITED AND BIBLIOGRAPHY

Abcarian, Richard. "Innocence and Experience in *Winesburg, Ohio*." *The University Review—Kansas City* 35 (Winter 1968): 95–105.

Anderson, David D., ed. *Critical Essays on Sherwood Anderson*. Boston: Hall, 1981.

———. "Moments of Insight." *Sherwood Anderson: An Introduction and Interpretation*. New York: Holt, 1967. 37–54. Partially rpt. as "The Grotesques and George Willard" in Ferres 421–31; rpt. in David D. Anderson, *Critical Essays*, 155–71.

———, ed. *Sherwood Anderson: Dimensions of His Literary Art*. East Lansing: Michigan State UP, 1976.

———. "Sherwood Anderson's Grotesques and Modern American Fiction." *MMisc* 12 (1984): 53–65.

Anderson, Sherwood. *The Letters of Sherwood Anderson*. Ed. Howard Mumford Jones and Walter B. Rideout. Boston: Little, 1953.

———. *Letters to Bab: Sherwood Anderson to Marietta D. Finley 1916–33*. Ed. William A. Sutton. Urbana: U of Illinois P, 1985.

———. *Sherwood Anderson: Selected Letters*. Ed. Charles E. Modlin. Knoxville: U of Tennessee P, 1984.

————. *Sherwood Anderson's Memoirs: A Critical Edition*. Ed. Ray Lewis White. Chapel Hill: U of North Carolina P, 1969.

This book differs substantially from the *Sherwood Anderson's Memoirs* published in 1942 by Paul Rosenfeld, who rearranged and heavily edited the unfinished manuscript of Anderson's memoirs, even adding short published essays to fill in apparent gaps.

————. *Sherwood Anderson: The Writer at His Craft*. Ed. Jack Salzman, David D. Anderson, and Kichinosuke Ohashi. New York: Appel, 1979.

————. *A Story Teller's Story: A Critical Text*. Ed. Ray Lewis White. Cleveland: P of Case Western U, 1968.

————. *Winesburg, Ohio*. Rev. ed. New York: Viking, 1960.

Quotations are taken from the Viking Critical edition. *Winesburg, Ohio: Text and Criticism* (1966).

Arcana, Judith. " 'Tandy': At the Core of *Winesburg*." *SSF* 24.1 (Winter 1987): 66–70.

Asselineau, Roger. "Langue et Style de Sherwood Anderson dans *Winesburg, Ohio*." *Configuration Critique de Sherwood Anderson*. *La Revue des Lettres Modernes* No. 78–80 (1963): 121–35. Trans. and rpt. in Ferres 345–56.

————. "Réalisme, Rêve et Expressionnisme dans *Winesburg, Ohio*." *Archives des Lettres Modernes* 2 (Apr. 1957): 1–32.

Atlas, Marilyn Judith. "Sherwood Anderson and the Women of Winesburg." David D. Anderson, *Critical Essays*, 250–66.

Baker, Carlos. "Sherwood Anderson's Winesburg: A Reprise." *VQR* 48 (Autumn 1972): 568–79.

Berland, Alwyn. "Sherwood Anderson and the Pathetic Grotesque." *Western Review* 15 (Winter 1951): 135–38.

Bort, Barry D. "*Winesburg, Ohio*: The Escape from Isolation." *MQ* 11 (July 1970): 443–56.

Bredahl, A. Carl. " 'The Young Thing Within': Divided Narrative and Sherwood Anderson's *Winesburg, Ohio*." *MQ* 27.4 (Summer 1986): 422–37.

Bresnahan, Roger J. "The 'Old Hands' of Winesburg." *MMisc* 11 (1983): 19–27.

Browning, Chris. "Kate Swift: Sherwood Anderson's Creative Eros." *TSL* 13 (1968): 141–48. Rpt. in White, *Merrill Studies*, 74–82.

Bunge, Nancy. "Women in Sherwood Anderson's Fiction." David D. Anderson, *Critical Essays*, 242–49.

Burbank, Rex J. "*Winesburg, Ohio*." *Sherwood Anderson*. New York: Twayne, 1964. 61–77.

Carabine, Keith. " 'A Pretty Good Unity': A Study of Sherwood Anderson's *Winesburg, Ohio* and Ernest Hemingway's *In Our Time*." Diss. Yale U, 1978. *DAI* 39 (1978): 2936A–37A.

Carabine suggests that the novel was not the appropriate form for Anderson, since he wanted to describe characters estranged from one another. Even loosely constructed novels such as the picaresque "possessed an opinionated stance and a simple narrative line that was inimical to Anderson, who lacked any sense of time or scale or narrative flow" (24). In addition, Anderson's work habits—that is, his inability to write except when inspired and his inability to revise except by rewriting an entire piece—made the form of the short story cycle attractive.

————. "Sherwood Anderson's 'Adventure': An Appreciation." *Society for the Study of Midwestern Literature Newsletter* 10 (1980): 1–12.

Chase, Cleveland B. *Sherwood Anderson*. New York: R. M. McBride, 1927.

Ciancio, Ralph. " 'The Sweetness of the Twisted Apples': Unity of Vision in *Winesburg, Ohio*." *PMLA* 87 (Oct. 1972): 994–1006.

Cowley, Malcolm. Introduction. *Winesburg, Ohio*. By Sherwood Anderson. New York: Viking, 1960. 1–15. Rpt. as "Sherwood Anderson's Book of Moments" in *A Many-Windowed House: Collected Essays on American Writers and American Writing*. Ed. Henry Dan Piper. Carbondale: Southern Illinois UP, 1970. 166–77. Also rpt. in Ferres 357–68, and in Rideout, *Collection of Critical Essays*, 49–58.

Curry, Martha Mulroy. "Anderson and Joyce: *Winesburg, Ohio* and *Dubliners*." *AL* 52 (May 1980): 236–49.

————. "Anderson's Theories on Writing Fiction." David D. Anderson, *Dimensions of Literary Art*, 90–109.

Dickerson, Mary Jane. "Sherwood Anderson and Jean Toomer: A Literary Relationship." *SAF* 1 (Autumn 1973): 163–65.

Enniss, Stephen C. "The Implied Community of *Winesburg, Ohio*." *ON* 11 (Spring-Summer 1985): 51–60.

Faulkner, William. "Sherwood Anderson: An Appreciation." *Essays, Speeches and Public Letters*. Ed. James B. Meriwether. New York: Random, 1965. 3–10. Rpt. in Ferres 487–94; in White, *Achievement of Sherwood Anderson*, 194–99; and in Rideout, *Collection of Critical Essays*, 166–70.

Ferres, John H., ed. *Winesburg, Ohio: Text and Criticism*. New York: Viking, 1966.

Fertig, Martin J. " 'A Great Deal of Wonder in Me': Inspiration and Transformation in *Winesburg, Ohio*." *MarkhamR* 6 (Summer 1977): 65–70.

Frank, Waldo. "Homage to Sherwood Anderson." *Story* 19 (Sept.-Oct. 1941): 29–33. Rpt. as "*Winesburg, Ohio* after Twenty Years" in Ferres 369–76; in White, *Achievement of Sherwood Anderson*, 116–21; and in White, *Merrill Studies*, 84–89.

Fussell, Edwin. "*Winesburg, Ohio*: Art and Isolation." *MFS* 6 (Summer 1960): 106–14. Rpt. in Ferres 383–95; in White, *Achievement of Sherwood Anderson*, 104–13; and in Rideout, *Collection of Critical Essays*, 39–48.

Gochberg, Donald. "Stagnation and Growth: The Emergence of George Willard." *Expression* (U of Maryland) 4 (Winter 1960): 29–35. Rpt. in White, *Merrill Studies*, 42–48.

Gold, Herbert. "*Winesburg, Ohio*: The Purity and Cunning of Sherwood Anderson." *Hudson Review* 10 (Winter 1957–58): 548–49. Rpt. in Ferres 396–404, and in David D. Anderson, *Critical Essays*, 138–45.

Gregory, Horace. Introduction. *The Portable Sherwood Anderson*. Ed. Horace Gregory. New York: Viking, 1949. 1–31. Partially rpt. in Ferres 301–8.

Hoffman, Frederick J. "Anderson—Psychoanalyst by Default." *Freudianism and the Literary Mind*. Baton Rouge: Louisiana State UP, 1957. 230–55. Rpt. as "Anderson and Freud" in Ferres 309–20, and in White, *Achievement of Sherwood Anderson*, 174–92.

Holladay, Sylvia A. "The 'New' Realism: A Study of the Structure of *Winesburg, Ohio*." *CEA* 41 (1979): 9–12.

Howe, Irving. "The Book of the Grotesque." *PR* 18 (Jan.-Feb. 1951): 32–40. Rpt. in *Sherwood Anderson*. New York: Sloane, 1951. 91–109; in Ferres 405–20; in

White, *Achievement of Sherwood Anderson*, 90–101; and in White, *Merrill Studies*, 101–13.

Huebsch, B. W. "Footnotes to a Publisher's Life." *The Colophon* ns 2.3 (Summer 1937): 406–26.

Ingram, Forrest L. "Sherwood Anderson: *Winesburg, Ohio.*" *Representative Short Story Cycles of the Twentieth Century: Studies in a Literary Genre*. The Hague: Mouton, 1971. 143–99.

Laughlin, Rosemary M. " 'Godliness' and the American Dream in *Winesburg, Ohio.*" *TCL* 13 (July 1967): 97–103. Rpt. in White, *Merrill Studies*, 52–60.

Lemmon, Dallas Marion, Jr. "The Rovelle, or the Novel of Interrelated Stories: M. Lermontov, G. Keller, S. Anderson." Diss. Indiana U, 1970. *DAI* 31 (1971): 3510A.

    Winesburg is classified as a "chain-rovelle," one of three subdivisions of the rovelle, because it contains "a sequence of self-contained but linked and cumulatively interrelated short tales using no framework structure" (6). Lemmon identifies George Willard as the book's chief unifying device. Not only does he appear in seventeen stories as protagonist, listener, or observer, but he represents Winesburg and he matures in the process of the book. The point of view used in the book is ultimately George's. There is a shift from an omniscient "multi-selective" to a selective or limited-omniscient narrator who focuses on George's consciousness.

Lorch, Thomas M. "The Choreographic Structure of *Winesburg, Ohio.*" *CLAJ* 12 (Sept. 1968): 56–65.

Love, Glen Allen. "Sherwood Anderson's American Pastoral." Diss. U of Washington, 1964. *DA* 25 (1965): 7247.

———. "*Winesburg, Ohio* and the Rhetoric of Silence." *AL* 40 (Mar. 1968): 38–57.

McAleer, John J. "Christ Symbolism in *Winesburg, Ohio.*" *Discourse: A Review of the Liberal Arts* (Concordia College) 4 (Summer 1961): 168–81. Rpt. in White, *Merrill Studies*, 60–74.

McDonald, Walter R. "*Winesburg, Ohio*: Tales of Isolation." *The University Review—Kansas City* 35 (Spring 1969): 237–40.

Mahoney, John J. "An Analysis of *Winesburg, Ohio.*" *JAAC* 15 (Dec. 1956): 245–52.

Maresca, Carol J. "Gestures as Meaning in Sherwood Anderson's *Winesburg, Ohio.*" *CLAJ* 9 (Mar. 1966): 279–83.

Meindl, Dieter. "Der kurzgeschichtenzyklus als modernistisches Genre." *GRM* 33.2 (1983): 216–28.

Mellard, James M. "Narrative Forms in *Winesburg, Ohio.*" *PMLA* 83 (Oct. 1968): 1304–12.

Murphy, George D. "The Theme of Sublimation in Anderson's *Winesburg, Ohio.*" *MFS* 13 (Summer 1967): 237–46.

O'Neill, John. "Anderson Writ Large: 'Godliness' in *Winesburg, Ohio.*" *TCL* 23 (Feb. 1977): 67–83.

Papinchak, Robert Allan. "Something in the Elders: The Recurrent Imagery in *Winesburg, Ohio.*" *WE* 9.1 (Nov. 1983): 1–7.

Pawlowski, Robert S. "The Process of Observation: *Winesburg, Ohio* and *The Golden Apples.*" *University Review* 37 (Summer 1971): 292–98.

Phillips, William L. "The Editions of *Winesburg, Ohio.*" *Sherwood Anderson: Centen-*

nial Studies. Ed. Hilbert H. Campbell and Charles E. Modlin. Troy, NY: Whitston, 1976. 151–55.

————. "How Sherwood Anderson Wrote *Winesburg, Ohio*." *AL* 23 (Mar. 1951): 7–30. Rpt. in Ferres 263–86; in White, *Achievement of Sherwood Anderson*, 62–84; in White, *Merrill Studies*, 2–24; and in Rideout, *Collection of Critical Essays*, 18–38.

Picht, Douglas R. "Anderson's Use of Tactile Imagery in *Winesburg, Ohio*." *RS* 35 (June 1967): 176–78. Rpt. in White, *Merrill Studies*, 48–51.

Pickering, Samuel. "*Winesburg, Ohio*: A Portrait of the Artist as a Young Man." *SoQ* 16 (Oct. 1977): 27–38.

Reed Pleasant Larus, III. "The Integrated Short-Story Collection: Studies of a Form of Nineteenth- and Twentieth-Century Fiction." Diss. Indiana U, 1974. *DAI* 35 (1975): 6730A.

Labeling the book as an integrated short-story collection, Reed provides a detailed analysis of what he argues is the chief unifying device in *Winesburg*: George Willard's development and the manner in which it is influenced by the grotesques. Other unifying patterns include the theory of the grotesque (as defined in "The Book of the Grotesque"), the narrator's constant sympathy for the grotesques, and the setting.

Rideout, Walter B., ed. *Sherwood Anderson: A Collection of Critical Essays*. Englewood Cliffs, NJ: Prentice, 1974.

————. "The Simplicity of *Winesburg, Ohio*." *Shenandoah* 13 (Spring 1962): 20–31. Rpt. in Ferres 287–300, and in David D. Anderson, *Critical Essays*, 146–54.

————. "Talbot Whittingham and Anderson: A Passage to *Winesburg, Ohio*." David D. Anderson, *Dimensions of Literary Art*, 41–60.

Rigsbee, Sally Adair. "The Feminine in *Winesburg, Ohio*." *SAF* 9 (Autumn 1981): 233–44.

Rogers, Douglas G. "Development of the Artist in *Winesburg, Ohio*." *Studies in the Twentieth Century* 10 (Fall 1972): 91–99.

San Juan, Epifanio, Jr. "Vision and Reality: A Reconsideration of *Winesburg, Ohio*." *AL* 35 (May 1963): 137–55. Rpt. in Ferres 468–81.

Schevill, James. "*Winesburg, Ohio*." *Sherwood Anderson: His Life and Work*. Denver: U of Denver P, 1951. 93–108.

Shawver, Jurgen Michael. "Sexuality and Human Development in *Winesburg, Ohio*." Diss. U of Nebraska at Lincoln, 1978. *DAI* 39 (1979): 6767A.

Using the work Peter Blos and Erik H. Erikson have done in psychoanalysis to elucidate Anderson's handling of sexuality, Shawver discusses each story in *Winesburg*, primarily to focus on two stages of development—adolescence and marriage.

Shilstone, Frederick W. "Egotism, Sympathy, and George Willard's Development as Poet in *Winesburg, Ohio*." *West Virginia University Philological Papers* 28 (1982): 105–13.

Silverman, Raymond Joel. "The Short Story Composite: Forms, Functions, and Applications." Diss. U of Michigan, 1970. *DAI* 31 (1971): 6633A.

In the chapter on *Winesburg*, Silverman suggests that there are four major divisions in the book: in the first ("Hands" through "Nobody Knows"), George Willard is unable to comprehend what other characters try to teach him; in the second ("Godliness"), a historical account of the town contributes to the reader's understanding of George's background; in the third ("Man of Ideas" through "Teacher"), George begins to reflect on his experiences and those of others; and in the fourth ("Loneliness" through "Sophistication"), George acknowledges his ignorance and becomes more determined than ever to find out about life. "Departure" functions as epilogue.

Sniderman, Stephen Lee. "The 'Composite' in Twentieth-Century American Literature." Diss. U of Wisconsin, 1970. *DAI* 31 (1970): 403A.

Sniderman identifies numerous unifying patterns in *Winesburg*. In addition to the pervasiveness of sexual initiation and the desire of characters to leave town, he cites "a distinct rhythm in the arrangement of the stories" (46): the first, fourth, ninth, and fourteenth stories depict an old man talking about himself to a young man; the third, sixth, eleventh, and eighteenth involve the relationship of parent and child; and the second, eighth, twelfth, and sixteenth describe a lonely character attempting to connect with another person. Sniderman denies that George Willard is the book's primary unifying device; instead, he argues that George and the grotesques are equally important, one of the major reasons why the book could not be written as a novel.

Stouck, David. "*Winesburg, Ohio* and the Failure of Art." *TCL* 15 (Oct. 1969): 145–51. Rpt. in White, *Merrill Studies*, 93–101; and in David D. Anderson, *Critical Essays*, 181–95.

———. "*Winesburg, Ohio* As a Dance of Death." *AL* 48 (Jan. 1977): 525–42. Rpt. in David D. Anderson, *Critical Essays*, 181–95.

Sutton, William A. *The Road to Winesburg: A Mosaic of the Imaginative Life of Sherwood Anderson*. Metuchen, NJ: Scarecrow, 1972.

Taylor, Welford Dunaway. "Re-inventing the American Soul." *Sherwood Anderson*. New York: Ungar, 1977. 19–43.

Thurston, Jarvis A. "Anderson and *Winesburg*: Mysticism and Craft." *Accent* 16 (Spring 1956): 107–28. Rpt. in Ferres 331–44.

Townsend, Kim. *Sherwood Anderson*. Boston: Houghton, 1987.

Walcutt, Charles Child. "Sherwood Anderson: Impressionism and the Buried Life." *American Literary Naturalism: A Divided Stream*. Minneapolis: U of Minnesota P, 1956. 222–39. Rpt. in White, *Achievement of Sherwood Anderson*, 156–71; and partially rpt. as "Naturalism in *Winesburg, Ohio*" in Ferres 432–43.

Weltz, Friedrich. "*Vier amerikanische Erzählungszyklen*." Diss. Universität München, 1953.

Identifying *Winesburg* as an *erzählungszyklen* or short story cycle, Weltz argues that the book's thematic center is George Willard's development and the struggle of the individual people (grotesques) against a hostile, threatening community. Because of their fixed relation to this thematic center, the stories are arranged in a definite pattern or sequence that could not be altered without damaging the development of theme.

White, Ray Lewis, ed. *The Achievement of Sherwood Anderson: Essays in Criticism*. Chapel Hill: U of North Carolina P, 1966.

———, ed. *The Merrill Studies in* Winesburg, Ohio. Columbus: Merrill, 1971.

———. "Of Time and *Winesburg, Ohio*: An Experiment in Chronology." *MFS* 25 (Winter 1979–80): 658–66.

———. "*Winesburg, Ohio*: First Impression Errors." *PBSA* 71 (1977): 222–23.

———. "*Winesburg, Ohio*: The Story Titles." *WE* 10 (Nov. 1984): 6–7.

————. *"Winesburg, Ohio*: The Table of Contents." *NMAL* 8.2 (Autumn 1984): Item 8.

Wilson, Raymond. "Rhythm in *Winesburg, Ohio." Great Lakes Review* 8.1 (Spring 1982): 31–43.

Yancey, Anita V. R. *"Winesburg, Ohio* and *The Pastures of Heaven*: A Comparative Analysis of Two Studies in Isolation." Diss. U of Southern Mississippi, 1971. *DAI* 32 (1972): 5249A.

Yancey suggests that even though the novel can develop the theme of isolation, the short story cycle "provides a freedom, a flexibility, remarkably conducive to the presentation of this theme" (123–24). *Winesburg*'s theme is defined in "The Book of the Grotesque": characters become grotesques when they take a truth and try to live their lives according to that single truth. Other unifying patterns include the use of enclosed spaces to suggest a character's isolation, the use of light and dark imagery to emphasize the contrast between reality and dream, and the use of contrasting characters (for example, Enoch Robinson and the old writer, or Doctor Parcival and Wing Biddlebaum).

Zlotnick, Joan. "Dubliners in Winesburg, Ohio: A Note on Joyce's 'The Sisters' and Anderson's 'The Philosopher.' " *SSF* 12 (Fall 1975): 405–7.

————. "Of Dubliners and Ohioans: A Comparative Study of Two Works." *BSUF* 17 (1976): 33–36.

3

Ernest Hemingway's
In Our Time

INTRODUCTION TO THE BOOK

Although reluctant to acknowledge those who helped him most substantially, Hemingway does eventually pay small tributes to two of the books that probably influenced his writing of *In Our Time*. Among the sixteen works of fiction that Hemingway said in a 1935 interview he " 'would rather read again for the first time' than be assured of a million-dollar annual income" were *Dubliners* and *Winesburg, Ohio*. Less publicly, he admitted in a conversion with F. Scott Fitzgerald that *Winesburg* was "his first pattern" (C. Baker's *Writer as Artist*: 25, 175).[1]

Although influenced by the forms of these books and some of the conventions associated with the short story cycle, *In Our Time* is a highly innovative work. Perhaps this is most obvious in Hemingway's decision to place the prose sketches or vignettes between his stories, but there are other examples.[2] Like *Dubliners* and *Winesburg, Ohio*, *In Our Time* is a *bildungsroman*, but there are subtle differences in the authors' concept of protagonist. *Winesburg* features the development of a single character—George Willard—while *Dubliners* focuses instead on the movement of an archetypal Dubliner from childhood to adolescence to maturity and "public life." *In Our Time* provides both, With Nick Adams, Hemingway provides a substantial, psychologically complex protagonist; and since most of the other major characters closely resemble Nick, the author also successfully creates a composite personality: the Middle American who is wounded in battle and has difficulty readjusting after the war is over.

Several other differences are worth noting at this point. Since Joyce, Anderson, and Hemingway are all concerned with the process of maturation—especially the development of the artist—it is not surprising that they emphasize initiation and the knowledge that results from being tested. However, there are crucial differences in emphasis. With the *In Our Time* stories the actual process of initiation is so important that it becomes the central focus in most of the stories. This is not the case with Joyce and Anderson, where in stories like "Eveline" and "Adventure" a character's psychological past is actually more important than the small part of the plot relating to the present tense. The present tense achieves greater importance in Hemingway. While characters are affected by their pasts, what is most important is the manner in which they are able to meet present challenges. Therefore, the actual test in the present tense—whether it is breaking off a relationship that isn't fun anymore or trying to maintain one's equilibrium as chaos threatens—is the heart of each story, its major plot and purpose.

In fact, the process of initiation is so centrally important in *In Our Time* that it almost overshadows the knowledge that should result from the test. Perhaps this is because the epiphanies or moments of recognition that end many of the *In Our Time* stories are often handled ironically. Since Hemingway's protagonists cannot tolerate too much truth—or like the doctor's wife, too much summer light—they often sidestep the difficulties that confront them at the ends of the stories. As a result, the characters' last thoughts often resemble deliberate parodies of Joycean epiphanies. Nick at the conclusion of "Indian Camp" comforts himself with the thought that he will never die. Similarly, at the end of "Soldier's Home," Harold Krebs convinces himself that he can escape his adjustment problems by leaving home for Kansas City. Even "Cross-Country Snow" and "Big Two-Hearted River"—stories where Nick genuinely seems to struggle with problems—are riddled with ambiguity, because with Hemingway it is often impossible to distinguish between escapism and the kind of temporary retreat one needs in order to regain a sense of equilibrium.

Hemingway had learned his lessons from Joyce and Anderson—as well as from others he cultivated as mentors—but there is no mistaking the originality of *In Our Time*. In many ways it is the quintessential Hemingway work. *In Our Time* probably succeeds better than any other single work in introducing the Hemingway hero, the world in which he lives, and the manner in which he attempts to order his experiences.

COMPOSITION AND PUBLICATION OF *IN OUR TIME*

The composition of *In Our Time* is not easily reconstructed.[3] Starting with *Selected Letters*, however, one can begin to see the development of Hemingway's intentions as he created this short story cycle. Further biographical and literary facts can be gleaned from Carlos Baker's *Ernest Hemingway: A Life Story*, Jeffrey Meyers's *Hemingway: A Biography*, and Michael Reynolds's *The Young Hemingway*.[4]

In his letters Hemingway insists that he consciously attempted to unify *In Our Time* and indicates some of his methods. He defines the major thematic pattern in the vignettes as a movement from innocence to experience and disillusionment: "The war starts clear and noble just like it did, Mons, etc., gets close and blurred and finished with the feller who goes home and gets clap. . . . The radicals start noble in the young Magyar story and get bitched'' (*Selected Letters* 91–92). In a frequently cited letter to Edmund Wilson, he also explains that the function of the vignettes in *In Our Time* is ''to give the picture of the whole between examining it in detail. Like looking with your eyes at something, say a passing coast line, and then looking at it with 15X binoculars. Or rather, maybe, looking at it and then going in and living in it—and then coming out and looking at it again'' (*Selected Letters* 128).

Although identifying no other unifying patterns, except to note that the stories begin and end with Nick in Michigan (*Selected Letters* 123), Hemingway was so convinced that the book was intricately unified that he became angry when his editor and publisher at Boni and Liveright asked for minor revisions and the deletion of the sexually explicit ''Up in Michigan.'' In response, he insisted that ''the stories are written so tight and so hard that the alteration of a word can throw an entire story out of key. . . . There is nothing in the book that has not a definite place in its organization . . . '' (*Selected Letters* 154).

Even though the vignettes were written earlier than most of the stories and were published separately in *in our time* (1924), Hemingway declared on several occasions that the vignettes were originally written with the intention that they would eventually preface the *In Our Time* stories (*Selected Letters* 123, 152). That this is an accurate statement seems unlikely, since Hemingway made this claim only after completing *In Our Time*. In his correspondence during 1923, he often mentions the *in our time* vignettes and occasionally refers to the short stories that he is writing and which will eventually be included in *In Our Time*, but there is never any suggestion that the two projects are related.

Most of the *In Our Time* vignettes were written between December 1922 and August 1923 and most of the stories between January and September 1924 (C. Baker's *Life Story*: sections 15 through 18), but it is impossible to determine exactly when Hemingway first thought of juxtaposing the various pieces of short fiction and publishing them together as a single unified work. What is clear, however, is that much of the book must have been written before Hemingway began consciously to design *In Our Time*.[5] Although the thematic shape of the third book (*In Our Time*) is partially determined by that of the second (*in our time*), it took Hemingway some time to recognize the advantages of juxtaposing both series—vignettes sandwiched around each story—and of publishing them together as a single work.[6]

As critics become increasingly familiar with the Hemingway collection at the John F. Kennedy Library, more may be discovered about Hemingway's intentions and methods.[7] Since 1983, several essays have been based on the prepublication materials relating to *In Our Time*, and they give us glimpses of how Hemingway revised his early fiction. Nicholas Gerogiannis and Jim Steinke indicate that relatively few changes were made in ''The Battler,'' ''A Very Short Story,'' and ''The Revolutionist'' (the last two originally published as vignettes in *in our time*). In contrast, Paul Smith and Kathryn Derounian describe fairly extensive early revisions in ''Out of Season'' and the vignette in which Nick is wounded, "Nick sat against the wall of the church." However, no substantive changes occur after their publication, respectively, in *Three Stories and Ten Poems* and *in our time* and their appearance in *In Our Time*.[8]

One must be careful when making generalizations about how these stories and vignettes were written, especially since more work remains to be done on the manuscripts at the Kennedy. At present, however, it is safe to say that Hemingway made relatively few revisions as he consciously began to construct *In Our Time*. The vignettes from *in our time* are altered only minimally and are placed in basically the same order. The only major changes are that chapters II and IX in *in our time* are reversed, chapters X and XI are now classified as stories ("A Very Short Story" and "The Revolutionist"), and chapter XVIII becomes a more explicit epilogue entitled "L'Envoi." Some of Hemingway's later revisions in the stories resulted from demands made by his publisher, specifically the omission of a passage in "Mr. and Mrs. Elliot" and the deletion of the entire story "Up in Michigan" on the grounds that both contained overt sexual relations. In place of "Up in Michigan," Hemingway grudgingly substituted "The Battler," but eventually acknowledged that the substitution gave "additional unity to the book as a whole" (*Selected Letters* 154–55). A final addition came in 1930, five years after the book was first published, when Hemingway demonstrated continuing interest in *In Our Time* by adding a prologue, later entitled "On the Quai at Smyrna."

If few revisions were made after the vignettes and stories were originally written—sometimes for publication elsewhere—there is a good reason why this was the case: Hemingway's interests and obsessions were so well established and so specific by 1923–24 that his early fiction was necessarily unified by these preoccupations.

UNITY IN *IN OUR TIME*

It is more difficult to describe unifying patterns in *In Our Time* than it is to describe similar patterns in other cycles discussed here in detail. While the others generally consist of only eight to ten stories (*Winesburg, Ohio* is the exception), *In Our Time* contains thirty-two separate pieces of short fiction. Furthermore, *In Our Time*, unlike the others, contains two different kinds of short fiction (vignettes and short stories). In spite of the fact that there are more parts and more different kinds of parts juxtaposed in *In Our Time*, most readers have little trouble perceiving that the narratives are connected.

Character

Protagonist or Composite Personality

When one begins to read *In Our Time*, the most explicit unifying device is the character Nick Adams. While several of the characters appear in more than one story or vignette (Doctor Adams, Marjorie, Bill, and Maera all appear in two), Nick is the only character who appears frequently enough so that the reader anticipates his reappearance; he is featured in half of the stories and appears once in a vignette (chapter VI, which is essential to an understanding of the book). After the first five stories, all of which feature him, Nick appears irregularly, but his presence is almost continuously felt. Although the protagonists in ''A Very Short Story,'' ''Cat in the Rain,'' and ''Out of Season'' are not given names, they so closely resemble Adams that many readers assume he is the character involved. Also, some of the other protagonists (the revolutionist in the story by the same name, Harold Krebs in ''Soldier's Home,'' and Joe Butler in ''My Old Man'') remind us of Nick because even if they differ from him in some important ways, they still resemble him since they share similar experiences, personality traits, and family or social backgrounds. Since the reader is almost always in the presence of Nick or someone who invites a comparison with Nick—perhaps resulting from Hemingway's projection of himself in all of the male protagonists—Nick Adams does more to unify *In Our Time* than George Willard does in *Winesburg, Ohio*.

Because Nick Adams and characters such as Harold Krebs resemble one another, possessing similar but ultimately distinct personalities, Carl Wood argues that *In Our Time* is unified by a composite personality which is based primarily on Nick Adams but which extends beyond his individual personality. Wood stresses that the book's main characters are ''drifting and disillusioned member[s] of the lost generation'' (722). More specifically, they are generally expatriates, committed to some sport, and unhappily married or unhappy in some other relationship. According to Wood, Hemingway carefully organized the middle stories and vignettes so that the reader could easily execute the transition between the early stories exclusively about Nick to those featuring different though generally similar protagonists. Joseph DeFalco agrees that Nick Adams ''typifies'' his generation: ''a whole race of contemporary men who have encountered irrational elements in their environment and have been forced to deal with them'' (26).

Plot

In addition to character, certain plots are fairly explicit unifying devices. Most important is the general movement in *In Our Time* from peacetime America to war in Europe to postwar America and Europe. Another important plot that unifies the entire book is the maturation of Nick Adams. Not only does he appear in half of the stories, but he develops from a child (''Indian Camp,'' ''The Doctor and the Doctor's Wife'') to a teenager (''The End of Something,'' ''The Three-Day Blow,'' ''The Battler'') to an adult (chapter VI, ''Cross-Country Snow,'' and ''Big Two-Hearted River'').

In Our Time is unified not only by large-scale plots that continue from story to story, explicitly connecting large segments of the book. Also important, though less noticeable, is the recurrence of plot patterns used to unify individual stories.

Chaman Nahal and Sheldon Norman Grebstein offer similar descriptions of some of these patterns, the major difference between the two being that Nahal perceives the patterns in a broader and more abstract manner. The recurring patterns Nahal focuses on involve a contrast between systolic and diastolic action—that is, the contrast between physical activity and the contemplative, physical passivity that follows, in which "the individual returns to a deep mystery within himself through passivity and makes himself ready for the next systolic move" (26). In stories like "Indian Camp," the narrative is divided into two parts, the first containing systolic action and the second, diastolic; in others, systolic and diastolic action alternate throughout the story.

The two (overlapping) plot patterns Grebstein describes are the movement from "outside to inside to outside" (or from "inside to outside") and the movement toward a destination, the arrival, and the departure. Sometimes a story will contain just one (or part of one) of these plots; other times the two plots will be integrated within a single story. Also, the first pattern (outside to inside to outside) can be used to describe the movement from physical action to thought (Nahal's diastolic action) since the protagonist often becomes progressively more reflective as he moves inside. Grebstein's description of recurring plot patterns is useful because even though the patterns he describes are fairly common—and may simply correspond to the three-part divisions found in many stories of this period, especially those containing journeys—they do assume unusual importance in *In Our Time*. In fact, one or both of the patterns are of major importance in every story with the exception of "My Old Man," which contains a series of journeys that are only of secondary importance as far as the themes in the story or its total effect is concerned.

Setting and Chronology

In addition to character and large-scale plot, setting and time are fairly explicit unifying devices. *In Our Time* differs from cycles such as *Winesburg, Dubliners, Go Down, Moses*, or *The Golden Apples* because it is not limited to a single location; nevertheless, various groups of stories are connected because they share a common setting. For example, the first Nick Adams stories are located in the general area of Petoskey, Michigan, and the bullfighting vignettes in Spain. In addition, as Hemingway emphasized, the structure of the book is circular: in the last story ("Big Two-Hearted River") we return to the Petoskey area and to a Nick Adams who appears barely in control of his life after the war. In addition to geography, a single time frame connects the entire book. As E. R. Hagemann argues in "Time-and-History in . . . *In Our Time*," the stories and vignettes collectively reconstruct a decade, 1914–23: "The Great War and its aftermath were . . . *the* experience of his generation, the experience that dumped his peers and his elders into graves, shell-holes, hospitals, and onto gallows" (255).

Theme or Topic

Vignettes

Originally published as a separate book, the vignettes have always been perceived as unified by recurring topics. The major difference among critics is whether they perceive the unity as predominantly biographical or ideological. Given the degree to which *In Our Time* was based on Hemingway's personal experiences, it is not surprising that Young argues that the vignettes are arranged "at least roughly according to the order in which their author experienced them" ("Hemingway's *In Our Time*"). Young, however, fails to demonstrate that this is the case, and those who have more extensively discussed biographical elements in the book do not substantiate his claim.[9] He is correct that there are vague correspondences between Hemingway's life and the vignettes (he goes to war, is wounded, returns to the States, and goes back to Europe, where he passionately enjoys bullfighting); but with the exception of chapter VI, the events described in the vignettes are not directly related to Hemingway's personal life. Instead, most of the events are based on stories told to Hemingway by friends such as Captain Dorman-Smith (dedicatee of *in our time*), Mike Strater, and Shorty Wornall and on events which Hemingway personally observed but did not participate in, such as some of the bullfights.

Charles A. Fenton entirely dismisses the idea that the vignettes are arranged in the order in which Hemingway experienced the events. To begin with, they do not preserve an accurate chronology: "A vignette derived from Kansas City is placed after vignettes drawn from the war and from European newspaper work; bullfighting sketches, based upon episodes observed in Spain in 1922 and 1923, precede the sketch of Nick Adams being wounded in Italy in 1918" (228). Furthermore, Fenton notes that the vignettes can be divided into three groups representing Hemingway's three "basic themes and attitudes": war, bullfighting, and journalism. While Fenton deserves credit for being the first to define specifically how subject matter or theme unifies the vignettes, there are some weaknesses in his method of dividing the vignettes into groups. As Burhans points out in "The Complex Unity of *In Our Time*," when Fenton divides the vignettes into groups (war, bullfighting, journalism), he is actually using two organizational principles rather than one: the first two groups are organized according to content, while the third (journalism) is based on Hemingway's "compositional source" (315). Burhans suggests that the vignettes be organized entirely on the basis of content. Therefore, according to him, there would be three groups consisting of nine vignettes on war, six on bullfighting, and two on crime.

In addition to noting that the vignettes are unified because they contain very similar content, Burhans thinks that the overall organization of the vignettes (from war to crime to bullfighting to crime) serves to emphasize the entire book's major theme: "By surrounding bullfighting with war and crime, Hemingway places violence and death on which man imposes order and meaning at the center of a world of chaotic disorder and violence, thus implying subtly that from the first—bullfighting—he can learn something about the second—the world—and about how to live in it'' (315).

Like Burhans, Robert M. Slabey and Keith Carabine (''Hemingway's *in our time*'') emphasize that the bullfighting vignettes are used by Hemingway to give an example of how violence and death can be controlled and sometimes mastered through the use of ritual. For example, convinced that the book is unified by the protagonists' attempts to order their lives, Slabey divides the vignettes into the following groups: (1) chapters I–VIII depict the loss of values; (2) chapters IX–XIV, the search for a code that would help characters confront and organize experience; and (3) chapter XV and ''L'Envoi,'' ''an ironic postscript-picture of decadence and impotence'' (41). Carabine, who offers one of the most detailed and perceptive descriptions of the vignettes, agrees that the Villalta and Maera vignettes (chapters XII–XIV) contrast with most of the other vignettes, which ''strip away and deny the customary guides and alignments—church, social justice, politics, love, revolution—that would make contemporary life bearable'' (320). Carabine differs from the others, however, because he emphasizes that even though the bullfighting vignettes offer a positive alternative to the suffering and uncontrolled violence in the rest of the book, the alternative is available to only a few, and to them only rarely. Carabine's reading of the vignettes is more pessimistic than either Burhans's or Slabey's but nonetheless convincing.

The Relationship between the Stories and Vignettes

Those critics who discuss the short stories as a separate unit generally perceive that they are unified by the same subjects as the vignettes. For example, David J. Leigh, Raymond Joel Silverman, and Slabey argue that the stories can be divided into the following categories on the basis of their content:

LEIGH

1. ''Indian Camp'' through ''Soldier's Home'': ''The Education of Nick Adams to Violence.''
2. ''The Revolutionist'' through ''My Old Man'': ''Results of this education: The Disillusioned Life of the Expatriate.''
3. ''Big Two-Hearted River'': ''Readjustment and Re-education by Return to Basic Sensations in Former Environment.''

SILVERMAN

1. ''Indian Camp'' through ''The Battler'': the disillusionment of Nick Adams.
2. ''A Very Short Story'' through ''The Revolutionist'': the shift from Nick Adams to other similar characters for the purpose of universalizing Nick's disillusionment.
3. ''Mr. and Mrs. Elliot'' through ''Out of Season'': the subject of failure is emphasized in addition to disillusionment.
4. ''Cross-Country Snow'' through ''Big Two-Hearted River'': Villalta's success in chapter XII and Nick's in ''Cross-Country Snow'' are followed by a series of failures.

SLABEY

1. "Indian Camp" through "The Battler": the youth of Nick Adams.
2. "A Very Short Story" through "The Revolutionist": the effect of war.
3. "Mr. and Mrs. Elliot" through "Cross-Country Snow": the failure of marriage.
4. "My Old Man" and "Big Two-Hearted River": the search for a code of behavior.

Even though their categories are somewhat arbitrary and vague, the critics indicate that the stories are unified by a limited number of subjects, that some of the stories based on a particular subject are grouped together, and that the subjects discussed form a general thematic pattern: as mentioned before, the movement from innocence to initiation to disillusionment to an attempt to reestablish values or a code of behavior.

Most critics perceive that the vignettes, the stories, and the book as a whole are unified by this theme. Briefly restated, it involves the loss of traditional values and the search for new ones or at least a code of behavior that allows one to maintain a minimum of dignity in a world that resists attempts to establish values or meaning. In addition to the bullfighters Villalta and Maera, Nick Adams (in "Cross-Country Snow" and "Big Two-Hearted River") and the revolutionist in the story by the same title are other characters who confront potentially violent or chaotic situations but are not overwhelmed by them. They survive—temporarily fending off chaos—because of their defense mechanisms or codes of behavior, specifically through the use of ritual, including acquired skills such as bullfighting and fishing.

While acknowledging the importance of the protagonists' attempts to order experience or establish codes of behavior, there are those who argue that the book is primarily unified as it depicts the psychological condition of Nick Adams or the general psychological condition of people in post–World War I America and Europe. Moving from specific to general, we can begin with Young, Richard Drinnon, and David Gordon, whose comments pertain specifically to Nick Adams but are also intended to describe Hemingway.

According to Young, *In Our Time* is unified through the psychological development of Nick Adams, who is the prototype of the Hemingway hero. The key to understanding Nick's development, as well as the development of subsequent protagonists such as Jake Barnes, Frederic Henry, or Robert Jordan, is the recognition of the symbolic function of Nick's war wound. In chapter VI of *In Our Time* Nick is wounded in the spine and declares a "separate peace" with the enemy. This traumatic experience, according to Young, symbolizes Nick's wounds both past and present, physical as well as psychic: "This culminating blow in the spine is symbol and climax for a process that has been going on since we first met Nick; it is an outward and visible sign of an inward and spiritual dis-grace" (*A Reconsideration* 41).

Although Young's reading of *In Our Time* has been highly influential because it establishes a convincing series of psychological cause and effect relationships in the Nick Adams stories, it has a weakness. Young tends to ignore any part of the book that does not feature Nick. As a result, in chapter 1 of *A Reconsideration* ("Adventures of Nick Adams"), Young discusses only several of the *In Our Time* vignettes, and he does not deal with any of the material between chapter VI and "Cross-Country Snow."

Although he stresses that Nick's experiences as a child and an adolescent have a long-term crippling effect on him, Young does not emphasize Nick's childhood to the extent Drinnon and Gordon do. Using Freudian approaches, Drinnon and Gordon both argue that Nick's relationship with his father, as described in "Indian Camp," "The Doctor and the Doctor's Wife," and "The Three-Day Blow," is an earlier and more important influence. In fact, Drinnon even suggests that Nick's war wound is traumatic to some extent because Nick associates the event with his father: "When he thought of his father, he also thought of hunting, guns, and his father's shooting" (12). Although the evidence he presents in support of his claim is often taken from Nick Adams stories not included in *In Our Time* (including "Fathers and Sons" and "A Way You'll Never Be"), Drinnon's description of Nick comes closer to approximating the reader's experience with the book than Gordon's more detailed but undemonstrated thesis. Gordon maintains that *In Our Time* "traces the essential psychological history of the Hemingway hero's relationship with his father: the child's need and admiration for his father; his fears, as rivalrous feelings emerge, of retaliatory aggression; and his efforts to rid himself of such dangerous feelings . . . " (123–24).

Leigh, on the other hand, focuses on the existential neurosis of Europeans as well as Americans after World War I. The major symptom is "a cognitive vacuum of 'meaninglessness' in which the person feels unable to believe in any truths or values beyond the simplest sensations . . . " (6). Because people suffering from this disorder can only trust their senses, characters in *In Our Time* who experience this existential neurosis—Nick Adams, Harold Krebs, the Elliots, the husband and wife in "Cat in the Rain"—display obsessive interest in sports and other activities that require no complex personal commitments. As a result, Leigh questions whether or not Nick's fishing trip in "Big Two-Hearted River" is as therapeutic as many critics suggest: "Nick has to learn to feel and reflect all over again, beginning with the simplest experiences. The difficulty with such therapy is, of course, that it might be a further symptom of the neurosis itself" (8).

Among those critics who employ psychological approaches, there is a tendency to perceive sporting events in *In Our Time* as the means whereby characters can avoid reality, a sharp contrast from the majority of critics, who argue that the ritual and skill demanded in a sport like bullfighting give characters' lives dignity and meaning.

Point of View

As is the case with theme, it is necessary to approach the use of point of view as a unifying device by considering each of the book's two major divisions separately. Although only six of the vignettes are written in the first person, while ten are in the third, most of the vignettes function as dramatic monologues, or they simulate the first person by using a covert narrator who reveals the characters' thoughts and dialogue. Thus, even though a variety of points of view and markedly distinct speakers are used, the vignettes are unified to some extent because (1) most feature or simulate a first-person speaker; (2) most feature anonymous speakers about whom the reader is given no background information; (3) and some feature speakers who resemble one another because of their tone or language habits.[10]

As far as the series of short stories is concerned, unity is achieved through similar means. In spite of the fact that all but three are told in the third-person point of view, the stories are not unified by a narrator, since the narrator infrequently makes his presence felt. Instead, they are linked to one another through the narrator's omniscience. Since many of these protagonists resemble one another, forming, as Carl Wood suggests, a composite personality, then the stories in *In Our Time* are unified by the consciousness of this composite personality as it is revealed through the first person and through the third-person limited-omniscient narrator. Therefore, while the point of view in both the stories and the vignettes is manipulated so that the protagonist's consciousness is revealed, there is a crucial difference between the points of view in the book's two major divisions: one composite personality is emphasized in the stories, but distinct personalities are juxtaposed in the vignettes.

Imagery

Image patterns and symbols contribute subtly to the unity of *In Our Time*. Among those discussed, many are juxtaposed (both within individual stories or vignettes and within the book as a whole) with diametric opposites: the campfire, which is a symbol of security, is juxtaposed with the threatening swamp in both "The Battler" and "Big Two-Hearted River"; the home, ironically suggesting "Not-Home," is juxtaposed with the forest, which suggests "Home" to at least Nick Adams, his father, and Ad and Bugs in "The Battler" (C. Baker's *Writer as Artist*: 131–34); images associated with the masculine principle—fishing poles, logs, towers, sharp-cutting instruments—are juxtaposed with images of the feminine—rain, pools, lakes, swamps (Benson's "Patterns of Connection"); various images of birth are juxtaposed with images of death (Benson's "Patterns," Lowry, Silverman); sexual imagery is juxtaposed with images of impotence, sterility, illness, and death (Benson's "Patterns," Silverman); light is juxtaposed with dark (Benson's "Patterns," Silverman); cold is juxtaposed with hot. Other important patterns, described in some detail by Jackson J. Benson and Silverman, include rigidity and stiffness (once again, sexuality and death are paired), the leaning or sitting against a wall or a building, screaming or moaning, and sport used as a metaphor (for the last item, also see Lewis). Charles G. Hoffman and A. C. Hoffman have noted the importance of the road motif, generally used to signify the beginning of an initiation.

Imagery clearly contributes to the tension in *In Our Time* between the masculine and feminine principle and between life and death. Further consideration needs to be given to the almost obsessive juxtaposition of opposites, especially the frequent inversion of the significance of certain archetypal symbols, such as water that is described as stagnant or births that result in death or which we associate with death. Also, subsequent criticism needs to provide more extensive descriptions of the recurrence of some of these images and symbols and the effect that such repetitions have on the way we read individual stories. Imagery seems to develop from story to story, and some of Hemingway's most ironic effects result from his ability to thwart the reader's expectations. For example, the reader who perceives the woods as a safe retreat for Nick in "The Doctor and the Doctor's Wife" does not anticipate—much as Nick himself—the danger that the woods represent in "The Battler."

CONCLUSION

Further discussion of Hemingway's juxtaposition of the stories and the vignettes in *In Our Time* is needed. Hemingway himself recognized that this was one the book's most experimental features. When finishing the last stories in September 1924, he was particularly enthusiastic about the interaction of the two series of narratives:

All the stories have a certain unity, the first five are in Michigan . . . and in between each one comes bang! the In Our Time [*in our time*]. It should be awfully good, I think. I've tried to do it so you get the close up very quietly but absolutely solid and the real thing but very close, and then through it all between every story comes the rhythm of the in our time chapters. (*Selected Letters* 123)

Following Hemingway's suggestion that the vignettes "give the picture of the whole between examining it in detail," a few critics suggest that the juxtaposition of both series of narratives results in the simultaneous depiction in *In Our Time* of individual experience and the generalizations that can be made concerning that experience. For example, Pleasant Larus Reed III notes that there is "a sense of simultaneity between stories and vignettes, a feeling of a rhythm of public events which pulls Nick or his substitute from one story to the next, from private to public, individual to universal 'time' " (183–84).

More attention to the thematic function of juxtaposed narratives would help readers better understand the book's most ambiguous stories, especially "Big Two-Hearted River." The pessimistic epilogue ("L'Envoi") that follows Nick's return to Michigan should serve to temper the more positive interpretations of the last Nick Adams story. Even if convinced that Nick retreats only temporarily, preparing himself so that he can fish in deeper and more treacherous water tomorrow, the reader must acknowledge that Hemingway chose an epilogue that by all accounts suggests defeat.

The thematic function of the juxtaposition of the vignettes and stories has been touched upon briefly, but it is clear—as it was in *Dubliners* and *Winesburg, Ohio*—that repetition in the book serves to emphasize content. The sense of meaninglessness, the pain, and the violence that characters experience in the individual stories is intensified as well as made more universal when the parts are juxtaposed. As Richard Hasbany describes the total effect:

Life is so single mindedly awful it seems a conscious, cosmic prank; it starts in pain, is pervaded by painful initiation, dislocation, guilt, desire, fear of responsibility, and isolation; and it is always threatened by bestial violence and death. Man emerges from . . . the cumulative effects of the juxtaposed images as a wounded creature in an ugly and treacherous world. (239)

Primarily because of Hemingway's decision to juxtapose thirty-two vignettes and short stories, the form of *In Our Time* is more complex than the forms of most other cycles. Not only are there more parts in *In Our Time* than in these other books, but there are also more wholes. Readers must consider how these stories (or vignettes) are to be read, how the parts are related to the self-sufficient whole. We may see, for instance, the story (or vignette) in relation to a series of stories (or a series of vignettes). We may also see an individual story (or vignette) in relation to the entire book. Furthermore, readers must decide whether or not a story and its preceding or following vignette function as a unit, thereby creating another series of parts and wholes.[11] The complexities are enormous; but if critics can provide increasingly precise descriptions of these inner-relationships, our appreciation of this intricate book will surely be enhanced.

Although the generic form of *In Our Time* is not distinct from the forms of *Dubliners*, *Winesburg, Ohio*, and the other books included in this study, it is certainly a more extreme example of the form. Instead of one series or cycle, *In Our Time* contains two—and possibly three—that are interrelated.

NOTES

1. In his recent biography, Jeffrey Meyers cites *Dubliners* as a more important influence on *In Our Time* than short fiction written by Anderson or Gertrude Stein (82–83).

2. I consistently use "vignette" to describe the brief pieces of fiction that are sandwiched around the short stories in *In Our Time*. Since the vignettes are identified by Hemingway as "Chapter 1," "Chapter 2," and so forth, I use "chapter" only when referring to vignettes by number.

3. Some of the stories and vignettes were based loosely on "Cross Roads," an early (late 1919 to early 1920) series that Hemingway wrote about Horton Bay (Reynolds, Introduction to *Critical Essays*); and some of the vignettes were also based on newspaper stories (1917–1923). Six of the vignettes were first published in *The Little Review* (Spring 1923); two of the stories in *Three Stories and Ten Poems* (Summer 1923), and eighteen vignettes in *in our time* (1924).

4. Other critics who discuss the composition and publication of individual stories or vignettes include Derounian, Hagemann, and Paul Smith. Also see Reynolds's introduction to *Critical Essays*.

5. Material completed at this time would include the stories published in *Three Stories and Ten Poems* ("Up in Michigan," "Out of Season," and "My Old Man"), the vignettes first published in *in our time*, probably "Indian Camp" (the first of the Nick Adams stories), and some of the other early 1924 stories that do not feature Nick.

6. In *Selected Letters*, the first mention of *In Our Time* is in a 2 May 1924 letter to Edward J. O'Brien. At this point Hemingway is interested in producing a work that is more substantial than either of his first two books, *Three Stories and Ten Poems* and *in our time*. He has only the vaguest idea of the new book's overall design: "What I would like to do would be bring out a good fat book in N.Y. with some good publisher who would tout it and have In Our Time [*in our time*] in it and the other stories, My Old Man and about 15 or 20 others. How many would it take?" (117).

7. Hemingway material at the archive is listed in the *Catalog of the Ernest Hemingway Collection at the John F. Kennedy Library*, 2 vols. (Boston: Hall, 1982).

8. According to Paul Smith (in both "Practice of Omission" and "Misconceptions"), the typescript of "Out of Season" reveals that Hemingway's early prose developed "through a process of accretion rather than, as many readers have assumed, through deletion" ("Misconceptions" 240). Kathryn Derounian's discussion of "Nick sat against the wall" does not support Smith's thesis. Working with three drafts of vignette VI, she explains that Hemingway revises to excise irrelevant details or unnecessary repetition and to emphasize Nick's perspective.

9. See Carlos Baker's *Hemingway: A Life Story*, Sheridan Baker's *An Introduction and Interpretation*, Hagemann's "Time-and-History," Montgomery, and Reynolds's "Two Sources."

10. Carabine describes several instances of a "laconic, easy, bemused" British officer's voice and "an extremely matter-of-fact" voice (" 'Pretty Good Unity' " 313).

11. Most critics do not acknowledge this as an organizational plan, as evidenced by the fact that they frequently call the vignettes "chapters" or "interchapters." Even though critics such as Sheridan Baker and Wood note that the book is divided into vignette-story chapters, they fail to establish one-to-one relationships between the stories and the vignettes that precede them. (Silverman is the exception, but his comments are restricted to his dissertation.)

WORKS CITED AND BIBLIOGRAPHY

Adair, William. "Landscapes of the Mind: 'Big Two-Hearted River.' " *College Literature* 4 (1977): 144–51. Rpt. in Reynolds, *Critical Essays*, 260–67.

———. "Lying Down in Hemingway's Fiction." *NConL* 16.4 (Sept. 1986): 7–8.

Backman, Melvin. "Hemingway: The Matador and the Crucified." *MFS* 1 (Aug. 1955): 2–11. Rpt. in Carlos Baker, *Hemingway and Critics*, 245–58; and in Carlos Baker, *Critiques of Four Novels*, 135–43.

Baker, Carlos. *Ernest Hemingway: A Life Story*. New York: Scribner's, 1969.

———, ed. *Ernest Hemingway: Critiques of Four Major Novels*. New York: Scribner's, 1962.

———, ed. *Hemingway and His Critics: An International Anthology*. New York: Hill and Wang, 1961.

————. *Hemingway: The Writer as Artist*. 4th ed. Princeton: Princeton UP, 1972.

Baker, Sheridan. *Ernest Hemingway: An Introduction and Interpretation*. New York: Holt, 1967.

————. "Hemingway's Two-Hearted River." *Michigan Alumnus Quarterly Review* 65 (Winter 1959): 142–49. Rpt. in Benson, *Short Stories*, 150–59.

Benson, Jackson J. "Ernest Hemingway as Short Story Writer." Benson (see below), *Short Stories*, 272–310.

————. "Patterns of Connection and Their Development in Hemingway's *In Our Time*." *Rendezvous* 5.2 (Winter 1970): 37–52. Rpt. in Reynolds, *Critical Essays*, 103–19.

————, ed. *The Short Stories of Ernest Hemingway: Critical Essays*. Durham: Duke UP, 1975.

Boutelle, Ann Edwards. "Hemingway and 'Papa': Killing of the Father in the Nick Adams Fiction." *JML* 9.1 (1981–1982): 133–46.

Bredahl, A. Carl. "Divided Narrative and Ernest Hemingway." *LHY* 24 (Jan. 1983): 15–21.

Burgess, Anthony. *Ernest Hemingway and His World*. London: Thames and Hudson, 1978.

Burhans, Clinton S., Jr. "The Complex Unity of *In Our Time*." *MFS* 14 (Ernest Hemingway Special Number) (Autumn 1968): 313–28. Rpt. in Benson, *Short Stories*, 15–29; and in Reynolds, *Critical Essays*, 88–102.

Camati, Anna Stegh. "Ritual as Indicative of a Code of Values in Hemingway's *In Our Time*." *RLet* 31 (1982): 11–25.

Carabine, Keith. " 'Big Two-Hearted River': A Re-interpretation." *Hemingway Review* 1.2 (Spring 1982): 39–44.

————. "Hemingway's *in our time*: An Appreciation." *Fitzgerald/Hemingway Annual 1979*. Ed. Matthew J. Bruccoli and Richard Layman. Detroit: Gale, 1980. 301–26.

————. " 'A Pretty Good Unity': A Study of Sherwood Anderson's *Winesburg, Ohio* and Ernest Hemingway's *In Our Time*." Diss. Yale U, 1978. *DAI* 39 (1978): 2936A–37A.

    Examines the composition of *In Our Time* and its unifying themes. Explains why Hemingway's talent and training lead in the direction of the short story, not the novel. Ultimately, Carabine claims that *In Our Time* is Hemingway's most successful work of fiction.

Catalog of the Ernest Hemingway Collection at the John F. Kennedy Library. 2 vols. Boston: Hall, 1982.

Cooper, Stephen. *The Politics of Ernest Hemingway*. Ann Arbor, MI: UMI, 1987.

Cowley, Malcolm. "Hemingway's Wound—and Its Consequences for American Literature." *GaR* 38.2 (Summer 1984): 223–39.

Dawson, William Forrest. "Ernest Hemingway: Petoskey Interview." *Michigan Alumnus Quarterly Review* 64 (Winter 1958): 114–23.

DeFalco, Joseph. *The Hero in Hemingway's Short Stories*. Pittsburgh: U of Pittsburgh P, 1963. Sections on "Indian Camp" and "The Doctor and the Doctor's Wife" are rpt. in Benson, *Short Stories*, 159–67.

Derounian, Kathryn Zabelle. "An Examination of the Drafts of Hemingway's Chapter 'Nick sat against the wall of the church. . . .' " *PBSA* 77.1 (1983): 54–65. Rpt. in Reynolds, *Critical Essays*, 61–75.

Drinnon, Richard. "In the American Heartland: Hemingway and Death." *Psychoanalytic Review* 52 (Summer 1965): 5–31.

Dupre, Roger. "Hemingway's *In Our Time*: A Contextual Explication." Diss. St. John's U, 1979. *DAI* 40 (1979): 2662A.

    Dupre examines in detail five of the eighteen vignettes and eleven of the fourteen stories, demonstrating that various sources are used as "subsurface contexts," including the following: Carl G. Jung's *Symbols of Transformation*; Sir James G. Frazer's *The Golden Bough*; Sigmund Freud's *The Interpretation of Dreams, Three Essays on the Theory of Sexuality*, and *Beyond the Pleasure Principle*; and John Bunyan's *The Pilgrim's Progress*.

Egri, Peter. "The Relationship between the Short Story and the Novel, Realism and Naturalism in Hemingway's Art. Part I: 1923–1929." *Hungarian Studies in English* (L. Kossuth U) 4 (1969): 105–26.

Fenton, Charles A. "Paris." *The Apprenticeship of Ernest Hemingway: The Early Years*. New York: Farrar, 1954. 224–41. The section on chapter III (from *in our time*) is rpt. in Benson, *Short Stories*, 80–84.

Ficken, Carl. "Point of View in the Nick Adams Stories." *Fitzgerald/Hemingway Annual 1971*. Ed. Matthew J. Bruccoli and C. E. Frazer Clark, Jr. Washington, DC: NCR Microcard Editions, 1971. 212–35. Rpt. in Benson, *Short Stories*, 93–112.

Flora, Joseph M. *Hemingway's Nick Adams*. Baton Rouge: Louisiana State UP, 1982.

Fox, Stephen D. "Hemingway's 'The Doctor and the Doctor's Wife.' " *ArQ* 29 (Spring 1973): 19–25.

Fuchs, Daniel. "Ernest Hemingway, Literary Critic." *AL* 36 (Jan. 1965): 431–51. Rpt. in Waldhorn, *Collection of Criticism*, 92–111; and in Wagner, *Five Decades*, 39–56.

Fulkerson, Richard. "The Biographical Fallacy and 'The Doctor and the Doctor's Wife.' " *SSF* 16 (Winter 1979): 61–65. Rpt. in Reynolds, *Critical Essays*, 150–54.

Gajdusek, Robert E. "Dubliners in Michigan: Joyce's Presence in Hemingway's *In Our Time*." *Hemingway Review* 2.1 (Fall 1982): 48–61.

Gerogiannis, Nicholas. "Nick Adams on the Road: 'The Battler' as Hemingway's Man on the Hill." Reynolds, *Critical Essays*, 176–88.

Gibb, Robert. "He Made Him Up: 'Big Two-Hearted River' as Doppelganger." *Hemingway Notes* 5.1 (Fall 1979): 20–24. Rpt. in Reynolds, *Critical Essays*, 254–59.

Gordon, David. "The Son and the Father: Patterns of Response to Conflict in Hemingway's Fiction." *L&P* 16 (Summer 1966): 122–38.

Grebstein, Sheldon Norman. "The Structure of Hemingway's Short Stories." *Hemingway's Craft*. Carbondale: Southern Illinois UP, 1973. 1–26. Rpt. in *Fitzgerald/Hemingway Annual 1972*. Ed. Matthew J. Bruccoli and C. E. Frazer Clark, Jr. Washington, DC: NCR Microcard Editions, 1973. 173–93.

Griffin, Peter. *Along with Youth: Hemingway, the Early Years*. Oxford: Oxford UP, 1985.

Grimes, Larry E. *The Religious Design of Hemingway's Early Fiction*. Ann Arbor, MI: UMI, 1985.

Groseclose, Barbara S. "Hemingway's 'The Revolutionist': An Aid to Interpretation." *MFS* 17 (Winter 1971–1972): 565–70.

Hagemann, E. R. "A Collation, with Commentary, of the Five Texts of the Chapters in

Hemingway's *In Our Time*. 1923–1938.'' *PBSA* 70 (1979): 443–58. Rpt. in Reynolds, *Critical Essays*, 38–51

———. '' 'Dear Folks . . . Dear Ezra': Hemingway's Early Years and Correspondence, 1917–1924.'' Oldsey, *Papers of a Writer*, 25–35.

———. '' 'Only let the story end as soon as possible': Time-and-History in Ernest Hemingway's *In Our Time*.'' *MFS* 26 (Summer 1980): 255–62. Rpt. in Reynolds, *Critical Essays*, 52–60.

———. ''Word-Count and Statistical Survey of the Chapters in Ernest Hemingway's *In Our Time*.'' *LRN* 5 (Winter 1980): 21–30.

Halliday, E. M. ''Hemingway's Ambiguity: Symbolism and Irony.'' *AL* 28 (Mar. 1956): 1–22. Rpt. in Carlos Baker, *Critiques of Four Novels*, 61–74; in Waldhorn, *Collection of Criticism*, 35–55; and in Weeks, *Collection of Critical Essays*, 52–71.

———. ''Hemingway's *In Our Time*.'' *Expl* 7 (Mar. 1949): Item 35. Rpt. in Reynolds, *Critical Essays*, 29–30.

Hannum, Howard L. ''Dating Hemingway's 'The Three-Day Blow' by External Evidence: The Baseball Dialogue.'' *SSF* 21.3 (Summer 1984): 267–68.

———. ''Soldier's Home: Immersion Therapy and Lyric Pattern in 'Big Two-Hearted River.' '' *Hemingway Review* 3.2 (Spring 1984): 2–13.

Harrison, James M. ''Hemingway's *In Our Time*.'' *Expl* 18 (May 1960): Item 51. Rpt. in Reynolds, *Critical Essays*, 141–43.

Hasbany, Richard. ''The Shock of Vision: An Imagist Reading of *In Our Time*.'' Wagner, *Five Decades*, 224–40.

Hedeen, Paul M. ''Moving in the Picture: The Landscape Stylistics of *In Our Time*.'' *Lang&S* 18.4 (Fall 1985): 363–76.

Hemingway, Ernest. *Ernest Hemingway: Selected Letters 1917–1961*. Ed. Carlos Baker. New York: Scribner's, 1981.

———. *The Nick Adams Stories*. Preface by Philip Young. New York: Scribner's, 1972.

———. *In Our Time*. New York: Scribner's, 1930.

Hoffman, Charles G., and A. C. Hoffman. '' 'The Truest Sentence': Words as Equivalents of Time and Place in *In Our Time*.'' *Hemingway: A Revaluation*. Ed. Donald R. Noble. Troy, NY: Whitson, 1983. 99–113.

Hoffman, Frederick J. ''No Beginning and No End: Hemingway and Death.'' *EIC* 3 (Jan. 1953): 73–84.

Hunt, Anthony. ''Another Turn for Hemingway's 'The Revolutionist': Sources and Meanings.'' *Fitzgerald/Hemingway Annual 1977*. Ed. Margaret M. Duggan and Richard Layman. Detroit: Gale, 1977. 119–35. Rpt. in Reynolds, *Critical Essays*, 203–17.

Ingram, Forrest L. *Representative Short Story Cycles of the Twentieth Century: Studies in a Literary Genre*. The Hague: Mouton, 1971.

Jackson, Paul R. ''Hemingway's 'Out of Season.' '' *Hemingway Review* 1.1 (Fall 1981): 11–17.

Johnson, Edgar. ''Farewell the Separate Peace.'' *SR* 48 (July–Sept. 1940): 289–300.

Johnston, Kenneth G. ''Hemingway and Cézanne: Doing the Country.'' *AL* 56 (Mar. 1984): 28–37.

———. ''Hemingway's 'Out of Season' and the Psychology of Errors.'' *L&P* 21 (1971): 41–46. Rpt. in Reynolds, *Critical Essays*, 227–34.

————. "In the Beginning: Hemingway's 'Indian Camp.' " *SSF* 15 (Winter 1978): 102–4.

————. "Nick/Mike Adams? The Hero's Name in 'Cross-Country Snow.' " *AN&Q* 20 (Sept.–Oct. 1981): 16–18.

————. " 'The Three-Day Blow': Tragicomic Aftermath of a Summer Romance." *Hemingway Review* 2.1 (Fall 1982): 21–25.

————. *The Tip of the Iceberg: Hemingway and the Short Story*. Greenwood, FL: Penkevill, 1987.

Joost, Nicholas. *Ernest Hemingway and the Little Magazines: The Paris Years*. Barre, MA: Barre, 1968.

Killinger, John. *Hemingway and the Dead Gods: A Study in Existentialism*. Lexington: U of Kentucky P, 1960.

Kruse, Horst H. "Ernest Hemingway's 'The End of Something': Its Independence as a Short Story and Its Place in the 'Education of Nick Adams.' " *SSF* 4 (Winter 1967): 152–66. Rpt. in Benson, *Short Stories*, 210–22; and in Reynolds, *Critical Essays*, 159–71.

Kyle, Frank B. "Parallel and Complementary Themes in Hemingway's Big Two-Hearted River Stories and 'The Battler.' " *SSF* 16 (Fall 1979): 295–300.

Lawrence, D. H. Rev. of *In Our Time*, by Ernest Hemingway. *Calendar of Modern Letters* 4 (Apr. 1927): 72–73. Rpt. in *Phoenix: The Posthumous Papers of D. H. Lawrence*. Ed. Edward D. McDonald. London: Heinemann, 1936. 365; and in Weeks, *Collection of Critical Essays*, 93–94.

Lebowitz, Alan. "Hemingway's *In Our Time*." *YR* 58 (Mar. 1969): 321–41.

Lee, A. Robert, ed. *Ernest Hemingway: New Critical Essays*. London: Vision; Totowa, NJ: Barnes, 1983.

Leigh, David J. "*In Our Time*: The Interchapters as Structural Guides to a Psychological Pattern." *SSF* 12 (Winter 1975): 1–8. Rpt. in Reynolds, *Critical Essays*, 130–37.

Leiter, Louis H. "Neural Projections in Hemingway's 'On the Quai at Smyrna.' " *SSF* 5 (Summer 1968): 384–86. Rpt. in Reynolds, *Critical Essays*, 138–40.

Lewis, Robert W., Jr. "Hemingway's Concept of Sport and 'Soldier's Home.' " *Rendezvous* 5.2 (Winter 1970): 19–27. Rpt. in Benson, *Short Stories*, 170–80; and in Reynolds, *Critical Essays*, 189–98.

Lohani, Shreedhar Prasad. "The Narrator in Fiction: A Study of the Narrator's Presence in Joyce's *Dubliners* and Hemingway's *In Our Time*." Diss. Southern Illinois U, 1984. *DAI* 45 (1985): 2517A.

Lowry, E. D. "Chaos and Cosmos in *In Our Time*." *L&P* 26.3 (1976): 108–17.

Lynn, Kenneth S. *Hemingway: The Life and the Work*. New York: Simon, 1987.

McComas, Dix. "The Geography of Ernest Hemingway: 'Out of Season.' " *Hemingway Review* 3.2 (Spring 1984): 46–49.

Meindl, Dieter. "Der kurzgeschichtenzyklus als modernistisches Genre." *GRM* 33.2 (1983): 216–28.

Meyers, Jeffrey. *Hemingway: A Biography*. New York: Harper, 1985.

Monteiro, George. "Dating the Events of 'The Three-Day Blow.' " *Fitzgerald/Hemingway Annual 1977*. Ed. Margaret M. Duggan and Richard Layman. Detroit: Gale, 1977. 207–10. Rpt. in Reynolds, *Critical Essays*, 1972–75.

————. " 'This Is My Pal Bugs': Ernest Hemingway's 'The Battler.' " *SSF* 23.2 (Spring 1986): 179–83.

Montgomery, Constance Cappel. *Hemingway in Michigan*. New York: Fleet, 1966.

Muller, Gerald H. "*In Our Time*: Hemingway and the Discontents of Civilization." *Renascence: Essays on Value in Literature* 29 (Summer 1977): 185–92.

Nagel, James. "Literary Impressionism and *In Our Time*." *Hemingway Review* 6.2 (Spring 1987): 17–26.

Nahal, Chaman. "The Short Stories." *The Narrative Pattern in Ernest Hemingway's Fiction*. Rutherford, NJ: Fairleigh Dickinson UP, 1971. 80–119.

Nakajima, Kenji. "The Bullfight, a Test of Manhood: On Hemingway's 'Chapter IX,' *In Our Time*". *KAL* 28 (Oct. 1987): 19–27.

———. "Literary Bravery in Hemingway's 'Chapter III' and 'Chapter IV' of *In Our Time*." *KAL* 27 (1986): 47–56.

———. "To Discipline Eyes against Misery: On Hemingway's 'Chapter II,' *In Our Time*." *KAL* 26 (Oct. 1985): 11–19.

Noble, Donald R., ed. *Hemingway: A Revaluation*. Troy, NY: Whitson, 1983.

Oldsey, Bernard, ed. *Ernest Hemingway: The Papers of a Writer*. New York: Garland, 1981.

———. "Hemingway's Beginnings and Endings." *CollL* 7 (1980): 213–38. Rpt. in his *The Papers of a Writer* 37–62.

Parker, Alice. "Hemingway's 'The End of Something.' " *Expl* 10 (Mar. 1952): Item 36. Rpt. in Reynolds, *Critical Essays*, 157–58.

Pearsall, Robert Brainard. *The Life and Writings of Ernest Hemingway*. Amsterdam: Rodopi, 1973.

Penner, Dick. "The First Nick Adams Story." *Fitzgerald/Hemingway Annual 1977*. Ed. Margaret M. Duggan and Richard Layman. Detroit: Gale, 1977. 195–202.

Reed, Pleasant Larus, III. "The Integrated Short-Story Collection: Studies of a Form of Nineteenth- and Twentieth-Century Fiction." Diss. Indiana U, 1974. *DAI* 35 (1975): 6730A.

  Reed defines *In Our Time* as an integrated short story collection: (1) the vignettes are unified because they depict "the innocent character's immersion in violence" (175); (2) the interaction between the stories and the vignettes serves to connect private and public worlds; (3) the relationship between the bullfighting vignettes and the marriage stories serves to contrast acceptable and unacceptable manners of handling "self-contained, institutionalized, violent conflict" (192); and (4) the decision to delete the expository prose in "Two-Hearted River" underscores Hemingway's attempt to connect the narratives implicitly rather than explicitly.

Reynolds, Michael S., ed. *Critical Essays on Ernest Hemingway's* In Our Time. Boston: Hall, 1983.

———. "Two Hemingway Sources for *In Our Time*." *SSF* 9 (Winter 1972): 81–86. Rpt. in Reynolds, *Critical Essays*, 31–37.

———. *The Young Hemingway*. New York: Basil Blackwell, 1986.

Roberts, John J. "In Defense of Krebs." *SSF* 13 (Fall 1976): 515–18. Rpt. in Reynolds, *Critical Essays*, 199–202.

Rovit, Earl, and Gerry Brenner. *Ernest Hemingway*. Rev. ed. Boston: Twayne, 1986.

Sanderson, Stewart F. "The Loss of Innocence." *Ernest Hemingway*. New York: Grove; Edinburgh: Oliver & Boyd, 1961. 27–39.

Scafella, Frank. "Imagistic Landscape of a Psyche: Hemingway's Nick Adams." *Hemingway Review* 2.2 (Spring 1983): 2–10.

Seed, David. " 'The Picture of the Whole': *In Our Time*." *Ernest Hemingway: New*

Critical Essays. Ed. A. Robert Lee. London: Vision; Totowa, NJ: Barnes, 1983. 13–35.

Shtogren, John Alexander, Jr. "Ernest Hemingway's Aesthetic Use of Journalism in His First Decade of Fiction." Diss. U of Michigan, 1971. *DAI* 32 (1972): 6454A.

Silverman, Raymond Joel. "The Short Story Composite: Forms, Functions, and Applications." Diss. U of Michigan, 1970. *DAI* 31 (1971): 6633A.

Silverman identifies key unifying imagery—rain, light and dark, figures leaning against walls or lying under blankets. He also provides a sequential reading of the vignettes and stories, attempting to define relationships between each story and the vignettes around it. As a result of this approach, he perceives correspondences that no one else notes: e.g., he points out that Villalta's triumph in chapter XII is echoed in the beginning of "Cross-Country Snow" and in chapter XIII.

Slabey, Robert M. "The Structure of Hemingway's *In Our Time*." *SDR* 3 (Autumn 1965): 38–52. Rpt. in Reynolds, *Critical Essays*, 76–87.

Smith, B. J. " 'Big Two-Hearted River': The Artist and the Art." *SSF* 20 (Spring–Summer 1983): 129–32.

Smith, Julian. "Hemingway and the Thing Left Out." *JML* 1.2 (1970–1971): 169–82. Rpt. in Wagner, *Five Decades*, 188–200; and in Benson, *Short Stories*, 135–47.

Smith, Paul. "Hemingway's Early Manuscripts: The Theory and Practice of Omission." *JML* 10.2 (June 1983): 268–88.

———. "Some Misconceptions of 'Out of Season.' " Rpt. in Reynolds, *Critical Essays*, 235–51.

Smith, Peter A. "Hemingway's 'On the Quai at Smyrna' and the Universe of *In Our Time*." *SSF* 24.2 (Spring 1987): 159–62.

Sniderman, Stephen Lee. "The 'Composite' in Twentieth-Century American Literature." Diss. U of Wisconsin, 1970. *DAI* 31 (1970): 403A.

Sniderman labels *In Our Time* a composite. He perceives Philip Young's *The Nick Adams Stories* as an adjunct to *In Our Time*, arguing that Nick becomes a three-dimensional character only when he is perceived in the context of the entire body of Nick Adams stories.

Sojka, Gregory Stanley. "Who Is Sam Cardinella and Why Is He Hanging between Two Sunny Days at Seney?" *Fitzgerald/Hemingway Annual 1976*. Ed. Matthew J. Bruccoli. Englewood, CO: Indian Head, 1978. 217–23.

Stein, William Bysshe. "Ritual in Hemingway's 'Big Two-Hearted River.' " *TSLL* 1 (Winter 1960): 555–61.

Steinke, Jim. "The Two Shortest Stories of Hemingway's *In Our Time*." Reynolds, *Critical Essays*, 218–26.

Vijgen, Theo. "A Change of Point of View in Hemingway's 'Big Two-Hearted River.' " *NMAL* 6.1 (Spring–Summer 1982): Item 5.

Wagner, Linda Welshimer, ed. *Ernest Hemingway: Five Decades of Criticism*. East Lansing: Michigan State UP, 1974.

———. "Juxtaposition in Hemingway's *In Our Time*." *SSF* 12 (Summer 1975): 243–52. Rpt. in *Hemingway and Faulkner: Inventors/Masters*. Metuchen, NJ: Scarecrow, 1975. 55–65; and in Reynolds, *Critical Essays*, 120–29.

———. " 'Proud and friendly and gently': Women in Hemingway's Early Fiction." In Oldsey, *Papers of a Writer*, 63–71.

Waldhorn, Arthur, ed. *Ernest Hemingway: A Collection of Criticism*. New York: McGraw, 1973.

————. *A Reader's Guide to Ernest Hemingway*. New York: Farrar, 1972.

Watts, Emily Stipes. *Ernest Hemingway and the Arts*. Urbana: U of Illinois P, 1971.

Weeks, Robert P., ed. *Hemingway: A Collection of Critical Essays*. Englewood Cliffs, NJ: Prentice, 1962.

Weltz, Friedrich. "Vier amerikanische Erzählungszyklen." Diss. Universität München, 1953.

> By considering a story's context in *In Our Time*, readers do not understand the individual story better; instead, they experience a heightening of the story's tragic intensity or its universal validity. This feeling of universality in the work is also achieved by placing a variety of protagonists in similar situations and through the juxtaposition of stories and vignettes. The book's cyclical structure is most evident in "My Old Man," the next to last story, where we return to childhood and are reminded of Nick's disillusionment with his father in "Indian Camp" and "The Doctor and the Doctor's Wife."

Westbrook, Max. "Grace under Pressure: Hemingway and the Summer of 1920." *Ernest Hemingway: The Writer in Context*. Ed. James Nagel. Madison: U of Wisconsin P, 1984. 77–106.

Whitlow, Roger. *Cassandra's Daughters: The Women in Hemingway*. Westport, CT: Greenwood, 1984.

Whitt, Joseph. "Hemingway's 'The End of Something,' " *Expl* 9 (June 1951): Item 58. Rpt. in Reynolds, *Critical Essays*, 155–56.

Wilkinson, Myler. *Hemingway and Turgenev: The Nature of Literary Influence*. Ann Arbor, MI: UMI, 1986.

Williams, Wirt. "*In Our Time*: Ranging Shots on the Near Side." *The Tragic Art of Ernest Hemingway*. Baton Rouge: Louisiana UP, 1981. 29–39.

Winchell, Mark Royden. "Fishing the Swamp: 'Big Two-Hearted River' and the Unity of *In Our Time*." *SCR* 18.2 (Spring 1986): 18–29.

Winn, Harlan Harbour, III. "Short Story Cycles of Hemingway, Steinbeck, Faulkner, and O'Connor." Diss. U of Oregon, 1975. *DAI* 36 (1976): 4500A.

> In addition to discussing unity, Winn outlines what may have been Hemingway's intentions when constructing *In Our Time*. His comments are useful because they are fairly comprehensive, but he does not go beyond what is said elsewhere.

Wood, Carl. "*In Our Time*: Hemingway's Fragmentary Novel." *NM* 74.4 (1973): 716–26.

Young, Philip. " 'Big World out There': *The Nick Adams Stories*." *Novel: A Forum on Fiction* 6 (Fall 1972): 5–19. Rpt. in Benson, *Short Stories*, 29–45.

————. *Ernest Hemingway*. Rev. ed. Pamphlets on American Writers 1. Minneapolis: U of Minnesota P, 1965. Earlier ed. rpt. in *Seven Modern American Novelists*. Ed. William Van O'Connor. Minneapolis: U of Minnesota P, 1964. 153–88.

————. *Ernest Hemingway: A Reconsideration*. University Park: Pennsylvania State UP, 1966.

————. "Hemingway's *In Our Time*." *Expl* 10 (Apr. 1952): Item 43.

4

John Steinbeck's
The Pastures of Heaven

For a decade, John Steinbeck devoted himself to writing short stories and cycles of stories. *The Pastures of Heaven* (1932) was the first cycle (and the second book) that he published, but another (unpublished) cycle, "Dissonant Symphony," was written at approximately the same time. Not long after this came *Tortilla Flat* (1935), Steinbeck's first book to win national recognition, containing a cycle of stories that compares Danny and his friends to the knights of King Arthur's Round Table. In 1938, Steinbeck completed *The Long Valley*, which includes three of the four stories that were later published separately as *The Red Pony* (1945), describing a boy's growth as he is exposed to death and unpredictable nature.

INTRODUCTION TO THE BOOK

Occurring more than a hundred years before the events that follow, the prologue to *Pastures of Heaven* introduces us to the valley and the book's ironic tone. The valley is named by a cruel Spanish corporal, sent to capture runaway Indians and force them back to the clay pits as slaves. Coming upon the valley accidentally, he is overwhelmed and declares, " 'Here are the green pastures of Heaven to which our Lord leadeth us' " (2).

In each of the stories that follow,[1] there is a disparity between the richness of the land and the impoverished, desperate, and sometimes petty lives of the inhabitants. Obsessed with a fortune that exists only in his imagination, "Shark" Wicks ignores his wife and prizes his daughter as a commodity. Mrs. Munroe's philanthropic zeal destroys the happiness that the Maltbys experienced before charity was offered. Molly Morgan succumbs to voices from the past, forcing her to relive a disastrous childhood. Pat Humbert creates an imaginary world in which a relationship is possible between himself and Mae Munroe; he is then crushed when reality intrudes in the person of Bert Munroe, announcing Mae's engagement to Bill Whiteside.

The epilogue also describes how outsiders perceive the Pastures of Heaven. Passengers on a tour bus stop and look longingly at the tranquility and the fruitfulness of the Pastures of Heaven and imagine how much better their lives would be if they only lived in the valley. From the sparse information we are given about these passengers—their ambitions, their desire to escape from problems that are inescapable, their inability to make sense out of their lives thus far—it appears doubtful that their lives would be significantly changed by a move to the Pastures of Heaven.

COMPOSITION OF *PASTURES OF HEAVEN*

There are relatively few comments about how the book was written in the letters preserved in *Steinbeck: A Life in Letters*. Furthermore, critics of *Pastures of Heaven* have shown little interest in the evolution of the work: there is no complete description or analysis of Steinbeck's revisions even though there are extant manuscript versions of the stories available at Stanford and the University of Texas at Austin.

The most insightful comments appear in Jackson J. Benson's biography, *The True Adventures of John Steinbeck, Writer*, and Peter Lisca's *The Wide World of John Steinbeck*. According to Benson, Steinbeck appropriated the idea for the book from a friend, Beth Ingels. Beth had grown up in a valley called Corral de Tierra and planned to write stories about events that had special impact on her, "gather[ing] them together in the fashion of *Winesburg, Ohio*" (208). Although Benson is the only person who argues that the idea for *Pastures of Heaven* originated with Ingels, the suggestion is plausible.[2] Unlike many writers of short story cycles, Steinbeck seems to have been aware almost from the beginning that he was writing a series of unified stories.

Lisca's comments in *The Wide World of John Steinbeck* suggest that the book changed direction several times as Steinbeck worked on the first drafts. Before beginning to write, he apparently did not intend to introduce the Munroe family (or the Morans, as they were originally called) until the end of the book. While working on the first stories, however, Steinbeck must have changed his mind, recognizing the value of the Munroes as a unifying device (Lisca 58; Benson 210; *Life in Letters* 43).[3] The title page of the first draft also indicates that the stories were originally placed in a slightly different order, that some of the stories listed on the title page were not included in the final version, and that stories VII (about the Lopez sisters), X (Pat Humbert), XI (the Whitesides), and XII (the epilogue) were written and added after the first draft (*Wide World* 56–60).

Although "Dissonant Symphony" and several other projects that Steinbeck was working on at this time have apparently been destroyed, Benson emphasizes that the early 1930s were a period during which Steinbeck experimented with point of view: "he was trying out various ways of dramatizing the subjective nature of experience'' (200). Perhaps this explains, at least in part, Steinbeck's attraction to the form of the short story cycle. While each story in *Pastures of Heaven* focuses on a different individual or family and their particular way of perceiving reality, ''Dissonant Symphony'' described the ways in which a single man (based on Steinbeck's father) is perceived by different observers. In both cases, the form of the cycle—specifically, the independent short stories—helps the writer simultaneously maintain divergent points of view.[4]

UNITY IN *PASTURES OF HEAVEN*

Character

The Munroes, the Whitesides, and Other Recurring Characters

The stories are most obviously unified by their location in the Pastures of Heaven. Another explicit unifying device is the use of recurring characters, especially the Munroe family. With the exception of the prologue and epilogue, each story contains a Munroe. In some stories, such as VII (about the Lopez sisters), VIII (Molly Morgan), and X (Pat Humbert), the Munroes are relatively minor figures; but they are centrally important in the book because their actions dramatically affect the lives of other protagonists. The Whitesides are the only other family that assumes major importance throughout *Pastures of Heaven*. Although appearing in only half of the stories and functioning as protagonists in only one, they provide a continual contrast to the Munroes. The Whitesides are the most civilized family in the valley, widely respected throughout the community, and they are prominently featured, since the long penultimate story (XI), which describes three generations of their family and summarizes the valley's history, is devoted exclusively to them and their place in the community.

In addition to the Munroes and the Whitesides, there are other characters— Molly Morgan, Pat Humbert, and Raymond Banks—who appear in at least several stories and who have a story devoted primarily to them. Not only do these characters reappear, but, as Harlan Harbour Winn III argues, ''the behavior of each in stories in which he recurs as a minor character reinforces his characterization in his own story'' (61). Steinbeck apparently chose to focus on these characters because they represent the community of the Pastures of Heaven itself: Molly Morgan is the local schoolteacher, and Pat Humbert, Raymond Banks, Bert Munroe, and John Whiteside serve together on the school board. In other words, those characters who receive the greatest attention in *Pastures of Heaven* are those who serve the community and, as a result, exert the greatest influence or control over others. More transient and less influential characters are featured in a single story and are generally not mentioned elsewhere in the book; for example, Tularecito (IV), the Maltbys (VI), and the Lopez sisters (VII) appear only in the stories devoted to them, and they leave the Pastures of Heaven at the end of their narratives.

Resemblances among the Characters

The characters resemble one another in various ways and can be compared accordingly. Mimi Reisel Gladstein, for example, argues that the women characters are similar. Although they do not play a major role in the book, female characters such as Helen Van Deventer, the Lopez sisters, and Alicia Whiteside typify strong and apparently indestructible women who use their strength in order to nourish others. Raymond Joel Silverman also classifies characters in groups based on the qualities of their imaginations. As will be discussed later in the section on theme, Silverman suggests that the imaginations of the first protagonists—Shark Wicks (III), Tularecito (IV), and Helen Van Deventer (V)—create neurotic illusions; the imaginations of the next group—the Maltbys (VI), the Lopez sisters (VII), and Molly Morgan (VIII)—produce romantic dreams; and the imaginations of the final group—Raymond Banks (IX), Pat Humbert (X), and John Whiteside (XI)—are responsible for visions that are more creative and broader in scope than the dreams in the first two groups.[5]

Chronology and Plot

The stories in *Pastures of Heaven* are sequentially ordered. As Joseph Fontenrose explains in some detail in *Steinbeck's Unhappy Valley*, ''Though the beginning of each story goes back in time, even to 1850 in 'The Whitesides,' each ends a little later in time than the preceding story . . . '' (307). Generally restricting background information about the protagonist(s) to the first few paragraphs, Steinbeck quickly shifts to the present tense action of the story. Through this method, a sense of progression in time is gradually achieved.

Another important unifying device involves plot or, more specifically, the Munroes' actions. In every story, the Munroes do or say something that triggers disillusionment or disaster in some other character's life: for example, Bert Munroe's visit welcoming the Van Deventers to the valley prompts Hilda to run away from home; the Munroes' gift to Robbie Maltby causes the Maltbys to feel shame because of their poverty; and Bert Munroe's joke about the Lopez sisters, taken too seriously by a jealous wife, results in the sisters' exile from the valley. Therefore, the involvement of the Munroes in other characters' lives is part of the major recurring plot line in *Pastures of Heaven*. In story after story, the protagonist's dreams or illusions are revealed, and then something is done or said by one of the Munroes that shatters these dreams or forces the protagonist to retreat further into the world of illusion. Whether or not the Munroes are actually responsible for what happens is a question I will return to in the section on theme. What is most important is that the Munroes' actions are repeated again and again and that they produce similar results in different contexts.

This same plot line—introduction of the protagonist's dreams, the intervention of the Munroes, the protagonist's disillusionment or desperate attempt to escape from the real world—recurs throughout *Pastures of Heaven* with the exception of the prologue, story XI, and the epilogue. In the penultimate story (XI), featuring the Whitesides, there is a reversal of the plot pattern. As Melanie Mortlock explains, even though three generations of the Whitesides have pursued the same dream, John Whiteside is realistic enough to recognize the point at which the dream becomes unattainable, and "he is wise enough to let it go and strong enough to carry on, to survive" (14). John Whiteside's example is all the more impressive because it follows nine stories describing other characters who are crippled by shattered dreams or incapable of recognizing when dreams are no longer possible.

Theme

Even though most attempts to identify a unifying theme are based on the general tension between dream or illusion and reality, interpretations differ both in the degree of generality in which they are expressed and in the extent to which the critic focuses on the source of the dream's failure.

Silverman is primarily interested in examining the protagonists' dreams; for him, identifying the reasons why dreams fail is of secondary importance. As noted before, Silverman argues that the characters reveal markedly different imaginations:

Progressively, we moved from the impractical (Junius's dream of irresponsibility), to the active but socially unrealizable (the Lopez dream of romantic prostitution), to the vision of ultimate vitality (Molly's dream of virtue, courage, and beauty). With the story of Raymond Banks, we have passed from the worlds of illusion and dream, to the world of vision. (43)

While Silverman establishes a logical progression in *Pastures of Heaven*, his approach appears flawed. It is not always possible to accept the manner in which he assigns stories to categories: for example, he is not very convincing when he suggests that the Raymond Banks narrative (IX) reveals "what Steinbeck regards as the truly creative imagination" (43). After all, the narrator encourages the reader to respond skeptically to Banks's "vision," which amounts to little more than his bizarre enjoyment of San Quentin hangings.

Instead of focusing primarily on the quality of the protagonists' dreams or imagination, one is better advised to concentrate on the reasons why dreams fail. While it is difficult to accept the categories and the logical progression that he tries to establish, Silverman does underscore several reasons why aspirations in *Pastures of Heaven* go unfulfilled. In addition to stressing that characters are impractical, he describes the extent to which many are solipsistic. Lisca, on the other hand, maintains that dreams are by definition attainable only briefly, if at all: "Human happiness and fulfillment are tenuous; it is a condition so frail that it can be shattered even by good intentions" (*Nature and Myth* 53).

Warren French, who perceives *Pastures of Heaven* as unified by Steinbeck's naturalistic vision, provides a similarly general and pessimistic statement of theme. Employing Donald Pizer's definition of naturalism,[6] French identifies the book's unifying theme as the characters' ability to " 'feel and strive painfully' " (39), while at the same time being unable to confront and deal rationally with their situations. Characters such as the Munroes are " 'feeling' rather than 'thinking' characters,'' French maintains, because they are sufficiently unconscious and inarticulate that they cannot analyze themselves or events (39–40). This sense of individual helplessness makes it difficult for characters to achieve their dreams or to comprehend others' aspirations, creating the naturalistic tone or vision in the book.

In addition to observing the characters' helplessness, one needs to consider their dependency on religion or superstition. Clearly, the supernatural pervades the book. As Fontenrose explains in his chapter "Religion and Myth" in *Steinbeck's Unhappy Valley*, almost every protagonist introduced in the book believes in a particular religion, superstition, legend, or myth. In the prologue and epilogue, the Spanish corporal and the young priest from the Carmel Mission are visibly Catholics; the *paisanos* throughout the book (such as Pancho, Tularecito's godfather, and the Lopez sisters) are also Catholics; the Battles are "devoted to a struggle with devils" (*Pastures of Heaven* 7); the Humberts and Helen Van Deventer are devotees of "a mortuary religion like that of ancient Egypt" (Fontenrose 38); the entire community believes that there is a curse on the Battle farm, and some are convinced that the Munroes have inherited this curse along with the land; and Tularecito believes in gnomes and fairies, while Molly Morgan wishes that she could believe as he does.

Throughout *Pastures in Heaven* religion is important primarily as a crutch: it helps people avoid confronting their weaknesses and circumstances. As Richard Astro suggests, the protagonists are "dreamers whose fantasies are annihilated by the hard facts of reality" (104). When these dreams are destroyed, most of them blame their misfortunes on something that is larger and more powerful than they are—whether it is the Munroe curse or the doctrine of Original Sin. In fact, Mortlock suggests that the Munroe curse is introduced into the book in such a manner that the readers, like the characters, are tempted to accept the curse as a serious explanation of the events that occur, "thereby proving the points he is making about his characters—that people believe in what they need to believe in, that they create their own gods and devils" (7).

Finally, it appears clear that religion and the supernatural are treated ironically, because in *Pastures of Heaven*, as Fontenrose stresses, "no religion is efficacious":

The Whitesides failed to establish a family dynasty in the new land. . . . There were no gnomes and elves for Tularecito to find. Alice Wicks was not a special gift from heaven. Though Helen Van Deventer, Molly Morgan, and Pat Humbert clung to or lapsed back into the old religion, it gave them no satisfaction. (*Unhappy Valley* 42)

In summary, then, although most of the characters in *Pastures of Heaven* believe in religion or act in response to superstition, the book itself ultimately discourages the reader from taking their devotion to the supernatural seriously.

Although most critics stress the characters' weaknesses as well as their tendency to blame their problems on someone or something else, there are some critics who blame the misfortunes in the book on the Munroes and their typically middle-class expectations. As mentioned earlier, in almost every story some action of the Munroes triggers misfortune in another character's life. Because of this, critics such as French, Randall R. Mawer, and Paul McCarthy suggest that Steinbeck's criticism of the Munroes is one of the major unifying themes. One must be careful, however, not to overemphasize the role that the family plays. Because the Munroes often do or say things that produce unhappy consequences for others, this does not mean that they are necessarily responsible for everything that happens. In several stories they function merely as catalysts. For example, (in story X) is Mae Munroe responsible for Pat Humbert's obsession with her? This hardly seems to be the case, since she does not know that Pat is eavesdropping when she tells her mother that the Humberts' house is attractive. Similarly, Bert Munroe cannot be blamed for asking Pat to assist at Mae's wedding; after all, no one knows about Pat's fantasies concerning Mae.

Capable of both insensitivity and stupidity, the Munroes are not attractive characters. Nevertheless, they should not be blamed for all misfortune. If we do so, we are responding in much the same way as the characters who blame superstition for all of their problems. In spite of the fact that the Munroes are largely responsible for the unhappiness that the Maltbys and the Lopez sisters experience, we should keep in mind that there are multiple explanations why disillusionment seems inescapable in *Pastures of Heaven*. As already indicated, some characters (such as Pat Humbert or Shark Wicks) base their dreams on thin air; therefore, it is not surprising when they fail to breathe life into them. Others (such as Tularecito, the Maltbys, and even the Lopez sisters) seem damned because their lives deviate too much from the norm accepted by the entire community—not just the Munroes. Still other characters (Molly Morgan, Helen Van Deventer, Pat Humbert) are largely victims of debilitating events in the past which continue to direct their lives.

We also need to keep in mind that not all the characters in *Pastures of Heaven* are overwhelmed by disillusionment. In spite of the fact that he has lost the house in which he envisioned future generations, John Whiteside does not blame Bert Munroe for the fire that Bert encouraged him to start. John Whiteside refuses to blame himself or others because he recognizes that his dream was attainable only temporarily. When his son and daughter-in-law moved to their new stucco house in Monterey immediately after their marriage, it became unlikely that descendants of the Whitesides would continue to live in the family home. Unlike most of the other characters in the book, John Whiteside is able to relinquish a dream because he has lived a life that is basically satisfying, promising other satisfactions in the future. This is why he responds as he does, at the very end of the story, when Bert Munroe stresses the value of his meerschaum pipe as an antique:

"I wish I could have saved my pipe," he [John] said.
"Yes, sir," Bert broke in effusively. "That was the best colored meerschaum I ever saw. They have pipes in museums that aren't colored any better than that. That pipe must have been smoked a long time."
"It was," John agreed. "A very long time. And you know, it had a good taste, too." (237)

At the moment of greatest disappointment, John Whiteside focuses on pleasure experienced in the past. He can respond to the fire with "horrified amusement" (236), because he has achieved, during his life, a kind of contentment through his study of philosophy and the companionship of family and friends.

Point of View, Myth, Imagery

Point of View

The distance the narrator maintains from his characters is crucially important as far as the book's ironic tone is concerned. Although the narrator rarely speaks in the first person and does not develop a fictional personality, the reader is occasionally aware of his presence. As Fontenrose, Winn, and Anita V. R. Yancey explain, even though the narrator seems at first invisible, remaining distant and aloof from the story he narrates, one becomes increasingly aware of his presence and his indirect method of commenting on characters and events: "There is a caustic touch in his description of Hubert Van Deventer, 'a florid, hunting man who spent six months out of every year trying to shoot some kind of creature or other' (p. 58). 'Helen could hear him telling the stupid, pointless stories . . . ' (p. 67). There is no moralizing or editorializing: the irony and the humor are in the narrative statements" (Fontenrose's *Unhappy Valley*: 5).

Although damaging information about or unflattering descriptions of most characters are included, the narrator and implied author treat the characters with varying degrees of irony. Those who are most clearly victims—Tularecito, the Maltbys, the Lopez sisters, and Molly Morgan—are handled gently, their virtues extolled and their weaknesses or foibles revealed compassionately. The Whitesides are also treated less ironically than most other families. Although situational irony influences the story's (XI) major plot, the narrator demonstrates his respect for the manner in which the Whitesides (especially John) respond to circumstances beyond their control. John is even allowed to speak ironically himself, demonstrating that he is capable of distancing himself from his experiences.

Myth

Because of the pervasive ironic tone, achieved by the narrator's ability to distance himself from the story he tells, the reader is not initially certain how to respond to the myths that reverberate throughout *Pastures of Heaven*. This is especially true of the Edenic myth, the only myth that attempts to unify the entire book.

Emphasized by the book's title as well as by both the prologue and epilogue, this myth is alluded to in all of the stories. As mentioned before, the characters are surrounded by a plentitude that ironically contrasts with their own impoverished and painful lives: "The land was rich and easy to work. The fruits of their gardens were the finest produced in central California" (*Pastures of Heaven* 3). Even the curse on the Battle farm and the Munroes evokes the Edenic myth since, as Lisca and others point out, "the second chapter identifies the curious curse that hangs over the valley to be original sin, for John Battle discovers a large snake that he knows is 'the damned serpent' and 'devil' " (*Nature and Myth* 54). While some explain that the Edenic myth is introduced to emphasize man's fallen condition or the theme that "human happiness and fulfillment are tenuous," others argue that the myth is used to dramatize man's refusal to confront his own limitations, as explained in the section on theme.

Imagery

Although noted by few critics, throughout the stories there is repeated emphasis on orchards, gardens, and cultivation in general. While rereading the book, I noted thirty-seven different instances where gardens, orchards, and produce are described. In his chapter "The Battle Farm" (*Unhappy Valley*), where he traces the continuing effect that the story about the farm has on subsequent stories, Fontenrose briefly compares references to cultivation. He does not, however, attempt to analyze the significance of the correspondences.

As I have suggested, throughout the stories the valley's richness is underscored. Unfortunately, many who enjoy the financial rewards gained from cultivating this veritable Garden of Eden seem incapable of appreciating the valley in any other way. George Battle, young Mustrovic, Bert Munroe, Shark Wicks, Raymond Banks, and the Humberts joylessly farm their land in their attempts to create order and financial security. The few who enjoy the natural beauty, the tranquility, the remoteness of the valley—such as the Maltbys—are forced away from the Pastures of Heaven because others are intolerant of the manner in which they live, communing with nature and refusing to work. With the exception of the Whitesides (and briefly, the Maltbys and Molly Morgan), the inhabitants are eager to profit financially from the valley, but they do not allow their personal lives to be otherwise enriched by the overwhelming natural beauty and abundance.

In addition to farming and gardening imagery, there are several other image patterns that should be at least noted. Joyce D. C. Brown explains how animal imagery is used in *Pastures of Heaven* to stress man's predatory nature, his reliance on superstition, and his ultimate helplessness and servility. More important, Winn argues that in almost every story, the description of the house or farm is used to illuminate characterization:

The townspeople regard the Battle and Mustrovics house as run-down, lonely and haunted just as its occupants exist on the fringe of society as mysterious recluses. When the Munroes move in and remodel it, their middle-class, Sears-Roebuck-catalogue mentality results in a home that looks ''like a thousand other country houses in the West'' ([*Pastures*] p. 13). (80–81)

One by one, Winn reviews the stories, demonstrating that setting is used symbolically to further character development.

CONCLUSION

As is true of most short story cycles, the tension between the stories' self-sufficiency and interdependence in *Pastures of Heaven* is a complex matter. Even though the cycle contains a prologue and epilogue, it is not a framed tale, not a story within a story.

The prologue serves to introduce the valley and explain how it was named in 1776. The irony of the name—given by a corporal distinguished only by his cruelty—establishes the ironic tone that is maintained throughout the book. Additionally, the prologue's last two paragraphs, describing the prosperous valley as it exists in the present tense, function as a transition into the stories themselves. When used in short story cycles, prologues are not generally self-sufficient. Therefore, they are exempt from the tension that critics describe in cycles between self-sufficiency and interdependence. They exist, one understands even on a first reading, entirely because of the contribution they make to the rest of the work.

The epilogue in *Pastures of Heaven* maintains the ironic tone introduced by the prologue. Most of the bus passengers who look longingly down on the Pastures of Heaven would be incapable of leading contented lives there. Unlike the prologue, however, the epilogue does achieve a satisfactory closure. Although only five pages long, the epilogue's plot consists of the bus passengers' imaginative attempts to project themselves into the Pastures. For example, the young husband recognizes that his own ambition and his wife's would prevent them from enjoying life in such an out-of-the-way place. The priest, too, desires to go there but knows that he cannot escape his difficult mission among the urban poor. Finally, as they begin to leave their scenic overlook, the bus driver expresses his dreams, ones that are attainable and reveal that he, unlike the passengers, could possibly be contented in such a place.

In addition to underlining irony, the most important purpose that the prologue and epilogue serve is to give us a broader historical perspective, transporting the reader from the discovery of the valley to a future that extends beyond the time period described in the stories.

In spite of the roles that the prologue and epilogue play, *Pastures of Heaven* does not achieve its unity primarily through its frame: the major connections exist within the stories themselves. The most important forms of unity that emerge are the pervasive ironic tone, the recurring tension between dream or illusion and reality, and the effect the leading families have on the community. Instead of being unified by a single protagonist or composite personality (as George Willard or Nick Adams function in *Winesburg, Ohio* or *In Our Time*), or by a particular kind of relationship (parent-child relations in *Everything That Rises Must Converge* or the Maples' marriage in *Too Far to Go*), *Pastures of Heaven* is unified by the actions of two central families.

The role that the Munroes play has been described in detail, but the Whitesides deserve greater attention than they usually receive. They are the only family that transcend the book's ironic structure. Just as George Willard stands out in *Winesburg, Ohio* because of his ability to leave town, the Whitesides seem unique in their ability to create lives worth living in the Pastures of Heaven. They are not impervious to unhappiness or bad luck, but they minimize its effect. They are the only characters that remain in the valley who are capable of responding appropriately to the natural setting. If its Edenic quality seems illusory to others, it is because of the lives that they live in the valley. It is never nature—bad crops, storms, drought—that ruins lives. Instead, it is individuals themselves and the community who are responsible for the unhappiness that many experience.

The recurring plot—introduction of the protagonist's dreams, the intervention of the Munroes, the protagonist's disillusionment or desperate attempt to escape from the real world—is repeated throughout *Pastures of Heaven*. This repetition, as we have seen with other cycles, intensifies the statement: the kind of defeat that the characters experience seems inescapable. Only with the penultimate story (XI), featuring the Whitesides, is there a reversal of the plot pattern. The Whitesides have lost their home and the dream it signifies, but John is not defeated. He remains realistic about the future. John's combination of idealism and practicality is, thus, echoed in the bus driver's remarks at the end of the epilogue: " 'You know,' the driver said, 'I always think it would be nice to have a little place down there. A man could keep a cow and a few pigs and a dog or two. A man could raise enough to eat on a little farm' " (242).

NOTES

1. Since the stories are untitled but numbered, this list may prove useful. Each story features a different person or family:

story II	(the Battle farm) the introduction of the Munroes
story III	the Wicks
story IV	Tularecito or "Little Frog"
story V	Helen Van Deventer and her daughter, Hilda
story VI	Junius Maltby and his son, Robbie
story VII	the Lopez sisters, Maria and Rosa
story VIII	Molly Morgan
story IX	Raymond Banks

story X   Pat Humbert

story XI   three generations of the Whitesides

2. Benson's source appears to be Carol (Steinbeck) Brown, the writer's first wife. Kiernan maintains that Steinbeck was encouraged by his lifelong friend and mentor, Ed Ricketts, to write a book about the legendary curse on the Valley of Corral de Tierra. Kiernan never indicates the source of his information, and what he says does not agree with Astro's detailed description of Ricketts's relationship with Steinbeck.

3. I have seen the early, incomplete draft of *Pastures of Heaven* at the Humanities Research Center, University of Texas at Austin, and in this version the Munroes are introduced at the beginning of the book.

4. Even though descriptions of "Dissonant Symphony" are brief and frequently conflicting, it seems that "Dissonant Symphony" contained a group of independent and juxtaposed narratives. (See Benson 202 and Kiernan 162–65.) At one point, Steinbeck asked his agent to market "Dissonant Symphony" and ten of the *Pastures of Heaven* stories together as a single volume (*Life in Letters* 43, 45–46).

5. Carpenter also establishes a classification system based on the characters' dreams, but his groups are not well defined.

6. "Late Nineteenth-Century Naturalism." *Realism and Naturalism in Nineteenth-Century American Literature*. Carbondale: Southern Illinois UP, 1966.

WORKS CITED AND BIBLIOGRAPHY

Astro, Richard. "The Pastures of Pleasure and Illusion." *John Steinbeck and Edward F. Ricketts: The Shaping of a Novelist*. Minneapolis: U of Minnesota P, 1973, 95–118.

Benson, Jackson J. *The True Adventures of John Steinbeck, Writer: A Biography*. New York: Viking, 1984.

Brown, Joyce Diann Compton. "Animal Symbolism and Imagery in John Steinbeck's Fiction from 1929 through 1939." Diss. U of Southern Mississippi, 1972. *DAI* 33 (1972): 1716A

Carpenter, Frederic L. "The Pastures of Heaven." *Steinbeck and His Critics: A Record of Twenty-Five Years*. Ed. Ernest W. Tedlock, Jr., and C. V. Wicker. Albuquerque: U of New Mexico P, 1957. 71–73.

Cherulescu, Rodica. "Man and Nature in *The Pastures of Heaven* by John Steinbeck." *AUB-LG* 22 (1973): 199–205.

Ditsky, John M. "Music from a Dark Cave: Organic Form in Steinbeck's Fiction." *JNT* 1.1 (Jan. 1971): 59–67.

Ferrell, Keith. *John Steinbeck: The Voice of the Land*. New York: M. Evans, 1986.

Fontenrose, Joseph. "*The Pastures of Heaven*." *John Steinbeck: An Introduction and Interpretation*. American Authors and Critics Series 8. New York: Barnes, 1963. 20–29.

————. *Steinbeck's Unhappy Valley: A Study of* The Pastures of Heaven. Berkeley, CA: Albany, 1981.

French, Warren. "Naturalism—The Story Cycles." *John Steinbeck*. 2nd ed. Boston: Twayne, 1975. 54–75.

Geismar, Maxwell. "John Steinbeck: Of Wrath or Joy." *Writers in Crisis: The American Novel between 1925–1940*. Boston: Houghton, 1942. 239–70.

Gladstein, Mimi Reisel. "Female Characters in Steinbeck: Minor Characters of Major Importance?" *Steinbeck's Women: Essays in Criticism*. Ed. Tetsumaro Hayashi. Steinbeck Monograph Series 9. Muncie: Ball State UP, 1979. 17–25.

Hughes, R. S. "*Pastures of Heaven*." *Beyond the Red Pony: A Reader's Companion to Steinbeck's Complete Short Stories*. Metuchen, NJ: Scarecrow, 1987. 29–51.

Ingram, Forrest L. *Representative Short Story Cycles of the Twentieth Century: Studies in a Literary Genre*. The Hague: Mouton, 1971. (See especially 39–43.)

Jain, Sunita. *John Steinbeck's Concept of Man: A Critical Study of His Novels*. New Delhi: New Statesman, 1979.

Kiernan, Thomas. *The Intricate Music: A Biography of John Steinbeck*. Boston: Little, 1979.

Levant, Howard. *The Novels of John Steinbeck: A Critical Study*. Columbia: U of Missouri P, 1974.

Lisca, Peter. *John Steinbeck: Nature and Myth*. New York: Crowell, 1978.

———. "*The Pastures of Heaven*." *The Wide World of John Steinbeck*. New Brunswick, NJ: Rutgers UP, 1958. 56–71.

McCarthy, Paul. *John Steinbeck*. New York: Ungar, 1980.

Mawer, Randall R. "Takashi Kato, 'Good American': The Central Episode in Steinbeck's *The Pastures of Heaven*." *StQ* 13 (Winter–Spring 1980): 23–31.

Moore, Harry Thornton. *The Novels of John Steinbeck: A First Critical Study*. Port Washington, NY: Kennikat, 1968.

Mortlock, Melanie. "The Eden Myth as Paradox: An Allegorical Reading of *The Pastures of Heaven*." *StQ* 11 (Winter 1978): 6–15.

Nakayama, Kiyoshi. "Steinbeck's *The Pastures of Heaven*: On the Relation between the Structure and the Theme." *SELit* 11 (Feb. 1973): N. pag.
Reviewed in *SQ* 10 (Spring 1977).

Owens, Louis. "John Steinbeck's *The Pastures of Heaven*: Illusions of Eden." *ArQ* 41.3 (Autumn 1985): 197–214. The article appears as a chapter in his *John Steinbeck's Re-Vision of America*. Athens: U of Georgia P, 1985. 74–89.

Peterson, Richard F. "The Turning Point: *The Pastures of Heaven*." *A Study Guide to Steinbeck: A Handbook to His Major Works*. Ed. Tetsumaro Hayashi. Metuchen, NJ: Scarecrow, 1974. 87–106.

Pugh, Scott. "Ideals and Inversions in *The Pastures of Heaven*." *KAL* 28 (Oct. 1987): 70–72.

Rahn, Walter. *Die Funktionen der Kalifornischen Landschaft im epischen Frühwerk John Steinbecks*. Münich: Max Hueber, 1962.
    15–35. Rahn emphasizes two major contrasts: (1) the city is often seen as evil and unhealthy, while the valley is depicted as healthy; and (2) the landscape, especially as one looks down into the valley when entering it, is sometimes dreamlike in appearance and other times quite realistic.

Schumann, Hildegard. *Zum Problem des kritischen Realismus bei John Steinbeck*. Halle, East Germany: Niemeyer Verlag, 1958.
    26–44. Schumann labels *Pastures of Heaven* a "kurzgeschichtenroman" and emphasizes that its stories are unified by a framing device. Brief comparisons are made between this work and *Winesburg*.

Silverman, Raymond Joel. "The Short Story Composite: Forms, Functions, and Applications.'' Diss. U of Michigan, 1970. *DAI* 31 (1971): 6633A.

Silverman argues that there are several progressive developments in *Pastures of Heaven*:

> Although it is possible to find a progression in which the Munroe family becomes increasingly "guilty" as their actions move from indirect to direct, it is better to concentrate upon the imaginative lives of the main character in each story and find our sequence there. As our progression moves from characters with truly creative imaginations, we do not find the Munroe family more and more guilty, but we do find their "bad company" to be increasingly destructive. (22)

Snell, George. "John Steinbeck: Realistic Whimsy." *The Shapers of American Fiction 1798–1947*. New York: Dutton, 1947. 187–97.

Steinbeck, John. *The Pastures of Heaven*. Rev. ed. New York: Viking, 1963. Quotations are taken from the Penguin paperback.

————. *Steinbeck: A Life in Letters*. Ed. Elaine Steinbeck and Robert Wallsten. New York: Viking, 1975.

Timmerman, John H. "Dreams and Dreamers: The Short Stories." *John Steinbeck's Fiction: The Aesthetics of the Road Taken*. Norman: U of Oklahoma P, 1986. 58–72.

Watt, F. W. *Steinbeck*. Writers and Critics Series. London: Oliver & Boyd; New York: Grove, 1962.

Weltz, Friedrich. "Vier amerikanische Erzählungszyklen." Diss. Universität München, 1953.

> Weltz stresses that while each story in *Pastures* is structured around a single character or family, it also functions as part of the larger story of the community of Pastures of Heaven, which assumes mythic significance. Apparently realistic details, such as the view of the valley from the hill, often serve symbolic purposes.

Winn, Harlan Harbour, III. "Short Story Cycles of Hemingway, Steinbeck, Faulkner, and O'Connor." Diss. U of Oregon, 1975. *DAI* 36 (1976): 4500A.

> Winn's chapter on *Pastures of Heaven* is a detailed and convincing analysis of the book's unity. Winn specifies several formal ways in which the book is connected, including the prologue and epilogue. He also focuses on recurring character, chronology, point of view, themes and motifs, and the ironic treatment of the myth of Eden and the promise of the New World. Winn suggests that the stories represent symbolically a period in American history, since the Pastures were discovered in 1776 and the last story takes place in 1929 at the beginning of the Great Depression.

Yancey, Anita V. R. "*Winesburg, Ohio* and *The Pastures of Heaven*: A Comparative Analysis of Two Studies in Isolation." Diss. 1 U of Southern Mississippi, 1971. *DAI* 32 (1972): 5249A

> In comparing the two cycles, Yancey discusses the unity of *Pastures of Heaven* by describing setting, recurring characters, theme, plot, point of view, prologue, epilogue, and irony. The predominant theme she defines as follows: "Each person creates his own idea of paradise and projects it into a real world, ironically unaware that he himself is the curse that will destroy his paradise" (214). Unlike critics such as Fontenrose and French, she denies that the stories are arranged chronologically or sequentially. Yancey's major contribution is her description of point of view, explaining how the narrator's distance from the characters and reader reinforces the pervasive irony.

5

William Faulkner's
The Unvanquished

INTRODUCTION TO THE BOOK

The first four or five stories in *The Unvanquished* feature two protagonists, the young Bayard Sartoris and his constant companion Ringo. Together they experience a series of initiations. As children in "Ambuscade" they fail disastrously when trying to defend their home from Yankee soldiers. When several years older, they are compelled by the code of the Old South to revenge Granny's death. Although Ringo responds more quickly and intelligently in the earlier stories, he is forced to assume the subordinate position when they grow older. *The Unvanquished* becomes a series of stories about the maturation of Bayard Sartoris, specifically about his ability to reject the code of violent revenge endorsed not only by Ringo but also by Colonel Sartoris, Drusilla, and Uncle Buck McCaslin.

COMPOSITION AND PUBLICATION OF
THE UNVANQUISHED

The first three stories in *The Unvanquished*—"Ambuscade," "Retreat," and "Raid"—were written in the spring of 1934. According to David Minter, the stories came easily, "in a matter of weeks" (144–46). Contrary to what critics have assumed, Faulkner's correspondence and interviews make it clear that he must have envisioned the stories as a cycle almost from the beginning. Responding to a question asked at the University of Virginia, Faulkner insisted that when he was writing "Ambuscade," the first story, he was already thinking of it as a part of at least a three-story series: "When I got into the first one I could see two more, but by the time I'd finished the first one I saw it was going further than that . . . " (Gwynn and Blotner 252). Also, in a letter to his agent, Morton Goldman, which was written soon after he had finished the second story ("Retreat''), Faulkner clearly states that he has a six-story series in mind and demonstrates his awareness of how marketable and lucrative short story series were at the time (Faulkner's *Selected Letters*: 80).

After his initial enthusiasm and productivity, Faulkner had difficulty writing the fourth story, primarily because he could not find an appropriate transition from the Civil War (this "War-Silver-Mule business") to Reconstruction, presumably the subject of the last three stories (*Selected Letters* 80–81). When *The Saturday Evening Post* was unwilling to pay as much as he demanded for the series, Faulkner temporarily abandoned it. After spending part of the summer of 1934 in Hollywood, Faulkner finished the fourth and fifth stories ("Riposte in Tertio" and "Vendée") by late September, and the sixth ("Skirmish at Sartoris") by mid-October. Also, at this time, the *Post* published the first three stories—"Ambuscade," "Retreat," and "Raid."

In January 1936 Faulkner finished the manuscript of *Absalom, Absalom!*, and it was published in October. In December, soon after "Vendée" and "Riposte in Tertio"[1] were published in the *Post*, Faulkner wrote his editor at Random House, Bennett Cerf, to see if he would be interested in publishing the Civil War stories as a book. It was not, however, until early summer that Cerf decided to do so. Most of the revisions were apparently made by Faulkner in June and July. The first three stories were most substantially reworked—"Ambuscade" gained twelve pages, and "Retreat" and "Raid" each approximately nine—but all of the stories were revised: while "Vendée" and "Riposte in Tertio" each gained 500 to 1,000 words, "Skirmish at Sartoris" lost about 500.[2] Random House encouraged Faulkner to write another story, a conclusion (*Selected Letters* 100), and "An Odor of Verbena" was written by late July. In February 1938 *The Unvanquished* was published.[3]

UNITY IN *THE UNVANQUISHED*

Character

Bayard appears in every story, and because he is a Sartoris and acts to reinforce and reshape community values, he functions symbolically to unify his community. Also, as Forrest L. Ingram describes in detail, there is a large cast of recurring characters. Colonel John Sartoris and Miss Rosa Millard (Granny) occasionally assume the role of protagonist, and they are present throughout the book—either literally or in someone's memory. Ringo, Bayard's counterpart, also appears in each story and is given a more prominent role than Bayard in "Raid" and "Riposte in Tertio." Drusilla Hawks, Bayard's cousin and, at the end of the book, his stepmother, plays a major role in three stories ("Raid," "Skirmish at Sartoris," and "An Odor of Verbena") and appears at the end of "Vendée." Loosh and Philadelphy, Colonel Dick, Uncle Buck McCaslin, Louvinia, and Joby all appear in at least two stories, and like the major characters demonstrate believable, plot-related character development.

Setting, Time, and Plot

Although characters frequently are forced to leave the book's central locale, Yoknapatawpha County in Mississippi, Yoknapatawpha is "the place from which all journeying proceeds and to which all journeying ultimately returns" (Ingram 114). The action is limited to a ten-year period—the second half of the Civil War and early Reconstruction (July 1863–October 1873)—and events are generally told in chronological order.[4]

Action is further unified because the book is a *bildungsroman*, tracing the maturation of Bayard, and many events are interrelated as they contribute to the progressively more difficult initiation process. For example, in the first story, Bayard and Ringo shoot a horse instead of a Yankee in their misguided attempt to protect themselves and Granny. Although their actions have repercussions, they are protected from any severe punishment by Granny and the gentlemanly Yankee colonel. Later, the Sartorises leave home and discover themselves swept along with hordes of blacks, emancipated but homeless. When they eventually return home, new hardships await them.

Most important, Bayard and Ringo must now revenge Granny's murder, which they felt impotent to prevent. Their mutilation of Grumby, restoring the honor of the Sartorises and making the countryside presumably safer, is followed by further tests of valor. The ultimate task, one that can be performed by Bayard alone, occurs in "An Odor of Verbena" when Colonel Sartoris is killed by Redmond. Considerably older and now a law student in Oxford, Bayard is once again forced to deal with the issue of family honor and revenge. Contrasting his earlier actions, Bayard confronts his father's murderer, but he refuses to take a weapon, thereby ending the cycle of violence that killed his father.

Subsequent analyses of initiation, so far as it relates to Bayard or Ringo, might also consider the following questions. Does the protagonist proceed on his own, or is he assisted by others? How far—physically and psychologically—must he travel from the family or the Sartoris house in each episode? Is the route chosen direct, or, as in the case of "Vendée," repetitious and confused? Are goals established in advance, and are they based on external standards or personal experience? Finally, if the episode involves confrontation with an antagonist, what criteria establish the protagonist's success or failure?

Mythology, Comedy, and Tragedy

More subtle dynamic structure is achieved by Faulkner's appropriation of ideas, situations, and character traits associated with Christian mythology as well as with comedy and Greek tragedy. Faulkner's description of Drusilla Hawks as "the Greek amphora priestess of a succinct and formal violence" (*The Unvanquished* 252) alerts most readers to the possibility of the influence of the mode of tragedy, at least in "An Odor of Verbena."

That Colonel John Sartoris displays the characteristics of a classical tragic hero has been well established by John Lewis Longley, Jr., in his chapter on Colonel Sartoris in *The Tragic Mask*. Longley also, supported later by Gorman Beauchamp, argues convincingly that the mode of comedy and Christian myth contrast with and finally supplant tragedy in the work. He explains that the tragedy in *The Unvanquished* results from the corruption of Edenic innocence, and that while Colonel John Sartoris achieves full status as a tragic hero, his son, Bayard, makes restitution for his loss by refusing to try to kill Redmond and therefore regains his innocence. Beauchamp, through a detailed comparison of *The Unvanquished* with Aeschylus's *Oresteia*, explains that the central conflict in both works is between emotion and reason: the tension between an emotional, primitive code of violent vengeance, common to Greek tragedy and fading Southern aristocracy, and a rational, civilized insistence on nonviolence and adherence to the law, typical of Apollonian thought as well as comedy. The forcefulness or the broad scope of *The Unvanquished* results, to a large extent, from Faulkner's ability to evoke simultaneously contradictory or mutually exclusive ideas and patterns.

Beauchamp's description of comic and tragic patterns in *The Unvanquished* is reinforced by Albert James Memmott's comparison of various instances of game playing in the stories. As already noted, both Longley and Beauchamp describe the final movement of *The Unvanquished* as a movement from tragedy to comedy. It should also be mentioned that Beauchamp describes the first six stories as moving from "light to dark" (277). When he refers to "light," one assumes that he is referring to young Bayard's romantic point of view as well as his playful though potentially dangerous antics, such as Bayard and Ringo firing at Union troops and then fleeing from them to hide under Granny's skirts. Memmott's analysis of play is primarily important because in addition to acknowledging this change in tone, he identifies and traces one of the subtle means by which the work remains tightly unified as it moves from comedy to tragedy. Games are played throughout *The Unvanquished*, but as Bayard and Ringo grow older and as social, political, and economic upheaval makes it more difficult to organize one's experiences, the games become increasingly dangerous and difficult.

Other Related Themes and Motifs

The Unvanquished contains a network of related motifs and themes concerning various kinds of conflict or opposition. Civil war affects everything, and as Esteban and Lorenzo Peraile (also Ingram 121) stress, the warring factions in the book include virtually every person, group, and institution—Bayard against Ringo, Bayard against his father, Colonel Sartoris against Redmond, the South against Grumby and the Reconstructionists.

The issue of race and racial tension is extremely important for at least the first half of the book. Faulkner heightened the significance of the issue when revising the early stories for inclusion in *The Unvanquished* (Backman, Blotner,

Creighton, and Holmes). As Joanne V. Creighton has argued convincingly, it is not through Bayard (either as character or narrator) that the issue is presented; rather, it is through the work's continual comparison of Bayard and Ringo as well as through other random and juxtaposed characters and situations: Colonel Sartoris's condescending treatment of slaves; Louvinia's refusal to believe that the Yankees—or anyone else—could free slaves; and Loosh's angry evaluation of the immorality of slavery. While Faulkner revised in order to emphasize the situations of blacks, one must also acknowledge that his revisions seem to have lacked direction. He breathes life into Ringo but then allows him to disappear almost entirely from the book during the last two stories. The issue of slavery and the treatment of blacks is abandoned as Faulkner grows increasingly preoccupied with the issue of violent revenge. Creighton accurately identifies one of the sources of the problem when she faults Faulkner for not better unifying his two major kinds of revisions, "the introduction of the retrospective narrator and the heightening of the significance of race" (*Craft of Revision* 83). As she argues, the adult narrator should be more perceptive when it comes to racial inequality, especially in his relationship with Ringo.

A more abstract but related conflict is the tension in the book between romanticism and realism. There are a few who have unsuccessfully attempted to dismiss *The Unvanquished* as sentimental, a Hollywood re-creation of the Old South. Irving Howe, for example, says, "It is as if *The Unvanquished* had been composed to deal with the matter of *Huckleberry Finn* in terms of *Tom Sawyer*" (43). Nevertheless, most critics have maintained that the work contains elements of both romanticism and realism. From what we know about Faulkner's revisions during the summer of 1936, it is clear that at least two of his goals were to exaggerate further young Bayard's tendency to romanticize events, especially in the first three stories, and to create distance between young Bayard the character and the older Bayard who relates events from his past (Creighton's *Craft of Revision*: 74–78; Holmes 48; Ingram 107).

Point of View

The critical controversy over romanticism and realism in *The Unvanquished* can be understood only through further consideration of point of view. Those few early critics who saw the work as slick and sentimental are not only damning it merely because parts of it appeared originally in popular magazines. In addition to overlooking the final story, they do not differentiate between the work's implied author, the character or actor Bayard (who ages from twelve to twenty-four in the book), and an older Bayard (of undetermined age), who reflects on these events.

If one keeps these distinctions in mind, much of the romanticism in *The Unvanquished* exists as a result of the child's (young Bayard's) idealistic or inexperienced point of view: a way of looking at the world that is questioned or qualified by the older narrator as well as by the implied author (Brooks,

Creighton, Joseph W. Reed, Jr.).[5] In general Faulkner presents an idealistic conception of the South merely to reject or demythify it. In fact, Arthur F. Kinney sees the romanticism as not just Bayard's point of view, but as symbolic of "a South dedicated to romantic absolutism—John's sense of honor; Granny's sense of property; Drusilla's sense of vengeance" (85). Joseph W. Reed, Jr., differs slightly from the other critics in his insistence that the older Bayard completely dissociates himself from his younger counterpart: he "takes the rather cold view that a narrative presence might take toward his protagonist (178)."[6]

Ultimately, for some critics the importance of point of view—that is, the depiction of a single complex consciousness—eclipses the significance of themes and ideas, regardless of whether the focus is on war, racial inequality, or the complex of ideas associated with the work's romanticism and realism or its use of comic and tragic modes. As William Currie Ramsey puts it, the stories are "concerned with bringing us into immediate contact with the complex agonies of Bayard's consciousness. . . . While Bayard never penetrates the minds of the . . . characters who surround him, he gives us an extremely elaborate picture of his own."

Imagery

Although there have been brief, isolated comments on unifying imagery in *The Unvanquished*, there has been no comprehensive effort to describe how the book's overall unity depends to a great extent on interconnected imagery.[7] One example of such a network of imagery involves the daily and seasonal cycles, which contribute to the development of Christian and regeneration myth as well as comedy and tragedy. The recurring visual and tactile imagery associated with these cycles—light and dark, warm and cold, dry and wet imagery—is important because it is used throughout the book to signal and intensify changes in the work's action and ideas.

In fact, all of the stories can be placed in a single seasonal cycle. In the first story, "Ambuscade," the season is summer: the hot temperatures and the dryness of the earth are repeatedly mentioned. There is a lazy quality to the story, almost as if it is told in slow motion, which is of course appropriate, since Bayard and Ringo are still children, dependent on others, and since they are slow to perceive what is happening around them. In the next two stories, taking place approximately one year later, the weather continues to be summerlike, even though the seasons are never mentioned in "Retreat" or "Raid."[8] In these stories Bayard and Ringo continue to be protected from the war by figures like Granny, Colonel Sartoris, Drusilla, and even the Yankee officer Colonel Dick.

Not long after this, Granny is murdered, her funeral is held, and Ringo and Bayard are sent to hunt down Grumby. Throughout these sections of the book, the falling rain is mentioned so frequently that it becomes oppressive.[9] The search for Grumby continues until February: "we rode . . . in the wet and the iron frost, and nights . . . we slept in the same wet and the same freeze and (once) in the snow, beneath whatever shelter we found when night found us'' (186). When they finally discover Ab Snopes, Grumby's accomplice, the weather is warmer, but the rain becomes steady (''now it began to rain all the time'' [202]). A cold snap directly precedes the confrontation with Grumby, and as soon as he is killed the rain returns. Repeatedly, the burden of vengeance and the hardships Bayard and Ringo bear are intensified by the season and weather. The bleakness of the season underscores Bayard's sense of loss and impotence as well as his desperation when forced to perform an impossible task. Such a mission fills Ringo and Bayard with a sense of impending doom, which is largely communicated by the unremitting weather.

After Bayard and Ringo are forced to defend not only themselves but also the community in ''Riposte'' and ''Vendée,'' the mood and the season change in the next story, ''Skirmish at Sartoris.'' Now it is spring, and the war is over. Throughout the story there are illustrations of how people are attempting to rebuild their lives: the men, assisted by Drusilla, are putting up a house to replace the one burned down by the Yankees; and the middle-aged women are applying pressure to force Drusilla to assume the role of wife and mother. The difficulty with which the community is being reborn is evidenced not only in Drusilla's struggle against marriage: even more important, the roles that the newly ''freed'' blacks will assume are ill-defined, and whites are quick to manipulate the situation to their own advantage.

This struggle for power among the surviving whites continues into the final story, demonstrating that Reconstruction in the South involves questions that are much more difficult than those introduced in ''Skirmish at Sartoris.'' One of these questions is actually resolved in ''Odor of Verbena.'' The violence and chaos resulting from civil war can only be exorcised through a return to peace and a rational acceptance of civil law. This is why Faulkner chooses to emphasize spring and summer in the last story, even though the season is fall. Although we are told that ''Skirmish at Sartoris'' takes place in the springtime, Faulkner waits until the next story to introduce his images of rebirth: warmth, water, restorative sleep, singing birds, gardens in full bloom, and the pervasive smell of flowers. The autumnal equinox is poetically delayed in ''Odor of Verbena'' because, following the demise of the Confederacy, the fall of the year continues the rebuilding and reordering of society.

While serious issues remain even at the end of *The Unvanquished*—especially the question of racial injustice—the process of change has been initiated. The inevitability and desirability of such change is foreshadowed from the beginning of the book by Faulkner's use of the seasonal cycle as a structural device. The natural world in general plays a larger role throughout *The Unvanquished* than previously acknowledged. While in earlier stories nature is used largely to reflect human psychology and morality, it becomes clear in ''Odor of Verbena'' that Bayard's sensitivity to the natural world encourages him to choose life over death. The natural and human worlds increasingly coalesce until we reach the point in ''Odor of Verbena'' where they become interdependent: while the equinox will not come until Bayard rejects violence, his rejection is largely the result of his sensitivity to the natural world around him. Although he is primarily motivated by his hatred of killing—especially when it is performed in order to justify questionable codes of honor—it is through Bayard's responses to the natural world that he is reminded of the worth of an individual life.

CONCLUSION

As the description of seasonal and cyclical imagery demonstrates, the final story in *The Unvanquished* forces the reader to reconsider the entire book. While this is not always the case, many cycles end with final stories that dramatically change the direction of the work. This is why the final or penultimate story is often considerably longer than the other stories, as is most obviously the case with "The Dead" in *Dubliners* and the two parts of "Big Two-Hearted River" in *In Our Time*. While cycles often intensify a theme or a situation or an incident by evoking it again and again, story after story, they also frequently use a final story (or several stories) to emphasize that one can escape vicious or deadening forms of repetition.

As illustrated in the cycles discussed so far, Gabriel Conroy achieves a perspective much broader than those attained by other characters in *Dubliners*; George Willard finally leaves Winesburg after observing others who long to go but are never able to do so; and John Whiteside in *Pastures of Heaven* refuses to accept the kind of defeat that cripples those around him, recognizing that his life does not depend on a single dream. Similarly, Bayard Sartoris's rejection of the code of revenge in "Odor of Verbena" must be understood in the context of *The Unvanquished*. The pattern of revenge, established in previous stories, is reversed in the final story. It is primarily through indirect means such as the seasonal imagery that Faulkner communicates Bayard's motivation when he goes to meet Redmond unarmed. Although he is influenced by his father's example, it is clear that Bayard behaves as he does primarily because of his own past actions in "Vendée": the killing as well as the ritualistic mutilation of Grumby. Repudiating his past ("Riposte in Tertio," "Vendée") and the associations previously established in his own mind between nature and death or dying, Bayard embraces everyday life, choosing to live and to let live.

NOTES

1. "Riposte in Tertio" was originally entitled "The Unvanquished."

2. Ingram 106. Not only does Ingram provide the most complete description available of unifying patterns in the book, but he also offers the only well-developed, systematic alternative to viewing *The Unvanquished* as a novel.

3. For information about the composition process, also see Blotner, Creighton, Holmes, Meriwether, Jane Millgate, Pilkington (" 'Strange Times' "), and Wittenberg.

4. The calculation is based on Meriwether's dates ("Place of *The Unvanquished*," Appendix C).

5. Once again, the issue of race is the exception. The older Bayard may recognize that Ringo was superior to him in many ways when they were children, but the narrator never questions the fact that Ringo must ultimately play the role of a servant. Racial injustice is one part of the code of the Old South that goes unexamined by Bayard (both as character and narrator).

6. There are, of course, the exceptions, Trimmer and Ramsey, who distinguish between a younger and older Bayard but still maintain that the older man is as romantic and incapable of confronting reality as his younger counterpart. For Trimmer, whatever realism is introduced into the book is achieved only through the reader's awareness of an implied author who is considerably more realistic and ironic than his protagonist and narrator. For Ramsey, realism is introduced through the example of Colonel John Sartoris and through the informal sermons of Brother Fortinbride extolling constructive, realistic action.

7. Horse and mule imagery has been noted by Hinteregger; dueling and other medieval imagery by Longley and Wilson; snake imagery by Roberts and Scott; and the image of the Sartoris house by Ingram.

8. Meriwether's chronology places both the second and third stories in the summer; both occur in 1864, and "Raid" is said to take place in August (Appendix C).

9. Let me illustrate the point with several brief passages that also emphasize light and dark imagery:

There was no sound nor sign of life at all; just the huge rotting building with the gray afternoon dying wetly upon it. . . . (175)

Ringo and I stood there and watched Granny going down into the earth with the quiet rain splashing on the yellow boards until they quit looking like boards and began to look like water with thin sunlight reflected in it, sinking away into the ground. (179)

I sat there on the mule in the slow gray cold rain, in the dying daylight. (185)

WORKS CITED AND BIBLIOGRAPHY

Backman, Melvin. "*The Unvanquished.*" *Faulkner: The Major Years*. Bloomington: Indiana UP, 1966. 113–26.

Beauchamp, Gorman. "*The Unvanquished*: Faulkner's *Oresteia.*" *MissQ* 23 (Summer 1970): 273–77. Rpt. in *William Faulkner: Four Decades of Criticism*. Ed. Linda Welshimer Wagner. East Lansing: Michigan State UP, 1973. 298–302.

Beck, Warren. *William Faulkner: Essays*. Madison: U of Wisconsin P, 1976.

Birney, Earle. "The Two William Faulkners." Rev. of *The Unvanquished*, by William Faulkner. *Canadian Forum* 18 (June 1938): 84–85.

Blotner, Joseph. Vol. 2 of *Faulkner: A Biography*. 2 vols. New York: Random, 1974.

Boyle, Kay. "Tattered Banners." Rev. of *The Unvanquished*, by William Faulkner. *New Republic* 94 (9 Mar. 1938): 136–37. Rpt. in *The Critic as Artist: Essays on Books, 1920–1970*. Ed. Gilbert A. Harrison. New York: Liveright, 1972. 38–41.

Brooks, Cleanth. "The Old Order (*The Unvanquished*)." *William Faulkner: The Yoknapatawpha Country*. New Haven: Yale UP, 1963. 75–99.

———. "Short Stories." *William Faulkner: First Encounters*. New Haven: Yale UP, 1983. 7–42.

Brylowski, Walter. *Faulkner's Olympian Laugh: Myth in the Novels*. Detroit: Wayne State UP, 1968.

Bungert, Hans. *William Faulkner und die humoristische Tradition des amerikanischen Südens*. Heidelberg: Carl Winter, 1971.

205–12. Although Bungert makes no original contributions, he reiterates that the comedy ("veiled humor") and romance in *The Unvanquished* result from young Bayard's naive point of view, and that as Bayard becomes more experienced, comedy is less frequent and tragedy prevails.

Burch, Beth. "Rosa Millard and the Railroad: A Note on William Faulkner's *The Unvanquished*." *MSE* 8.2 (1982): 1–3.

Byrne, Mary Ellen. "An Exploration of the Literary Relationship between Sherwood Anderson and William Faulkner. Diss. Temple U, 1976. *DAI* 36 (1976): 8055A.

Suggests that Faulkner's work with "novel-short stories" could have been influenced by Anderson's *Winesburg* and *Poor White*.

Collins, Carvel. Introduction. *The Unvanquished*. By William Faulkner. New York: New American Library (Signet), 1959. vii–xii.

Cowley, Malcolm. *The Faulkner-Cowley File: Letters and Memories, 1944–1962*. New York: Viking, 1966.

Creighton, Joanne V. "*Dubliners* and *Go Down, Moses*: The Short Story Composite." Diss. U of Michigan, 1969. *DAI* 31 (1970): 1792A–93A.

In chapter 4, Creighton notes that *The Unvanquished* appears to defy the criteria she has established to differentiate between the novel and the short story composite: "Like the novel, the book is centered not upon ordinary representative individuals within a single society, but on an extraordinary single individual. The book, in other words, assumes the form of the composite while portraying the subject of a novel" (158).

———. "*The Unvanquished*: Revision, Retrospection, and Race." *William Faulkner's Craft of Revision: The Snopes Trilogy, "The Unvanquished" and "Go Down, Moses."* Detroit: Wayne State UP, 1977. 73–84.

Duclos, Donald P. "Colonel Falkner: Prototype and Influence." *FJ* 2.2 (Spring 1987): 28–34.

———. "Son of Sorrow: The Life, Works, and Influence of Colonel William C. Falkner, 1825–1889." Diss. U of Michigan, 1962. *DA* 23 (1962): 233.

One of the most detailed and accurate accounts available of the life of Colonel William C. Falkner, Faulkner's great-grandfather and the prototype for Colonel John Sartoris.

Faulkner, William. *Selected Letters of William Faulkner*. Ed. Joseph Blotner. New York: Random, 1977.

———."Sherwood Anderson: An Appreciation." *Essays, Speeches and Public Letters*. Ed. James B. Meriwether. New York: Random, 1965. 3–10. Rpt. in Ferres 487–94; in White, *Achievement of Sherwood Anderson*, 194–99; and in Rideout, *Collection of Critical Essays*, 166–70.

———. *The Unvanquished*. 1938. New York: Vintage, 1966.

Frazer, Winifred L. "Faulkner and Womankind—'No Bloody Moon.' " *Faulkner and Women: Faulkner and Yoknapatawpha, 1985*. Ed. Doreen Fowler and Ann J. Abadie. Jackson: UP of Mississippi, 1986. 162–79.

Friedman, Alan Warren. "Twice-Told Tales: *The Unvanquished, The Wild Palms*, and *Go Down, Moses*." *William Faulkner*. New York: Ungar, 1984. 117–36.

Gwynn, Frederick L., and Joseph L. Blotner, eds. *Faulkner in the University: Class*

Conferences at the University of Virginia 1957–1958. Charlottesville: U of Virginia P, 1959.

Harbison, Sherrill. "Two Sartoris Women: Faulkner, Femininity, and Changing Times." *Critical Essays on William Faulkner: The Sartoris Family*. Ed. Arthur F. Kinney. Boston: Hall, 1985. 289–303.

Hawkins, E. O. "Rosa Millard and Ann Franklin." *SoQ* 23.2 (Winter 1985): 87–93.

Hinkle, James. "Reading Faulkner's *The Unvanquished*." *CollL* 13.3 (Fall 1986): 217–39.

Hinteregger, Gerald. "Das Land und die Menschen in William Faulkners erzählenden Werken." Diss. Karl-Farnzens-Universität (Graz, Austria), 1953.

Hoar, Victor. "Colonel William C. Falkner in the Civil War." *JMissH* 27 (Feb. 1965): 42–62.

Hoffman, Frederick J. "The Negro and the Folk." *William Faulkner*. 2nd ed. New York: Twayne, 1966. 80–101.

Holder, Alan. "An Odor of Sartoris: William Faulkner's *The Unvanquished*." *William Faulkner*. Ed. Harold Bloom. New York: Chelsea, 1986. 207–19.

Holmes, Edward Morris. "Riposte in Seconde." *Faulkner's Twice-Told Tales: His Re-Use of His Material*. The Hague: Mouton, 1966. 46–57.

Howe, Irving. *William Faulkner: A Critical Study*. 3rd ed. New York: Vintage, 1975.

Howell, Elmo. "William Faulkner and the Andrews Raid in Georgia, 1862." *Georgia Historical Quarterly* 49 (June 1965): 187–92.

Hunter, Edwin R. *William Faulkner: Narrative Practice and Prose Style*. Washington, DC: Windhover, 1973.

Ingram, Forrest L. "William Faulkner: *The Unvanquished*." *Representative Short Story Cycles of the Twentieth Century: Studies in a Literary Genre*. The Hague: Mouton, 1971. 106–42.

Irwin, John T. *Doubling and Incest/Repetition and Revenge: A Speculative Reading of Faulkner*. Baltimore: Johns Hopkins UP, 1975.

Kinney, Arthur F. *Faulkner's Narrative Poetics: Style as Vision*. Amherst: U of Massachusetts P, 1978.

Knoll, Robert E. "*The Unvanquished* for a Start." *CE* 19 (May 1958): 338–43.

Longley, John Lewis, Jr. "Colonel John Sartoris: The Classic Tragic Hero." *The Tragic Mask: A Study of Faulkner's Heroes*. Chapel Hill: U of North Carolina P, 1963. 177–91.

McHaney, Thomas L. "An Episode of War in *The Unvanquished*." *FJ* 2 (Spring 1987): 35–44.

Memmott, Albert James. "Sartoris *Ludens*: The Play Element in *The Unvanquished*." *MissQ* 29 (Summer 1976): 375–87.

Meriwether, James B. "The Place of *The Unvanquished* in William Faulkner's Yoknapatawpha Series." Diss. Princeton U, 1958. *DA* 19 (1959): 2957.

    Chapter 1 outlines the publication history of the stories as well as the initial critical reaction to *The Unvanquished*. Recurring characters and themes are discussed in the next two chapters.

———. "The Short Fiction of William Faulkner: A Bibliography." *Proof* 1 (1971): 293–329.

    Notes whether or not the stories in *TU* have been published elsewhere and if there are any extant manuscript, typescript, or proof versions of the stories.

Millgate, Jane. "Short Stories into Novels: A Textual and Critical Study of Some Aspects of Faulkner's Literary Method." M.A. Thesis. U of Leeds, 1962.

310–16. In the conclusion, Millgate briefly considers Faulkner's revisions of the magazine stories, stressing that they do not significantly contribute to *The Unvanquished*'s unity. The book is labeled as a "story sequence," not a novel.

Millgate, Michael. *"The Unvanquished." The Achievement of William Faulkner*. New York: Random, 1966. 165–70.

———. *William Faulkner*. Rev. ed. New York: Grove, 1966.

Miner, Ward L. *The World of William Faulkner*. Durham: Duke UP, 1952.

Minter, David. *William Faulkner: His Life and Work*. Baltimore: Johns Hopkins UP, 1980.

Nordanberg, Thomas. "Exploration of the Morality of the Old South: *The Unvanquished*." *Cataclysm as Catalyst: The Theme of War in William Faulkner's Fiction*. Stockholm: Uppsala, 1983. 74–91.

Oates, Stephen B. *William Faulkner: The Man and the Artist*. New York: Harper, 1987.

O'Brien, Matthew C. "A Note on Faulkner's Civil War Women." *NMW* 1 (Fall 1968): 56–63.

Organ, Dennis. "The Morality of Rosa Millard: Inversion in Faulkner's *The Unvanquished*." *PAPA* 1.2 (1975): 37–41.

Peavy, Charles D. *Go Slow Now: Faulkner and the Race Question*. Eugene: U of Oregon P, 1971.

Peraile, Esteban, and Lorenzo Peraile. "Una lectura de *Los invictos*." *CHA* 291 (1974): 692–701.

Pikoulis, John. "The Sartoris War." *The Art of William Faulkner*. Totowa, NJ: Barnes, 1982. 112–36.

Pilkington, John. "The Civil War and Reconstruction: *The Unvanquished*." *The Heart of Yoknapatawpha*. Jackson: UP of Mississippi, 1981. 189–215.

———. " 'Strange Times' in Yoknapatawpha.' " *Fifty Years of Yoknapatawpha: Faulkner and Yoknapatawpha, 1979*. Ed. Doreen Fowler and Ann J. Abadie. Jackson: UP of Mississippi, 1980. 71–89.

Powers, Lyall H. *"The Unvanquished." Faulkner's Yoknapatawpha Comedy*. Ann Arbor: U of Michigan P, 1980. 125–41.

Pryse, Marjorie. "Miniaturizing Yoknapatawpha: *The Unvanquished* as Faulkner's Theory of Realism." *MissQ* 33 (Summer 1980): 343–54.

Ramsey, William Currie. "Coordinate Structure in Four Faulkner Novels." Diss. U of North Carolina at Chapel Hill, 1971. *DAI* 33 (1972): 283A–84A.

Three devices of coordination are used in the book: (1) the presentation of two or more characters facing similar situations and reacting in contrasting ways; (2) the recurrence of similar situations facing the same character; and (3) the contrast between Bayard's actions and his speech, and the contrast of both against the words and actions of others. Ramsey also argues that there are not significant differences between Bayard the narrator and Bayard the participant in the action.

Reed, Joseph W., Jr. "Uncertainties: *The Unvanquished* and *Go Down, Moses*." *Faulkner's Narrative*. New Haven: Yale UP, 1973. 176–200.

Reed, Pleasant Larus, III. "The Integrated Short-Story Collection: Studies of a Form of Nineteenth- and Twentieth-Century Fiction." Diss. Indiana U, 1974. *DAI* 35 (1975): 6730A

288–89. *The Unvanquished* is labeled a "short story novel."

Roberts, John J., and R. Leon Scott, Jr. "Faulkner's *The Unvanquished*." *Expl* 34 (Mar. 1976): Item 49.

Rollyson, Carl E., Jr. "The Presentation of the Past and of Historical Process as Legend and Fact in *Flags in the Dust* and *The Unvanquished*." *Uses of the Past in the Novels of William Faulkner*. Ann Arbor, MI: UMI, 1984. 17–32.

Ruzicka, William T. "*The Unvanquished*: 'The Aura of Father's Dream.' " *Faulkner's Fictive Architecture: The Meaning of Place in the Yoknapatawpha Novels*. Ann Arbor, MI: UMI, 1987. 19–28.

Taylor, Nancy Dew. " 'Moral Housecleaning' and Colonel Sartoris's Dream." *MissQ* 37.3 (Summer 1984): 353–64.

Tick, Stanley. "The Unity of *Go Down, Moses*." *TCL* 8 (July 1962): 67–73. Rpt. in *William Faulkner: Four Decades of Criticism*. Ed. Linda Welshimer Wagner. East Lansing: Michigan State UP, 1973. 327–34.

Trimmer, Joseph Francis. "*The Unvanquished*: The Teller and the Tale." *BSUF* 10 (Winter 1969): 35–42.

Tuck, Dorothy. "*The Unvanquished*." *Crowell's Handbook of Faulkner*. New York: Crowell, 1964. 67–71.

Van Devender, George W. "William Faulkner's Black Exodus: Multiple Narratives in *The Unvanquished*." *SCB* 42.4 (Winter 1982): 144–48.

Vickery, Olga W. *The Novels of William Faulkner: A Critical Interpretation*. Rev. ed. Baton Rouge: Louisiana State UP, 1964.

Volpe, Edmond L. "Response to 'Colonel Falkner: Prototype and Influence' and 'An Episode of War in *The Unvanquished*.' " *FJ* 2.2 (Spring 1987): 45–46.

———. "*The Unvanquished*." *A Reader's Guide to William Faulkner*. New York: Farrar, 1978. 76–87.

Waggoner, Hyatt H. "Present as Past: *The Unvanquished, The Hamlet*." *William Faulkner: From Jefferson to the World*. Lexington: U of Kentucky P, 1959. 170–93.

Walker, William E. "*The Unvanquished*: The Restoration of Tradition." *Reality and Myth: Essays in American Literature in Memory of Richmond Croom Beatty*. Ed. William E. Walker and Robert L. Welker. Nashville: Vanderbilt UP, 1964. 275–97.

Watkins, Floyd C. "Faulkner's Inexhaustible Voice." *The Flesh and the Word*. Nashville: Vanderbilt UP, 1971. 234–53.

Watson, James G. "Faulkner's Short Stories and the Making of Yoknapatawpha County." *Fifty Years of Yoknapatawpha: Faulkner and Yoknapatawpha, 1979*. Ed. Doreen Fowler and Ann J. Abadie. Jackson: UP of Mississippi, 1980. 202–25.

———. *William Faulkner: Letters and Fiction*. Austin: U of Texas P, 1987.

Williams, David. "Fall of the Goddess: The Rise of a Female Personality in the Snopes Trilogy and 'An Odor of Verbena.' " *Faulkner's Women: The Myth and the Muse*. Montreal: McGill-Queen's UP, 1977. 197–226.

Wilson, G. Jennifer. "Faulkner's 'Riposte in Tertio.' " *AN&Q* 16 (Feb. 1978): 88.

Winn, Harlan Harbour, III. "Short Story Cyles of Hemingway, Steinbeck, Faulkner, and O'Connor." Diss. U of Oregon, 1975. *DAI* 36 (1976): 4500A.
    The Unvanquished is labeled a short story cycle, but the book is not discussed.

Wittenberg, Judith Bryant. "Repudiation and Catharsis: *The Unvanquished*." *Faulkner: The Transfiguration of Biography*. Lincoln: U of Nebraska P, 1979. 156–66.

6

William Faulkner's
Go Down, Moses

INTRODUCTION TO THE STORIES

Journeys or hunting episodes are as important in *Go Down, Moses* as initiations in *Winesburg, Ohio*, *In Our Time*, and *The Unvanquished*. All of the stories are constructed around at least one thematically significant trip. In "Was," the two major (and overlapping) plot patterns are Uncle Buck McCaslin's trip to Hubert Beauchamp's to fetch Tomey's Turl, and Miss Sophonsiba's (and Turl's) elaborate scheme for trapping Uncle Buck into marriage. The action in both cases is described as a hunt, and both Turl and "Buck" are followed, lured, and cornered as if they were animals. "The Fire and the Hearth" also contains a series of hunting or trapping trips: Lucas is tracked by his daughter, Nat, as he hides his own still in an attempt to trap his son-in-law, George Wilkins; Lucas, and then the salesman from the city, hunt for gold with a metal divining machine; and, finally, Molly Beauchamp tries to end Lucas's obsession with the divining machine by hunting for the gold herself until she drops from physical exhaustion.

The entire plot of "Pantaloon in Black" consists of one intense journey as Rider keeps running in the night, attempting to outdistance his grief over his wife's death. "The Old People," "The Bear," and "Delta Autumn" are based on a series of hunting trips Ike McCaslin takes, which are retold in chronological order to emphasize what Ike learns from the woods, the bear, and Sam Fathers. In the final story, "Go Down, Moses," the journey is of secondary importance, but it is the problem that preoccupies Mollie Beauchamp's and Gavin Stevens's attention: how to find Samuel Worsham Beauchamp and bring him home to be buried.

In all cases the journey or hunt has both literal and metaphoric meaning. Only in "The Old People" and the first three sections of "The Bear" does the hunt resemble the initiation stories of Hemingway or Anderson or Faulkner himself in "The Odor of Verbena." Here Ike becomes a hunter but, more important, he learns the humility and awe that are necessary if one is to transcend this world and discover truth and beauty that is timeless. (This discovery of the eternal as a result of one's sensitivity to nature is identified by critics as the primitive nature myth or the totemic myth.)

In other stories, journeys do not lead to self-discovery. Instead, they serve to emphasize certain points for the reader: for example, that slaves are treated like animals ("Was" and "Pantaloon in Black"), that Lucas seeks hidden connections between himself and the father who never acknowledged his existence ("Fire and the Hearth"),[1] that the only way Rider can escape his pain is through self-annihilation, and that the family remains responsible for Butch Beauchamp even though he is a murderer.

Although the plot pattern of the hunt is complicated and is discussed further in the section on imagery, one should at least begin by understanding that it is used by the author as a means of intensifying his social criticism as well as a method of character development and self-realization.

COMPOSITION AND PUBLICATION OF THE BOOK

The composition history of *Go Down, Moses* demonstrates that Faulkner created the book by extensively rearranging and revising stories that he had written for magazine publication and by combining these fragments with a considerable amount of original material. Critics who have provided thorough analyses of Faulkner's revisions include Jane Millgate, Henry Alden Ploegstra, James Early, Joseph Blotner, Warren Beck, John T. Matthews, and Michael Grimwood. Most important, as this section reveals, are Blotner's comments in the biography as well as the *Selected Letters of William Faulkner*.

Exactly when Faulkner began to think about the book that was to become *Go Down, Moses* is not clear, but he does mention it for the first time during the spring of 1940 (*Selected Letters* 122, 124). In these letters to his editor at Random House (Robert K. Haas), Faulkner is extremely vague, merely saying that the book will include stories about "Negroes" and that it will resemble *The Unvanquished*. He does not specify which stories he has in mind at this time, but he was probably referring to four written the past year: three Lucas Beauchamp–Roth Edmonds stories ("The Fire on the Hearth," "A Point of Law," and "Gold Is Not Always," all of which are eventually incorporated into "The Fire and the Hearth") and a story ("Pantaloon in Black") about Rider, one of Roth Edmonds's tenants. Late in the summer, Faulkner indicates that he needs only one more story ("a novella, actually") to complete the book (Blotner 1056).

Faulkner returned to the stories in December 1940, when he wrote "Delta Autumn." The sense of exhaustion that permeates this story may well be the result of an almost fatal hunting trip that Faulkner took to the Big Sunflower River, according to Michael Grimwood, the previous November.[2] Whether or not he is accurate about the date of this particular hunting trip, Grimwood correctly emphasizes the change in tone introduced by "Delta Autumn." Suddenly, when one reaches this story, the subject of exhaustion—the depletion of land, of physical strength, of psychological and moral strength—overwhelms all other concerns, including the issue of racial injustice. It is known for certain that Faulkner was frustrated at this time by continuing financial difficulties and his growing awareness that the United States would soon be involved in World War II.[3]

At the beginning of May 1941, Faulkner wrote to Random House and outlined the book's contents, including (in this order) "The Fire and the Hearth," "Pantaloon in Black," "The Old People" (written April 1939), "Delta Autumn," and "Go Down, Moses" (July 1940). A few weeks later he informed his editor that he would also include "Almost" (eventually retitled "Was" and placed at the beginning of the book) (*Selected Letters* 140–41). The story had originally been written in the first person from Bayard Sartoris's point of view, but was revised so that it is told in the third person while at the same time presenting Cass Edmonds's recollections (Blotner 1074).

In June and July, Faulkner rewrote the first four stories in the order in which they appear in *Go Down, Moses*. As mentioned earlier, "The Fire and the Hearth" grew out of a series of Lucas Beauchamp stories that he had written earlier, but it contains much new material, including a description (in the second section) of Lucas's relationship with Zack Edmonds. More than any of the stories upon which it is loosely based, "The Fire and the Hearth" is preoccupied with the issue of racial injustice and the relations between the black (Beauchamp) and white (McCaslin, Edmonds) branches of a single family. Lucas Beauchamp, through the revisions, is transformed from a primarily comic figure into a character worthy of respect.

Repeatedly, Faulkner tightened connections among the stories by developing the McCaslin-Beauchamp-Edmonds genealogy and the complex sense of anger and guilt and impotence that surrounded the family. In "The Old People," as in "Was," Faulkner changed the point of view from first to third, and the young boy who had previously been nameless became Ike McCaslin. Only "Pantaloon in Black" remained basically unaltered.

Faulkner began revising "Delta Autumn" in the beginning of July. Two changes were crucially important: Roth Edmonds was given the part earlier assigned to Don Boyd, and Boyd's (Roth's) black mistress became the granddaughter of Tennie's Jim, instead of merely an anonymous black woman. After reworking only half of "Delta Autumn," Faulkner suddenly stopped. Blotner best describes what probably happened at this point: "[Faulkner] decided to change the plan. Assembling *The Unvanquished* he had realized he needed new material for climactic effect. Now he arrived at the same conclusion about *Go Down, Moses*. Reaching back to the material of 'The Old People,' he began a new hunting story, again featuring Ike McCaslin and Sam Fathers" (1080).

This story became "The Bear." Although some critics have assumed that the shorter *Saturday Evening Post* version of the story was written before the one in *Go Down, Moses*, all circumstantial evidence emphasizes that this was not the case.[4] Section III of "The Bear" was submitted to Random House at the beginning of November 1941, and Faulkner, perhaps convinced that he was through with the story, requested his publisher's copy of "Was" to make final adjustments (*Selected Letters* 144; Blotner 1085). Before long, however, Faulkner began writing a new section for "The Bear," no doubt aware that there were issues in the book—especially Ike's repudiation of his inheritance—that warranted further discussion. After finally completing sections IV and V of "The Bear," Faulkner once again revised "Delta Autumn," making Ike McCaslin nearly eighty, instead of seventy, and providing more extensive allusions to earlier events in his life (Blotner 1093). By mid-December, not long after the bombing of Pearl Harbor, the entire manuscript was completed and sent to Random House, and *Go Down, Moses* was published in March 1942.

Although he chronically needed money and was under pressure to complete *Go Down, Moses* as soon as possible, Faulkner refused all of the easy solutions that offered themselves as the book proved considerably more difficult than he had anticipated. He ended up including more stories and considerably longer and more complex ones than originally planned. Although the idea for the book began with a character who was a racial stereotype, *Go Down, Moses* evolved into a lengthy and serious consideration of racial injustice. Repeatedly, Faulkner tried to conclude *Go Down, Moses* prematurely, but he must have been driven on by the compelling individuals he had created and their unresolved—and perhaps for him unresolvable—conflicts.

UNITY IN *GO DOWN, MOSES*

Because it contains stories which are constructed in unusually complex ways (in particular the subdivisions used in the long stories, "The Fire and the Hearth" and "The Bear"), and because it is largely unified by implicit rather than explicit means, *Go Down, Moses* presents difficulties when one begins assessing and describing its unity. This is especially true since it apparently lacks a single unifying theme and since its use of multiple points of view appears to promote fragmentation.

Character, Setting, and Chronology

Most readers eventually acknowledge their appreciation of *Go Down, Moses*'s complex and subtle forms of unity, but it sometimes takes several readings before this happens. Upon an initial reading, the first and most obvious unifying pattern is genealogy, the complex family relationships that exist among the McCaslin, Edmonds, and Beauchamp descendants of (Lucius Quintus) Carothers McCaslin. Although it may appear that genealogy would be a static pattern, its unraveling in *Go Down, Moses* is dynamic, for family relationships are revealed only gradually, and relations are sometimes unclearly defined in both the readers' and the characters' minds.[5]

Since *Go Down, Moses* is limited to McCaslin descendants, slaves, and tenants as well as a few residents of Jefferson, Mississippi, the town closest to the McCaslin plantation, the book is also explicitly unified by its Yoknapatawpha setting. In fact, the only scene that takes place outside Yoknapatawpha County (the one that begins "Go Down, Moses" and takes place in jail in Joliet, Illinois) is only a couple of pages long, and its protagonist is soon executed and returned to Jefferson to be buried.

Of those explicit unifying patterns common to fiction, chronological order and a central character are relatively unimportant in *Go Down, Moses*. Although events within individual stories are more or less chronologically ordered, Faulkner generally does not order the stories in the book temporally. "Was" occurs in 1859; "The Fire and the Hearth," between 1940 and 1941, not long after "Delta Autumn"; "Pantaloon in Black," at approximately the same time as "The Fire and the Hearth" and "Delta Autumn"; "The Old People," in 1878–1888; "The Bear," in 1877–1888; "Delta Autumn," in 1940; and "Go Down, Moses," some time after "The Fire and the Hearth" and "Delta Autumn." The only exception to Faulkner's achronological approach is his use of rough chronological order when retelling Ike McCaslin's story ("The Old People," "The Bear," and "Delta Autumn"), which may be one of the reasons some readers think of Ike as the book's protagonist even though he is a character in only three out of the seven stories.

Faulkner's decision generally to avoid chronological order has certain specific thematic functions. Most important, it demonstrates how one's perceptions of the past and one's perceptions of the present continue to influence one another. In addition, Faulkner's decision to de-emphasize chronology serves to strengthen further other elements of the book, such as myth and theme. Since the reader is not assisted from story to story with transitions that illustrate how the events in the second story are temporally or causally related to the events in the first, the reader must work to discover other more implicit transitions.

Theme, Myth, and Point of View

The Wilderness and Black-White Relations

Of these implicit, atemporal unifying patterns (myth, point of view, imagery, and theme), theme has received the most critical attention. Covering almost a hundred years of Southern history and tracing three to six generations of the McCaslins, Edmondses, and Beauchamps, the book is rich with ideas and philosophies. Because there is such a wide range of material, it is a tribute to the book's coherence that so many critics agree that the same two subjects—the wilderness and black-white relations—are most pervasive. The stories featuring Ike McCaslin as protagonist and center of consciousness ("The Old People," "The Bear," "Delta Autumn") develop the two key themes related to the wilderness: the role of the wilderness as a spiritual or moral instructor, and man's violation of the wilderness. The other four stories ("Was," "The Fire and the Hearth," "Pantaloon in Black," "Go Down, Moses"), each featuring a different protagonist, are devoted to the subject of black-white relations and collectively develop the theme of the white person's inability to recognize the black person's humanity and behave justly toward the black.

Even though these two subjects (the wilderness and black-white relations) are undeniably important, generating many of the book's ideas and themes, critics tend to disagree over the manner in which the subjects interact and the extent to which they unify *Go Down, Moses*. Everyone agrees that the book's preoccupation with the subjects results in innumerable connections among the stories, but it appears unlikely that either of these subjects—or any other important ones, such as love and domestic felicity, land ownership, atonement, or the desire to transcend the world—single-handedly unifies the book. For example, although black-white relations are of major importance in most of the stories, the subject is relatively unimportant in "The Old People," just as love is not a major theme in "The Old People" and "The Bear" and atonement is irrelevant in "Pantaloon in Black."

It is also doubtful that two or more of the major subjects combine or merge during the process of the book, producing a single theme which unifies *Go Down, Moses*. Such an argument is attractive to those who perceive the book as divided into two parts—the first three stories focusing on black-white relations and the second three focusing on the wilderness—but attempts to synthesize the major subjects and produce a single unifying theme prove dissatisfactory. For example, some critics argue that the wilderness sections of the book provide solutions for problems outlined in the remainder of the book, specifically the problem of racial prejudice and injustice in twentieth-century America. It is, according to Kenneth E. Richardson and Walter F. Taylor, Jr. ("Let My People Go"), the spiritual and moral training that Ike McCaslin receives in the wilderness which enables him to be the only white McCaslin almost free from racial prejudice.

Other critics, such as T. H. Adamowski, Gloria R. Dussinger, Joan S. Korenman, William Van O'Connor, and Edmond L. Volpe, are willing to accept that there are lessons to be learned from the wilderness, but they deny that these experiences have value when taken out of context. As Volpe explains in *A Reader's Guide*, "the very structure of the novel reflects the isolated experience that Ike undergoes in the woods: social man and natural man cannot merge" (252).

Presentation of Consciousness and Conflicting Philosophies

Although it appears unlikely that *Go Down, Moses* is unified by a single subject or theme, this does not mean that the book was carelessly constructed or that it is an "incompletely unified whole," as Early, Stanley Sultan, and Floyd C. Watkins have alleged. What it does mean, however, is that critics have frequently misunderstood Faulkner's intentions and the function of the book. *Go*

Down, Moses, as the Chicago critics would explain, is primarily a mimetic or presentational—not a didactic—work. Therefore, it should not be faulted because theme is not the single most important unifying principle of the work. Instead of being unified because it advocates a particular theme or philosophic argument, *Go Down, Moses* is unified in its presentation of consciousness, specifically its description of how myth enables a character to structure experience.[6] *Go Down, Moses* depicts multiple consciousnesses, comparing the myths or philosophies that characters represent, but refuses to endorse one myth over another. Ike McCaslin's asceticism is repeatedly contrasted to Cass Edmonds's materialism (especially in section IV of "The Bear"), and Ike McCaslin's Christianity is compared and contrasted with Sam Fathers's totemism. No approach to life is depicted as inherently superior or inferior—all are taken seriously. This explains why so much disagreement exists among critics concerning which philosophy Faulkner advocates.

The juxtaposition or the tension between conflicting philosophies has been widely recognized by critics as a key organizational or structural device.[7] But thus far most critics have merely emphasized that the major characters' life-styles and philosophies are irreconcilable. They have not, with few exceptions, attempted either a rigorous description of the structures of the myths involved or a description of the manner in which certain myths are used to structure large portions of *Go Down, Moses*.

To my knowledge, there has been only one rigorous attempt to compare the actual structures of some of the myths, Wesley Morris's in *Friday's Footprint: Structuralism and the Articulated Text*. In his chapter on *Go Down, Moses*, Morris isolates two myths as most important—Sam Fathers's totemic myth and Ike McCaslin's and Lucas Beauchamp's genealogical myth (which defines one's relation to the world on the basis of patrimony and descent). According to Morris, these myths "stand in tension throughout *Go Down, Moses*" (39). Using an approach which is inspired by Lévi-Strauss (focusing on the binary opposition of nature and culture, on myth's mediation of contraries), Morris identifies the major similarities and differences in the manners in which the two myths structure experience. Such an analysis of myth is important because understanding the structure of the totemic and genealogical myths enables the reader to comprehend better the motivation and behavior of Ike McCaslin, Sam Fathers, and Lucas Beauchamp ("the pattern of complex moral commitments" [39]). In fact, in a story such as "The Old People," which attempts to do little more than express Sam Fathers's and Ike McCaslin's mythic consciousness, the entire story is elucidated by Morris's description of the structure of the myth.

Other critics who discuss myth extensively focus, instead, on the Christian myth, and these critics are primarily interested in demonstrating that the myth is responsible for the organization of large portions of *Go Down, Moses*. Defining "myth" in the broad sense as a synonym for "philosophy," Donald Kartiganer explains that although other myths can be found in the book, it is primarily Ike McCaslin's interpretation or use of Christian myth that structures most of the book. "The Old People" and "The Bear" define Ike's belief in "those patterns [that] effectively preside over our lives" (135). In the last two stories, "Delta Autumn" and "Go Down, Moses," Ike confronts his own complicity in evil; and, in spite of this recognition, he reaffirms his faith in God because he knows that evil plays a part in God's plan of redemption, which is only possible through emulation of Christ's sacrifice.

Lynn Gartrell Levins and James M. Mellard also explain how the overall organization of the book is based on Christian myth, but they differ from Kartiganer because they use the term "myth" in its narrower sense as a symbolic narrative.[8] Levins and Mellard argue that substantial portions of the book are structured according to the narrative pattern associated with Christianity (the broad biblical rhythms of "life in an unfallen Edenic setting, the fall from that innocent existence, the exile and death which follow, and the concluding suggestion of redemption or restoration" [Mellard 135]). Levins's description of how the narrative organizes *Go Down, Moses* is less ambitious than Mellard's, focusing only on the first three stages outlined above (Eden, the Fall, exile and death) and dealing only with Ike McCaslin stories, "The Old People," "The Bear," and "Delta Autumn."

Mellard attempts to demonstrate that the entire plot of *Go Down, Moses* is based on the four stages or acts of the biblical narrative. There are two revolutions of the cycle: "Was" depicts a world of innocence, "pure myth" (141); "The Fire and the Hearth" and "Pantaloon" depict the real world and progressively establish a movement from innocence to experience; "The Old People" (which begins the second revolution and marks a movement from the Old Testament to the New) and "The Bear" depict Ike in a fallen world; "Delta Autumn" finds Ike in exile and near death; and "Go Down, Moses" shows redemption and regeneration, primarily through the fire and hearth imagery and the concerted effort of blacks and whites to bring Butch Beauchamp home and bury him. Although making a detailed case for the book's unity, Mellard is not always convincing as he explains how each story fits into his masterplan.

Third-Person Point of View as a Unifying Device

In addition to creating separate consciousnesses and philosophical stances, point of view is an important structural device in at least one other way. Although using the protagonist in each story as the center of consciousness, Faulkner maintains the third-person point of view throughout, enabling him subtly to remind the reader of the story's context. As Jane Millgate explains, "Within each section there is a unity of point of view which gives it internal pattern, and the uniform narrative mode of the third person integrates these individually unified elements into a total work which achieves its own unity of tone and manner without limiting the variety and richness of its components" (305).

Imagery

Imagery, much like point of view, is used not only to create self-sufficient and discrete worlds (e.g., in "The Old People," the hunting imagery and the symbolic action related to the hunt), but also to connect the worlds. The two symbols and metaphors which have received the most attention are the fire and the hearth and the hunt. Expressing and emphasizing the value love and domestic felicity have for certain characters (Lucas and Molly Beauchamp, Rider, Miss Worsham), the symbol of the fire and the hearth binds those stories ("The Fire and the Hearth," "Pantaloon in Black," and "Go Down, Moses") in which the symbol is used to connote "human coherence and solidarity" (*Go Down, Moses* 380). Furthermore, as Michael Millgate has suggested in his introduction to the concordance, the use of fire imagery in the hunting stories serves to emphasize Ike McCaslin's inability to comprehend the significance of love.

The hunt also functions as a metaphor or symbol for a particular philosophy or myth, the totemic or primitive nature myth. As suggested earlier, in the hunting trilogy ("The Old People," "The Bear," and "Delta Autumn"), the plot pattern is used to suggest that this world can be transcended for another where the individual is freer and able to discover durable truths. When the pattern appears in other stories, it is frequently used ironically to contrast another character's myth or attitude to Sam Fathers's or Ike McCaslin's—for example, the racism of those who hunt blacks in "Was" and "Pantaloon in Black."

In this way the hunt, both as plot pattern and symbol, becomes an especially subtle means whereby Faulkner can both describe how myths work in the individual consciousness and emphasize other things that he wants to say through the stories. For example, although the criticism of slavery is veiled in "Was," since it is told from Cass Edmonds's point of view, it becomes more powerfully rendered when the reader compares the goal of the hunt (for Tomey's Turl) in "Was" to the transcendence briefly achieved in "The Old People" and "The Bear." More important, the manner in which blacks are hunted down and executed in the tragic stories "Pantaloon in Black" and "Go Down, Moses" makes the reader further distrustful of the light comedy that Cass employs when describing Uncle Buck's trip to "Warwick" to fetch his runaway slave.[9]

Other unifying imagery in *Go Down, Moses*—the commissary books, the coffeepot legacy, animal imagery (especially the deer, bear, and snake)—is used in much the same way to define and contrast the major characters' values and philosophies.

CONCLUSION

Although some critics have focused exclusively on "The Bear" and other stories in the book that are frequently anthologized, most critics recognize that *Go Down, Moses* is an achievement almost as important as Faulkner's major novels, *The Sound and the Fury*, *As I Lay Dying*, and *Absalom, Absalom!* Not everyone agrees with Warren Beck that *Go Down, Moses* is "the most subtly integrated and hauntingly attuned of all Faulkner's novels" (333), but those who have demonstrated sustained interest in the book argue that *Go Down, Moses* deserves to be considered a major work because of its broad scope, its experimental structure, and its intentionally ambiguous or open-ended treatment of characters, situations, and ideas. Faulkner himself, at the University of Mississippi in 1947, labeled it one of his most important works, just behind *Absalom, Absalom!* and *As I Lay Dying* (Meriwether and Millgate 53–54).

Several explicit connections among the stories in *Go Down, Moses* are especially significant. These include the setting in Yoknapatawpha, the characters who are descendants of Carothers McCaslin, and the exposition provided in section I of "Was" and section IV of "The Bear." The most subtle and probably the most profound connection is the juxtaposition of the major characters' ideas or, rather, the myths that they use in order to structure experience. Although it promotes no single theme or myth, *Go Down, Moses* does not suggest that such attempts to structure life are without validity or meaning. On the contrary, "one is not necessarily condemned to the dissipation of energies in a chaotic world that defies meaningfulness. If anything, Faulkner depicts a world of surplus meaningfulness where general systems and discrete experiences abound" (Morris 73).

The independent and interdependent stories in *Go Down, Moses* allow the book to present multiple themes or ways of looking at the world without recognizing one as more important than the others or without fusing them. Although the novel can accommodate more than one theme or preoccupation simultaneously, the form of the cycle has certain advantages over the novel in this area: the independent stories can promote philosophies that are different from what is expressed in other parts of the book. This is because the parts of the cycle remain as important as the book's overall effect, unlike the novel, where the importance of the parts is necessarily subordinated to the whole.

As the composition history of *Go Down, Moses* demonstrates, Faulkner's extensive revisions and additions served primarily to emphasize key characters and their ways of looking at life. Ike McCaslin, Lucas and Molly Beauchamp, Sam Fathers, and Cass (or Roth) Edmonds are developed so that they transcend stereotypes and their relationships with one another become more substantial. Written at a time when Faulkner thought his manuscript almost complete, his publisher impatiently awaiting its delivery, "The Bear" was extended because it was absolutely necessary for Faulkner to articulate more clearly and emphatically the conflicting philosophies the characters represent. This is especially true of the long debate between Ike McCaslin and Cass Edmonds in section IV, which provides exposition to complement what is said symbolically elsewhere in the book.

Taken all together, the stories in *Go Down, Moses* create an extraordinary cycle in which the parts illuminate each other and the entire work. *Go Down, Moses* demonstrates a remarkable achievement in the development of the short story cycle genre.

NOTES

1. This point is argued convincingly by Matthews in *The Play of Faulkner's Language*.
2. The evidence in Blotner's biography, upon which Grimwood depends heavily,

indicates that the nearly fatal hunting trip definitely took place, but it is impossible to be certain what year it occurred. According to all accounts, Faulkner began to hemorrhage in his sleep, and only a series of fortunate coincidences saved his life.

3. In December 1940 Faulkner briefly mentions a hunting trip he took in November as a means of escaping from the war: "One nice thing about the woods: off there hunting, I don't fret and stew so much about Europe. But I'm only 43, I'm afraid I'm going to the damn thing yet" (*Selected Letters* 138).

4. Since the *Post* version is limited to material covered in sections I and II of the version in *Go Down, Moses*, and since typesetting copy for sections I and II had been sent to Random House several months before the shorter version of the story was submitted to the *Post*, it is unlikely that the *Post* version was written first.

5. Walton Litz and Meredith Smith provide useful genealogical summaries.

6. Here and throughout the next paragraph I use the term "myth" in its broadest sense as a synonym for "philosophy" or "cognitive strategy" (it is simply "a basic way of envisaging experience, and carries no necessary connotation of storytelling" [*Princeton Encyclopedia of Poetry and Poetics* 538]).

7. See Adams, Benert, Breaden, Canfield, Hamilton, Harter, Howe, James, Kartiganer, Kinney (*Narrative Poetics*), Matthews ("Creative Responses"), Morris, and Walter.

8. "Myth," as I use it here, is defined as "a story or a complex of story elements taken as expressing, and therefore as implicitly symbolizing, certain deep-lying aspects of human and transhuman existence" (*Princeton Encyclopedia of Poetry and Poetics* 538).

9. One of the best recent analyses of the pattern of the hunt is the chapter on *Go Down, Moses* in Matthews's *The Play of Faulkner's Language*. Matthews suggests that hunting, like other rituals employed in the book, is used to give the characters a language in which they can mourn irretrievable losses.

WORKS CITED AND BIBLIOGRAPHY

Ackerman, R. D. "The Immolation of Isaac McCaslin." *TSLL* 16 (Fall 1974): 557–65.

Adamowski, T. H. "Isaac McCaslin and the Wilderness of the Imagination." *CentR* 17 (Winter 1973): 92–112.

Adams, Richard P. *Faulkner: Myth and Motion*. Princeton: Princeton UP, 1968.

Akin, Warren, IV. " 'Neither We from Them nor They from Us': An Interpretation of *Go Down, Moses*." Diss. Bryn Mawr, 1975. *DAI* 36 (1976): 6094A.

    There are three major divisions: (1) the first three stories focus on the relations between black and white McCaslins before and after 1888; (2) the second three deal with the life of Ike McCaslin; and (3) the last story moves beyond the McCaslins to examine racial conflict in a larger context. The tone moves from comedy to tragedy as the situations in which blacks are placed become more intolerable and the validity of Ike's relinquishing the land is questioned.

———. " 'The Normal Human Feelings': An Interpretation of Faulkner's 'Pantaloon in Black.' " *SSF* 15 (Fall 1978): 397–404.

———. "Providence and the Structure of *Go Down, Moses*." *SoR* ns 18.3 (July 1982): 495–505.

Backman, Melvin Abraham. "The Wilderness and the Negro in Faulkner's 'The Bear.' " *PMLA* 76 (Dec. 1961): 595–600. Rpt. in *Faulkner: The Major Years*. Bloomington: Indiana UP, 1966. 160–74; and in *William Faulkner: A Collection of Criticism*. Ed. Dean Morgan Schmitter. New York: McGraw, 1973. 136–46.

Bassett, John Earl. "*Go Down, Moses*: Experience and the Forms of Understanding." *Kentucky Review* 3.1 (1981): 3–22.

Beck, Warren, IV. "Short Stories into Novels" and "*Go Down, Moses*." *William Faulkner: Essays*. Madison: U of Wisconsin P, 1976. 275–582.

Benert, Annette. "The Four Fathers of Isaac McCaslin." *SHR* 9 (Fall 1975): 423–33.

Blotner, Joseph. Vol. 2 of *Faulkner: A Biography*. 2 vols. New York: Random, 1974.

Bradford, Melvin E. "All the Daughters of Eve: 'Was' and the Unity of *Go Down, Moses*." *ArlQ* 1 (Autumn 1967): 28–37.

———. "The Gum Tree Scene: Observations on the Structure of 'The Bear.' " *SHR* 1 (Spring 1967): 141–50.

Breaden, Dale G. "William Faulkner and the Land." *AQ* 10 (Fall 1958): 344–57. Rpt. in Utley, 1st ed., 273–79.

Brogunier, Joseph. "A Source for the Commissary Entries in *Go Down, Moses*." *TSLL* 14 (Fall 1972): 545–54.

Brooks, Cleanth. "*Go Down, Moses*." *William Faulkner: First Encounters*. New Haven: Yale UP, 1983. 129–59.

———. "The Story of the McCaslins (*Go Down, Moses*)." *Faulkner: The Yoknapatawpha Country*. New Haven: Yale UP, 1963. 244–78, 414–20.

Butor, Michel. "Les relations de parenté dans 'L'ours' de William Faulkner." *LetN* 4 (May 1956): 734–45.

    Emphasizes that *Go Down, Moses*, like *Absalom, Absalom!*, is a novel of process or reader participation, since the reader must work to define characters (from vague pronoun references) and their relationships. At the end of the work, it is the reader—not Ike McCaslin or Roth Edmonds—who may be able to transcend racial prejudice.

Canfield, J. Douglas. "Faulkner's Grecian Urn and Ike McCaslin's Empty Legacies." *ArQ* 36 (Winter 1980): 359–84.

Chakovsky, Sergei. "Lucas Beauchamp and Jim: Mark Twain's Influence on William Faulkner." *Faulkner and Race: Faulkner and Yoknapatawpha, 1986*. Ed. Doreen Fowler and Ann J. Abadie. Jackson: UP of Mississippi, 1987. 236–54.

Claridge, Laura P. "Isaac McCaslin's Failed Bid for Adulthood." *AL* 55 (May 1983): 241–51.

Cleman, John L. " 'Pantaloon in Black': Its Place in *Go Down, Moses*." *TSL* 22 (1977): 170–81.

Corrick, James A., III. "Thematic Patterning as a Structuring Device in William Faulkner's *Go Down, Moses*." Diss. U of Arizona, 1981. *DAI* 42 (1981): 1633A.

    "Since literary criticism has no terminology for describing thematic patterning, this study employs terms used in musical composition. By constructing a model similar to the fugue form in music, we can show how the acceptance or rejection of love and understanding functions as one of the unifying elements in *Go Down, Moses*" (*DAI*).

Cowley, Malcolm. *The Faulkner-Cowley File: Letters and Memories, 1944–1962*. New York: Viking, 1966.

———. "Go Down to Faulkner's Land." Rev. of *Go Down, Moses*, by William Faulkner. *New Republic* 106 (29 June 1942): 900.

Creighton, Joanne V. "*Dubliners* and *Go Down, Moses*: The Short Story Composite."

Diss. U of Michigan, 1969. *DAI* 31 (1970): 1792A–93A.

The dissertation contains four chapters, assigned the following tasks: (chapter 1) a reading of the first three stories in *Go Down, Moses* for the purpose of demonstrating the extent to which they are open-ended and enriched by their context in the book; (chapter 2) an analysis of unifying principles in *Go Down, Moses* through discussion of the last four stories; (chapter 3) a comparison of the dramatic form of *Go Down, Moses* with the lyrical form of *Dubliners*; and (chapter 4) a discussion of the fiction of Faulkner and Joyce in order to differentiate between the short story composite and the novel.

————. "*Go Down, Moses*: Construction of a Short Story Composite." *William Faulkner's Craft of Revision: The Snopes Trilogy, "The Unvanquished" and "Go Down, Moses."* Detroit: Wayne State UP, 1977. 85–148. Sections on "The Fire and the Hearth," "The Old People," "The Bear," and "Delta Autumn" appeared earlier, in slightly different form, in *TSLL* 15 (Fall 1973): 577–92; and in *SSF* 11 (Spring 1974): 161–72.

Dabney, Lewis M. "Sam Fathers and *Go Down, Moses*." *The Indians of Yoknapatawpha: A Study in Literature and History.* Baton Rouge: Louisiana UP, 1974. 118–57.

————. " 'Was': Faulkner's Classic Comedy of the Frontier." *SoR* ns 8 (Autumn 1972): 736–48.

Davis, Thadious M. "Set Patterns: *Go Down, Moses* and Beyond." *Faulkner's "Negro": Art and the Southern Context.* Baton Rouge: Louisiana State UP, 1983. 239–47.

Denniston, Dorothy L. "Faulkner's Image of Blacks in *Go Down, Moses*." *Phylon* 44 (Spring 1983): 33–43.

Devlin, Albert J. "Faulknerian Chronology: Puzzles and Games." *NMW* 5 (Winter 1973): 98–101.

————. " 'How Much It Takes to Compound a Man': A Neglected Scene in *Go Down, Moses*." *MQ* 14 (Summer 1973): 408–21.

Donaldson, Susan V. "Isaac McCaslin and the Possibilities of Vision." *SoR* ns 22.1 (Jan. 1986): 37–50.

Donnelly, Sheila Hurst. "Isaac McCaslin: Fugitive from Responsibility, Poet of Cloistered Virtue." *MHLS* 7 (1984): 65–74.

Dunn, Margaret M. "The Illusion of Freedom in *The Hamlet* and *Go Down, Moses*." *AL* 57 (Oct. 1985): 407–23.

Dussinger, Gloria R. "Faulkner's Isaac McCaslin as Romantic Hero Manqué." *SAQ* 68 (Summer 1969): 377–85.

Early, James. *The Making of* Go Down, Moses*: William Faulkner's Creative Imagination at Work.* Dallas: Southern Methodist UP, 1972.

Fant, Joseph L., III, and Robert Ashley, eds. *Faulkner at West Point.* New York: Random, 1964.

Faulkner, William. *Go Down, Moses.* New York: Random, 1942.

————. *Selected Letters of William Faulkner.* Ed. Joseph Blotner. New York: Random, 1977.

————. "Sherwood Anderson: An Appreciation." *Essays, Speeches and Public Letters.* Ed. James B. Meriwether. New York: Random, 1965. 3–10. Rpt. in Ferres 487–94; in White, *Achievement of Sherwood Anderson*, 194–99; and in Rideout, *Collection of Critical Essays*, 166–70.

Fisher, Richard E. "The Wilderness, the Commissary, and the Bedroom: Faulkner's Ike

McCaslin as Hero in a Vacuum." *English Studies* (Amsterdam) 44 (Feb. 1963): 19–28.

Ford, Daniel G. "Faulkner's Sense of 'Was.' " *PAPA* 10.1 (Spring 1984): 45–56.

Foster, Thomas C. "History, Private Consciousness, and Narrative Form in *Go Down, Moses*." *CentR* 28.1 (Winter 1984): 61–76.

Friedman, Alan Warren. "Twice-Told Tales: *The Unvanquished, The Wild Palms*, and *Go Down, Moses*." *William Faulkner*. New York: Ungar, 1984. 117–36.

Grimwood, Michael. " 'Delta Autumn': Stagnation and Sedimentation in Faulkner's Career." *SLJ* 16.2 (Spring 1984): 93–106.

———. *"Go Down, Moses." Heart in Conflict: Faulkner's Struggles with Vocation*. Athens: U of Georgia P, 1987. 223–98.

———. "Pastoral and Parody: The Making of Faulkner's Anthology Novels." Diss. Princeton U, 1976. *DAI* 37 (1977): 5828A.

Gwynn, Frederick L., and Joseph L. Blotner, eds. *Faulkner in the University: Class Conferences at the University of Virginia 1957–1958*. Charlottesville: U of Virginia P, 1959.

Hamilton, Gary D. "The Past in the Present: A Reading of *Go Down, Moses*." *SHR* 5 (Spring 1971): 171–81.

Harter, Carol Clancey. "The Diaphoric Structure and Unity of William Faulkner's *Go Down, Moses*." Diss. State U of New York at Binghamton, 1970. *DAI* 31 (1971): 6057A–58A.

   Harter agrees with Tick (see below) that *Go Down, Moses* is well unified but rejects his label "short story blend." Harter argues that the book should be considered a novel, more specifically a novel with diaphoric instead of temporal structure. (Her terminology is based on Philip Wheelwright's *Metaphor and Reality*.) Different versions of the stories are compared in order to describe how the diaphoric structure evolved, especially so far as the central tension between Ike McCaslin and Roth Edmonds is concerned.

———. "The Winter of Isaac McCaslin: Revisions and Irony in Faulkner's 'Delta Autumn.' " *JML* 1.2 (1970–1971): 209–25.

Hochberg, Mark R. "The Unity of *Go Down, Moses*." *TSL* 21 (1976): 58–65.

Hoffman, Daniel. "Faulkner's 'Was' and Uncle Adam's Cow." *Faulkner and Humor: Faulkner and Yoknapatawpha, 1984*. Ed. Doreen Fowler and Ann J. Abadie. Jackson: UP of Mississippi, 1986. 57–78.

Holmes, Edward Morris. "The Hunt." *Faulkner's Twice-Told Tales: His Re-Use of His Material*. The Hague: Mouton, 1966. 58–79.

Howe, Irving. *William Faulkner: A Critical Study*. 3rd ed. New York: Vintage, 1975.

Hunter, Edwin R. *William Faulkner: Narrative Practice and Prose Style*. Washington, DC: Windhover, 1973.

Idei, Yasuko. "Faulkner's *Go Down, Moses*: An Interrelation between Content and Structure." *KAL* 17 (Sept. 1976): 29–41.

Ingram, Forrest L. *Representative Short Story Cycles of the Twentieth Century: Studies in a Literary Genre*. The Hague: Mouton, 1971.

James, Stuart. "The Ironic Voices of Faulkner's *Go Down, Moses*." *SDR* 16.3 (Autumn 1978): 80–101.

Jenkins, Lee. *"Go Down, Moses." Faulkner and Black-White Relations: A Psychoanalytic Approach*. New York: Columbia UP, 1981. 221–60.

Kartiganer, Donald M. *The Fragile Thread: The Meaning of Form in Faulkner's Novels*. Amherst: U of Massachusetts P, 1979.

Kerr, Elizabeth M. "*Go Down, Moses*: Paradise Lost, or, The Secret of the Ledgers." *William Faulkner's Gothic Domain*. Port Washington, NY: Kennikat, 1979. 137–61.

———. *William Faulkner's Yoknapatawpha: "A Kind of Keystone in the Universe."* New York: Fordham UP, 1983.

King, Richard H. "Working through Faulkner's *Go Down, Moses*." *A Southern Renaissance: The Cultural Awakening of the American South, 1930–1955*. Oxford: Oxford UP, 1980. 130–45. Rpt. in *William Faulkner*. Ed. Harold Bloom. New York: Chelsea, 1986. 193–205.

Kinney, Arthur F. " 'Delta Autumn': Postlude to 'The Bear.' " Utley, 1st ed., 384–95.

———. " 'Delta Autumn': William Faulkner's Answer for David H. Stewart." *Papers of the Michigan Academy of Science, Arts and Letters* 49 (1963): 541–49. Rpt. in *Modern Short Stories: The Uses of Imagination*. Ed. Arthur Mizener. 3rd ed. New York: Norton, 1971. 625–28.

———. "Faulkner and the Possibilities for Heroism." *SoR* ns 6 (Autumn 1970): 1110–25. Rpt. in Utley, 2nd ed., 235–51.

———. *Faulkner's Narrative Poetics: Style as Vision*. Amherst: U of Massachusetts P, 1978.

Klotz, Marvin. "Procrustean Revision in Faulkner's *Go Down, Moses*." *AL* 37 (Mar. 1965): 1–16.

Korenman, Joan S. "Faulkner's Grecian Urn." *SLJ* 7 (Fall 1974): 3–23.

Kreiswirth, Martin. "Centers, Openings, and Endings: Some Faulknerian Constants." *AL* 56 (Mar. 1984): 38–50.

Kuyk, Dirk, Jr. *Threads Cable-Strong: William Faulkner's* Go Down, Moses. Lewisburg: Bucknell UP, 1983.

Latimer, Kathleen. "Comedy as Order in *Go Down, Moses*." *PCL* 10 (1984): 1–8.

Lawson, Richard Alan. "Patterns of Initiation in William Faulkner's *Go Down, Moses*." Diss. Tulane U, 1966. *DA* 27 (1966): 1372A.

Leahy, Sharon L. "Poker and Semantics: Unravelling the Gordian Knot in Faulkner's 'Was.' " *AL* 57.1 (Mar. 1985): 129–37.

Levins, Lynn Gartrell. *Faulkner's Heroic Design: The Yoknapatawpha Novels*. Athens: U of Georgia P, 1976. 75–94.

Limon, John. "The Integration of Faulkner's *Go Down, Moses*." *CritI* 12.2 (Winter 1986): 422–38.

Lindholdt, Paul J. "Isaac McCaslin and the Burden of Influence." *UMSE* 5 (1984–1987): 172–81.

Litz, Walton. "Genealogy as Symbol in *Go Down, Moses*." *Faulkner Studies* 1 (Winter 1952): 49–53.

Longley, John Lewis, Jr. "The Comic Hero: McCaslin." *The Tragic Mask: A Study of Faulkner's Heroes*. Chapel Hill: U of North Carolina P, 1963. 79–101, 105–10.

McGee, Patrick. "Gender and Generation in Faulkner's 'The Bear.' " *FJ* 1 (Fall 1985): 46–54.

Matthews, John T. "Creative Responses to Time in the Novels of William Faulkner." Diss. Johns Hopkins U, 1976. *DAI* 37 (1977): 6486A–87A.

    The stories in *Go Down, Moses* are unified by the various protagonists' creative attempts to remember what was valuable in the past and to retain what is valuable in the present. The fragmented form of the book—"the stories occupy some as yet poorly defined space between a collection of related stories and a novel"— serves to emphasize "the fracturing power of time" (219).

———. "The Ritual of Mourning in *Go Down, Moses*." *The Play of Faulkner's Language*. Ithaca: Cornell UP, 1982. 212–73.

Meindl, Dieter. "Der kurzgeschichtenzyklus als modernistisches Genre." *GRM* 33.2 (1983): 216–28.

Mellard, James M. "The Biblical Rhythm of *Go Down, Moses*." *MissQ* 20 (Summer 1967): 135–47.

Meriwether, James B. "The Short Fiction of William Faulkner: A Bibliography." *Proof* 1 (1971): 293–329. Rev. and rpt. in *The Literary Career of William Faulkner*. Columbia: U of South Carolina P, 1971.

    Notes whether or not the stories in *Go Down, Moses* have been published elsewhere and if there are any extant manuscript, typescript, or proof versions of the stories.

Meriwether, James B., and Michael Millgate, eds. *Lion in the Garden: Interviews with William Faulkner, 1926–1962*. New York: Random, 1968.

Mickelsen, David. "The Campfire and the Hearth in *Go Down, Moses*." *MissQ* 38.3 (Summer 1985): 311–27.

Millgate, Jane. "*Go Down, Moses*." "Short Stories into Novels: A Textual and Critical Study of Some Aspects of Faulkner's Literary Method." M.A. Thesis. Leeds, 1962. 148–308. The section on "Gold Is Not Always" is rev. and rpt. in *ES* 45 (Aug. 1964): 310–17.

    The chapter explains how Faulkner revised preexisting stories for inclusion in *Go Down, Moses*. Millgate's detailed analyses of revisions remain extremely useful.

Millgate, Michael. "*Go Down, Moses*." *The Achievement of William Faulkner*. New York: Random, 1966. 201–14. Rpt. (in part) in Utley, 2nd ed., 222–35.

———. Introduction. Vol. 1 of *Go Down, Moses: A Concordance to the Novel*. 2 vols. Ed. Jack L. Capps. Ann Arbor, MI: UMI, 1977.

———. *William Faulkner*. Rev. ed. New York: Grove, 1966.

Minter, David. *William Faulkner: His Life and Work*. Baltimore: Johns Hopkins UP, 1980.

Morris, Wesley. "The Pilgrimage of Being." *Friday's Footprint: Structuralism and the Articulated Text*. Columbus: Ohio State UP, 1979. 1–83.

Muste, John M. "The Failure of Love in *Go Down, Moses*." *MFS* 10 (Winter 1964–65): 366–78.

Nilon, Charles H. *Faulkner and the Negro*. New York: Citadel, 1965.

Oates, Stephen B. *William Faulkner: The Man and the Artist*. New York: Harper, 1987.

O'Connor, William Van. "The Wilderness Theme in Faulkner's 'The Bear.' " *Accent* 13 (Winter 1953): 12–20. Rev. and rpt. in *The Tangled Fire of William Faulkner*. Minneapolis: U of Minnesota P, 1954. 125–34; and in *William Faulkner: Three Decades of Criticism*. Ed. Frederick J. Hoffman and Olga W. Vickery. East Lansing: Michigan State UP, 1960. 322–30.

Ono, Kiyoyuki. "The Secret of 'Was' Is." *Faulkner Studies in Japan*. Ed. Thomas L. McHaney. Athens: U of Georgia P, 1985. 148–73.

Orloff, Kossia. "Ring Composition: The Structural Unity of William Faulkner's *Go Down, Moses*." Diss. U of Iowa, 1977. *DAI* 38 (1978): 4184A.

Go Down, Moses is a ring composition, achronological but unified and coherent because of thematic connections. The structural pattern that best describes the overall design of *Go Down, Moses* is chiasmus. Each of the stories in the second half of the book (beginning with "The Bear") is "structurally balanced" by a particular story in the first half. The book's center is "Delta Autumn," which provides the key to the book's thematic coherence: "the tension between love and pride, not a tension limited to race or time or condition" (*DAI*).

Pascal, Richard. "Love, Rapacity, and Community in *Go Down, Moses*." *ArielE* 15.3 (July 1984): 63–79.

Phillips, K. J. "Waste Land in Faulkner's *Go Down, Moses*." *International Fiction Review* 9.2 (Summer 1982): 114–19.

Pikoulis, John. "The Keatsian Moment." *The Art of William Faulkner*. Totowa, NJ: Barnes, 1982. 192–226.

Pilkington, John. "Pensioners of History: *Go Down, Moses*." *The Heart of Yoknapatawpha*. Jackson: UP of Mississippi, 1981. 243–88.

Ploegstra, Henry Alden. "William Faulkner's *Go Down, Moses*: Its Sources, Revisions, and Structure." Diss. U of Chicago, 1966. (No abstract in *DA*.)

The dissertation contains three divisions: (1) a detailed description of the magazine stories upon which *Go Down, Moses* is based; (2) a thorough comparison of the typescript, magazine, and book (*Go Down, Moses*) versions of the stories; and (3) an analysis of unifying devices in *Go Down, Moses*. According to Ploegstra, "there is no term extant which describes it [the book] adequately. To enlarge the term 'novel' to include works like *Go Down, Moses* does more to weaken literary classifications than it does to clarify the nature of the book" (325–26).

Powers, Lyall H. "*Go Down, Moses*." *Faulkner's Yoknapatawpha Comedy*. Ann Arbor: U of Michigan P, 1980. 162–91.

Ragan, David Paul. "The Evolution of Roth Edmonds in *Go Down, Moses*." *MissQ* 38.3 (Summer 1985): 295–309.

Reed, Joseph W., Jr. "Uncertainties: *The Unvanquished* and *Go Down, Moses*." *Faulkner's Narrative*. New Haven: Yale UP, 1973. 176–200.

Reed, Pleasant Larus, III. "The Integrated Short-Story Collection: Studies of a Form of Nineteenth- and Twentieth-Century Fiction." Diss. Indiana U, 1974. *DAI* 35 (1975): 6730A.

The Unvanquished and *Go Down, Moses* are labeled "short story novels," and *These 13, Doctor Martino*, and *Collected Stories* are called "integrated short story collections." The difference between the two groups is that the stories in *The Unvanquished* and *Go Down, Moses* "must be read together for their full effect," while stories in the last three volumes are "enhanced" when read together, but their "full effect" does not depend on their being read in this context.

Richardson, Kenneth E. "The Wilderness and the Spiritual Father." *Force and Faith in the Novels of William Faulkner*. The Hague: Mouton, 1967. 45–61.

Rollyson, Carl E., Jr. "The Dramatization of the Past and of Historical Process in *Go Down Moses*" and "Historical Research and the Evolution of History in *Go Down, Moses*." *Uses of the Past in the Novels of William Faulkner*. Ann Arbor, MI: UMI, 1984. 99–152.

Roth, Russell. "The Brennan Papers: Faulkner in Manuscript." *Perspective* 2 (Summer 1949): 219–24.

Ruzicka, William T. *"Go Down, Moses." Faulkner's Fictive Architecture: The Meaning of Place in the Yoknapatawpha Novels*. Ann Arbor, MI: UMI, 1987. 83–110.

Sams, Larry Marshall. "Isaac McCaslin and Keats's 'Ode on a Grecian Urn.' " *SoR* ns 12 (Summer 1976): 632–39.

Schleifer, Ronald. "Faulkner's Storied Novel: *Go Down, Moses* and the Translation of Time." *MFS* 28.1 (Spring 1982): 109–27.

Sederberg, Nancy B. " 'A Momentary Anesthesia of the Heart': A Study of the Comic Elements in Faulkner's *Go Down, Moses." Faulkner and Humor: Faulkner and Yoknapatawpha, 1984*. Ed. Doreen Fowler and Ann J. Abadie. Jackson: UP of Mississippi, 1986. 79–96.

Selzer, John L. " 'Go Down, Moses' and *Go Down, Moses*.' " *SAF* 13 (Spring 1985): 89–96.

Skei, Hans H. "Cycles of Stories and Stories for Novels 1933–1941." *William Faulkner: The Short Story Career: An Outline of Faulkner's Short Story Writing from 1919 to 1962*. Oslo: Dept. of Literature, U of Oslo, 1981. 78–99.

———. *William Faulkner: The Novelist as Short Story Writer*. Oslo: Dept. of Literature, U of Oslo, 1985.

> Brief chapters are devoted to "William Faulkner and the Short Story," "Cycles of Stories, or Novels?," and "The Novelist as Short-Story Writer."

Slatoff, Walter Jacob. *Quest for Failure: A Study of William Faulkner*. Ithaca, NY: Cornell UP, 1960.

Smith, Meredith. "A Chronology of *Go Down, Moses." MissQ* 36.3 (Summer 1983): 319–28.

Snead, James A. *"Go Down, Moses." Figures of Division: William Faulkner's Major Novels*. London: Methuen, 1986. 180–211.

Sniderman, Stephen Lee. "The 'Composite' in Twentieth-Century American Literature." Diss. U of Wisconsin, 1970. *DAI* 31 (1970): 403A.

> *Go Down, Moses* is discussed in detail and identified as a model composite because each story is essential to an understanding of the book, because the stories must be read sequentially, and because the book maintains a continuous balance between the parts and the whole.

Stephens, Rosemary. "Ike's Gun and Too Many Novembers." *MissQ* 23 (Summer 1970): 279–87.

———. "Mythical Elements of 'Pantaloon in Black.' " *UMSE* 11 (1970): 45–51.

Sultan, Stanley. "Call Me Ishmael: The Hagiography of Isaac McCaslin." *TSLL* 3 (Spring 1961): 50–66.

Sundquist, Eric J. "Half Slave, Half Free: *Go Down, Moses." Faulkner: The House Divided*. Baltimore: Johns Hopkins UP, 1983. 131–59.

Tangum, Marion Mast. "Voices in *Go Down, Moses*: Faulkner's Dialogic Rhetoric." Diss. U of Texas at Austin, 1986. *DAI* 47 (1986): 1731A.

Taylor, Walter F., Jr. "Faulkner's Pantaloon: The Negro Anomaly at the Heart of *Go Down, Moses." AL* 44 (Nov. 1972): 430–44.

———. *Faulkner's Search for a South*. Urbana: U of Illinois P, 1983.

———. "Let My People Go: The White Man's Heritage in *Go Down, Moses." SAQ* 58 (Winter 1959): 20–32. Rpt. in Utley, 1st ed., 290–301.

Thompson, Lawrance R. *"Go Down, Moses." William Faulkner: An Introduction and Interpretation*. 2nd ed. New York: Holt, 1967. 81–98.

Thornton, Weldon. "Structure and Theme in Faulkner's *Go Down, Moses.*" *Costerus* 3 (1975): 73–112.

Tick, Stanley. "The Unity of *Go Down, Moses.*" *TCL* 8 (July 1962): 67–73. Rpt. in *William Faulkner: Four Decades of Criticism.* Ed. Linda Welshimer Wagner. East Lansing: Michigan State UP, 1973. 327–34.

Toolan, Michael. "The Functioning of Progressive Verbal Forms in the Narrative of *Go Down, Moses.*" *Language and Style: An International Journal* 16.2 (Spring 1983): 211–30.

———. " 'Pantaloon in Black' in *Go Down, Moses*: The Function of the 'Breathing' Motif." *CNv* 2 (Jan. 1984): 155–66.

Utley, Francis Lee, et al., eds. *Bear, Man, and God: Seven Approaches to William Faulkner's "The Bear."* New York: Random, 1964. The 2nd ed. (1971) is entitled *Bear, Man, and God: Eight Approaches to William Faulkner's "The Bear."*

Vashchenko, Alexandre. "Woman and the Making of the New World: Faulkner's Short Stories." *Faulkner and Women: Faulkner and Yoknapatawpha, 1985.* Ed. Doreen Fowler and Ann J. Abadie. Jackson: UP of Mississippi, 1986. 205–19.

Vickery, Olga W. "Initiation and Identity." *The Novels of William Faulkner: A Critical Interpretation.* Rev. ed. Baton Rouge: Louisiana State UP, 1964. 124–34.

Vinson, Audrey L. "Miscegenation and Its Meaning in '*Go Down, Moses.*' " *CLAJ* 14 (Dec. 1970): 143–55.

Volpe, Edmond L. "*Go Down, Moses.*" *A Reader's Guide to William Faulkner.* New York: Farrar, 1978. 230–52.

Waggoner, Hyatt H. *William Faulkner: From Jefferson to the World.* Lexington: U of Kentucky P, 1959.

Wagner, Linda Welshimer. *Hemingway and Faulkner: inventors/masters.* Metuchen, NJ: Scarecrow, 1975.

Walker, David. "Out of the Old Time: 'Was' and *Go Down, Moses.*" *JNT* 9 (Winter 1979): 1–11.

Walter, James. "Expiation and History: Ike McCaslin and the Mystery of Providence." *LaS* 10 (Winter 1971): 263–73.

Watkins, Floyd C. "Faulkner's Inexhaustible Voice." *The Flesh and the Word.* Nashville: Vanderbilt UP, 1971. 234–53.

Watson, James G. "Faulkner's Short Stories and the Making of Yoknapatawpha County." *Fifty Years of Yoknapatawpha: Faulkner and Yoknapatawpha, 1979.* Ed. Doreen Fowler and Ann J. Abadie. Jackson: UP of Mississippi, 1980. 202–25.

———. *William Faulkner: Letters and Fiction.* Austin: U of Texas P, 1987.

Weinstein, Philip M. "Meditations on the Other: Faulkner's Rendering of Women." *Faulkner and Women: Faulkner and Yoknapatawpha, 1985.* Ed. Doreen Fowler and Ann J. Abadie. Jackson: UP of Mississippi, 1986. 81–99.

Wheeler, Otis B. "Faulkner's Wilderness." *AL* 31 (May 1959): 127–36.

Willis, Susan. "Aesthetics of the Rural Slum: Contradictions and Dependency in 'The Bear.' " *Faulkner: New Perspectives.* Ed. Richard H. Brodhead. Englewood Cliffs, NJ: Prentice, 1983.

Winn, Harlan Harbour, III. "Short Story Cycles of Hemingway, Steinbeck, Faulkner, and O'Connor." Diss. U of Oregon, 1975. *DAI* 36 (1976): 4500A.
  Go Down, Moses is labeled a short story cycle, but the book is not discussed.

Wittenberg, Judith B. "The End of the Major Period: *Go Down, Moses.*" *Faulkner: The Transfiguration of Biography.* Lincoln: U of Nebraska P, 1979. 190–204.

Zender, Karl F. "Faulkner at Forty: The Artist at Home." *SoR* ns 17 (Spring 1981): 288–302.

———. "A Hand of Poker: Game and Ritual in Faulkner's 'Was.' " *SSF* 11 (Winter 1974): 53–60.

———. "Reading in 'The Bear.' " *Faulkner Studies* 1 (1980): 91–99.

7

Eudora Welty's
The Golden Apples

Of all her own works, Eudora Welty describes *The Golden Apples* as "closest to [her] heart" (*Conversations with Eudora Welty* 42–43, 192). Even the writing process was noteworthy, described by Welty as both intense and liberating:

I liked the sort of freedom out of which I wrote that whole book—being able to give everything, unhesitatingly, to what I was trying to say. . . .

I think the time when I went through the most intense, sustained writing was when I did the collection called *The Golden Apples*. (*Conversations* 285, 326)

What Welty enjoyed most—after she had written several stories—was discovering that the lives in which she had become involved were connected and must be told together: "All this time in the back of my head these connections had worked themselves out. I had just to get the clue like a belated detective: this story's people were that story's people at a different period in their lives" (*Conversations* 192).

INTRODUCTION TO UNIFYING FORMS

Eudora Welty also gives some clues for understanding the connections among the stories in *The Golden Apples*. While stressing the importance of myth, she warns those who exaggerate its importance or who attempt to explain the entire book in terms of myth: "In *The Golden Apples* I used mythology, but the stories weren't meant to illustrate a myth. I just used mythology, just as I used Mississippi locations and names. . . . it is kind of frightening to think that people see ponderous allegorical meanings" (*Conversations* 189). Given the extent to which criticism has dwelt upon her use of myth, Welty's warnings are appropriate. While certain myths are centrally important to any discussion of *The*

Golden Apples, they are no more significant than other unifying forms such as character, setting, or imagery.

UNITY IN *THE GOLDEN APPLES*

Character, Chronology, Setting

The importance of characters as a unifying device is immediately obvious. Almost all of the characters or dramatis personae are listed on a separate page, immediately after the table of contents. They are arranged according to family, with the MacLain and Stark families heading the list. At the bottom of the page is a postscript listing additional families, generally from the lower or working class, that play minor roles in the stories.

Recurring and developing characters provide much of the book's unity. The MacLain family appears more frequently than any other: they are featured as major characters in four stories—"Shower of Gold," "Sir Rabbit," "The Whole World Knows," and "Music from Spain"—and make at least cameo appearances in all of the others. The Rainey family is similarly important even though they function as protagonists (or centers of consciousness) only in the first and the last story.[1] They contribute to the overall cyclical organization achieved in the book: it begins with Katie Rainey's first-person narrative and ends with her funeral and her daughter Virgie's perceptions of the past and present.

Several other families play important roles in more than one story. Cassie and Loch Morrison function as the centers of consciousness in "June Recital," and Loch is featured in "Moon Lake," while Cassie is used as a foil to Virgie Rainey in "The Wanderers." Mrs. Lizzie Stark presides over the Morgana middle class in all but two stories, being the person who does the most to keep the working class (and men of all classes) in their places. Her daughter, Jinny Stark MacLain, exhibits her own style of narcissism in "June Recital," "Moon Lake," "The Whole World Knows," and "The Wanderers." Similarly, Nina Carmichael appears in several stories ("June Recital," "The Whole World Knows," "The Wanderers") but is important only in "Moon Lake."

A variety of characters appear frequently but serve merely as a backdrop for the action: they represent those people who never make any real impact on our lives even though they are part of its everyday fabric. The scolding busy-body, Miss Perdita Mayo, is mentioned in more than half of the stories and taken seriously in none of them. Although eminently forgettable, Parnell Moody is allowed to develop in convincing ways within the framework of the book: depicted in "June Recital" as a pupil who cries if Miss Eckhart gives her a harsh look, she is the camp counsellor in "Moon Lake" who wears her underclothes beneath her bathing suit and proves helpless when Easter nearly drowns. Even the Holifields, who achieve no importance other than the clownlike role that Junior plays in "Sir Rabbit," appear in virtually every story, performing small tasks (such as the handyman at Moon Lake) that no one really notices.

Welty frequently uses recurring characters and their relationships to help execute a transition from story to story. The most obvious example is the transition between "The Whole World Knows" (#5) and "Music from Spain" (#6). The first story chronicles Ran MacLain's unhappy marriage to Jinny Stark, focusing on a brief period of separation soon after they are married; the second describes the other twin's, Eugene's, equally dissatisfactory marriage. The transitional device is sometimes less noticeable. For example, both of the first two stories ("Shower of Gold" and "June Recital") involve most of the same characters. The major difference is that Welty, in the second story, adds to the original cast of MacLains, Raineys, and Starks presented in the first. By including newcomers such as the Morrisons and Miss Eckhart in "June Recital," the author is able to emphasize the more than fifteen years that have elapsed between the first two stories.

In addition to reappearing, characters are further revealed or developed in the process of the book. I suggested this above, briefly, when describing Jinny Stark and Parnell Moody. Better examples would be Virgie Rainey, Cassie Morrison, or Ran MacLain, because these characters undergo more substantial and sustained changes. As developed, they achieve a kind of internal consistency which appears organic: they are allowed to grow in ways—not always predictable—that prove absolutely convincing. Although Virgie Rainey appears only in the second and the last stories, she is evoked so powerfully at the beginning of "The Wanderers" that the gaps between the two stories are easily bridged. What she has become in her early forties fulfills in unexpected ways the potential she displayed as a gifted young pianist. Even though she does not play the piano now, she has retained her passion, her willfulness, her harmonious relationship with nature, and her ability to distance herself from others and perceive them objectively. Furthermore, she has matured: for example, she assumes responsibility for her mother after her stroke. By the end of the book, Virgie also reveals herself as the book's most perceptive character. She is even capable of viewing her own past in comprehensive mythic terms, as illustrated by her fascination with the roles that heroes and victims (Medusa and Perseus) play.

Chronology and Setting

The stories are arranged chronologically, covering approximately a forty-year time span:

"Shower of Gold"	Virgie is a baby; Ran and Eugene are young children.
"June Recital"	In the present tense, Loch is a young boy with malaria and Cassie is beginning college. Virgie is the same age as Cassie. Cassie recollects the June piano recitals when she, Virgie, Eugene, and Jinny were children. (Virgie is thirteen at her last recital; Jinny is younger than the others.)

"Sir Rabbit"	In the first part, Mattie Will Sojourner is fifteen; Ran and Eugene are about the same age. In the second, Mattie is somewhat older, described as a "girl-wife not tied down yet" (104).
"Moon Lake"	Loch Morrison, a teenager, is the lifeguard, and Ran is apparently in his twenties. Easter, Nina, and Jinny are pubescent—Easter has "started her breasts" (119).
"The Whole World Knows"	Ran is now about thirty-five; Jinny is twenty-five. Nina and Junior Nesbitt are courting.
"Music from Spain"	Eugene—living in San Francisco—has been married for twelve years and is in his forties.
"The Wanderers"	Eugene has returned to Morgana and died of tuberculosis. Virgie is in her forties; Ran has put on weight and is now the mayor of Morgana; Jinny is in her thirties; Nina is married to Junior and pregnant; Katie Rainey is dead; Snowdie is nearly seventy.

None of the stories can be dated with absolute certainty. However, the events described—from King MacLain's apparent suicide to Katie Rainey's death—span a period of forty years, from the early 1900s to the early 1940s.

Most of the stories take place in a small Mississippi town named Morgana, intended, as Eudora Welty explains, to emphasize "the idea of *fata morgana*, to show that they were living absorbed in illusions" (*Conversations* 214). They reveal the restrictions, the hypocrisy, the petty snobbery associated with small-town life. Although Virgie Rainey demonstrates her talent as a pianist, everyone is convinced that she will never amount to anything, simply because she comes from a relatively poor family. Miss Eckhart, on the other hand, is condemned from the beginning because she is a stranger who doesn't acknowledge the unspoken rules of behavior; "Missie Spights said that if Miss Eckhart had allowed herself to be called by her first name, then she would have been like other ladies. Or if Miss Eckhart had belonged to a church that had ever been heard of . . . Or if she had been married to anybody at all, just the awfullest man . . . " (*The Golden Apples* 66).

In addition to Morgana, the surrounding areas occasionally function as settings. The county seat, MacLain, is important not only as the place where Snowdie and King MacLain grew up, but also as the setting for the last scene in the book. Virgie Rainey stops here briefly after leaving Morgana and notes the cemetery where the MacLains and Miss Eckhart are buried. The wood on the outskirts of Morgana that is owned by Mrs. Lizzie Stark is also important in "Shower of Gold" and "Sir Rabbit." In both cases, it represents a place apart from the community, where there are fewer restraints: in the first story, Snowdie is lured here by her husband and impregnated; in the second, it is where Mattie Will Sojourner has sexual relations with the twins and, later, with their father. Finally, there is Moon Lake: "it was a strange place, Nina thought, unlikely—and three miles from Morgana, Mississippi, all the time" (115). A place suggesting both adventure and danger, this is where the orphan Easter is brought back to life by Loch after she nearly drowns in the lake.

The only story that does not take place in Morgana or its environs is "Music from Spain," which describes Eugene MacLain's life in San Francisco after he leaves Morgana. This story demonstrates that the characters' difficulties are not entirely the result of life in Morgana. Eugene feels no less trapped by his marriage and job than Ran was in "The Whole World Knows."

Theme and Myth

As suggested by the book's title, some of the most important ideas in *The Golden Apples* are highlighted through Welty's use of W. B. Yeats's "The Song of the Wandering Aengus." Cassie, in "June Recital," repeats certain lines while tie-dying her scarf and daydreaming about the past. The poem has such a profound effect on her that she sits up in bed later that night, and, still half-asleep, recites the second line: " 'Because a fire was in my head.' " After she lies down again, she sees in her dreams a "grave, unappeased, and radiant face . . . the face that was in the poem" (97). The face belongs to Aengus, the Celtic god associated with poetry, youth, and beauty, but in the poem he comes to represent all those who give up everything for their dream of great beauty, or love, or art. This longing—never satisfied—can also never be abandoned:

> Though I am old with wandering
> Through hollow lands and hilly lands,
> I will find out where she has gone,
> And kiss her lips and take her hands;
> And walk among long dappled grass,
> And pluck till time and times are done
> The silver apples of the moon,
> The golden apples of the sun.[2]

Yeats's poem gains further significance when we learn that "June Recital" was first published separately as "Golden Apples" in *Harper's Bazaar* (September 1947). In addition, the title of the last story—which brings together virtually the entire cast—is "The Wanderers," and in this story, as Franklin D. Carson notes, we find the only reference given to King MacLain's grandfather: "Didn't he kill a man, or have to, and what would be the long story behind it, the vaunting and the wandering from it?" (*The Golden Apples* 274; Carson's "Wandering Aengus": 16).

While various myths are evoked in *The Golden Apples*, especially the one that Yeats improved upon, myths are never used to give structure to the stories or the book.[3] Loosely employed, they instead serve as analogies to underscore character traits, events, or themes in the stories. For example, as Ruth Vande Kieft makes clear, the most important characters in *The Golden Apples* are "wanderers" of one variety or another:

There are the wanderers who are expressive in action, wild, rebellious, free, over-flowing, self-determining; but they are driven by fierce hungers and yearnings. The characters who serve as their foils appear to be re-actors more than actors. They tend to be passive, helpless, outreaching; their characteristic activity is quietly unobtrusive and inward, for they observe and learn, feel, and wonder. But they have their own kind of power. (98)

Although Vande Kieft avoids using the word "wanderer" to describe characters such as Snowdie MacLain, Cassie Morrison, or Nina Carmichael, I find it appropriate for these characters as well as the more obvious candidates, such as King MacLain, Virgie Rainey, and Ran and Eugene MacLain. Journeys within can be as passionate and as frustrating as those that are external. After all, Virgie Rainey qualifies as a wanderer not simply because she is active and capable of leaving Morgana: as indicated earlier, the most impressive thing about Virgie in "The Wanderers" is her perceptiveness about both the past and the present.

Regardless of whether or not they leave Morgana, the wanderers in *The Golden Apples* often discover that their dreams are unattainable—at least for them. King MacLain spends most of his life trying to escape the restrictions that marriage and small-town life impose: "King MacLain, an old man, had butted like a goat against the wall . . . " (264). By the end of his life, however, King has returned to Morgana to live in spite of the fact that he did not want to come home and frequently mistakes his wife for Nellie Loomis. Although old with wandering, King has sufficient vitality to resist the town's way of looking at things and to thumb his nose, so to speak, at death: "[King] made a hideous face at Virgie, like a silent yell. It was a yell at everything—including death . . . " (257). Still, in spite of the fact that he maintains his integrity when coming home to Morgana, the reader senses that whatever King MacLain sought away from home he never discovered. His dissatisfaction seems to have increased with old age.

King's wife, Snowdie, also appears disappointed with the outcome of her quest. As she tells Virgie in "The Wanderers," Snowdie has spent all of her parents' money searching for King, and when he returns home in his sixties, she doesn't know what to do with him. Miss Eckhart's dreams also prove illusory, except for the flushed pleasure that she experiences every year as her pupils perform at the June recital. Her love for Virgie and Mr. Sissum—the only two people she cares about—continues unrequited. Perhaps the most important of the wanderers, Virgie Rainey does eventually acknowledge that her emotional reaction to Miss Eckhart includes love, but she does not do so until she is in her forties and her teacher is dead. Nevertheless, Miss Eckhart's influence on Virgie is strong enough that it continues to affect her in "The Wanderers," as revealed by Virgie's statements: especially what she says about herself and her decision to leave Morgana, about the interconnectedness of love and hate (or heroes and victims), and about the ability of art to transmute tragedy in order to create beauty. Where Virgie will go and what she will do are less important than her ability "to accumulate and assimilate the dual aspects of her world because she comes to see these dual aspects as parts of a whole" (Pugh 446).

Both the MacLain twins—Ran and Eugene—suffer from dreams that cannot be realized. In "The Whole World Knows," Ran longs for a variety of things, living as he does in a highly subjective dream world that is emphasized through the first-person point of view. Ran longs for a relationship with Jinny that does not involve dishonesty, he longs for Jinny to know what it is like to experience pain, he longs to be free of the guilt that he feels over Maideen Sumrall's suicide, and, most of all, he longs to know himself, which he thinks might be possible if he knew his father first. Our last glimpse of Ran in "The Wanderers" suggests that the improvements in his life are superficial. His marriage still seems impossible even though he and Jinny are back together and have several children. Instead of being a wanderer herself, Jinny seems so self-occupied that she is incapable of being interested in anything beyond herself.[4]

Eugene MacLain's restlessness takes him across the country to San Francisco, but he seems only slightly more successful than Ran in pursuing his dreams. He too feels trapped in a dissatisfactory marriage, which has deteriorated because he and his wife Emma are unable to let go of the grief they feel over their daughter's death. "Music from Spain" describes Eugene's attempt to do exactly this. By attaching himself to a true wanderer who functions as a father figure— a Spaniard whose appetite for life seems both large and well satisfied—Eugene achieves a sense of wholeness that could be described as an epiphany. During these brief moments, Eugene experiences the kind of exhilaration and imaginative sympathy that he needs to renew his life with Emma. Unfortunately, however, he is unable to share the experience when he returns home, partly because of his own inability to communicate and partly because Emma's petty criticism of the Spaniard discourages any intimacy between them.[5]

Loch Morrison is another wanderer who actually leaves Morgana. We hear from Cassie that he lives in New York City and that he likes it there" (261). Given no more information than this, and aware that King and Eugene MacLain returned home dissatisfied, readers may be reluctant to come to conclusions about Loch's life after Morgana. He is, however, one of the most imaginative characters, and one of the few willing to take risks. His point of view alternates with Cassie's in "June Recital," and his subjective way of observing the world is only partially the result of his malaria. Loch's ability to take risks for the sake of adventure is demonstrated in "June Recital" when he picks up the metronome even though he suspects it might be dynamite. His separateness and capacity for heroism are also emphasized in "Moon Lake," where he brings Easter back to life after she nearly drowns. In this story, we are never told what Loch is thinking or feeling, but his musical ability suggests that his imagination is still active: "He played taps for them . . . so beautifully they wept together, whole tentfuls some nights" (113).

Although wandering often proves disappointing, characters such as Virgie Rainey or King MacLain still long for greater passion or adventure. As "The Song of Wandering Aengus" emphasizes, the search itself becomes as important as its goal. Only exceptional wanderers, such as Virgie or W. B. Yeats, realize that the search cannot, finally, be distinguished from the dream.

Imagery

Elaine Upton Pugh provides the most coherent explanation of the sun and moon imagery in *The Golden Apples*, especially as it relates to the end of "The Song of Wandering Aengus."[6] ("And pluck till time and times are done / The silver apples of the moon / The golden apples of the sun.") The set of opposites (silver/golden, sun/moon) represents an Apollonian-Dionysian duality: "sunrise and daylight can . . . be associated with the Nietzschean Apollonian mode of order, decorum, and reason which is set in contrast to the Dionysian mode of chaos, passion, fertility, and intuition" (436). Characters such as Cassie Morrison and Snowdie MacLain are typical of those who operate in the world of daylight or the sun, while Virgie Rainey and the orphan Easter ("Moon Lake") can be identified with the worlds of nighttime and moonlight.

Characters associated with the Dionysian mode repeatedly demonstrate their ability to seize life in spite of the restraints placed upon it in a small town. The most powerful imagery in *The Golden Apples* communicates the immediacy of sensuous experience: images of birds, butterflies, flowers, and, most important of all, ripe fruit. Eugene in "Music from Spain" imagines the musician as "floating bird-like up into the pin-point distance" (203), which prefigures the end of the story where Eugene is swung around in the air by the Spaniard. Hummingbirds are used in "Music from Spain," "June Recital," and "The Wanderers" to describe an epiphanic moment when one is suspended in the air: "as the small aerial wanderers suck sweetness from flowers, so their human counterparts try to suck sweetness from life" (Vande Kieft 120). Butterflies are also used several times to underline a character's intricate beauty as well as her refusal to be pinned down. For example, the butterfly pin that Miss Eckhart gives to Virgie ("made of cut-out silver, like silver lace" [64]) has a broken safety-catch.

The ripeness or overripeness of fruit is used by a variety of characters to emphasize that the moment must be seized or its potential will be wasted. Virgie in particular is associated with figs: her mother sells fig ice cream, Virgie picks figs for Miss Eckhart in exchange for her lessons, and Virgie goes to her music lesson "peeling a ripe fig with her teeth" (41). In "June Recital," Loch perceives the fig tree close to where Snowdie and Miss Eckhart used to live as "a magic tree with golden fruit" (25).[7] Ripe pears are used to mean much the same thing. In "Moon Lake," just as the girls take the leaking boat out for an adventure,

Nina describes her attempt to seize the moment by comparing it to an absolutely ripe pear: "so juicy and tender that to eat one baptized the whole face, and so delicate that while you urgently ate the first half, the second half was already beginning to turn brown" (131). Sensuous pleasure and the capacity to participate actively in life are also evoked by flower imagery, especially the magnolia that Virgie brings to Miss Eckhart that "smelled too sweet and heavy for right after breakfast" (41).

Finally, water imagery is used several times to emphasize that a character is reborn or resurrected. The most important event in "Moon Lake" is Easter's near drowning. She is resuscitated only by Loch's remarkable persistence. Virgie Rainey's new sense of freedom, experienced the night her mother dies, is signaled when she takes off her clothes and bathes by moonlight in the river. Eugene's adventure with the Spaniard also takes him closer and closer to the ocean, and when Eugene is taken up into his arms and swung around in the air, "the sweet and the salt, the alyssum and the sea affected him as a single scent" (223).

CONCLUSION

Far from finding the issue of genre inconsequential, Welty emphasizes the advantages gained from the short story cycle's form: "In *The Golden Apples* they [the parts of the book] exist on their own as short stories; they have independent lives. They don't have to be connected, but I think by being connected there's something additional coming from them as a group with a meaning of its own" (*Conversations* 43).[8] As was the case with *Dubliners, Winesburg, Ohio,* and *The Pastures of Heaven,* the form of *The Golden Apples* reinforces the characters' essential separateness or isolation from one another. The appropriateness of the cycle form for *The Golden Apples* is shown in the final paragraph of the book as Virgie sits under a tree with an old beggar woman who is taking shelter from the rain. The significance of the scene, reminiscent of the end of Joyce's "The Dead,"[9] is cogently explained by Pugh: "The stories in *The Golden Apples,* like Virgie and the old woman, or like Virgie and Cassie, exist 'alone and together.' Taken together, they frame a picture which suggests that history and personality are a composite of contrasting qualities recognized in contrasting but associated images" (450).

Also resembling the conclusions to *Dubliners, Winesburg, Ohio, The Pastures of Heaven,* and *The Unvanquished,* the final story in *The Golden Apples* is used to reverse patterns repeated throughout the book. Virgie is not the first character who leaves Morgana, but she is the first character who departs with an understanding of herself and what she wants. Her perceptiveness suggests that she may fare better than King or Eugene MacLain. "The Wanderers" is also used to bring the large cast of characters together one more time so that readers can observe what they have become or represent. Finally, in addition to its role as summary, the last story is cyclical, forcing us to return to the beginning of the book and see the stories as integrated in a manner that defies chronology. While the initial story ("Shower of Gold") is a first-person narrative by Mrs. Fate (Miss Katie) Rainey, the last story describes her death and funeral. While the first story is preoccupied with the impregnation of Snowdie MacLain, the last focuses on Mrs. Rainey's death and Virgie's rebirth. While Mrs. Lizzie Stark makes the arrangements for the birth of Snowdie's twins in the first story, in the last Snowdie has to prepare Mrs. Rainey's body for the funeral after Mrs. Stark refuses to come. While the first story describes the manner in which King MacLain abandons his family, the last records his eventual return home when he is too old for wandering. The parallels are so abundant that Welty must have written or revised the last story while keeping one eye on "Shower of Gold."[10] More than any other book discussed here in detail, Eudora Welty's *The Golden Apples* illustrates the aptness of the term short story cycle.

NOTES

1. Virgie Rainey is also prominently featured in "June Recital" as Cassie Morrison recollects the piano lessons they took together.

2. *The Poems of W. B. Yeats*. Rev. ed. Ed. Richard J. Finneran. New York: Macmillan, 1983. 59–60.

3. While Aengus remains most important, the stories also allude to two other mythic figures whose quests involve apples. Hercules literally pursues golden apples, since his most difficult task is to obtain the golden apples from the Hesperides; Hippomenes, on the other hand, receives golden apples from Venus, and they enable him to win the race against Atalanta, thereby winning her love.

4. Jinny's narcissism is repeatedly emphasized in *The Golden Apples*. She is the only child in "June Recital" who refuses to give up the flowers that are symbolically presented. She is described as kissing herself in "Moon Lake" (118, 125); and when she waves the towel over Easter, Jinny is more concerned with drawing attention to herself than helping someone who may be dying (148–52). Similarly, in "The Wanderers," Jinny is more concerned with her new diamond ring than with the funeral for Mrs. Rainey (243).

5. The final word about Eugene is delivered in "The Wanderers." Like his father, his last days in Morgana reveal his cynicism (273).

6. Other critics who discuss this imagery include Appel, Carson (" 'The Song of Wandering Aengus' " and "Recurring Metaphors"), Demmin and Curley, McHaney, Morris, Pitavy-Souques ("Technique as Myth"), Skaggs, and Vande Kieft.

7. Characters think about figs or fig trees in most of the stories. For example, at camp in "Moon Lake" Jinny Stark "cried into her pillow for her mother, or perhaps for the figs" (138). In "The Wanderers," just after her mother dies, Virgie Rainey compares flowers on the window to "a jar of figs in syrup held up" (236).

8. Welty has definite ideas concerning generic labels as they are applied to *The Golden Apples*. When doctoral students wrote to her suggesting that the book was a novel, she had no patience with them, responding that "It doesn't matter with a thesis, I guess" (*Conversations* 43).

9. The rain at the end of "The Wanderers" is described as "October rain on Mississippi fields. The rain of fall, maybe on the whole South, for all she knew on the everywhere. She stared into its magnitude" (276).

10. Other less important parallels include the activity of sewing, the preoccupation with "decent" grieving, and the fact that both stories take place in October. Furthermore, the forest in which Snowdie and King rendezvous in "Showers of Gold" is described in "The Wanderers" as partially destroyed by the logging business owned by Mr. Nesbitt, Virgie's boss.

WORKS CITED AND BIBLIOGRAPHY

Appel, Alfred, Jr. "The Wanderers and the Golden Apples." *A Season of Dreams: The Fiction of Eudora Welty*. Baton Rouge: Louisiana State UP, 1965. 205–37.

Arnold, Marilyn. "When Gratitude is No More: Eudora Welty's 'June Recital'. " *SCR* 13.2 (Spring 1981): 62–72.

Blackwell, Louise. "Eudora Welty: Proverbs and Proverbial Phrases in *The Golden Apples.*" *SFQ* 30 (Dec. 1966): 332–41.

Bryant, J. A., Jr. *Eudora Welty*. Minneapolis: U of Minnesota P, 1968.

———. "Seeing Double in *The Golden Apples.*" *SR* 82 (Spring 1974): 300–15.

Carson, Franklin D. "The Passage of Time In Eudora Welty's 'Sir Rabbit.' " *SSF* 12 (Summer 1975): 284–86.

———. "Recurring Metaphors: An Aspect of Unity in *The Golden Apples.*" *NConL* 5 (Sept. 1975): 4–7.

———. " 'The Song of Wandering Aengus': Allusions in Eudora Welty's *The Golden Apples.*" *NMW* 6 (Spring 1973): 14–18.

Corcoran, Neil. "The Face That Was in the Poem: Art and 'Human Truth' in 'June Recital.' " *DeltaES* 5 (1977): 27–34.

Cothran, Dianne Allbritton. "Myth and Eudora Welty's Mississippi: An Analysis of *The Golden Apples.*" Diss. Florida State U, 1982. *DAI* 46 (1985): 151A.

Daniel, Robert. "The World of Eudora Welty." *Southern Renascence: The Literature of the Modern South*. Ed. Louis D. Rubin, Jr., and Robert D. Jacobs. Baltimore: Johns Hopkins UP, 1953. 306–15.

Demmin, Julia L., and Daniel Curley. "Golden Apples and Silver Apples." Prenshaw, *Eudora Welty: Critical Essays*, 242–57. Rpt. in Prenshaw, *Eudora Welty: Thirteen Essays*, 130–45.

Desmond, John F., ed. *A Still Moment: Essays on the Art of Eudora Welty*. Metuchen, NJ: Scarecrow, 1978.

Devlin, Albert J. *Eudora Welty's Chronicle: A Story of Mississippi Life*. Jackson: UP of Mississippi, 1983.

———, ed. *Welty: A Life in Literature*. Jackson: UP of Mississippi, 1987.

Etter, Kathryn. "Genre of Return: The Short Story Volume." Diss. U of Iowa, 1985. *DAI* 47 (1986): 898A.

Evans, Elizabeth. *Eudora Welty*. New York: Ungar, 1981.

Feld, Bernard David, III. "The Short Fiction of Eudora Welty." Diss. Columbia U, 1978. *DAI* 39 (1978): 278A.

Fritz-Piggott, Jill. "The Sword and the Song: Moments of Intensity in *The Golden Apples.*" *SLJ* 18.2 (Spring 1986): 27–39.

Harris, Wendell V. "The Thematic Unity of Welty's *The Golden Apples.*" *TSLL* 6 (Spring 1964): 92–95.

Howard, Zelma Turner. *The Rhetoric of Eudora Welty's Short Stories*. Jackson: UP of Mississippi, 1973.

Isaacs, Neil D. *Eudora Welty*. Southern Writers Series 8. Austin, TX: Steck-Vaughn, 1969.

———. "Four Notes on Eudora Welty." *NMW* 2 (Fall 1969): 42–54.

Jones, William M. "The Plot as Search." *SSF* 5 (Fall 1967): 37–43.

Kerr, Elizabeth M. "The World of Eudora Welty's Women." Prenshaw, *Eudora Welty: Critical Essays*, 132–48.

Kreyling, Michael. "The Way Things Emerge in *The Golden Apples*." *Eudora Welty's Achievement of Order*. Baton Rouge: Louisiana State UP, 1980. 77–105.

McDonald, W. U., Jr. "Eudora Welty Manuscripts: A Supplementary Annotated Finding List." *BB* 31 (1974): 95–98, 126.

    Identifies and describes Welty manuscripts and typescripts added to major collections since 1963.

———. "Textual Variants in the *Collected Stories: The Golden Apples*." *EuWN* 9.2 (Summer 1985): 3–6.

McHaney, Thomas L. "Eudora Welty and the Multitudinous Golden Apples." *MissQ* 26 (Fall 1973): 589–624.

MacKethan, Lucinda H. "To See Things in Their Time: The Act of Focus in Eudora Welty's Fiction." *AL* 50 (May 1978): 258–75.

Manning, Carol S. *With Ears Opening Like Morning Glories: Eudora Welty and the Love of Storytelling*. Westport, CT: Greenwood, 1985.

Mark, Rebecca. "From the 'I' of the Hero to the Eye of the Story: Eudora Welty's Search for the Voice of the Woman Artist in *The Golden Apples*." Diss. Stanford U, 1986. *DAI* 47 (1986): 2159A.

Messerli, Douglas. "Metronome and Music: The Encounter between History and Myth in *The Golden Apples*." Desmond, *A Still Moment*, 82–102.

Moreland, Richard C. "Community and Vision in Eudora Welty." *SoR* ns 18 (Winter 1982): 84–99.

Morris, Harry C. "Zeus and the Golden Apples: Eudora Welty." *Perspective* 5 (Autumn 1952): 190–99.

Neault, D. James. "Time in the Fiction of Eudora Welty." Desmond, *A Still Moment*, 35–50.

Pawlowski, Robert S. "The Process of Observation: *Winesburg, Ohio* and *The Golden Apples*." *University Review* 37 (Summer 1971): 292–98.

Pei, Lowry. "Dreaming the Other in *The Golden Apples*." *MFS* 28.3 (Autumn 1982): 415–33.

Phillips, Robert L., Jr. *An Introduction to Eudora Welty's* The Golden Apples. Jackson: Mississippi Library Commission, 1977.

Pitavy-Souques, Danièle. "A Blazing Butterfly: The Modernity of Eudora Welty." *Miss Q* 39.4 (Fall 1986): 537–60. Rpt. in Devlin, *Life in Literature*, 113–38.

———. "A Structural Approach to Myth in the Fiction of Eudora Welty." Prenshaw, *Eudora Welty: Critical Essays*, 56–67.

———. " 'Shower of Gold' ou les ambiguites de le narration." *DeltaES* 5 (Nov. 1977): 63–81.

———. "Technique as Myth: The Structure of *The Golden Apples*." Prenshaw, *Eudora Welty: Critical Essays*, 258–68. Rpt. in Prenshaw, *Eudora Welty: Thirteen Essays*, 146–56; and in *Eudora Welty*. Ed. Harold Bloom. New York: Chelsea, 1986. 109–18.

————. "Watchers and Watching: Point of View in Welty's 'June Recital.' " Trans. Margaret Tomarchio. *SoR* ns 19.3 (July 1983): 483–509.

Polk, Noel. "A Binding Variant for the English *The Golden Apples*." *EuWN* 10.1 (Winter 1986): 1–2.

————. "Sending Schedule for the Stories in *The Golden Apples*." *EuWN* 8.1 (Winter 1984): 1–3.

Prenshaw, Peggy Whitman, ed. *Eudora Welty: Critical Essays*. Jackson: UP of Mississippi, 1979.

————, ed. *Eudora Welty: Thirteen Essays. Selected from Eudora Welty: Critical Essays*. Jackson: UP of Mississippi, 1983.

Pugh, Elaine Upton. "The Duality of Morgana: The Making of Virgie's Vision, the Vision of *The Golden Apples*." *MFS* 28.3 (Autumn 1982): 435–51.

Rubin, Louis D., Jr. "Art and Artistry in Morgana, Mississippi." *MissR* 4.3 (Summer 1981): 101–16. Rpt. in his *A Gallery of Southerners*. Baton Rouge: Louisiana State UP, 1982. 49–66.

Skaggs, Merrill Maguire. "Morgana's Apples and Pears." Prenshaw, *Eudora Welty: Critical Essays*, 220–41.

Vande Kieft, Ruth M. "The Search for the Golden Apples." *Eudora Welty*. Rev. ed. New York: Twayne, 1987. 87–125.

Welty, Eudora. *Conversations with Eudora Welty*. Ed. Peggy Whitman Prenshaw. Jackson: UP of Mississippi, 1984.

————. *The Eye of the Story: Selected Essays and Reviews*. New York: Random, 1978.

————. *The Golden Apples*. New York: Harcourt, 1949. Quotations are taken from the Harvest paperback.

————. *One Writer's Beginnings*. Cambridge, Mass.: Harvard UP, 1984.

Westling, Louise. *Sacred Groves and Ravaged Gardens: The Fiction of Eudora Welty, Carson McCullers, and Flannery O'Connor*. Athens: U of Georgia P, 1985.

Yaeger, Patricia S. " 'Because a Fire Was in My Head': Eudora Welty and the Dialogic Imagination." *PMLA 99.5 (Oct. 1984): 955–73. Rpt. in MissQ* 39.4 (Fall 1986): 561–86; and in Devlin, *Life In Literature*, 139–67.

————. "The Case of the Dangling Signifier: Phallic Imagery in Eudora Welty's 'Moon River.' " *TCL* 28.4 (Winter 1982): 431–52.

8

Flannery O'Connor's *Everything That Rises Must Converge*

INTRODUCTION TO UNIFYING FORMS

After examining her manuscripts at Georgia College, Stuart L. Burns concludes that Flannery O'Connor "was best able to exercise her particular talents through the medium of the short story or the short story cycle" ("How Wide" 26). Throughout her life, this preference for stories is demonstrated. Her first sustained work of fiction, her M.F.A. thesis at the State University of Iowa, consisted of a group of related stories, and two of her most important books—*A Good Man Is Hard to Find and Other Stories* (1955) and *Everything That Rises Must Converge* (1965)—are cycles in which stories are connected by a growing awareness that one's sense of superiority must be transcended in order to gain essential knowledge about oneself and one's position in the world. Even O'Connor's novels, *Wise Blood* (1952) and *The Violent Bear It Away* (1960), are largely based on short stories, many of them published separately elsewhere.

Everything That Rises Must Converge contains Flannery O'Connor's last stories, and because she was working on the book at the time of her death, some critics have suggested that it does not accurately represent O'Connor's intentions or that her intentions were never fully realized. This does not seem to be the case. The last entries included in *Letters of Flannery O'Connor: The Habit of Being* make it clear that the writer wished to include all of the nine stories in *Everything That Rises* and that she controlled the basic order in which they appear.[1]

UNITY IN *EVERYTHING THAT RISES MUST CONVERGE*

Character

Parent-Child Relations

All of the stories in *Everything That Rises* describe strained relationships between different generations, usually parents and children. Furthermore, in most of these families a conflict develops between characters who represent traditional Southern orthodoxy (or the dying aristocracy) and those considered liberal "do-gooders." Three of the first four stories contrast sons who believe themselves to be more sensitive or intellectual than their philistine mothers. Additionally, in each of these first three stories, the adult child presents enlightened views, especially on the question of race and class, while the mother is entrenched in what her son considers archaic values and prejudices.

For example, Julian in "Everything That Rises Must Converge" despairs because his mother, living in much reduced circumstances, still assumes an air of superiority toward blacks. Asbury in "The Enduring Chill" feels permanently tainted by his mother's bourgeois complacency and, like Julian, he makes a show of his tolerance toward the blacks who work in his mother's dairy. Wesley, one of the two sons in "Greenleaf," is described as "thin and nervous and bald and being an intellectual was a terrible strain on his disposition" (34). Although frustrated by his mother's practical, down-to-earth nature and her materialism, each of these sons is completely dependent—financially and emotionally—on the central role that the mother plays in his life.

"The Comforts of Home" follows this same pattern in that Thomas is dependent on a mother whom he severely criticizes, but the story differs from the earlier tales in one major way: the son—not the mother—is conservative in his social thinking. Insisting that his mother must turn out the young woman (Star Drake) whose parole she has arranged, Thomas resembles his dead father more closely than he imagines: "The old man would have . . . pulled the necessary strings with his crony, the sheriff, and the girl would have been packed off to the state penitentiary . . . " (121).

Only two of the stories—the third and the sixth—focus on the relationship between parents and young children. "A View of the Woods" presents three generations of the same family but concentrates primarily on the grandfather, Mr. Fortune, and the granddaughter who he thinks resembles him exactly. Here, as in the stories that surround it ("Greenleaf " and "The Enduring Chill"), the older generation is described as materialistic and insensitive. Throughout the story Mr. Fortune's granddaughter opposes his determination to sell the land that serves as the family's front yard to Tilman so that he can use it for "a combination country store, filling station, scrap metal dump, used-car lot and dance hall" (67). As Forrest L. Ingram stresses, the story is linked also to "Greenleaf," because both Mr. Fortune and Mrs. May "are finally frustrated in their attempt to control the future of their land and of the people who live on it" ("Seven-Story Cycle" 26).

The only other story featuring a young child is "The Lame Shall Enter First." This one, like the story that directly precedes it ("The Comforts of Home"), contains a socially aware parent. There are, however, big differences between the genuine compassion that Thomas's mother feels for Star Drake and Sheppard's trendy liberalism, which only serves to gratify his ego. Sheppard helps Rufus Johnson because he believes that attention paid to Rufus will produce larger dividends than time wasted on his own son, Norton, whom he considers spoiled and dull. Although Thomas's mother and Sheppard may bear a superficial resemblance when first introduced, it soon becomes clear that they are motivated for different reasons. It also becomes clear that while O'Connor may poke fun at a do-gooder who brings boxes of candy to people in jail because it is the "nice" thing to do, the writer judges harshly only those characters who demonstrate an inability to transcend their own egos: those who cannot move beyond themselves and their own needs. This is true of both parents and grown children, of so-called conservatives and liberals.

Apart from "A View of the Woods," there are two other stories containing daughters—"Judgement Day" and "Revelation." The father-daughter relationship in "Judgement Day," the last story in the book, echoes the mother-son relationships in "Everything That Rises" and "The Enduring Chill." The daughter, who has moved up to New York City from Georgia, assumes an air of liberalism toward blacks; however, as we soon learn, her live-and-let-live attitude demonstrates practical rather than ethical considerations. Warning her father, she insists, "I don't want any trouble with niggers, you hear me? If you have to live next to them, just you mind your business and they'll mind theirs" (261). It is also the daughter's insensitive, exceedingly practical nature that refuses Tanner's final request to be buried at home in Georgia.

The single story dealing with a mother-daughter relationship is "Revelation," the seventh story and the one originally designated to end the book. The daughter here closely resembles many of the other adult children in the sense that she is a sullen intellectual and treats her mother condescendingly. Mary Grace—ironically named, as are many of the major characters—resents her mother's attempts to make her grateful for all that she has done for her. And, most of all, she despises her mother's and Mrs. Turpin's self-satisfaction and air of superiority, especially when it is directed toward blacks and poor whites. Because Mrs. Turpin represents the same negative qualities that the mother possesses—and she displays them more freely—it is Mrs. Turpin who is attacked by Mary Grace in the doctor's office.

"Parker's Back" is the only story that does not include an explicit parent-child relationship. In the story, however, the protagonist, O. E. Parker, assumes an almost childlike apprehensiveness around his authoritarian wife, who beats him at the end of the story and leaves him "crying like a baby" (244). The wife, Sarah Ruth, also demonstrates in exaggerated form the insensitivity and the self-righteousness that a variety of other characters in the book exhibit. She is a religious bigot, rejecting any form of worship that includes an icon.

To summarize, then, the characters in *Everything That Rises* display similar personality traits: self-righteousness or condescension, egoism or insularity, and a sense of inadequacy or dependency that is concealed by their attempts to dominate others.

If the characters in the book resemble one another—or are said to bear a family resemblance—there are good reasons why this is the case. As Burns has argued successfully, much of *Everything That Rises* is prefigured in a novel that O'Connor started but never finished entitled "The Heathen":

The *extent* to which O'Connor created her stories out of unmalleable novel-material has not perhaps been appreciated. Perusal of "The Heathen" indicates that the extent was considerable. In fact, of the last ten stories O'Connor wrote, one, "The Enduring Chill," was extracted almost verbatim from the projected novel; another, "Parker's Back," clearly had its genesis in the novel; a third, "Judgement Day," contains a sizable extract from the novel; and most of the rest manifest some relationship to that work. ("How Wide" 30–31; also see Marian Burns)

The characters in *Everything That Rises*, Burns explains, are the direct literary descendants of several characters in the novel. For example, Julian Chestny, Asbury Fox, and Thomas ("Comforts of Home") are described as the "grandchildren, so to speak" (31) of Walter Tilman, the novel's young protagonist. Tilman's mother, as one would expect, is said to function as the prototype for Mrs. Chestny, Mrs. Fox, and Thomas's mother.

There are, no doubt, other reasons for the strong resemblances that O'Connor's characters share. Since she wished to concentrate on relationships that are sufficiently intense and volatile that they lead to violence, it is not surprising that she focuses on family conflicts involving parents and children. It is also appropriate that she chooses almost exclusively to discuss relationships between a widowed parent and his or her children. In families containing a single parent, the relationship between the parent and child can be extremely close and, at least in some cases, encourage greater dependency than might be the case with two parents. Additionally, the tensions that exist between the generations in *Everything That Rises* are exacerbated by the fact that grown children such as Julian and Thomas continue to live with their mother and allow her to support them.[2]

Doubling[3]

Similarities between characters are also emphasized within individual stories. First of all, an important relationship (such as Julian's with his mother) is often emphasized by comparing it with another less important one (for example, the black woman with the young boy on the bus). In that first story, both sons seem to flirt with the possibility of exchanging mothers, and the overall purpose of the parallel relationships is to emphasize Julian's dependency on his own mother. In the next story, "Greenleaf," Mrs. May's two grown sons (Wesley and Scofield) are constantly compared to the Greenleafs' twins (O. T. and E. T.), who are considerably more enterprising. This comparison serves to undercut Mrs. May's ideas about social hierarchy: in spite of the fact that she considers Mr. and Mrs. Greenleaf white trash, their grandchildren will attend convent schools and end up in "society" (33), while she shudders to contemplate what sort of grandchildren she might have.

Furthermore, in several stories a parent's relationship with a child is illuminated when it is compared with another relationship that either the parent or the child has. For example, Sheppard's criminal neglect of Norton in "The Lame Shall Enter First" is stressed by his eagerness to help Rufus, and Mary Grace's feelings for her mother in "Revelation" are acted out when the daughter attacks Mrs. Turpin, someone who identifies closely with her mother and possesses her negative qualities. Similarly, Thomas's covert plotting with Farebrother, the local sheriff, says a great deal about Thomas and the extent to which he has been influenced by his own father without being aware of it. The two father figures emphasize manipulative and cruel aspects of Thomas's personality that he refuses to acknowledge.

Finally, in other stories, characters often have a look-alike or someone who seems to resemble them. In these cases, as with the parallel relationships described above, the purpose of the double is to reveal certain truths: to force characters such as Mrs. Chestny, Mr. Fortune, and Thomas to see themselves as they are. For example, in "Everything That Rises" Julian Chestny correctly assesses the significance of the resemblance his mother bears to the black woman on the bus: " 'That was the whole colored race which will no longer take your condescending pennies. That was your black double' " (21).

Although doubles sometimes appear to be exact replicas, more often they are "presented as the *alter ego* of another, the embodiment of qualities suppressed or ignored by the first, a mirror image or inverse reflection" (Asals's "The Double": 50). Mr. Fortune and his granddaughter Mary Fortune Pitts are the best example. Initially in the story, Fortune believes that Mary is "thoroughly of his clay" (58), and they are described as resembling each other physically. Eventually, however, as Mary opposes his desire to sell family land to amass wealth and perpetuate his name, Fortune must acknowledge that she is part Pitts, powerless and long-suffering. Mary comes to represent aspects of the Pittses— and even of Fortune himself—that he has refused to acknowledge.

Other stories contain doubles that function in similar ways as alter egos. In "Comforts of Home," Thomas (meaning twin) and Star Drake seem so entirely different that they represent polar opposites. Star is a self-proclaimed nymphomaniac whom Thomas's mother has befriended; Thomas is a president of the local historical society who prizes above all the chaste domestic comfort his mother provides. Before very long, however, the reader understands why Thomas finds Star so threatening. She represents the sexuality he has repressed. Additional instances of characters who have doubles serving as alter egos include Mrs. Turpin (Mary Grace) in "Revelation" and Tanner (Coleman) in "Judgement Day."

Plot

Conflict that Leads to Violence

The stories in *Everything That Rises* are further unified because the plots in the individual stories resemble one another: the conflicts that the characters experience often lead to violence. Furthermore, it is frequently the protagonist's self-centeredness, self-righteousness, or intolerance that triggers the violence.

In "Everything That Rises," the black woman punches Mrs. Chestny only after the white woman has treated her condescendingly. This act of violence is immediately followed by another when Julian brutalizes his mother verbally: " 'You got exactly what you deserved,' he said, 'Now get up' " (20). Mrs. May also comes to a violent end in "Greenleaf." Her resentment of her shiftless sons and dissatisfaction with the Greenleafs is dramatized when she demands that Mr. Greenleaf kill his sons' bull. The violence that she directs against the Greenleafs changes course, however, and the bull charges her, piercing her heart with his horn. In "A View of the Woods," the conflict involves the sale of the front lawn and Mr. Fortune's refusal to see that his granddaughter represents his own capacity for failure and submission. Denying that he resembles the Pittses, Mr. Fortune strangles Mary, a struggle that brings on his own apparently fatal heart attack.

With the exception of the fourth story, "The Enduring Chill," all the other stories contain conflicts that trigger similar violent exchanges. Thomas's desire to get rid of Star Drake impels him to plant his gun in her purse; when the young woman discovers what he has done, she lunges at his throat and Thomas accidentally shoots his mother, who has moved in order to protect Star. In the next story, "The Lame Shall Enter First," Rufus Johnson commits a series of violent acts to demonstrate that Sheppard is not his Savior. More disturbing is the suicide of Sheppard's son Norton, who hangs himself in a desperate attempt to regain his mother's love.

The violence in "Revelation" is as unexpected as Norton's suicide. Mary Grace throws her college textbook at Mrs. Turpin and then proceeds to try to strangle her. Although she has said little before this point, Mary Grace's growing hostility has been revealed by her facial expressions as the two women carry on their self-congratulatory conversation. Parker in "Parker's Back" is the victim of violence twice in rapid succession. After just barely escaping death when his tractor turns over and explodes, he is subjected to a torrent of verbal and physical abuse when his wife accuses him of getting a new tattoo that is idolatrous. Finally, in the last story, "Judgement Day," Tanner is attacked twice by the black actor who lives in the same apartment building and whom Tanner insists on calling "preacher."[4]

The Possibility of Enlightenment

Conflict and violence are important in *Everything That Rises* because they lead toward the possibility of enlightenment. As suggested above, most of the stories follow the same pattern:

• The protagonist is convinced that he or she is superior (spiritually, intellectually, socially) to others.

• This air of superiority causes conflicts that trigger violence.

• The violent encounter is a potentially humbling experience, and if it is survived, then there is the possibility that self-knowledge may result.

As Flannery O'Connor explains in *Mystery and Manners*: "I have found that violence is strangely capable of returning my characters to reality and preparing them to accept their moment of grace. Their heads are so hard that almost nothing else will do the work" (112).

Since everything in the stories is geared toward the possibility of enlightenment or *anagnorisis*, Flannery O'Connor's handling of this part of the stories warrants more discussion. This is especially true since readers do not always interpret the ends of the stories in the same way. Additionally, analysis of the movement toward enlightenment demonstrates the importance of the way the stories are ordered in *Everything That Rises*: the characters become progressively more capable of vision.

In the first stories O'Connor seems to tease the reader with the possibility of enlightenment. Characters move in the direction of epiphany but fall short of the final destination. At the end of "Everything That Rises," Julian is at the brink of discovery, but he is too overwhelmed by his mother's condition to grasp what has happened. After she becomes disoriented and collapses on the pavement, Julian runs to find help. Although he heads toward "a cluster of lights," the lights seem to "drift" further and further away: "The tide of darkness seemed to sweep him back to her, *postponing from moment to moment his entry into the world of guilt and sorrow*" (23; emphasis mine).

Mrs. May's situation in "Greenleaf" is described more ambiguously. She too is given virtually no time to appreciate her situation; before she can comprehend what is happening, the bull has attacked her and she is dying. There is not even time for the expression on her face to change (52). At the very end of the story, two statements (both descriptions of Mrs. May) puzzle some readers. The first underlines Mrs. May's failure of vision: "she had the look of a person whose sight has been suddenly restored but who finds the light unbearable" (52). The second emphasizes the same point but does so ironically. The final view we have of Mrs. May is an unreliable one from Mr. Greenleaf's point of view: "she seemed, when Mr. Greenleaf reached her, to be bent over whispering some last discovery into the animal's ear" (53).

"A View of the Woods" ends with Mr. Fortune's refusal to admit what he knows must be the case: that he, like Mary Fortune, is part Pitts. After killing his granddaughter in his crazed attempt to deny what she represents, Mr. Fortune (like the first protagonists) is given little time for reflection. The heart attack that rapidly follows gives him only seconds to observe the natural symbols that tower over him: "he saw that the gaunt trees had thickened into mysterious dark files that were marching across the water and away into the distance" (81). The mystery—perceived even by the Pittses—entirely eludes Mr. Fortune.

The character Asbury in "The Enduring Chill' is more perceptive when it comes to interpreting symbols. As a result, this story takes us almost to the point of epiphany, although it stops just before the exact moment in which we are led to believe it will take place. In it, the last image that we receive of Asbury is that of him acknowledging the descent of the Holy Ghost:

The old life in him was exhausted. He awaited the coming of new. . . . The fierce bird which through the years of his childhood and the days of his illness had been poised over his head, waiting mysteriously, appeared all at once to be in motion. Asbury blanched and the last film of illusion was torn . . . from his eyes. He saw that for the rest of his days, frail, racked, but enduring, he would live in the face of a purifying terror. (114)

The story represents a significant progression. In all of the previous ones, the protagonists have been too overwhelmed or too willful to learn from their experiences.

In "Comforts of Home," the struggle for the gun and the accidental shooting of Thomas's mother all happen so quickly that there is not time for *anagnorisis*. Since the story ends only seconds after Thomas has shot his mother, the only character who experiences an epiphany is the sheriff. In what amounts to a parody of the moment of enlightenment, the sheriff mistakenly believes that he can at a glance understand this psychologically complex *ménage à trois*: "He saw the facts as if they were already in print: the fellow had intended all along to kill his mother and pin it on the girl" (141). Like Mr. Fortune, Thomas destroys all that he values when he attempts to deny a part of his personality that he wishes to repress.

In the next three stories, characters demonstrate progressively greater understanding as a result of the violence they experience. Sheppard in "The Lame Shall Enter First" recognizes that "he had stuffed his own emptiness with good works like a glutton. He had ignored his own child to feed his vision of himself" (190). Mrs. Turpin ("Revelation") is also forced to see herself clearly. Unlike many other protagonists, Mrs. Turpin survives her violent experience and reflects upon it in the tranquility of her modern "pig-parlor" (198). Although at first angry, scowling and grunting, Ruby Turpin is eventually silenced by a vision in which she is forced to recognize that God does not condone her method of classifying people according to race, the amount of property they own, or whether or not they have sunny dispositions. At the very end of the story, O'Connor takes pains to emphasize that Ruby's vision will have a lasting impression. Although the visual images begin to "fade," their effect on her remains vivid: "In the woods around her the invisible cricket choruses had struck up, but what she heard were the voices of the souls climbing upward into the starry field and shouting hallelujah" (218). "Revelation" seems to follow logically after "The Enduring Chill" and "The Lame Shall Enter First," the former ending in limited insight and pointing toward a more substantial religious experience and the latter ending just at the moment Sheppard is able to see himself for the first time.

"Parker's Back" also describes a vision that seems to have an enduring influence over a protagonist. At the same time it shows the altered behavior that can result from such a traumatic experience. O. E. Parker not only perceives that the eyes of the Byzantine Christ tattooed on his back are ''eyes to be obeyed'' (241), but he also demonstrates that his entire life is transformed after he is ''reborn.'' This is the only story that moves beyond the moment of vision and describes the difficulties resulting from one's submission to Christ. After perceiving himself changed—''It was as if he were himself but a stranger to himself, driving into a new country though everything he saw was familiar to him'' (241)—Parker is rejected and abused by his wife, who is convinced that only idolaters seek God's presence in the physical world.

O'Connor in *Everything That Rises* establishes a rhythmic pattern: the failure of or incapacity for vision in the first stories is followed by a group of stories in which most of the protagonists are able to move beyond their egos and, as a result, see more clearly. The pattern is in no way mechanical, as demonstrated by the inclusion of ''The Comforts of Home'' in the middle of stories containing epiphanies. O'Connor repeatedly demonstrates the difficulty of achieving vision. As she said herself, it is hard to jolt us out of our habitual self-complacency. Although I would not argue that each of the stories in *Everything That Rises* is logically ordered, there does seem to be a definite progression. This progression is completed by the last story, ''Judgement Day.'' Consideration of final things, including the moment of judgment, logically follows the spiritual development traced in the rest of the book. Like Julian's mother in ''Everything That Rises'' and Mr. Fortune in ''A View of the Woods,'' Tanner is too old and fragile and narrow-minded to change. Although he never experiences the kind of self-understanding achieved by Asbury, Sheppard, or Ruby Turpin, Tanner does express a kind of longing for home which is sufficiently broad that it includes a desire for death and resurrection.

This final story is a complex one that necessitates further discussion.[5] Although he does not transcend his sense of superiority toward blacks, Tanner demonstrates that belief in God and in the Resurrection can lead the sinner toward salvation in spite of his failure to comprehend fully his sins—much less make his confession.[6] The black man's violence against Tanner is deplorable, but it does represent a kind of justice given Tanner's history of racism. Therefore, the end of the story includes a final judgment and an act of penance, even though Tanner does not consciously confess his sins or perform penance. While his daughter may not take ''morbid stuff, death and hell and judgement'' (258) seriously, Tanner does. And although he realizes that he will never get home to Georgia alive, he forces himself to begin the journey, convinced he is ''on [his] way home'' (269). Tanner achieves a kind of grace—including eventual burial in Corinth, Georgia—entirely on the basis of belief.

Imagery

Imagery is generally used in the same way from story to story. As illustrated below, the cumulative effect of various image patterns can be powerful in *Everything That Rises*.

Imagery Evoking the Moment of Epiphany

Most important is the imagery associated with the moment of epiphany. Repeatedly, sun imagery—often involving a sun setting or rising directly above a dark wood—heralds the possibility that a character may perceive spiritual realities within this world. Although he does not take into account the significance of the woods, a subject that few critics have commented upon, Stuart Burns provides the best general introduction to the subject of sun imagery in Flannery O'Connor's fiction.

As Burns notes, the only stories in *Everything That Rises* that do not contain sun imagery are "The Comforts of Home" and "Judgement Day," stories that do not culminate in epiphany. In the other stories the presence of the sun invariably introduces the possibility of epiphany. In "Greenleaf," for example, just moments before Mrs. May is attacked by the bull she is made dizzy by the intense "red-hot sun" (51). And, as Burns emphasizes, the sun itself becomes identified with the bull, a symbol of both pagan fertility and Christ: "The sun, a scrub bull and a silver bullet combine to dramatize the divine agency of Christ in this story" (161).

When describing how the sun imagery works in *Everything That Rises*, I must stress that it introduces the *possibility* of epiphany. As mentioned before, many of O'Connor's characters are unwilling or unable to see. Just as we are never told what—if any—vision Mrs. May experiences at the end of the first story, sun imagery is also used in "A View of the Woods" and in the beginning of "The Enduring Chill" to emphasize opportunities for vision that go unrealized. As Mr. Fortune tries to understand why his family opposes his decision to sell their "front yard," he looks out over the land, focusing on the sun setting just beyond the woods: "The old man stared for some time . . . held there in the midst of an uncomfortable mystery that he had not apprehended before. He saw it, in his hallucination, as if someone were wounded behind the woods and the trees were bathed in blood" (71). He never recognizes the significance of what he glimpses, however, for at that moment the sound of Pitts's truck brings him back into the world of buying and selling.

An equally fleeting and undecipherable moment is perceived at the beginning of "The Enduring Chill." As Asbury returns home, he is greeted by a sunrise ("a startling white-gold sun") that awakens him and, ultimately, disappoints him:

[The sun] cast a strange light over the single block of one-story brick and wooden shacks. Asbury felt that he was about to witness a majestic transformation, that the flat of roofs might at any moment turn into the mounting turrets of some exotic temple for a god he didn't know. The illusion lasted only a moment before his attention was drawn back to his mother. (82)

Since Asbury is unwilling to move beyond his own stunted imagination—just as he is unwilling to see any priest other than the one who grips his imagination—he is not, at this point in the story, susceptible to any truths beyond himself.

Elsewhere in *Everything That Rises* sun imagery triggers or introduces epiphanies. At the end of "The Enduring Chill," Asbury's movement toward vision is initiated both by his submissiveness and the sunset he sees from his bedroom window: "A blinding red-gold sun moved serenely from under a purple cloud" (114). Similarly, in both "Revelation" and "Parker's Back," sunsets and sunrises are described vividly, and they mark the moment when the protagonist becomes aware of some inescapable truth.

In "Parker's Back," "Revelation," "A View of the Woods," and "Greenleaf," the sun imagery works in conjunction with images of trees or of the woods. Generally, as is clearly the case in "A View of the Woods," the distant forest is perceived as a place of mystery. From the woods the bull appears in "Greenleaf"; with a final view of the trees around the lake ("mysterious dark files" [81]), Mr. Fortune dies in "Greenleaf"; and from the woods Mrs. Turpin hears choruses of hallelujah. Ultimately, the woods represent a borderline or the point that connects both the material world and the spiritual realities that the characters find so frightening. Both Asbury and Mrs. May perceive the woods as the final defense against potentially overwhelming experiences. As the narrator in "The Enduring Chill" explains, "Below [the sunset] the treeline was black against the crimson sky. It formed a brittle wall, standing as if it were the frail defense he had set up in his mind to protect him from what was coming" (114).

Imagery Emphasizing the Character's Solipsism

Several related images are used to stress the characters' inability to transcend their own egos. Julian in "Everything That Rises," for example, is described several times as retreating into an inner compartment or mental bubble: "Behind the newspaper Julian was withdrawing into the inner compartment of his mind where he spent most of his time. This was a kind of mental bubble in which he established himself when he could not bear to be a part of what was going on around him" (11). Similarly, Julian escapes from everyday humiliations by returning imaginatively to the ancestral house that his family used to own: "He retired again into the high-ceilinged room sparsely settled with large pieces of antique furniture" (14).

CONCLUSION

Everything That Rises is tightly unified in ways typical of O'Connor's fiction. Because of her preoccupation with parent-child relations, with doubling, and with plot patterns that advance the protagonist to the point of revelation, many of the stories in the book resemble one another. In fact, it is only a slight exaggeration to say that one encounters the same basic parent-child relationship and plot in each story. Conflict leads to violence, which introduces the possibility of enlightenment. The differences among the stories involve this question of enlightenment: some characters are too brutalized by the violence to be capable of vision; some are too set in their ways to see things anew; still others glimpse some truth about themselves and their situations at the last moment.

After witnessing a series of characters who fail to achieve any kind of vision, the reader is given several examples of protagonists who recognize their own weaknesses and transcend their egos. The last of these stories is "Parker's Back."[7] In it, O'Connor features a character who not only acknowledges his limitations but who is also profoundly transformed when he submits his will to Christ's. The last story in the book, "Judgement Day," reverses the kind of progression experienced in the other stories. Tanner never gains insight into his relationship with Coleman and his own bigotry; nevertheless, the story represents an advance over the entire book in other ways. Its central preoccupation is with "last things": death, final judgment, penance, and the possibility of damnation or salvation. Through this story, written during the last months of her life, O'Connor stresses that faith is as important as the recognition and confession of sins.[8]

All of the last three stories—"Revelation," "Parker's Back," and "Judgement Day"—describe characters who develop spiritually. Collectively, they provide what Flannery O'Connor must have considered an optimistic conclusion to *Everything That Rises*. "Revelation" describes a vision that will have a lasting effect on Mrs. Turpin, destroying her illusion that God favors her over other people. "Parker's Back" reveals the difficulty that Parker's commitment to Christ involves. While his life may seem to be hell on earth, he is one of the few protagonists actually capable of vision and able to transform himself as a result. Finally, "Judgement Day" emphasizes the power of belief, through which Tanner achieves a kind of grace in spite of his inability to perceive his own flawed nature.

NOTES

1. There are only two exceptions. First, from the letters in *The Habit of Being*, it is not clear which of the two final stories O'Connor intended to use to end the book. Second, as Westarp explains in detail, *Everything That Rises* does not include O'Connor's last-minute revisions in "Judgement Day."

2. O'Connor's preoccupation with parent-child relations also results from the fact that this was the kind of relationship she observed most closely. She was compelled as an adult to return home and, for the last thirteen years of her life, be cared for by her widowed mother.

3. Asals's discussion of doubles in *Everything That Rises* is excellent and has strongly influenced my work. See "The Double" and *Imagination of Extremity*.

4. Tolomeo argues that O'Connor shifts the placement of the violent, consciousness-raising scenes in the last three stories in *Everything That Rises*. While these scenes typically occur near the end of the earlier stories, they are shifted to an earlier position in "Revelation," "Parker's Back," and "Judgement Day."

5. The following critics represent divergent views concerning "Judgement Day": Feeley (*Voice of the Peacock*), Getz (*Nature and Grace*), May, and Wood. The major

issue involved in the controversy is whether or not Tanner enjoys a relationship of equality with Coleman and, thus, achieves a kind of "convergence."

6. Although Tanner is no worse than other characters in the story, one has to remember that his close relationship with Coleman is based on their mutual recognition of the white's superiority. It is Tanner who sleeps in the bed while Coleman lies at the foot of the bed on a pallet. As the narrator tells us, Tanner can never quite confront the fact that Coleman is his equal or double: "[Tanner] had an instant's sensation of seeing before him a negative image of himself, as if clownishness and captivity had been their common lot. The vision failed him before he could decipher it" (255).

7. "Parker's Back" is one of the last two stories Flannery O'Connor wrote and one that pleased her immensely. (See the letters written in July 1964 in *The Habit of Being*.)

8. "Judgement Day" is a substantial reworking of "The Geranium," the title story from O'Connor's M.F.A. thesis.

WORKS CITED AND BIBLIOGRAPHY

Asals, Frederick. "The Double in Flannery O'Connor's Stories." *FCB* 9 (Autumn 1980): 49–86.

———. "Flannery O'Connor's 'The Lame Shall Enter First'. " *MissQ* 23 (1970): 103–20.

———. *Flannery O'Connor: The Imagination of Extremity*. Athens: U of Georgia P, 1982. The section devoted to "The Double" is rpt. in *Flannery O'Connor*. Ed. Harold Bloom. New York: Chelsea, 1986. 93–109.

———. "The Mythic Dimensions of Flannery O'Connor's 'Greenleaf.' " *SSF* 5 (Summer 1968): 317–30.

Ashley, Jack Dillard. "Throwing the Big Book: The Narrator Voice in Flannery O'Connor's Stories." Westarp and Gretlund 73–81.

Blasingham, Mary V. "Archetypes of the Child and of Childhood in the Fiction of Flannery O'Connor." Westarp and Gretlund 102–12.

Bleikasten, André. "Writing on the Flesh: Tattoos and Taboos in 'Parker's Back.' " *SLJ* 14.2 (Spring 1982): 8–18.

Browning, Preston, Jr. *"Everything That Rises Must Converge."* *Flannery O'Connor*. Carbondale: Southern Illinois UP, 1974. 99–131.

———. " 'Parker's Back': Flannery O'Connor's Iconography of Salvation by Profanity." *SSF* 6 (Fall 1969): 525–35.

Burke, John J., Jr. "Convergence of Flannery O'Connor and Chardin." *Renascence* 19 (1966): 41–47, 52.

Burns, Dan G. "Flannery O'Connor's 'Parker's Back': The Key to the End." *NConL* 17.2 (Mar. 1987): 11–12.

Burns, Marian. "The Chronology of Flannery O'Connor's 'Why Do the Heathen Rage?' " *FCB* 11 (Autumn 1982): 58–75.

———. "O'Connor's Unfinished Novel." *FCB* 11 (Autumn 1982): 76–93. Rpt. in Friedman and Clark 169–80.

Burns, Stuart L. "How Wide Did 'The Heathen' Range?" *FCB* 4 (Autumn 1975): 25–41.

———. " 'Torn by the Lord's Eye': Flannery O'Connor's Use of Sun Imagery." *TCL* 13 (Oct. 1967): 154–66.

Cash, Jean W. "O'Connor on 'Revelation': The Story of a Story." *ELN* 24.3 (Mar. 1987): 61–67.

Casper, Leonard. "The Unspeakable Peacock: Apocalypse in Flannery O'Connor." *The Shaken Realist: Essays in Modern Literature in Honor of Frederick J. Hoffman*. Ed. Melvin J. Friedman and John B. Vickery. Baton Rouge: Louisiana State UP, 1970. 287–99.

Coulthard, A. R. "Flannery O'Connor's 'A View of the Woods': A View of the Worst." *NConL* 17.1 (Jan. 1987): 7–9.

Denham, Robert D. "The World of Guilt and Sorrow: Flannery O'Connor's 'Everything That Rises Must Converge.' " *FCB* 4 (Autumn 1975): 42–51.

Desmond, John F. "The Lessons of History: Flannery O'Connor's *Everything That Rises Must Converge*." *FCB* 1 (1972): 39–45.

———. *Risen Sons: Flannery O'Connor's Vision of History*. Athens: U of Georgia P, 1987.

Driggers, Stephen G. "The Catalog of the Flannery O'Connor Manuscripts at Georgia College." *FCB* 14 (1985): 59–61.

Driskell, Leon. " 'Parker's Back' vs. 'The Partridge Festival': Flannery O'Connor's Critical Choice." *GaR* 21.4 (Winter 1967): 476–90.

Driskell, Leon V., and Joan T. Brittain. *The Eternal Crossroads: The Art of Flannery O'Connor*. Lexington: UP of Kentucky, 1971.

Dunleavy, Janet Egleson. "A Particular History: Black and White in Flannery O'Connor's Short Fiction." Friedman and Clark 186–202.

Dunn, Robert J. "The Manuscripts of Flannery O'Connor at Georgia College." *FCB* 5 (Autumn 1976): 61–69.

Ebrecht, Ann. " 'The Length, Breadth, and Depth of the World in Movement': The Evolutionary Vision of Flannery O'Connor and Teilhard de Chardin." Westarp and Gretlund 208–16.

Eggenschwiler, David. *The Christian Humanism of Flannery O'Connor*. Detroit: Wayne State UP, 1972.

Farnham, James F. "Further Evidence for the Sources of 'Parker's Back.' " *FCB* 12 (Autumn 1983): 114–16.

Feeley, Kathleen. *Flannery O'Connor: Voice of the Peacock*. New Brunswick, NJ: Rutgers UP, 1972.

———. "Thematic Imagery in the Fiction of Flannery O'Connor." *SHR* 3.1 (Winter 1968): 14–32.

Fitzgerald, Robert. Introduction. *Everything That Rises Must Converge*. By Flannery O'Connor. New York: Farrar, 1965. vii–xxxiv.

Folks, Jeffrey J. "The Mechanical in *Everything That Rises Must Converge*." *SLJ* 18.2 (Spring 1986): 14–26.

Friedman, Melvin, J., and Beverly Lyon Clark, eds. *Critical Essays on Flannery O'Connor*. Boston: Hall, 1985.

Friedman, Melvin J., and Lewis A. Lawson, eds. *The Added Dimension: The Art and Mind of Flannery O'Connor*. 2nd ed. New York: Fordham UP, 1977.

Garson, Helen S. "Cold Comfort: Parents and Children in the Work of Flannery O'Connor." Westarp and Gretlund 113–22.

Gentry, Marshall Bruce. *Flannery O'Connor's Religion of the Grotesque*. Jackson: UP of Mississippi, 1986.

———. "Narration and the Grotesque in Flannery O'Connor's Stories." Westarp and Gretlund 82–91.

Getz, Lorine M. *Flannery O'Connor: Her Life, Library, and Book Reviews*. New York: Mellen, 1980.

———. *Nature and Grace in Flannery O'Connor's Fiction*. Vol. 2 of Studies in Art and Religious Interpretation. New York: Mellen, 1982.

Grimshaw, James A., Jr. *The Flannery O'Connor Companion*. Westport, CT: Greenwood, 1981.

Hendin, Josephine. "The Enduring Conflict: Parents and Children in *Everything That Rises Must Converge*." *The World of Flannery O'Connor*. Bloomington: Indiana UP, 1970. 97–130.

Howell, Elmo. "The Developing Art of Flannery O'Connor." *ArQ* 29 (Autumn 1973): 266–76.

Humphries, Jefferson. "Art, Delusion, Disease, and Reality: The Apotheosis of Asbury Fox in 'The Enduring Chill.' " *The Otherness Within: Gnostic Readings in Marcel Proust, Flannery O'Connor, and François Villon*. Baton Rouge: Louisiana State UP, 1983. 112–40.

Hyman, Stanley Edgar. *Flannery O'Connor*. U of Minnesota Pamphlets on American Writers 54. Minneapolis: U of Minnesota P, 1966.

Ingram, Forrest L. "American Short Story Cycles: Foreign Influences and Parallels." *Proceedings of the Comparative Literature Symposium, Vol. V: Modern American Fiction. Insights and Foreign Lights*. Ed. Wolodymyr T. Zyla and Wendell M. Aycock. Lubbock: Texas Tech P, 1972. 19–37.

———. "O'Connor's Seven-Story Cycle." *FCB* 2 (1973): 19–28.

———. *Representative Short Story Cycles of the Twentieth Century: Studies in a Literary Genre*. The Hague: Mouton, 1971.

Kessler, Edward. *Flannery O'Connor and the Language of Apocalypse*. Princeton: Princeton UP, 1986.

Kinney, Arthur F. *Flannery O'Connor's Library: Resources of Being*. Athens: U of Georgia P, 1985.

Logan, Jan H. "Flannery O'Connor and Flaubert: A French Connection." *NConL*. 13.5 (Nov. 1983): 2–5.

Lorch, Thomas M. "Flannery O'Connor: Christian Allegorist." *Crit* 10.2 (1968): 69–80.

McDermott, John V. "Julian's Journey into Hell: Flannery O'Connor's Allegory of Pride." *MissQ* 28 (Spring 1975): 171–79.

McFarland, Dorothy Tuck. *"Everything That Rises Must Converge." Flannery O'Connor*. New York: Ungar, 1976. 43–71.

Magistrale, Tony. "An Explication of Flannery O'Connor's Short Story 'A View of the Woods.' " *NConL* 17.1 (Jan. 1987): 6–7.

Maida, Patricia D. " 'Convergence' in Flannery O'Connor's 'Everything That Rises Must Converge.' " *SSF* 7.4 (Fall 1970): 549–55.

Marston, Jane. "Epistemology and the Solipsistic Consciousness in Flannery O'Connor's 'Greenleaf.' " *SSF* 21.4 (Fall 1984): 375–82.

Martin, Carter W. "The Genesis of O'Connor's 'The Partridge Festival.' " *FCB* 10 (Autumn 1981): 46–53. (O'Connor briefly considered including "The Partridge Festival" in *Everything That Rises* but chose "Judgement Day" instead.)

————. *The True Country: Themes in the Fiction of Flannery O'Connor*. Nashville: Vanderbilt UP, 1969.

May, John R. *The Pruning Word: The Parables of Flannery O'Connor*. Notre Dame, IN: U of Notre Dame P, 1976.

Montgomery, Marion. "O'Connor and Teilhard de Chardin: The Problem of Evil." *Renascence* 22 (Autumn 1969): 34–42.

————. "On Flannery O'Connor's 'Everything That Rises Must Converge.' " *Crit* 13 (1971): 15–29.

————. *Why Flannery O'Connor Stayed Home*. LaSalle, IL: Sherwood Sugden, 1981.

Muller, Gilbert H. *Nightmares and Visions: Flannery O'Connor and the Catholic Grotesque*. Athens: U of Georgia P, 1972.

Napier, James J. "Flannery O'Connor's Last Three: 'The Sense of an Ending.' " *SLJ* 14.2 (Spring 1982): 19–27.

————. "In 'Parker's Back': A Technical Slip by Flannery O'Connor." *NConL* 11.4 (Sept. 1981): 5–6.

Oates, Joyce Carol. "The Visionary Art of Flannery O'Connor." *SHR* 7.3 (Summer 1973): 235–46.

O'Connor, Flannery. *Everything That Rises Must Converge*. New York: Farrar, 1965.

————. *Letters of Flannery O'Connor: The Habit of Being*. Ed. Sally Fitzgerald. New York: Farrar, 1979.

————. *Mystery and Manners: Occasional Prose*. Ed. Sally Fitzgerald and Robert Fitzgerald. New York: Farrar, 1969.

————. *The Presence of Grace and Other Book Reviews*. Ed. Carter W. Martin. Athens: U of Georgia P, 1983.

Orvell, Miles. *Invisible Parade: The Fiction of Flannery O'Connor*. Philadelphia: Temple UP, 1972.

Ryan, Steven T. "The Three Realms of O'Connor's 'Greenleaf.' " *C&L* 29.1 (1979): 39–51.

Schleifer, Ronald. "Rural Gothic: The Stories of Flannery O'Connor." *MFS* 28.3 (1982): 475–85. Rpt. in Friedman and Clark 158–68.

Scouten, Kenneth. " 'The Partridge Festival': Manuscript Revisions." *FCB* 15 (1986): 35–41. (O'Connor briefly considered including "The Partridge Festival" in *Everything That Rises* but chose "Judgement Day" instead.)

Sederberg, Nancy B. "Flannery O'Connor's Spiritual Landscape: A Dual Sense of Nothing." *FCB* 12 (Autumn 1983): 17–34.

Shields, John C. "Flannery O'Connor's 'Greenleaf' and the Myth of Europa and the Bull." *SSF* 18.4 (Fall 1981): 421–31.

Shloss, Carol. "Epiphany." *Flannery O'Connor's Dark Comedies: The Limits of Inference*. Baton Rouge: Louisiana State UP, 1980. 102–23. Rpt. in *Flannery O'Connor*. Ed. Harold Bloom. New York: Chelsea, 1986. 65–80.

Sullivan, Walter. "Flannery O'Connor, Sin, and Grace: *Everything That Rises Must Converge*." *The Sounder Few: Essays from the Hollins Critic*. Ed. R. H. W. Dillard, George Garrett, and John Rees Moore. Athens: U of Georgia P, 1971. 101–19.

Tedford, Barbara Wilkie. "Flannery O'Connor and the Social Classes." *SLJ* 13.2 (Spring 1981): 27–40.

Tolomeo, Diane. "Home to Her True Country: The Final Trilogy of Flannery O'Connor." *SSF* 17 (1980): 335–41.

Vande Kieft, Ruth M. "Judgment in the Fiction of Flannery O'Connor." *SR* 76 (1968): 337–56.

Walters, Dorothy. *Flannery O'Connor*. New York: Twayne, 1973.

Werner, Craig Hansen. "Dublin(er)'s Joyce: Ernest Gaines, Flannery O'Connor, Russell Banks." *Paradoxical Resolutions: American Fiction since James Joyce*. Urbana: U of Illinois P, 1982. 34–50.

Westarp, Karl-Heinz. "Flannery O'Connor's Development: An Analysis of the Judgement-Day Material." Westarp and Gretlund 46–54.

———. " 'Judgement Day': The Published Text versus O'Connor's Final Version." *FCB* 11 (Autumn 1982): 108–22.

———. " 'Parker's Back': A Curious Crux Concerning Its Sources." *FCB* 11 (Autumn 1982): 1–9.

———. "Teilhard de Chardin's Impact on Flannery O'Connor: A Reading of 'Parker's Back.' " *FCB* 12 (Autumn 1983): 93–113.

Westarp, Karl-Heinz, and Jan Nordby Gretlund, eds. *Realist of Distances: Flannery O'Connor Revisited*. Aarhus, Denmark: Aarhus UP, 1987.

Westling, Louise. *Sacred Groves and Ravaged Gardens: The Fiction of Eudora Welty, Carson McCullers, and Flannery O'Connor*. Athens: U of Georgia P, 1985.

Winn, Harlan Harbour, III. "Short Story Cycles of Hemingway, Steinbeck, Faulkner, and O'Connor." Diss. U of Oregon, 1975. *DAI* 36 (1976): 4500A.

Wood, Ralph C. "From Fashionable Tolerance to Unfashionable Redemption: A Reading of Flannery O'Connor's First and Last Stories." *FCB* 7 (Autumn 1978): 10–25.

Wray, Virginia Field, "Flannery O'Connor in the American Romance Tradition." Diss. U of South Carolina, 1979. *DAI* 40 (1979): 1475A.

———. "Flannery O'Connor's Master's Thesis: Looking for Some Gestures." *FCB* 8 (Autumn 1979): 68–76. (The title story—"The Geranium"—is an early version of "Judgement Day.")

9

John Updike's
Too Far to Go: The Maples Stories

INTRODUCTION TO UNIFYING FORMS

John Updike published his first story about Richard and Joan Maple, ''Snowing in Greenwich Village,'' in 1956, and it was not until 1963 that he wrote the next story explicitly devoted to them. *Too Far to Go: The Maples Stories* evolved in much the same way as other story cycles by Updike: many of the episodes describing the Maples' marriage were first published in magazines and in other collections of Updike short stories.[1] Only gradually did the Maples require a book of their own, one which would preserve in some detail the integrity and complexity of that relationship.

Updike's interest in the form of the short story cycle has been demonstrated on a number of occasions. His stories about childhood and adolescence, most of which take place in a town resembling Updike's own hometown, Shillington, Pennsylvania, are collected in *Olinger Stories: A Selection* (1964). Two more recent cycles—*Bech: A Book* (1970) and *Bech is Back* (1982)—trace the wanderings of Henry Bech, a Jewish writer who is based in Manhattan but who travels all over the world as a cultural ambassador.[2] Furthermore, in his most recent volume of stories, *Trust Me* (1987), Updike attempts to connect the narratives by the twin topics, trust and betrayal.

ANALYSIS OF UNIFYING FORMS

The stories in *Too Far to Go*, as already indicated, are primarily unified by Richard and Joan Maple. As a result, many of the recurring elements—character, plot, imagery, theme—are used to chronicle the development of their relationship.

Character and Plot

The Maples' Marriage

The Maples' marriage functions as the book's protagonist as well as its major plot pattern. As the stories are ordered, Joan and Richard move closer and closer to separation and divorce, but potential flaws in the marriage are evident even in the first story, "Snowing in Greenwich Village," where Richard becomes flustered when their guest, Rebecca Cune, flirts with him. Years later, now living in the suburbs of Boston, Joan and Richard Maple find their marriage threatened in more serious ways. "Wife-wooing" describes the ways in which children and family life complicate sex and romance. In subsequent stories, infidelities and jealousies prove more damaging, especially since they necessitate elaborate lies. Even attempts at distancing themselves from one another—including celibacy—prove unsuccessful in "Twin Beds in Rome," "Sublimating," and "Nakedness."

The divorce itself does not come until the last story, and in many ways it does not end or close off the relationship. The marriage between Richard and Joan is terminated, but their connections with one another are not severed. Richard himself realizes, at the end of "Gesturing," that Joan "would never stop gesturing within him, never; though a decree come between them, even death . . . " (231). Just as Richard kisses Joan after their divorce decree is announced in court, the book itself celebrates a relationship at the point when it seems least successful. As Updike says of the Maples in his introduction to the book, "That a marriage ends is less than ideal; but all things end under heaven, and if temporality is held to be invalidating, then nothing real succeeds" (10).

Although events are told in the stories largely from Richard's frame of reference (third-person limited omniscient),[3] this does not prevent Updike from stressing the importance of both partners. In fact, this is one way in which *Too Far to Go* differs from any of the other books discussed at length here. In the Maples stories, it is a relationship—not a single protagonist or several families or a community—that demands and sustains the reader's attention. Although we are given considerably less access to Joan's thoughts than to Richard's, the narrator frequently moves beyond Richard's perceptions in his attempt to render events more objectively.

Children and Lovers

In addition to the marriage itself, various characters who influence the marriage appear in more than one story. Of these, the children are most important, and they appear or are mentioned in all of the stories except the one that takes place before they are born, "Snowing in Greenwich Village," and the one describing a vacation taken away from them, "Twin Beds in Rome." Apart from Richard and Joan, their children are the only characters in the book who are allowed to develop. The book repeatedly chronicles the amount of time that the Maples have been married and the ages of their children: for example, in the second story ("Wife-wooing"), they have been married for seven years and have three small children; in the next ("Giving Blood"), the marriage is nine years old; in the fifth ("Marching Through Boston"), twelve years have passed and there are four children.

More important, Updike is careful to provide indications of how the children change during this twenty-year period. Take the eldest, Judith, as an example. Her qualities—she is independent, straightforward, social-minded—are brought into sharper focus as she grows older. Additionally, in a series of stories, Richard expresses amazement at the process whereby she becomes an adolescent and then a woman (115, 126, 173, 183, 196–97). Similarly, Dickie Jr.'s and Judith's close relationship develops as it is described through several stories. The reader notices Dickie's resentment as Judith gradually outgrows him. Furthermore, Dickie's sensitivity and his tendency to function as the family conscience are stressed in both "Sublimating" and "Separating."

Considerably less protective of the Maples' marriage, a series of lovers are interwoven in the pattern of the stories. Seen with the greatest frequency are Ruth, the woman whom Richard wants to marry at the end of the book, and Eleanor and Mack Dennis. Ruth actually appears in only one story, "Gesturing," after Richard has moved by himself to Boston, but her presence is felt in most of the stories after "The Red-Herring Theory." For example, although her name is never mentioned, Ruth is clearly the major impediment to a reconciliation between Joan and Richard: "His skull cupped a secret, a white face, a face both frightened and soothing, both strange and known . . . which he felt all around him, solid as the sunlight" (195–96).

Eleanor and Mack Dennis appear or are mentioned in most of the stories, and they are also instrumental in the breakdown of the marriage. Eleanor is introduced in "The Taste of Metal," newly separated from her husband and eagerly initiating an affair with Richard. In the next story, "Your Lover Just Called," which occurs an indefinite amount of time later, Mack Dennis is installed in the local motel while Eleanor vacations in Wyoming awaiting their divorce. Although the cause and effect relationship between the two stories is never precisely defined, the stories work as companion pieces. Since the first story ends with Richard and Eleanor necking in the wrecked car as Joan is sent to get the police, the reader finds it difficult to take Richard's indignation seriously when he catches Mack kissing Joan in "Your Lover Just Called." After this point, the Dennises are replaced by other lovers, but the Maples never completely lose sight of them. For example, while dining with a new romantic possibility in "Eros Rampant," Richard spies Eleanor across the room with "a real thug" (132) and, later in the same story, accuses Joan of still seeing Mack.

Several other peripheral characters appear in more than one story, such as Joan's psychiatrist and Marlene Brossman, one of the women with whom Richard flirts at parties. Nevertheless, of the characters who influence the Maples' marriage, it is only the children who become more than flat characters. And even they are glimpsed at odd moments, occupying the center of the stage only in "Separating," the story in which Richard and Joan tell their children that they are going to live apart. The spotlight is almost exclusively on the husband and wife: others appear only as they throw light on that relationship.

Chronology

In addition to the fact that the stories are placed in rough chronological order, they are obviously connected by their time frame, covering the mid-fifties to the couple's divorce in 1976. "Wife-wooing" describes somewhat ironically the cozy domesticity of the fifties; "Marching through Boston" (first published in *The New Yorker* in 1966) emphasizes Joan's commitment to the civil rights movement and her desire for greater independence from Richard; all of the stories following "Marching" reveal the sense of greater sexual freedom that both Joan and Richard experience during the sixties and seventies. The Maples stories are more concerned with individual lives than with social or political history; nevertheless, references to various social trends help us understand how their relationship develops.

Setting

The stories are connected to some extent because they take place in the same New England town, unnamed but a commuting distance from Boston. With the exception of "Snowing in Greenwich Village," "Twin Beds in Rome," and "Nakedness," they all include descriptions of what life is like in a fashionable suburb for the middle class and wealthy. These details are often of secondary or incidental importance, but they do add up. Although readers never learn what Richard does to earn a living, it is clear that the Maples live in comfort: for example, Joan's part-time job at a museum is not taken out of financial necessity. There is also money for their own tennis court, for summer cottages on the beach, for Richard's convertible and Joan's new Volvo, for spur-of-the-moment trips to Rome, and, finally, for a separation and two different households. The time that they devote to leisure is best emphasized by the role parties and entertaining play in their lives.

Although the reader quickly understands the kind of life that the Maples enjoy, the town itself or the geographical area is never used symbolically, as is Winesburg in *Winesburg, Ohio*, Morgana, Mississippi, in *The Golden Apples*, or Olinger, Pennsylvania, in Updike's *Olinger: A Selection*. Richard makes a few snide comments about Joan's puritanical nature, but there is no sustained commentary on New England. Updike uses the town simply to locate the Maples socially and economically. In fact, apart from the Maples' house and yard, it is difficult to visualize the town.

Recurring Imagery and Other Motifs

Domestic Imagery

While the community in which the Maples live has limited significance, the description of their domestic life at home is extremely important. Their apartment or house, their yard, even their plumbing—all of these say a great deal about their relationship.

In the first story, "Snowing in Greenwich Village," there are repeated references to the places where people live. Married only a year and a half, the Maples have just moved to a new apartment, their first large enough to justify unpacking the wedding presents. Because of their shyness and awkwardness, it is also clear that they are just beginning to entertain and to present themselves socially as a couple. At the end of the story, Richard walks their visitor, Rebecca Cune, home, and we are also given a glimpse of her efficiency apartment. Richard's way of looking at the room reveals the sexual tension that exists between him and Rebecca: "Richard perceived, on his right, an unexpected area created where . . . a double bed was placed. Tightly bounded on three sides, the bed had the appearance not so much of a piece of furniture as of a permanently installed, blanketed platform" (26). Richard's attraction to Rebecca foreshadows his future unfaithfulness to Joan.

"Snowing in Greenwich Village" also includes descriptions of other places where all three characters have lived in the past. Given Rebecca's flirtatious nature, it is not surprising to learn that she used to live in an apartment with a couple who eventually separated, the boyfriend marrying someone else. We also hear about the log cabin that was the Maples' home for the first three months of their marriage. Rebecca even describes her uncle's house, made entirely out of metal because of his fear of fire. As unwittingly revealed, the characters are preoccupied with their need for a home.

The significance of the home is equally important in later stories, including "Eros Rampant," "Plumbing," "Separating," and "Gesturing." In the first, Richard learns that Joan has followed his example and has had extramarital affairs. He is initially disoriented by this discovery, and the final scene in the story juxtaposes his worst fears concerning Joan with the everyday reality that surrounds him. After waking from a nightmare that exaggerates the extent of Joan's unfaithfulness, he is reassured by the domestic contentedness to which their kitchen testifies (143).

In "Plumbing," the story that follows "Eros Rampant," the narrator (presumably Richard) reflects on the house they have just left. These thoughts lead to recollections of the house in which he grew up, and, eventually, to consideration of his own children's lives. Contemplation of these houses forces the narrator to remember, with some objectivity, moments from the past, especially inadequacies in himself and his wife that must have proven painful for the children: "Our house, in her [Bean, the youngest child], did surely possess the

dimension of dread that imprints every surface on the memory, that makes each
scar on the paint a clue to some terrible depth'' (152).

In this story, as its title suggests, the significance of the household imagery
extends even to the plumbing. At times Updike uses the metaphor to underscore
the temporary nature of human life: ''All around us, we are outlasted'' (154)—
not only by the natural world but also by our plumbing. Other times he concentrates on the complexity of his new house's plumbing system, about which
he and most home owners know nothing, in order to emphasize our imperfect
understanding of ourselves and our pasts: ''We think we have bought living
space and a view when in truth we have bought a maze, a history, an archaeology
of pipes and cut-ins and traps and valves'' (145). Throughout the story, the
speaker excavates the past as his plumber examines his pipes.

In ''Sublimating'' and ''Separating,'' the domestic imagery stresses Richard's
need to protect and to maintain access to his family at the same time that he is
in the process of abandoning or of moving away from them. In ''Separating,''
he worries about the foundation of their clay tennis court and replaces a lock on
the screened porch. In ''Sublimation,'' Richard's violent pruning of the rare
Japanese yews is, at least in part, an attempt to release pent-up frustration
resulting from Joan and Richard's self-imposed celibacy, a last-ditch effort to
make the marriage work. It is not incidental, however, that the yews block the
family's front door; as Richard says, '' 'It was them or me. I couldn't get in
my own front door' '' (171). Pruning the yews to the point that they are no more
than stumps, Richard unconsciously expresses his fear that he will be denied
entrance to what has been his family's house, a fear that is expressed in many
of Updike's stories about separation and divorce.

In ''Gesturing,'' Richard establishes another home for himself during his
separation from Joan. Here the apartment itself and the domestic routines associated with it—shopping for food, cooking dinner, doing the laundry—signify
Richard's attempt to maintain his equilibrium in spite of the fact that he is riddled
with guilt and sadness: ''Each hour had to be scheduled lest he fall through. He
moved like a waterbug, like a skipping stone, upon the glassy tense surface of
his new life'' (222). His apartment's best feature is the view it offers of the John
Hancock building: ''When the conversation finally ended, . . . he had to go lean
his vision against his inanimate, giant friend. . . . It spoke to him, as the gaze
of a dumb beast speaks, of beauty and suffering, of a simplicity that must perish,
of time'' (224). Most important, the building can only reflect what it sees, since
its windows are made out of glass. ''A companion of sorts'' (220), the Hancock
building places few demands on him, allowing him to spend his days in reflection.
The new apartment and the view that it offers emphasize his need to retreat
temporarily from relationships. His escape, however, is not complete. Previous
occupants of the apartment have cut with a diamond their initials, the date, and
the words ''With this ring / I thee wed'' (224) into one of the panes in his
window, thereby partially obscuring the view and forcing him to acknowledge
that Joan ''would never stop gesturing within him, never'' (231).

Although not all of the stories are equally preoccupied with household imagery, many employ domestic images that occasionally comment on the Maples. For example, twin beds are used in both "Giving Blood" and "Twin Beds in Rome," the third and fourth stories, to suggest the distance that exists between Joan and Richard. In "Your Lover Just Called," Richard looks into his own house from a distance, gaining an entirely new perspective on his family, especially since he sees Joan in the kitchen embracing Mack Dennis. In "Waiting Up," the house in which his lover lives—and where Joan has been summoned—is used to explain Richard's attraction to women other than his wife: "The house that had swallowed his wife was one where he had always felt comfortable and welcome, a house much like his own, yet different enough in every detail to be exciting . . . " (116–17).

Repeatedly, in story after story, Updike uses the simplest domestic details to evoke the woes that are in marriage. Consequently, not only does the house or household function as an especially apt metaphor for the relationship, but the reader is also given a vivid sense of the relationship as it existed during crucial moments.

The Journey Metaphor

Too Far to Go, the book's title, introduces another centrally important metaphor. Repeatedly, the marriage is described in terms of a journey, which may in fact be "too far" or too painful to undertake.

The first mention of the journey metaphor occurs in "Twin Beds in Rome." Even though there is also much traveling in this story—not only to Rome, but also the circuitous trip from the airport to their hotel in Rome—Updike is primarily interested in journeys that are interior:

"Where are we going?" He honestly wanted to know, honestly hoped she could tell him.

"Back to the ways things were?"

"No. I don't want to go back to that. I feel *we've come very far* and have only a little way more to go." (61; emphasis mine)

Although the "little way more to go" suggests how close they are to separation or divorce, the end of the story demonstrates that their route is not a direct one; their progress is complicated with much backtracking. Seeing how relaxed and happy Joan has become during their last days together in Rome, Richard, "jealous of her happiness, . . . again grew reluctant to leave her" (72).

In subsequent stories it becomes clear that the Maples—both separately and collectively—will continue on their journeys beyond the point of separation and divorce. In "Divorcing: A Fragment," Richard is confronted with Joan's suicidal depression after they have separated. His reaction is to continue on his separate path regardless of his desire to go with Joan: "His happiness and health seemed negligible, compared to the consecrated unhappiness they had shared. Yet there was no way out, no way but a numb marching forward . . . " (234).

The last use of the journey motif includes the suggestion that the Maples have finally arrived somewhere together. The title of the story, "Here Come the Maples," is taken from the wording of the joint affidavit they file in order to receive a no-fault divorce: " 'Now come Richard F. and Joan R. Maple and swear under the penalties of perjury that an irretrievable breakdown of the marriage exists' " (236). To Richard, the phrasing "conjured up a vision of himself and Joan breezing into a party" (236). While the journey myth is evoked in only a few stories, it is used to suggest the couple's confusion about the direction their lives have taken, their disillusionment and disorientation when separated, and their unexpected closeness achieved at the point of divorce.

The Motifs of Bleeding, Giving Blood, and Childbirth

Blood is mentioned frequently in the Maples stories, and it is generally used to signify the extent to which Joan and Richard are bound by flesh and blood even if they choose to separate or divorce.[4] The point is made explicitly by Richard at the end of "Gesturing": [Richard] saw through [Joan's] words to what she was saying—that these lovers, however we love them, are not us, are not sacred as reality is sacred. We are reality. We have made children" (231). Even in one of the earliest stories, "Wife-wooing," the narrator (presumably Richard) expresses awe that his wife (Joan) can be the mother of three children and still appear virginal: "Who would have thought, blood once spilled, that no barrier would be broken, that you would be each time healed into a virgin again" (33).

Blood is also associated with marriage and children in "Giving Blood." Lying in twin beds positioned at right angles, the Maples are connected only by Richard's imaginative sense that "his blood and Joan's merged on the floor, and together their spirits glided from crack to crack, from star to star on the ceiling" (48). Although not developed at length, the motifs of bleeding, giving blood, and childbirth are used together to reinforce a central theme: the Maples are irrevocably bound to one another because of their children.

The Motif of Illness

As Updike says in his general introduction to the book, one of the Maples (especially Richard) is frequently unwell. These recurring minor illnesses appear, at least in part, psychosomatic and are used to comment on the characters and their relationship.

This is best demonstrated by "Twin Beds in Rome," where Richard understands the connection between his stomach pains and his failing marriage. When Joan asks if the chestnuts he ate for breakfast are the source of his problem, he replies, " 'No. It's just, I think, being here, so far from anywhere, with you, and not knowing . . . why' " (68). Richard's illnesses are also occasionally devices to ensure Joan's undivided attention or to get his own way ("Marching Through Boston"). Colds are featured in "Snowing in Greenwich Village" and "Your Lover Just Called" and are used to underscore the extent to which one can become isolated within a marriage. In both stories, the spouse without the cold becomes preoccupied with another romantic partner.

CONCLUSION

Patterns such as those I have described—the setting, chronological order, recurring characters—do much to create a unified effect. Nevertheless, Updike's *Too Far to Go* seems more casually ordered than the other cycles discussed in earlier chapters. Perhaps the best example is the book's imagery. Although his symbolic use of domestic images is extensive and highly effective in evoking the Maples' relationship, other patterns—such as the motif of blood, glass imagery, even the extended metaphor of the journey, upon which the title is based—seem underdeveloped. The point is emphasized when readers remember the more coherent (and more complex) imagery in cycles such as *Dubliners*, *In Our Time*, *Go Down, Moses*, or *The Golden Apples*.

Part of the explanation, no doubt, is that Updike does not tend to rework his stories after deciding to include them in cycles.[5] Furthermore, and of greater significance, there is no evidence that he wrote any of the stories, except perhaps the Bech stories, with the intention of publishing them together. Therefore, Updike's composition method differs markedly from those employed by all of the other writers I have discussed earlier. If *Too Far to Go* lacks some of the unity that cycles such as *Dubliners* and *The Golden Apples* contain, one should still keep in mind that the Maples stories are tightly unified by their chronological account of the Maples' marriage and that there is much to be gained from reading them together. Updike must have sensed this by 1972, because his *Museums and Women and Other Stories* is divided into three sections; and in the third, under the heading "The Maples," he included "Marching Through Boston," "The Taste of Metal," "Your Lover Just Called," "Eros Rampant," and "Sublimating."[6]

As emphasized repeatedly in this chapter, it is Joan and Richard Maple that provide the strong connections among the stories. In spite of the fact that the narrator in two stories is never named (the first person in "Wife-wooing" and "Plumbing"), he closely resembles Richard elsewhere in the book. In fact, both members of the couple seem to be essentially the same from story to story; while the characters develop, their personalities, their styles of speaking ("darley," "sweetie"), their most important preoccupations remain the same. As Updike says, identifying one of the book's major themes, "People are incorrigibly themselves" (10).

Ultimately, it is the relationship between Richard and Joan Maple that most impresses, especially its vigor and their intelligent appreciation of one another at the point of divorce. An extremely perceptive critic of even his own work, John Updike best summarizes the overwhelming importance of their relationship in his preface to *Too Far to Go*: "A tribe segregated in a valley develops an accent, then a dialect, and then a language all its own; so does a couple. Let this collection preserve one particular dead tongue, no easier to parse than Latin'' (10). Never neglecting the anguish or even the boredom that it produces, Updike celebrates the marriage of Joan and Richard Maple in *Too Far to Go* because of its enduring quality.

NOTES

1. Updike's short story collection *The Same Door* (1959) included "Snowing in Greenwich Village"; *Pigeon Feathers* (1962), "Wife-wooing"; *The Music School* (1966), "Giving Blood" and "Twin Beds in Rome"; *Museums and Women* (1972), "Plumbing," "Marching through Boston," "The Taste of Metal," "Your Lover Just Called," "Eros Rampant," and "Sublimating." (Part III of *Museums and Women* is entitled "The Maples.")

2. Henry Bech was recently seen in the 20 April 1987 issue of *The New Yorker*. Perhaps readers can look forward to a trilogy of Bech stories.

3. There are two exceptions. The contemplative stories ("Wife-wooing" and "Plumbing") are told in the first person, presumably by Richard Maple.

4. It is not surprising to learn in the final story that Richard first courted Joan when she was hospitalized for platelet deficiency, an illness that made her unable to stop bleeding.

5. As Updike says in his introduction to his cycle *Olinger Stories: A Selection*: "I have let the inconsistencies stand in these stories. Each started from scratch. Grand Avenue here is the Alton Pike there. In 'Pigeon Feathers' the grandfather is dead, in 'Flight' the grandmother." He lets the stories stand as originally written because it "does not do to dote" (viii–ix).

6. The stories in Part III of *Museums and Women and Other Stories* are arranged in exactly the same order in which they will appear in *Too Far to Go*. Interestingly enough, though, Updike places "Plumbing" in the first section, indicating that he did not at this time consider it to be about the Maples.

WORKS CITED AND BIBLIOGRAPHY

Barnes, Jane. "John Updike: A Literary Spider." *VQR* 57.1 (Winter 1981): 79–98. Rpt. in *John Updike*. Ed. Harold Bloom. New York: Chelsea, 1987. 111–25.

Detweiler, Robert. "*Too Far to Go*: Getting There." *John Updike*. Rev. ed. Boston: Twayne, 1984. 166–71.

Greiner, Donald J. *The Other John Updike: Poems/Short Stories/Prose/Play*. Athens: Ohio UP, 1981.
   Although *Too Far to Go* is not included, many of the stories are discussed.

Hamilton, Alice, and Kenneth Hamilton. "Married Love: Introducing the Maples" and "The Sovereign State of Marriage." *The Elements of John Updike*. Grand Rapids: Eerdmans, 1970. 50–61, 62–77.

Theroux, Paul. "A Marriage of Mixed Blessings." Rev. of *Too Far to Go*, by John Updike. *NYTBR*. 8 Apr. 1979: 7. Rpt. in *Critical Essays on John Updike*. Ed. William R. Macnaughton. Boston: Hall, 1982. 86–88.

Updike, John. *Too Far to Go: The Maples Stories*. New York: Fawcett Crest, 1979.

Wilhelm, Albert E. "Narrative Continuity in Updike's *Too Far to Go*." *JSSE* 7 (Autumn 1986): 87–90.

————. "Rebecca Cune: Updike's Wedge between the Maples." *NMAL* 7.2 (Fall 1983): Item 9.

————. "Three Versions of Updike's 'Snowing in Greenwich Village.' " *AN&Q* 22 (Jan.-Feb. 1984): 80–82.

PART II

The Twentieth-Century Short Story Cycle: An Annotated Listing

Twentieth-Century Short Story Cycles

Adler, Renata. *Speedboat*. New York: Random, 1976.

    All of the stories are told in the first person by a woman in her mid-thirties who has been a political speechwriter, a visiting professor at a branch of City University of New York, and a reporter for a tabloid. Instead of developing characters, plots, or even scenes, the stories (through the narrator) comment on life among the intellectually elite in New York. Each story consists of a series of vignettes, often only a paragraph long. These vignettes are loosely connected as they develop a central topic: for example, the struggle for survival in a brownstone ("Brownstones") or the various literal and figurative ways in which people isolate themselves and their kind ("Islands").

Anderson, Jessica. *Stories from the Warm Zone and Sydney Stories*. New York: Viking, 1987.

    The book contains two series of stories: the first set in Brisbane; the second in Sydney. The first group ("from the Warm Zone") is told from Beatrice's point of view as she grows from childhood into adolescence. The second group, featuring different characters, is less well unified and describes adult domestic lives.

Anderson, Sherwood. *Winesburg, Ohio*. Rev. ed. New York: Viking, 1960. (First pub. in 1919)

    Major unifying devices include the Winesburg setting and the protagonist, George Willard. Although most stories feature a different protagonist, the characters resemble one another because of their inability to connect. Another important unifying device is the narrator, who creates a sense of community among the characters. (See chapter on *Winesburg*.)

————. *Death in the Woods and Other Stories*. New York: Liveright, 1933.

    All of the stories focus on male-female relations, and five of them demonstrate the effect a woman's death has on a male character. There is a sense of progression in the stories as the male protagonists (and narrators) become increasingly aware that women exist for purposes other than offering men emotional support. The first stories focus on the ways in which women help men survive or define themselves.

Auchincloss, Louis. *Tales of Manhattan*. Boston: Houghton, 1967

The stories are divided into three sections: "Memories of an Auctioneer," "Arnold & Degener" (law firm), and "The Matrons." All are about upper-class life in Manhattan and are told by the same first-person narrator, who is describing three different lives he has lived.

Babel, Isaac. *Red Calvary* [*Konarmiia*]. *The Complete Stories*. Ed. and trans. Walter Morison. New York: Criterion, 1955. (First pub. in Russian in 1926) 39–200.

The setting is the border area of the Polish front in 1920. The war is ubiquitous, affecting every landscape, character, and plot. Although there is a large cast in these thirty-five stories and sketches, one character (Ljutov) unifies the stories. Ljutov seeks out racially and religiously diverse Polish and Russian characters, and, gradually, they help us understand Ljutov's own background.

Baldwin, James. *Going to Meet the Man*. New York: Dial, 1965.

All of the stories deal with racial prejudice and dispossession in the United States between the mid–1950s and mid–1960s. They are arranged in chronological order, describing a period of gradual social change. The protagonists also appear to grow older: while the first stories feature children, the last ones are about adults. Although the first two stories contain the same family and community, the others deal with a variety of people and places. Most protagonists are male and black, but "Come Out the Wilderness" features a black woman, and "The Man Child" and "Going to Meet the Man" describe white males. The last stories try to explain the inhumanity of the white man.

Banks, Russell. *Searching for Survivors*. New York: Fiction Collective, 1975.

Contains fourteen stories and a series of companion pieces, which include "Searching for Survivors—I," "Searching for Survivors—II," and three "With Che" stories. As Craig Hansen Werner has explained, the stories are primarily unified by setting, theme, and style: the stories' "effectiveness stems from the tension between the abstract and concrete in the narrator's imagination" (*Paradoxical Resolutions: American Fiction since James Joyce*. Urbana: U of Illinois P, 1982. 48).

———. *Trailerpark*. Boston: Houghton, 1981.

Thirteen stories about the residents of a trailerpark in a New Hampshire town. The first story, "The Guinea Pig Lady" (70-pages long), introduces most of the characters. Each story is devoted to a single character or couple or family. The book is reminiscent of *Winesburg, Ohio*, and the characters are "grotesques" whose stories are objectively but sympathetically told. Chronology is not generally important, but several times previous events are noted. Characters such as Captain Dewey Knox, Terry Constant, Doctor Wickshaw, and Marcelle Chagnon appear in many of the stories. The last story, "The Fisherman," brings together most of the cast as they help Merle Ring decide how to spend the money he has won in the lottery.

———. *Success Stories*. New York: Harper, 1986.

A large number of the stories—"Queen for a Day," "My Mother's Memoirs," "Success Story," "Adultery," "Mistake," "Children's Story," and "Sarah Cole"—appear to be about the same first-person narrator, identified as Earl Painter. These are arranged chronologically, beginning with his response to his father's abandonment of the family and ending with his own adulteries, failed marriages, and inability to take care of his child. Some characters (Earl, Earl's parents,

Eleanor) appear in more than one story. All stories end with a revelation or a minor victory achieved against all odds.

Barth, John. *Lost in the Funhouse: Fiction for Print, Tape, Live Voice*. Garden City, NY: Doubleday, 1968.

The author's preface begins by insisting that the book is "neither a collection nor a selection, but a series; though several of its items have appeared separately in periodicals, the series will be seen to have been meant to be received 'all at once' and as here arranged" (ix). The stories comment self-consciously on the difficulties of storytelling. Ambrose, the only protagonist who appears in more than one story, contrasts with the other main characters who can only complain about their fate: in "Lost in the Funhouse," Ambrose devotes himself to fiction, to creating funhouses.

———. *Chimera*. New York: Random, 1972.

Contains three stories about telling stories. They are linked by characters (especially Dunyazade, Scheherazade, and the Genie or writer) and recurring heroic plots based on reworked myth. All stories contain framing devices, which become increasingly complex as the reader moves through the book.

Barthelme, Donald. *Sadness*. New York: Farrar, 1972.

Barthelme's story collections generally lack sufficient unity to be considered cycles. *Sadness* is better connected thematically than most of the others. Repeatedly, the stories demonstrate that dreams are not realized and dissatisfaction is the most constant state. Society encourages paralyzing conformity. The only escape, as the artist in the last story ("Daumier") demonstrates, is to avoid routine.

Barthelme, Steve. *And He Tells the Little Horse the Whole Story*. Baltimore: Johns Hopkins UP, 1987.

According to Tom LeClair, the stories are about failed communication: "[Barthelme's] characters are speakers and listeners who almost never exchange roles" (*NYTBR* [20 December 1987]: 8). LeClair also notes that half of the stories take place in automobiles, and most involve characters "drifting in and out of love."

Boyle, Kay. *The Smoking Mountain: Stories of Postwar Germany*. New York: McGraw, 1951.

The stories describe Americans and Germans living in Germany immediately after World War II. The occupying troops are revealed as insensitive to a culture different from their own and as capable of generosity but capricious in their giving. The Germans appear more complicated as they struggle to survive or to rise once again in the world: they are described as desperate, cunning, and unable to confront their collective guilt. Chronology is not important.

Bradbury, Ray. *The Martian Chronicles*. Garden City, NY: Doubleday, 1950.

The stories and sketches describe the establishment of a space colony on Mars. They proceed chronologically: the first ones explain how four expeditions are necessary before a settlement can be established; the middle ones describe the first colonies, especially the Americans' materialism and inability to tolerate anything unfamiliar; the final ones, the abandonment of Mars, the destruction of Earth, and the hope that a few Earth immigrants will begin life again on Mars, accepting the planet on its own terms. Although the stories take place in different locations on Mars and involve a large and changing cast, they are unified by more than plot and theme. The original settlers—Spender, Parkhill, Wider, and Hathaway—appear in several stories, including some of the last. Furthermore, the tone of the stories is consistent: repeatedly, the narrator criticizes American narrowness and greed.

———. *The October Country*. New York: Knopf, 1970. (1955)

The tone of the stories is eerie. Recurring subjects include death and other fantastic worlds that lure us away from familiar reality. Bradbury's October country, as summed up by Hazel Pierce, is "compartmentalized into small dark areas, the hidden places of human deprivation and depravation. His autumn people are void of hope or optimism. Occasionally one of them rouses himself for a cruel joke or last-ditch effort. But for the most part, they live static, sterile lives" ("Ray Bradbury and the Gothic Tradition," in *Ray Bradbury*, ed. Martin Harry Greenberg and Joseph D. Olander. [New York: Taplinger, 1980] 172).

———. *Dandelion Wine*. Garden City, NY: Doubleday, 1957.

All of the stories take place in Green Town during the summer of 1928. Although not appearing in every story, Doug is the protagonist and the writer of the book that we are reading. The stories are unified by a central theme: one's capacity for life is enhanced by an acceptance of death. Seasonal imagery underlines this theme.

Busch, Frederick. *Domestic Particulars: A Family Chronicle*. New York: New Directions, 1976.

As the title suggests, the stories are about a single family. Following chronological order, the stories trace Harry Miller's family life in Brooklyn; his graduation from college; his army physical; his relationships with women, including his wife Anna; his refusal to keep in touch with his parents; and his parents' deaths. Many of the stories are told in first person by people who know Harry well. These accounts—told by his mother, father, wife—explain why Harry behaves so strangely in the final stories.

———. *Rounds*. New York: Farrar, 1979.

The book represents an interesting variation on the short story cycle. It begins as a cycle with two alternating series of stories, the first about Eli Silver and the second about Annie and Phil Sorenson. Halfway through the book, however, the two series merge when the Sorensons become the adoptive parents of the baby born to Silver's lover.

Caldwell, Erskine. *Georgia Boy*. New York: Duell, Sloan, and Pearce, 1943.

A group of stories about rural Georgia. All of the stories are about the Stroups and their black servant, Handsome Brown, and are told from the first-person point of view by the son, who appears to describe the events shortly after they have happened. There is no evidence that the boy or narrator learns from past events.

Calvino, Italo. *Marcovaldo or the Seasons in the City* [*Marcovaldo, ovvero, Le stagioni in citta*]. Trans. William Weaver. New York: Harcourt, 1983. (First pub. in Italian in 1963)

The stories are connected by the seasonal cycle; by Marcovaldo, an unskilled laborer who dreams of beauty; and by the grim industrial (northern Italian) city in which Marcovaldo lives. In spite of Marcovaldo's attempts to rediscover nature—for example, mushrooms growing in cracks in the sidewalk—the city appears hostile to life of any sort. The first stories take place in the early 1950s, the last ones in the mid–1960s, during more economically prosperous times.

———. *Cosmicomics* [*Le cosmicomiche*]. Trans. William Weaver. New York: Harcourt, 1968. (First pub. in Italian in 1965)

A series of stories about the evolution of the universe. Each begins with an italicized paragraph describing a step in the evolutionary process, which is dramatized by the story that follows. The first-person narrator in all of the stories is Qfwfq, a protean being who is sometimes a simple cellular structure, sometimes a dinosaur, sometimes a personification of an abstract concept such as the sun's revolution around the galaxy. (Also see *t zero*.)

————. *t zero* [*Ti con zero*]. Trans. William Weaver. New York: Harcourt, 1969. (First pub. in Italian in 1967)

A second series of stories about the evolution of the universe (see *Cosmicomics*). The first four stories are about Qfwfq, and they dramatize events such as the creation of terrestrial continents on Earth, the origin of birds, and the power that the sea exercises over life on Earth. The second group of three stories describes Qfwfq's love for Priscilla, depicting the need organisms have for life outside themselves. The final four stories are also told in the first person, but not by Qfwfq. These narratives debate issues pertaining to time and space.

————. *The Castle of Crossed Destinies* [*Il castello dei destini incrociati*]. Trans. William Weaver. New York: Harcourt, 1976. (First pub. in Italian in 1973)

The book is divided into two parts—"The Castle" and "The Tavern"—and the first story in each section functions as a frame tale. In "The Castle" guests are each given part of a deck of cards, which are then used to communicate their stories. Since everyone is mute, only the narrator interprets the stories suggested by the positioning of the cards. The stories are connected by character and event, since similar cards (and combinations of cards) are read in each story. In "The Tavern," the tone is more pessimistic: the stories that are told describe people who are weak, or defeated, or lack direction. Even the narrator's tale ("I Also Try to Tell My Tale") stresses his inability to make sense out of the cards he places in front of the others.

————. *Mr. Palomar*. London: Picador, 1986. (First pub. in Italian in 1983)

Mr. Palomar's world is described in a series of brief stories arranged around topics such as "Palomar on the beach," "Palomar on the terrace," or "Palomar in society." The three major divisions of the book include *Palomar's Vacation*, *Palomar in the City*, and *The Silences of Palomar*. Things of this world are catalogued as Calvino explains how Mr. Palomar distances himself from the world.

Camus, Albert. *Exile and the Kingdom* [*L'Exil et le royaume*]. Trans. Justin O'Brien. New York: Knopf, 1958. (First pub. in French in 1957)

Forrest L. Ingram analyzes unifying devices of this book in *Representative Short Story Cycles* (The Hague: Mouton, 1971). He sees as most important the general movement toward the "kingdom," which could be defined as a harmonious relationship achieved by balancing one's own needs with those of the community. Ingram also notes the importance of setting and imagery: repeatedly, the environment is used symbolically to evoke the character's state of mind or situation. The first four stories take place in Algeria, the fifth in Montmartre (Paris), and the last in the jungles of Brazil.

Carter, Angela. *The Bloody Chamber*. New York: Harper, 1979.

Imaginative reworkings of fairy tales, most of them taken from Charles Perrault. They are connected by their explicit sexuality (often emphasizing the animal nature of sexuality) and their sadomasochism. The order in which the stories are placed does not seem important.

————. *Black Venus*. London: Hogarth, 1985. The same stories (in slightly different order) are published as *Saints and Strangers* in the United States (1986). Carter revised ''The Fall River Axe Murders'' for the American edition.

The stories are all highly imaginative, focusing on people out of distant times or places or on characters in literature. In addition to Lizzie Borden, Carter re-creates Baudelaire's relationship with his Creole mistress, Edgar Allan Poe's childhood, and the fairies in *A Midsummer Night's Dream* (transplanted from Athens to an English wood). While not linked by setting, character, or plot, the stories are connected because each demonstrates Carter's ability to take a legend, literary text, literary personality, or historical period and ''make it new.'' Often, as is especially the case with ''Edgar Allan Poe'' and ''Axe Murders,'' Carter demonstrates shrewd psychological insights into the characters she re-creates. Many of the stories feature women who are trapped and forced to behave desperately. The ordering of the stories does not seem important. (''Axe Murders'' is probably placed first in the American edition because Lizzie Borden has greater recognition value than some of the other protagonists.)

Cather, Willa. *The Troll Garden*. Ed. James Woodress. Lincoln: U of Nebraska P, 1983. (1905)

The introduction by Woodress stresses the extent to which the stories are unified: ''*The Troll Garden* is not simply a collection of stories all having something to do with art and artists. There is overall design and meaning and a careful arrangement of the tales to support the themes woven into the fabric of the text'' (xvi). The stories present a variety of artists (musicians, writers, sculptor) and patrons of the arts. Many characters are seduced by art; some are destroyed by it or by those barbarians who denigrate what they cannot understand; still others are revealed as incapable of distinguishing between good and bad art.

Connell, Evan S., Jr. *Mrs. Bridge*. New York: Viking, 1959.

The book consists of juxtaposed stories and vignettes about Mrs. Bridge. At times, the plot continues from story to story, but this is the exception and not the rule. A consistent picture of Mrs. Bridge's world evolves gradually: she is a snob and unrelentingly superficial. The tone is lightly ironic, mildly disapproving of the Bridges' narrow upper-middle-class world. Unified by setting, character, plot, tone and theme.

————. *Mr. Bridge*. New York: Knopf, 1969.

The book resembles Connell's *Mrs. Bridge* (see above). Stories and vignettes proceed in a roughly chronological manner, revealing various facets of Mr. Bridge's life: his prejudices, his fear that others will take advantage of him, his cheapness, and his self-justifying principles. Other forms of unity include setting and recurring characters (family, cook, minister, friends).

Coover, Robert. *A Night at the Movies: Or, You Must Remember This*. New York: Linden/Simon, 1987.

The various stories function as parts of an old-time night at the movies: ''Phantom of the Movie Palace'' contains previews of coming attractions; the cowboy adventure is ''Shootout at Gentry's Junction''; the comedy is ''Charlie in the House of Rue''; the romance is ''You Must Remember This''; and so on. The stories are connected by the writer's parodic use of film classics and their genres. Often, the old film conventions seem to self-destruct when they are reworked from a contemporary perspective.

Corrington, John Williams. *The Actes and Monuments*. Urbana: U of Illinois Press, 1978.

    Most of the stories are about lawyers practicing in the South. Although the same characters do not continue from story to story, the protagonists are concerned with the same problems, including the difficulty of defining truth, the acceptance of death, and the belief in grace.

Crane, Stephen. *Whilomville Stories. Tales of Whilomville. Works of Stephen Crane.* Vol. 7. Ed. Fredson Bowers, with Intro. by J. C. Levenson. Charlottesville: UP of Virginia. 1969. (1900)

    Stories are unified principally by their setting in small-town America (Whilomville) and through the Trescott family. Jimmie Trescott functions as protagonist: he is featured in all but one story, and his actions suggest that he develops in the process of the book. The book is further unified by the seasonal cycle: covering two years, the stories begin and end in summer. *Note*: Crane also published a series of Civil War stories entitled *The Little Regiment and Other Episodes of the American Civil War* in 1896.

de Beauvoir, Simone. *The Woman Destroyed* [*La femme rompue*]. Trans. Patrick O'Brian. New York: Putnam's, 1969. (First pub. in French in 1967)

    All three stories or novellas describe difficulties experienced by middle-aged women. All live in Paris, and their problems involve their relations with husbands and grown children. As they grow older, the women feel increasingly less important to their families. While their situations are similar—all are temporarily alone, and everything they believe in is revealed as illusory—they differ in the ways in which they respond to their situations. Only the first woman ("The Age of Discretion") regains her vitality. She has remained intellectually active and is not entirely dependent on her family for emotional support.

Doctorow, E. L. *Lives of the Poets: Six Stories and a Novella*. New York: Random, 1984.

    The first six stories are self-conscious fictions written by the protagonist in the final story, the novella-length "Lives of the Poets." Throughout the first six stories there are echoes of literary influences: for example, the unmistakable influence of *Dubliners* on "The Water Works" and *Leaves of Grass* on "Willi." "Lives of the Poets" chronicles the protagonist's writer's block, which may explain why all of the other stories feature anxiety-ridden characters.

Dos Passos, John. *U.S.A.* Boston: Houghton, 1946. (First pub. together in 1938)

    Contains three major divisions: *The 42nd Parallel, Nineteen Nineteen*, and *The Big Money*. Each division is subdivided into sections devoted to a single protagonist. The subdivisions or "chapters" include a story about the protagonist as well as vignettes entitled "Newsreel" and "Camera Eye" (occasionally a brief biography of a historic figure is also included). The diverse materials included in each "chapter" give the individual stories a larger social context. In addition to recurring characters, major unifying devices include the historical framework (1900 to early 1930s) and the criticisms the work makes of capitalistic greed, mindless conformity, the obscenity of war, and the breakdown of the family.

Dubus, Andre. *Adultery and Other Choices*. Boston: Godine, 1977.

    The book is divided into three parts. The first group of five stories takes place in rural Louisiana, featuring adolescent or young adult protagonists who are attempting to gain control of their lives. In the first three stories, the same protagonist (Paul) struggles to establish his identity, especially to become a man in his father's eyes. Female initiations are described in the next two stories, where protagonists become increasingly able to assert themselves against the pressure to conform.

The stories in the second group describe military life, especially the manner in which one is desensitized by mindless authority. The beginning story features Paul as a Marine officer-candidate.

The last division contains a novella entitled "Adultery," in which Edith discovers that she does not have to maintain a marriage that is dissatisfactory. Her recognition that she has a choice—that situations can be perceived from various points of view—echoes what is said in other stories.

Elkin, Stanley. *The Living End*. New York: Dutton, 1979.

The book contains three long stories. In the first, Ellerbee is killed by Ron, whose accomplice is Jay Ladlehaus. Ellerbee descends into hell, where he eventually discovers the accomplice and befriends him. In the second, "The Bottom Line," God evicts Ladlehaus from hell and he is buried alive in a grave, his complaints heard only by Quiz, a high school caretaker. Finally, in "The State of the Art," Quiz is smitten by God, he ascends from hell into heaven, and the book ends with God annihilating everything because he is dissatisfied with his creation. The characters and plots continue from story to story, and the entire book is a satire on the concept of an omnipotent and just God.

Evanier, David. *The One-Star Jew*. San Francisco: North Point, 1983.

Fourteen stories about (writer and a New Yorker) Bruce Orav, his wife and stepson, his mother and father, his friends and philanthropic activities, and his psychiatrist. All are told in the first person by Orav, in rough chronological order, and cover the years between his thirtieth and fortieth birthdays. In the stories, Orav considers what it means to be a Jew, he struggles to love his parents and stepson, and he criticizes the fund-raising organization that employs him.

Faulkner, William. *The Unvanquished*. New York: Random, 1965. (1938)

The protagonist, Bayard Sartoris, appears in every story, and he eventually acts to reshape community values. Bayard also functions as storyteller, looking back on events after they have happened. Other recurring major characters include Colonel John Sartoris, Granny, Ringo, Drusilla Hawks, Loosh, Colonel Dick, and Uncle Buck McCaslin. The action is limited to a chronological account of events during the Civil War and early Reconstruction. (See chapter on *The Unvanquished*.)

———. *Go Down, Moses*. New York: Random, 1942.

The most obvious unifying device is genealogy, the complex family relationships that exist among the descendants of Carothers McCaslin. All of the stories are also constructed around at least one thematically significant journey. In some cases the journey leads to self-knowledge, but in most it serves to emphasize the plight of blacks. In addition to black-white relations, the other major topic is the role of the wilderness as spiritual instructor. (See chapter on *Go Down, Moses*.)

———. *Knight's Gambit*. New York: Random, 1949.

Gavin Stevens prevents or detects crimes in Yoknapatawpha County, Mississippi. In each story, Stevens solves a mystery: in four, he discovers who has committed a murder and what the motivation involved; in one, "Tomorrow," he discovers why a juror votes as he does in a murder trial; in "Knight's Gambit," the final story, he prevents a murder before it can occur. Three of the stories are told in the first person by Stevens's nephew, and one ("Knight's Gambit") uses the nephew as the center of consciousness. The sense of progression in the stories results from the nephew's growing appreciation of his uncle, especially his philosophic attitude toward criminals, justice, and the truth. In the final story, "Knight's Gambit," Faulkner marries off his lawyer/detective and provides his most complete statement about Stevens's character.

Fitzgerald, F. Scott. *The Pat Hobby Stories*. New York: Scribner's, 1962.

All of the stories feature Pat Hobby, a Hollywood hack writer. Much the same thing happens in each: Hobby has a scheme for getting ahead that leads to disastrous results. As Stephen Sniderman suggests, the stories do not benefit from being published together: "These stories not only become repetitious and predictable, but they stretch the reader's sense of verisimilitude to the breaking point" ("The 'Composite' in Twentieth-Century American Literature." Diss. U of Wisconsin, 1970. *DAI* 31 [1970]: 403A).

————. *The Basil and Josephine Stories*. Ed. Jackson R. Bryer and John Kuehl. New York: Scribner's, 1973.

Although Fitzgerald designed these stories to work together as two juxtaposed series, they were not published as such during his lifetime. (*Taps at Reveille* contains seven of the Basil stories and four about Josephine. Omitted are the last two Basil stories and the last one about Josephine.) In the Basil stories, parallel situations are used to emphasize the protagonist's gradual maturation. In the Josephine stories, however, the protagonist behaves in the same manner in story after story; the only difference is her increased understanding of her position. Some other characters appear in more than one story.

Gaines, Ernest. *Bloodline*. New York: Dial, 1968.

All of the stories are unified by Bayonne, the Louisiana setting. The stories progress from a naive, young narrator with a limited perspective to a more mature narrator with greater control over events. As the book develops, it also becomes clear that the characters are rejecting the old order of black submissiveness and trying to establish something more humane.

————. *A Gathering of Old Men*. New York: Knopf, 1983.

While it is debatable whether or not the first and last stories are self-sufficient, the portraits of the old men are independent and connected. All describe the men's thoughts and actions when they hear that a white man has been killed by a black. The similarity with which they respond underlines their sense of community and the strength of their coordinated action at the end of the book.

Gallant, Mavis. *The Pegnitz Junction: A Novella and Five Short Stories*. Port Townsend, WA: Graywolf, 1984. (1973)

The stories describe the effect that World War II continues to have on Europeans, especially Germans. All of the main characters are Germans, and the question of collective guilt is brought up again and again. The most devastating example— dramatically placed as the final story—features a woman who can ignore or forget the past as long as she is comforted by material possessions. Other recurring topics or motifs include hunger (especially the inability to tolerate wasted food), a sense of vertigo, the naming of plants, the tragedy of the Jews in Silesia, and the division of Germany after the war. Most important, however, are the lies that everyone tells, either because they cannot confront the truth or because they no longer believe that truth exists.

————. *Home Truths: Selected Canadian Stories*. Toronto: Macmillan of Canada, 1981.

The stories feature Canadians. The first group focuses on children's and adolescents' perceptions; all six describe Canadians at home in Canada. The next group (entitled "Canadians Abroad") features young adults abroad for the first time. The final group is about Linnet Muir, a highly autobiographical character, who resembles some of the protagonists from the first section. In this third section, the stories are arranged chronologically, beginning in childhood and continuing into young adulthood. Throughout the book, Canadians are described as unable to express their emotions. Furthermore, compared to Europeans, they have a weak sense of national identity. Finally, they are divided against themselves because of language, religion, class, and geography. The stories also describe various dissatisfactory parent-child relations, emphasized by the presence of orphans (real or figurative), divorced parents, and potential stepparents.

————. *Overhead in a Balloon: Twelve Stories of Paris*. New York: Random, 1987. (Pub. in Canada in 1985)

The characters—whether French or expatriates—seem rootless. Many lack families or other substantial connections, and those who live with their families do so only out of habit or convenience. Isolation and a sense of loss are unifying themes.

Gardiner, John Rolfe. *Going on Like This*. New York: Atheneum, 1983.

The stories are arranged in five groups under the headings "Beltway," "Village," "Town," "The Near Country," and "On the Road." After the first group, describing people living in the shadow of the Washington beltway, the stories take us to a rural Virginia town, to the Virginia countryside, and, finally, on the road itself. Within each group, the stories generally feature the same characters and geographic location.

Gass, William H. *In the Heart of the Heart of the Country and Other Stories*. Boston: Godine, 1981. (1968)

All five stories are about solipsism and art as a refuge from a world that is chaotic, violent, and unresponsive to one's needs. Refuge is often purchased at a high price. In the first story, "The Pedersen Kid," the narrator appears to be freezing to death as he imagines himself tunneling through the world of snow. The narrator in "Mrs. Mean" becomes so obsessed with language that he denies the reality of others. With the exception of Charlie Fender—who wishes for an alternative reality in "Icicles" but lacks the imagination to create one—all the stories are told in the first person. In the final story, "In the Heart of the Heart," Gass presents his most complete statement about art: while it can help one create order and beauty, a devotion to art can also kill spontaneity and result in sterility.

Godwin, Gail. *Dream Children*. New York: Knopf, 1976.

All the protagonists are dreamers. The first six stories contain women who long to escape from dissatisfactory marriages or relationships. The wife in the title story believes that her child who was dead at birth comes back to her. Mrs. Wakeley in "Nobody's Home" envisions the day her husband will come home to an empty house. The dreams of the few male characters are both positive and negative: Eliott's in "Legacy of the Motes" helps him better understand himself; the protagonist in "Why Does a Great Man Love" uses dreams to help him deny the reality of others.

Hemingway, Ernest. *In Our Time*. New York: Scribner's, 1970. (1930. The 1925 publication of *In Our Time* does not include "On the Quai at Smyrna.")

In Our Time contains a series of short stories, each of which is framed by an italicized vignette. Both narrative series (stories, vignettes) are unified by the same theme: the loss of traditional values and the search for new ones, or at least a code of behavior that ensures a minimum of dignity in a world without values. The most explicit unifying device is Nick Adams, featured in at least seven stories. A historical framework connects the stories, taking us from peacetime America to war in Europe to postwar America and Europe. (See chapter on *In Our Time*.)

Herriot, James. *All Creatures Great and Small*. New York: St. Martin's, 1972. (1970)
———. *All Things Bright and Beautiful*. New York: St. Martin's, 1974.
———. *All Things Wise and Wonderful*. New York: St. Martin's, 1977.
———. *The Lord God Made Them All*. New York: St. Martin's, 1981.

According to a conversation I had with Brian Sinclair, the original Tristan Farnon, the stories are based on real incidents but reworked considerably. The stories are unified by recurring characters (Tristan and Sigfried, James, Helen, Mrs. Hall), the Yorkshire dales, Skeldale house, and the author's conviction—revealed in episode after episode—that the most ordinary people and their animals have a great deal to tell us about human nature. The episodes in each book are arranged chronologically: collectively they take us from pre– to post–World War II England.

Huggan, Isabel. *The Elizabeth Stories*. New York: Viking, 1987. (Pub. In Canada in 1984)

The eight stories describe Elizabeth Kessler growing up in rural Canada during the 1940s and 1950s. They are all told in the first person by Elizabeth and chronicle her struggle against her sense of helplessness and the injustices she experiences. Although various sexual initiations are described, the stories focus on Elizabeth's relationship with her parents.

Hughes, Langston. *Simple Speaks His Mind*. New York: Simon, 1950.
———. *Simple Takes a Wife*. New York: Simon, 1953.
———. *Simple Stakes a Claim*. New York: Rinehart, 1957.
———. *Simple's Uncle Sam*. New York: Hill and Wang, 1965.

Originally published in newspapers, these stories and anecdotes are about Jesse B. Semple, who represents the black man in Harlem during the forties, fifties, and sixties. As Phyllis R. Klotman suggests, the stories take the form of a comedy skit: "two stand-up comics playing against and to each other, fast-paced dialogue and a quick wit" ("Jesse B. Semple." *Critical Essays on Langston Hughes*. Ed. Edward J. Mullen. Boston: Hall, 1986). The verbal exchange in each story allows Semple to state his philosophy about life and to demonstrate how wit is used by the black person as self-defense. Various characters such as Boyd (the straight man) and Isabel (Semple's first wife) continue from story to story and book to book.

James, Henry. *The Finer Grain*. Ed. W. R. Martin and Warren U. Ober. Delmar, New York: Scholars' Facsimiles, 1986. (1910)

Employing Forrest L. Ingram's terminology, Martin and Ober argue in their Introduction that *The Finer Grain* is an early example of the short story cycle. The five stories are unified through their preoccupation with art, the imagination, and the relation between art and reality. Maintaining that the stories are logically ordered, Martin and Ober say that the first provides the most explicit comment on the function of the artist. The second illustrates that "intelligent, compas-

sionate—in short, *moral*—behavior is dependent on . . . imaginative insight . . . "
(xi). The middle story features a character (Winch) who attempts to achieve
immortality while the fourth describes "communal 'artistic consciousness.' " The
final story balances the first: while the latter is about "the success of the creative
imagination," (xiii) the former describes its failure.

Jewett, Sarah Orne. *The Country of the Pointed Firs and Other Stories*. Ed. Willa Cather.
Garden City, NY: Doubleday, 1956. "And other stories" did not appear in the
title when it was first published in 1896.

    The narrator in the book spends a summer in Dunnet Landing, a coastal village
in Maine that is no longer prosperous. This narrator and the sense of place best
unify the stories. Bowden Place and the schoolhouse are focal points, and the
community's cohesiveness is revealed in their ceremonies, including a funeral, a
wedding, and a family reunion. The sea's control over lives is emphasized. Although some of the transitions between stories resemble transitions in a novel,
there is no continuing plot. Contains a prologue and epilogue. Although published
in 1896, the book is included because it is mentioned in the Introduction and it
is generally not well known.

Joyce, James. *Dubliners*. Rev. ed. 1968. New York: Viking, 1982. (1914)

    Each story takes place in Dublin and describes Dubliners' responses to lives
that prove humiliating or suffocating. Because characters are placed in situations
where they must choose to act or remain passive, many of the individual plots
resemble one another. Although external situations do not seem to improve, some
protagonists achieve a degree of self-awareness. With the possible exception of
the first three stories, there is no protagonist who appears in more than one story.
Nevertheless, the book presents the gradual maturation of what might be called
the archetypal Dubliner. (See chapter on *Dubliners*.)

Kafka, Franz. *Ein Hungerkunstler: Vier Geschichten*. [*A Hunger Artist*] *Erzahlungen und
kleine Prosa*. Ed. Max Brood. New York: Schocken, 1953. (The four stories are
included in *Franz Kafka: The Complete Stories*. Ed. Nahum N. Glatzer. New
York: Schocken, 1971. (1924)

    Forrest Ingram provides an excellent discussion of unifying forms in the four
stories. Most important is the basic pattern that the stories follow: (1) initially the
protagonist appears secure; (2) then something occurs to emphasize how precarious
his or her situation actually is; (3) the body of the story consists of a series of
questions asked by the narrator; and (4) the conclusion contains a summary and
an attempt to regain a sense of equilibrium. This pattern is used to emphasize a
series of topics, including anxiety and security, isolation and communication,
freedom and restriction, and the common and the extraordinary (Ingram's *Representative Short Story Cycles*: 46–105).

Le Guin, Ursula K. *Orsinian Tales*. New York: Harper, 1976.

    Contains eleven stories about an imaginary but realistically drawn Eastern-bloc
country, resembling Yugoslavia or Czechoslovakia or Hungary. The stories are
not arranged chronologically: for example, the first ("The Fountains") takes place
in 1960, the second ("The Barrow") in 1150, and the third ("Ile Forest") in
1920. Only gradually does the reader begin to understand that these people—
century after century—are linked by common aspirations. Repeatedly, society
thwarts the individual's freedom and defines reality. The stories describe the
various ways in which individuals use their imaginations to try to protect or enlarge

their personal freedom. (Unfortunately, however, the imagination sometimes appears to be another form of oppression.) Recurring imagery includes forests, fountains, waterfalls, fortresses, and towers.

Lem, Stanislaw. *The Cyberiad: Fables for the Cybernetic Age [Cyberiada]*. Trans. Michael Kandel. New York: Seabury, 1974. (First pub. in Polish in 1967)

A series of science-fiction fairy tales about Turl and Klapaucius. They invent machines that help them prevent a war between two antagonistic kingdoms, that write poetry, that even isolate the tyrant King Krool from his country. Sometimes they create machines for their own amusement, sometimes for financial profit; at other times they are forced to do so. While the machines generally help them escape forms of oppression, a few prove to be monsters once created.

————. *Tales of Pirx the Pilot. [Opowiesci o pilocie Pirxie]*. Trans. Louis Iribarne. New York: Harcourt, 1979.

Five science-fiction stories. Arranged chronologically, the stories trace Pirx's development as an astronaut and pilot. In the first, he is terrified and barely competent, but he handles his test well. In subsequent stories, he is given increasingly difficult tasks to perform. There is a sequel: *More Tales of Pirx the Pilot*. Trans. Louis Iribarne. New York: Harcourt, 1982.

————. *A Perfect Vacuum*. Trans. Michael Kandel. New York: Harcourt, 1979.

A series of reviews of sixteen fictitious books, including a review of *A Perfect Vacuum*. Connected by the reviewer's consistently satiric and postmodern perspective.

Levi, Primo. *The Periodic Table. [Il sistema periodico]*. Trans. Raymond Rosenthal. London: Abacus, 1986. (First pub. in Italian in 1975)

Each story is named after one of the chemical elements in the periodic table. Discussion of the element (or chemistry) introduces characters and plot, and the point of the story is always closely linked to this element. A first-person narrator (resembling Levi) further unifies the narratives. The chronology take us from Levi's family background, to his training as a chemist, to his temporary jobs in industry during the beginning of World War II, to his imprisonment in a concentration camp, to his work as a chemist in postwar Italy.

————. *The Monkey's Wrench [La chiave a stella]*. Trans. William Weaver. New York: Summit, 1986. (First pub. in Italian in 1978)

These stories are about storytelling: how one tells stories as well as the difficulties and the rewards involved in being a storyteller. The main characters are the first-person narrator (a writer obviously resembling Levi) and a raconteur named Libertini Faussone, a self-educated Italian who has made his living constructing bridges and towers all over the world. As Faussone recounts his adventures, the narrator frequently interrupts to compare their experiences, philosophies, and the ways in which they tell stories.

————. *Moments of Reprieve [Lilit e altri racconti]*. Trans. Ruth Feldman. London: Abacus, 1987. (First pub. in Italian in 1981)

Moments of unexpected reprieve connect all of the stories. Each story features a different survivor of Auschwitz and the particular quality that enabled him to survive. The same first-person speaker (resembling Levi) narrates the events, which seem to be arranged in rough chronological order. The final story returns the speaker to Italy. Repeatedly there is a tension between the past and present: the first-person speaker often reminds us that he is narrating events from the past.

London, Jack. *Tales of the Fish Patrol*. Plainview, NY: Books for Libraries, 1976. (1905)

       This book illustrates that boundaries between genres are sometimes difficult to draw. Resembling both a short story cycle and an episodic novel, *Tales of the Fish Patrol* contains a series of escapades involving Charley Le Grant, Neil Partington, and the first-person narrator, a sixteen-year old who learns to become a better sailor. In their boat, the *Reindeer*, the crew pursues those who violate local fishing restrictions. Each story takes place on the water, generally San Francisco Bay, and features a chase scene. The law-breakers are inevitably immigrant Americans, and the Chinese receive especially harsh treatment. Transitions between stories resemble transitions in novels: the first paragraphs make frequent references to past incidents, especially the previous story.

McCarthy, Mary. *The Company She Keeps*. New York: Simon, 1942.

       The stories are about Margaret Sargent's attempt to understand herself. Between marriages, Sargent interacts with the New York intelligentsia of the 1930s. Characters are introduced and defined as they fit into Sargent's life. There is a sense of progression as she achieves greater self-knowledge. Most stories are devoted to a different character, and a comprehensive picture of the protagonist develops as other people view her from various perspectives.

Malamud, Bernard. *Pictures of Fidelman: An Exhibition*. New York: Farrar, 1969.

       The stories feature Fidelman in Italy as he tries one art form after another: painting, writing, art forgery and stealing, sculpture, and glass-blowing. They progress to make a statement in "Glass Blower of Venice": life is more important that art. Other recurring topics include mother-son relations (including the Madonna and child), the importance of the craftsman, and the extent to which art is based on imitation and chicanery.

Michener, James A. *Tales of the South Pacific*. New York: Macmillan, 1952. (1947)

       The parts of the book more closely resemble stories than chapters in a novel. Most delineate a particular character, relationship, or incident. Many of the characters appear in more than one story, especially the first-person narrator, Nellie Forbush, Bus Adams, Tony Fry, and Emile De Becque. The most important unifying device is the setting in the Pacific islands and its effect on the characters. The overall plot is unified by a military operation called "Alligator."

Moore, George. *The Untilled Field*. London: Unwin, 1903.

       A bleak and critical portrait of the Irish, which probably influenced Joyce's *Dubliners*. Each story deals with a different character, repeatedly emphasizing that Ireland and the Catholic Church stifle individual freedom and imagination. Exile seems unavoidable for those characters who are critical of Ireland, but, as soon as they leave, they long to return to the Irish countryside.

Munro, Alice. *Lives of Girls and Women*. New York: Penguin, 1984. (Pub. in Canada in 1971)

       The stories are about Del Jordan's maturation. They are arranged chronologically, and all of them take place in the same southern Ontario town. While the first four stories focus on the mother's influence, the remaining four deal primarily with peer pressure. Del's closest female friend, Naomi, demonstrates the ways in which people in a small town conform to community expectations. Her relationships with two boyfriends, Jerry and Garnet, illustrate Del's need to assert her own independence from potentially dominant figures. By the final story, Del matures to the point where she can begin to make her own decisions about work and love. She also reveals a greater understanding of how one writes fiction.

———. *The Beggar Maid: Stories of Flo and Rose*. New York: Knopf, 1979. (Pub. in Canada in 1978 as *Who Do You Think You Are?*)

The stories are about Rose, tracing her development from childhood to adult-hood. The first three as well as the last two take place in Hanratty, Ontario, but the town is significant in all of the stories, representing those things about herself of which Rose is both proud and ashamed. Rose leaves Hanratty for college in Ontario, marriage to the heir of a department store chain, and, after divorce, life on her own as a television personality, teacher, and actress. Flo (her stepmother), Patrick (her ex-husband), and Anna (her daughter) all appear in more than one story. Everything is told retrospectively by a third-person narrator, and Rose is generally the center of consciousness. As she accepts her past—especially Flo and Hanratty—Rose gains greater confidence in herself, especially in her ability to act.

Nabokov, Vladimir. *Pnin*. Garden City, NY: Doubleday, 1957.

Four parts of this book originally appeared as stories in *The New Yorker*. Although the parts are presented as chapters in a novel, they more closely resemble stories. For example, recurring characters are introduced in each story as if the reader has no knowledge of the rest of the book. In story after story we see Pnin behave in much the same way. Repeatedly, he is victimized by forces and bullies that he cannot control. Although often humiliated, he continues to struggle, never responding with anger.

Oates, Joyce Carol. *By the North Gate*. New York: Vanguard, 1963.

The first and last stories contrast an old man's response to mindless cruelty: in the last, Revere is able to rise above events. In the stories in between, characters discover evil in themselves and others. Most of the action takes place in Eden County, upper New York State, emphasizing the characters' inability to regain innocence.

———. *The Goddess and Other Women*. New York: Vanguard, 1974.

Contains twenty-five stories about the inability of women to deal with their own sexuality. Young women experiment with sex while trying to establish ident-ities. Older women tend to exploit men, to withdraw from the sexual arena, or to devote themselves masochistically to men. Such self-destruction often involves overt violence.

———. *The Hungry Ghosts: Seven Allusive Comedies*. Los Angeles: Black Sparrow, 1974.

These satires on academia have many targets—bored and paranoid poets on the lecture circuit; desperate and easily manipulated graduate students and assistant professors; hypocritical radicals; sadistic full professors, incapable of original work. All appear to lack substance ("ghosts") and to be insatiably hungry for recognition. Four of the stories take place at Hilberry University (southern Ontario) and contain recurring characters but no central protagonist. The titles of the stories refer ironically to literary works.

———. *The Poisoned Kiss and Other Stories from the Portuguese*. New York: Vanguard, 1975.

Supposedly translations from an imaginary work, *Azulejos* (by Fernandes de Briao). The stories deal with unlikely unions (or obsessions) with the unknown or alien. Many protagonists throw off the security of the known in order to embrace the unknown. Repeated use of an initial for a character's name.

————. *Last Days: Stories*. New York: Dutton, 1984.

The stories are divided into two parts: "Last Days" and "Our Wall." The first division contains five stories, each taking place in the United States and dealing with the subjects of solipsism, suicide, madness, and death. Four of these five stories also deal with the children who are affected by adult instability, insanity, and violence. In the other group, four are about Eastern-bloc countries (East Germany, the Soviet Union, Poland, and Hungary) and Abyssalia (North Africa). In the second division of stories, the situations grow progressively worse as we move from inexperienced travelers ("Ich bin ein Berliner") and cultural ambassadors (Antonia, the writer in "Détente") to professional State Department employees (Marianne in "Old Budapest" and the diplomat in "Lamb of Abyssalia") and actual citizens of those countries that are visited (only "Our Wall," the final story, focuses on the consciousness of an Eastern-bloc citizen). In the second group of stories, characters feels claustrophobic and cannot communicate with or trust one another. In both groups of stories, madness and violence result. Oates's purpose in linking these two groups of stories is to compare the sources of the characters' disorientation and madness.

————. *Raven's Wing*. New York: Dutton, 1987.

Parts of this collection are tightly unified but not the entire book. The first seven stories deal with marriages, always disastrous ones that are full of loneliness and sadomasochism. There are repeated instances of crying, throwing up, losing weight, and becoming pregnant. Some of the later stories also focus on sadistic sexual relations: in "Little Wife" events are told from a child's point of view, and in "Testimony" they are narrated by the third party in a bizarre sex-and-drugs triangle.

O'Connor, Flannery. *A Good Man Is Hard to Find and Other Stories*. New York: Harcourt, 1955.

Although more loosely connected than O'Connor's stories in *Everything That Rises Must Converge*, the stories in this volume are also preoccupied with evil and violence. Murders, accidents, drownings, abandonment—all are used to make characters (and readers) less complacent and more capable of vision.

————. *Everything That Rises Must Converge*. New York: Farrar, 1965.

Because of O'Connor's preoccupation with parent-child relations, with doubling, and with plot patterns that advance the protagonist to the point of self-recognition, many of the stories in the book resemble one another. With the exception of "The Enduring Chill," all of the stories contain conflicts that trigger violent exchanges that introduce the possibility of enlightenment. (See chapter on *Everything That Rises*.)

Paterson, Katherine. *Angels & Other Strangers: Family Christmas Stories*. New York: Harper, 1979.

Although advertised as children's literature, most of these stories are told from an adult's point of view and would interest various ages. All are about Christmas. Although the same characters do not appear more than once, similar types re-emerge: the difficult child who is sympathetically described, the lonely widower or aunt who wants to be with children at Christmas, the person who feels estranged from others because of race, religion, or political beliefs. Other recurring motifs include the empty manger, the guiding star, the breaking of Christmas ornaments, and, most important, the conquering of fear. The stories end in epiphanies: even the most wounded characters achieve a kind of wholeness.

Porter, Katherine Anne. *The Collected Stories of Katherine Anne Porter*. New York: Harcourt, 1965.

Contains "The Old Order," a sequence of stories including "The Source," "The Journey," "The Witness," "The Circus," "The Last Leaf," "The Fig Tree," and "The Grave." The first stories describe the old order, exemplified by Grandmother Rhea, whose power and discipline are both admirable and frightening. "The Circus," "The Fig Tree," and "The Grave" describe Miranda's initiation into a world less stable than the one Grandmother Rhea seemed to control. The concluding frame in the last story ("The Grave") is used to emphasize what Miranda has learned. Porter's *Pale Horse, Pale Rider* contains two stories ("Old Mortality" and "Pale Horse, Pale Rider") featuring Miranda when she is older.

Potter, Nancy. *Legacies*. Urbana: U of Illinois P, 1987.

Loosely connected, these stories are about the loss of community and family life in America during the 1980s. The adults in these stories have no satisfactory jobs, marriages, or friendships. They do not even seem to have a place to call home: for example, Fran ("A Thin Place") migrates westward until she reaches the Great Basin, where she settles in a trailer but dreams of her childhood home ("a real house with a large attic, a grape arbor, a root cellar" 33). Other characters are homeless, share someone else's home, or buy a prefabricated house for a retirement community. They all seem to be searching for some place where they can belong and be themselves.

Price, Reynolds. *Permanent Errors*. New York: Atheneum, 1970.

The stories and vignettes are divided into four parts. The first ("Fool's Education") contains Tamplin's unreliable recollections about his break-up with Sara. The second ("Elegies") includes three stories, one of which consists of brief vignettes describing a mother's death. The third ("Home Life") also includes a story made up out of discrete vignettes, collectively describing a husband's guilt after his wife's attempted suicide. In this section, there is also a story about a wife's unsuccessful attempt to blame her husband and his lover for the wife's unhappiness. The final section contains a single story, "Walking Lessons," describing the effect a suicide has on a husband. As Price explains in the preface, all of the narratives are connected by his "attempt to isolate in a number of lives the central error of act, will, understanding which, once made, had been permanent, incurable, but whose diagnosis and palliation are the hopes of continuance" (vii). One of these errors is the obsessive need for solitude, especially in cases where the protagonist is a writer.

Quiroga, Horacio. *The Exiles: And Other Stories* [*Los desterrados*]. Trans. J. David Danielson with Elsa K. Gambarini. Austin: U of Texas P, 1987. (First pub. in Spanish in 1926)

Repeatedly, characters are placed in oppressive situations that erupt in violence; nevertheless, some reveal a capacity for compassion. The stories are further unified by their setting in an outpost of Argentina.

Rosten, Leo. *The Education of H*y*m*a*n K*a*p*l*a*n*. New York: Harcourt, 1937.
―――. *Return of H*y*m*a*n* K*a*p*l*a*n*. New York: Harper, 1959.

Stories about the teacher and students at the American Night Preparatory School for adults. Hyman Kaplan, the enthusiastic if incorrigible star pupil, is prominently featured in all stories, as is Mr. Parkhill, the patient, plodding English language instructor. In addition to recurring character, the stories are unified by setting (the classroom), verbal humor (e.g., repeated use of malapropism, punning), and the clash between the ways in which America is perceived by the American academician and the old-world immigrant. There is little character development.

Saroyan, William. *My Name Is Aram*. New York: Penguin, 1944. (1940)

The stories take place in Fresno, California, between 1915 and 1925. They are about the eccentric Garoghlanian family, who are poor, imaginative, and generally happy. Aram is featured in all of them, and he gradually grows older as the stories progress. Collectively, they define the world as Aram knows it.

Stead, Christina. *The Salzburg Tales*. New York: Appleton-Century, 1934.

Resembling *The Decameron* and *The Canterbury Tales*, the book consists of "The Prologue," "The Personages," the tales which are told by thirty-one narrators over a seven-day period, and "The Epilogue." The setting is in Salzburg, as the title suggests, where people gather for the open-air performance of the medieval play *Jedermann*. The framed stories are also linked by interludes containing description and dialogue. Some correspondences are established between the narrators and the tales they relate.

Stein, Gertrude. *Three Lives*. New York: Random, 1936. (1909)

Three stories, each featuring a long-suffering, patient female who is devoted to taking care of another woman's family. Two of the three central characters are actually domestic servants (of German descent), and all of the stories take place in Bridgeport, Connecticut. Only the last story features a woman who marries, and when Lena is forced to leave service and marry, she loses all interest in life. The stories recreate the protagonist's consciousness and her manner of speaking.

Steinbeck, John. *The Pastures of Heaven*. New York: Viking, 1963. (1932)

In each of the stories there is a disparity between the richness of the land and the impoverished and desperate lives of the inhabitants. The stories are most obviously unified by their location in the Pastures of Heaven. The second most explicit unifying device is the use of recurring characters, especially the Munroe family. With the exception of the prologue and epilogue, each story contains a Munroe: their actions repeatedly have a disastrous effect on others. (See chapter on *The Pastures of Heaven*.)

————. *Tortilla Flat*. New York: Covici-Friede, 1935.

Set in a working-class Italian ghetto in Monterey, California, each of the stories focuses on Danny and his friends. They are primarily unified by their criticism of American materialism. Beginning with the book's preface, Danny's band is compared repeatedly to the knights of the Round Table in order to emphasize their positive qualities, such as protecting the helpless and homeless.

————. *The Red Pony*. New York: Viking, 1945. (When *The Red Pony* was published by Covici-Friede in 1937, it contained only the first three stories.)

The setting is the Tiflin ranch in California, where Jody lives with his father, mother, and Billy Buck, a hired hand. The stories are thematically unified, as they deal with the interrelated subjects of birth, old age, and death. Chronologically and thematically ordered, the stories trace Jody's ability to handle difficult tasks and accept the inevitability of death.

Stuart, Jesse. *Save Every Lamb*. New York: McGraw, 1964.

The stories describe incidents in W-Hollow, Kentucky, and the surrounding valley. Divided into three sections, *Save Every Lamb* focuses on (section one) the world of Jesse Stuart's youth, (section two) the Powderjay family (Jesse Stuart and his brothers and parents), and (section three) Stuart's own family, his wife Naomi and his daughter Jane. The book chronicles the changes in people and nature during an approximately fifty-year period (1910s to 1960s).

Tallent, Elizabeth. *In Constant Flight*. New York: Knopf, 1983.

The stories describe failed or failing romantic relationships between men and women. They are generally told by the same woman (or by women who closely resemble one another): a first-person narrator who is middle-class, well-educated, and physically attractive. The narrator feels as if men reject her, and the men and situations in the various stories resemble one another. The book consists of variations on a single theme.

―――. *Time with Children*. New York: Knopf, 1987.

Thirteen stories about American life. Several stories are devoted to an American couple living in London; two other families are described in a series of stories that take place around Sante Fe. These couples repeatedly place their families in jeopardy as they enjoy momentary flirtations.

Tarkington, Booth. *Penrod: His Complete Story: Penrod, Penrod and Sam, Penrod Jashber*. Garden City, NY: Doubleday, 1943. (1914, 1916, 1929)

The Penrod books are variations on the short story cycle. Tarkington combines the form of the novel and the story cycle. Each book contains a series of brief chapters devoted to a particular escapade: for example, the first six chapters in *Penrod* are devoted to the pageant of the Table Round; other series of chapters in the book are devoted to Penrod's adventures at home, at school, and in the neighborhood. The stories (groups of chapters) are unified by recurring character, setting, plot (the adventure), and theme (in most cases, Penrod and his friends' unrealized aspirations and dreams).

Taylor, Peter. *The Widows of Thornton*. New York: Harcourt, 1954.

Contains eight stories and one brief play about people who either live in Thornton or come from there. Primarily concerned with family relations, including the interaction of family and servants and visiting relatives. The stories are unified thematically by the ways in which women undervalue themselves. They tend to define themselves entirely by their roles as wives (or their inability to function as wives) and as social and cultural leaders in the community. Only in the final story, "The Dark Walk," does a woman perceive that she is trapped and begin to make her own decisions.

Thomas, Dylan. *Portrait of the Artist as a Young Dog*. New York: New Directions, 1955. (1940)

Almost all of the stories are first-person accounts of the artist as a young man. They proceed chronologically, beginning with stories about childhood and ending with five stories about young adulthood. Collectively, the stories describe the development of the artist's imagination and his skill with language. The location is always rural Wales, the town identified as Tawe, South Wales, in "Old Garbo" and as Swansea in "The Peaches."

Thomas, Maria. *Come to Africa and Save Your Marriage and Other Stories*. New York: Soho, 1987.

Features a group of foreigners living in Africa. Some have come to offer developing countries assistance, others to cure the sense of alienation they feel in their own countries. Many make valuable if unexpected discoveries about themselves.

Toomer, Jean. *Cane*. New York: University Place, 1967. (1923)

The book is divided into three parts: the first containing six stories about women in rural Georgia; the second, four stories set in Washington, D.C., or Chicago; and the third, a single long story (''Kabnis'') about a black intellectual from the urban North who returns to the South to teach. All of the women in the first stories, generally poor blacks, are examples of people who resist the restrictions placed upon them by the Old South. Although oppressed and sometimes destroyed, these women are described as physically and spiritually beautiful. They are depicted as superior to the urban blacks described in the second section, especially those who mimic middle-class whites. The third section returns us to the South, where a black attempts to regain his sense of himself and his past. The South is repeatedly defined in this book as rural Georgia, and strong, sensuous images of it pervade even stories taking place in the North. The book's three sections are thematically ordered; they are used by Toomer to argue that a black person's vitality is rooted in the South, based on his or her appreciation of physical (natural) beauty. Around many of the stories, especially in the first section of the book, there are lyric poems or sketches that enhance the material developed in the stories.

Updike, John. *Olinger Stories: A Selection*. New York: Vintage, 1964.

Although ten of these eleven stories had been published in other Updike story volumes, they do function as a cycle when brought together here. The primary unifying devices are the setting (Olinger) and the developing consciousness of the protagonist. They are arranged in rough chronological order, taking us from childhood through adulthood, the final story featuring the protagonist returning to a football game at the old high school.

————. *Bech: A Book*. New York: Knopf, 1970.

————. *Bech Is Back*. New York: Knopf, 1982.

Episodes in the life of Henry Bech, a middle-aged Jewish novelist. They are primarily concerned with the difficulty of writing and being a writer. In the first stories in *Bech: A Book*, the writer is on a State Department tour of Eastern Europe. *Bech Is Back* similarly begins with trips—to American universities, to Canada, to Third World countries—where he seems to fail in his role as cultural ambassador. Bumbling romantic interludes follow, and Bech marries Bea, who is first introduced in ''Bech Takes Pot Luck'' (*Bech: A Book*). Stories four, five, and six in *Bech Is Back* describe Bech with Bea in the Holy Land, in Scotland, and home again in Ossining. At the end of the book, Bech completes his long-awaited novel, *Think Big*.

————. *Too Far to Go: The Maples Stories*. New York: Fawcett Crest, 1979.

The most important unifying device is the Maples' marriage, which seems most impressive as they divorce one another. In addition to Richard and Joan Maple, other recurring characters include their children, their friends, and their lovers. The book also describes life among well-heeled suburbanites.The time period takes us through the fifties and into the sixties and seventies. Important recurring motifs and imagery include the Maples' homes and the journey. (See the chapter on *Too Far to Go*.)

————. *Trust Me: Short Stories*. New York: Knopf, 1987.

The first half of the book is well unified by the themes of trust and betrayal. After this point, however, some stories (such as "One More Interview" and "The Ideal Village") deal with entirely different topics.

Walker, Alice. *In Love and Trouble: Stories of Black Women*. New York: Harcourt, 1973.

The stories describe black women's attempts to maintain dignity in spite of the injustices they face. In one, an old woman is thrown out of a white church; in another, a young woman is publicly humiliated when she requests free food for her family. Frequently lovers and male figures of authority are abusive, denying the woman the love and respect she deserves. The book's unity breaks down in the last three stories.

Weaver, Gordon. *A World Quite Round: Two Stories and a Novella*. Baton Rouge: Louisiana State UP, 1986.

The three stories are about the relationship between art and reality. In the first, "Ah Art! Oh Life," a young boy is encouraged to believe that art (in this case, painting) makes life bearable and enables one to understand the past. Much of the story—especially the old artist's inability to paint at the end of the story— suggests that the worlds of art and reality have little effect on one another. The second story features an interpreter for the Chinese Voluntary Army who is so obsessed with language that he ignores the cruel results of his own words. The final story is linked to the second in various ways, including the part of Henry Pena's story that describes the freezing cold in Korea and the fighting with the Chinese. More important, however, the final story is the most extensive and self-conscious discussion of storytelling. It suggests that fiction can replace reality if stories are more compelling than the world around us. The title of the book is taken from Wallace Stevens's "The Man with the Blue Guitar."

Welty, Eudora. *The Golden Apples*. New York: Harcourt, 1949.

Recurring and developing characters provide much of the book's unity. The MacLain family appears more often than any other, but the Morrisons, Starks, and Raineys are important in a number of stories. The stories are arranged chronologically, covering a forty-year period from the early 1900s to the early 1940s. Most of the stories take place in a small Mississippi town named Morgana. As suggested by its title, some of the most important ideas in *The Golden Apples* are highlighted through Welty's use of W. B. Yeats's "The Song of the Wandering Aengus." (See chapter on *The Golden Apples*.)

West, Jessamyn. *The Friendly Persuasion*. New York: Harcourt, 1945.

———. *Except for Me and Thee: A Companion to The Friendly Persuasion*. New York: Harcourt, 1969.

Roughly arranged in chronological order, the stories are about the Birdwell family, each told from the point of view of a family member. They are unified by historical events, including the Civil War (the time frame is approximately 1845 to the early 1900s), the cohesiveness of the Birdwell family, the influence of the Quaker religion (especially its philosophy of nonviolence), the setting (Maple Grove nursery in Indiana), and the use of revealing incidents in most stories for character development or theme.

Wharton, Edith. *The Ghost Stories of Edith Wharton*. New York: Scribner's, 1973. (Originally pub. as *Tales of Men and Ghosts*, 1910)

All of the stories feature ghosts, which are frequently used to underscore the importance of "doubles" or alter egos. In several stories (such as "The Lady's Maid's Bell" or "The Eyes"), the concept of the double is centrally important. In others, the theme of the double is less significant, merely employed as a convention associated with the ghost story.

————. *Old New York. The Edith Wharton Omnibus*. New York: Scribner's, 1978. (The novellas were published separately in 1924 by Appleton.)

A cycle of four novellas about Old New York families: *False Dawn* (the 1840s), *The Old Maid* (1850s), *The Spark* (1860s), and *New Year's Day* (1870s). According to Adeline R. Tintner, each novella is "essentially two short stories linked by the passage of time with two incidents and two [retrospective] flashes, the second illuminating the first" ("The Narrative Structure of *Old New York*: Text and Pictures in Edith Wharton's Quartet of Linked Short Stories," *JNT* 17 [Winter 1987]: 77). The same first-person narrator is used in all of the stories except *The Old Maid*, and some characters and families appear in more than one novella.

Wilder, Thornton. *The Bridge of San Luis Rey*. New York: Boni, 1927.

The first and last stories function as a framing device, explaining the symbolic value of the bridge, what happens when it breaks apart, and the effect that the resulting deaths have on other people. The three stories in between are both independent and connected, delineating the lives of three of the people who have died. All of these characters' lives are connected, in part because each was involved with the actress Camila. More important, however, they were all extremely lonely and used language, literature, or theatre in their attempts to connect. Esteban and his brother, for example, created a language which they alone understood. Only through their deaths is their need for love communicated. The moral is stated explicitly by the Abbess in the final story: "There is a land of the living and a land of the dead and the bridge is love, the only survival, the only meaning" (235).

Windham, Donald. *Emblems of Conduct*. New York: Scribner's, 1963.

The stories are all first-person accounts of childhood and adolescence in Atlanta, Georgia. They generally proceed chronologically, the first eight or so focusing on the old family home and the protagonist's mother, aunt, and brother. The family home becomes a powerful symbol as it is described from story to story. The sources of the protagonist's security are defined, especially the sense of love he experiences with his mother's large family. Gradually the focus of the stories widens, and in the very last one he leaves home, against his family's wishes, to go to New York.

Wright, Richard. *Uncle Tom's Children*. New York: Harper, 1938. (The 1940 edition adds "The Ethics of Living Jim Crow" and "Bright and Morning Star.")

In the 1940 edition, "The Ethics of Living Jim Crow" appears to be a preface; it does not, however, function in this way, and its inclusion weakens the overall unity. The first three stories in the book ("Big Boy Leaves Home," "Down by the Riverside," and "Long Black Song") describe the responses of individual blacks to white oppression. The final two stories ("Fire and Cloud" and "Bright and Morning Star") suggest that blacks can achieve nothing by acting alone: racial injustice and cruelty can be combatted only by the unified effort of blacks and poor whites. In the first two stories nature appears hostile; in "Long Black Song" the black woman is in harmony with nature.

Index

Abcarian, Richard, 62 n.4, 63
Absalom, Absalom! (Faulkner), 108, 129, 130, 132
Ackerman, R. D., 131
The Actes and Monuments (Corrington), 193
Adair, William, 84
Adamowski, T. H., 126, 131
Adams, Richard P., 131 n.7, 131
Adams, Robert M., 39
Addison, Joseph, *The Spectator*, 4. *See also* Steele, Richard
Adicks, Richard, 34, 39
Adler, Renata, *Speedboat*, 187
Adultery and Other Choices (Dubus), 10, 63 n.9, 193–94
"Adventure" (Anderson, *Winesburg, Ohio*), 49, 71–72
Adventures of Sherlock Holmes (Doyle), 5
Aeschylus, *Oresteia*, 110, 115
"After the Race" (Joyce *Dubliners*), 25, 26, 29, 35, 36
Akin, Warren, IV, 131
All Creatures Great and Small (Herriot), 197
All Things Bright and Beautiful (Herriot), 197
All Things Wise and Wonderful (Herriot), 197

"Almost" (Faulkner, *Go Down, Moses*), 121
"Ambuscade" (Faulkner, *The Unvanquished*), 107, 108, 112
Amoretti (Spenser), 3
Anderson, Chester G., 39
Anderson, David D., 62 n.4, 63
Anderson, Jessica, *Stories from the Warm Zone and Sydney Stories*, x, 63 n.9, 187
Anderson, Sherwood, ix, xi, xv, 7, 11, 13, 71–72, 83 n.1, 116, 121, 133; *Death in the Woods*, 11, 187; "invents *Winesburg* form," 7; *Letters*, 20 n.12, 51, 63; *Letters to Bab: Sherwood Anderson to Marietta D. Finley 1916– 1933*, 63; *Marching Men*, 51; *Memoirs* (1942), 51, 64; *Memoirs: Critical Edition* (1969), 50, 51, 64, 121; *Men and Their Women*, 11; *Poor White*, 116; *Selected Letters*, 63; *Sherwood Anderson: The Writer at His Craft*, 64; *A Story Teller's Story*, 62 n.1, 64; *The Triumph of the Egg*, 62; *Windy McPherson's Son*, 51; *Winesburg, Ohio*, ix, x, xi, xii, 5, 7, 8, 9, 11, 14, 15, 20 nn.7, 9, 12, 21, 22, 41, 49–69, 71, 74, 75, 76, 83, 85, 94, 103, 106, 114, 116, 121, 149, 152, 176, 187, 188
And He Tells the Little Horse the Whole Story (Barthelme), x, xiv n.2, 189

Angels & Other Strangers: Family Christmas Stories (Paterson), 202–3

Appel, Alfred, Jr., 150 n.6, 151

"Araby" (Joyce, *Dubliners*), 17, 18, 25, 26, 28, 29, 31, 32, 33, 34, 36, 37, 39, 40, 41, 46, 47

Arcana, Judith, 64

Arnold, Marilyn, 151

Asals, Frederick, 159, 166 n.3, 167

Ashley, Jack Dillard, 167

Ashley, Robert, 133. *See also* Fant, Joseph L., III

As I Lay Dying (Faulkner), 129, 130

Asselineau, Roger, 64

Astrophel and Stella (Sidney), 3

Astro, Richard, 98, 104 n.2, 104

Atherton, James S., 31, 39

Atlas, Marilyn Judith, 54, 64

Atwan, Robert, x

Auchincloss, Louis, *Tales of Manhattan*, 188

"An Awakening" (Anderson, *Winesburg, Ohio*), 55

Babel, Issac, *Red Calvary*, 13, 188

Backman, Melvin, 84, 110, 115, 131–32

Baker, Carlos, 57, 64, 71, 72, 73, 81, 84 n.9, 84–85

Baker, James R., 27, 39 n.6, 40. *See also* Staley, Thomas F.

Baker, Sheridan, 84 nn.9, 11, 85

Baldwin, James, *Going to Meet the Man*, 10, 14, 188

Balzac, Honore de, 5

Banks, Russell, xv, 48, 171; *Searching for Survivors*, 14, 63 n.9, 188; *Success Stories*, 10, 14, 188–89; *Trailer Park*, 188

Barnes, Jane, 182

Barth, John, x; *Chimera*, 13, 189; *Lost in the Funhouse*, x, xiv, 13, 14, 189

Barthelme, Donald, *Sadness*, 189

Barthelme, Steve, *And He Tells the Little Horse the Whole Story*, x, xiv n.2, 189

The Basil and Josephine Stories (Fitzgerald), 9, 195

Bassett, John Earl, 132

"The Battler" (Hemingway, *In Our Time*), 73, 74, 75, 78, 79, 81, 82

Baudelaire, Charles, 192

"The Bear" (Faulkner, *Go Down, Moses*), 19, 121–22, 123, 124, 125, 126, 127, 128, 129, 130

Beattie, Ann, 16

Beauchamp, Gorman, 110, 115

Bech: A Book (Updike), 13, 17, 173, 206

Bech is Back (Updike), 13, 173, 206

Beck, Warren, 27, 40, 115, 122, 129, 132

Beckson, Karl, xiv n.2, 40

The Beggar Maid (or *Who Do You Think You Are?* Munro), 9, 201

Behn, Aphra, *The Rover*, 4

Beja, Morris, 39 n.8, 40

Benert, Annette, 131 n.7, 132

Benson, Jackson J., 81, 85, 94–95, 104 nn.2, 4, 104

Benstock, Bernard, 34, 40

Berland, Alwyn, 56, 64

Beyond the Pleasure Principle (Freud), 86

The Bible, 3

Bidwell, Bruce, 39 nn.6, 7, 40. *See also* Heffer, Linda

"The Big Two-Hearted River" (Hemingway, *In Our Time*), 38, 72, 75, 76, 78, 79, 80, 81, 82, 114

Bildungsroman, 8–9, 10, 71, 109

Birney, Earle, 115

Black Venus (or *Saints and Strangers*, Carter), 11–12, 13, 192

Blackwell, Louise, 151

Blasingham, Mary V., 167

Bleikasten, André, 167

Bloodline (Gaines), 195

The Bloody Chamber (Carter), 11–12, 191

Blos, Peter, 67

Blotner, Joseph L., 107, 110, 114 n.3, 115, 116–17, 122, 123, 124, 130–31 n.2, 132, 134. *See also* Gwynn, Frederick L.

"The Boarding House" (Joyce, *Dubliners*), 15, 26, 27, 28, 29, 30, 32, 36, 43

Boccaccio, *The Decameron*, 2, 3, 21
"The Book of the Grotesque" (Ander-
son, *Winesburg, Ohio*), 52, 56, 57,
61, 62 n.5, 65–66, 67, 69
Borden, Lizzie, 192
The Borough (Crabbe), 4
Bort, Barry D., 62 n.4, 64
Boutelle, Ann Edwards, 85
Bowen, Zack, 40. *See also* Carens,
James F.
Boyle, Kay, 115; *The Smoking Mountain*,
13, 189
Boyle, Robert, 29, 40
Bradbury, Ray: *Dandelion Wine*, 190;
The Martian Chronicles, 189–90; *The
October Country*, 190
Bradford, Melvin E., 132
Brandabur, Edward, 35–36, 39 n.10, 40
Breaden, Dale G., 131 n.7, 132
Bredahl, A. Carl, 64, 85
Breman, Brian A., 40
Brenner, Gerry, 89. *See also* Rovit, Earl
Bresnahan, Roger J., 64
The Bridge of San Luis Rey (Wilder), 7,
20 n.13, 208
Brittain, Joan T., 168. *See also* Driskell,
Leon
Brivic, Sheldon, 40
Brogunier, Joseph, 132
Brooks, Cleanth, 111, 115, 132
Brown (Steinbeck), Carol, 104 n.2
Brown, Homer Obed, 37, 38, 39 n.6, 40
Brown, Joyce D. C., 101, 104
Brown, Terence, 40
Browning, Chris, 64
Browning, Preston, Jr., 167
Browning, Robert, *The Ring and the
Book*, 4
Brugaletta, John J., 40. *See also* Hayden,
Mary H.
Bryant, J. A., Jr., 151
Brylowski, Walter, 115
Bunge, Nancy, 62 n.3, 64
Bungert, Hans, 116
Bunyan, John, *The Pilgrim's Progress*,
86
Burbank, Rex J., 58, 64
Burch, Beth, 116

Burgess, Anthony, 40, 85
Burhans, Clinton S., Jr., 77–78, 85
Burke, John J., Jr., 167
Burke, Kenneth, 39 n.10, 41
Burns, Dan G., 167
Burns, Marian, 158, 167
Burns, Stuart L., 155, 157–58, 164, 167
Busch, Frederick: *Domestic Particulars:
A Family Chronicle*, 9, 14, 190;
Rounds, 190
Butor, Michel, 132
By the North Gate (Oates), 201
Byrne, Mary Ellen, 116

Caldwell, Erskine, *Georgia Boy*, 14, 190
Calvino, Italo: *The Castle of Crossed
Destinies*, 13, 63 n.9, 191; *Cosmicom-
ics*, 190–91; *i zero*, 191; *Marcovaldo,
or the Seasons in the City*, 190; *Mr.
Palomar*, 15, 63 n.9, 191
Camati, Anna Stegh, 85
Camus, Albert, 13; *Exile and the King-
dom*, 20 n.13, 191
Cane (Toomer), 7, 17, 62, 63 n.10, 206
Canfield, J. Douglas, 131 n.7, 132
Canterbury Tales (Chaucer), 2, 21
Carabine, Keith, xiv n.1, 5, 7, 21, 62
n.4, 63 n.6, 64–65, 77, 84 n.10, 85
Carens, James F., xiv n.2, 40, 41. *See
also* Bowen, Zack
Carpenter, Frederic L., 104 n.5, 104
Carrier, Warren, 28, 41
Carson, Franklin D., 145, 150 n.6, 151
Carter, Angela: *Black Venus* (or *Saints
and Strangers*), 11–12, 13, 192; *The
Bloody Chamber*, 11–12, 191
Cash, Jean W., 168
Casper, Leonard, 168
The Castle of Crossed Destinies (Cal-
vino), 13, 63 n.9, 191
*Catalog of the Ernest Hemingway Collec-
tion at the John F. Kennedy Library*,
73, 84 n.7, 85
Cather, Willa, *The Troll Garden*, 7, 192
"Cat in the Rain" (Hemingway, *In Our
Time*), 75, 80
Cerf, Bennett, 108
Cervantes, Miguel de, 21

Cézanne, Paul, 87

Chakovsky, Sergei, 132

Chamber Music (Joyce), 26, 43

Chambers, Ross, 41

Chase, Cleveland B., 65

Chatman, Seymour, *Story and Discourse*, 62 n.1

Chaucer, Geoffrey, *Canterbury Tales*, 2, 21

Cheever, John, 16

Cherulescu, Rodica, 104

Chestnutt, Margaret, 41

Chimera (Barth), 13, 189

"Christmas Eve" (Joyce, *Dubliners*), 26. *See also* "Clay"

Church, Margaret, 41

Ciancio, Ralph, 56, 59, 63 n.6, 65

Cibber, Colley, *Love's Last Shift*, 4

Cixous, Hélène, 41

Claridge, Laura P., 132

Clark, Beverly Lyon, 168. *See also* Friedman, Melvin J.

"Clay" (Joyce, *Dubliners*), 11, 15, 25, 26, 29, 30, 32, 35, 36, 45, 48, 49. *See also* "Christmas Eve"

Cleman, John L., 132

Clements, Robert J., 2, 19 nn.2, 4, 21. *See also* Gibaldi, Joseph

Cohn, Alan M., 46. *See also* Epstein, Edmund L.; Peterson, Richard F.

Coleridge, Samuel Taylor, 1

Collected Stories (Faulkner), 20 n.17, 137

Collected Stories (Porter), 203

Collins, Ben L., 41

Collins, Carvel, 115

Come to Africa and Save Your Marriage (Thomas), x, xiv n.2, 205–6

"The Comforts of Home" (O'Connor, *Everything That Rises Must Converge*), 156–57, 158, 159, 160, 162, 163, 164

Coming to Terms with the Short Story (Lohafer), 17, 21 n.2, 22

The Company She Keeps (McCarthy), 200

"Composite personality," xii, 10, 71, 74–75, 80–81

Connell, Evan S., Jr.: *Mr. Bridge*, 192; *Mrs. Bridge*, 14, 192

Connolly, Thomas E., 41

The Conquest of Granada (Dryden), 4

Conversations with Eudora Welty (Welty), 141, 144, 149, 150 n.8, 153

Cooke, M. G., 41

Cooper, Stephen, 85

Coover, Robert, x; *A Night at the Movies*, 13, 192

Cope, Jackson I., 28, 41

Corcoran, Neil, 151

Corrick, James A., III, 132

Corrington, John William, 41; *The Actes and Monuments*, 193

Cosmicomics (Calvino), 190–91

Cothran, Dianne Allbritton, 151

Coulthard, A. R., 168

"Counterparts" (Joyce, *Dubliners*), 26, 29, 30, 32, 33, 36, 47

The Country of the Pointed Firs (Jewett), 7, 198

Cowley, Malcolm, ix-x, xiv, 8, 65, 85, 115, 132

Cowper, William, *The Task*, 4

Crabbe, George, *The Borough*, 4

Crane, Stephen, 7; *The Little Regiment and Other Episodes of the American Civil War*, 193; *Whilomville Stories*, 7, 193

Creighton, Joanne V., x, xi, xiv n.1, xiv, 10, 21, 22, 34, 39 n.6, 41, 111, 112, 114 n.3, 116, 132–33; *William Faulkner's Craft of Revision*, x, xiv, 21, 111, 116, 133

Cronin, Edward J., 31, 41

"Cross-Country Snow" (Hemingway, *In Our Time*), 72, 75, 78, 79, 80

"Cross Roads" (Hemingway), 83 n.3

Curley, Daniel, 150 n.6, 151. *See also* Demmin, Julia L.

Curry, Martha Mulroy, x, xiv, 41, 62 n.1, 65

The Cyberaid: Fables for the Cybernetic Age (Lem), 199

Cyclic literature, early history of, 2–7

Dabney, Lewis M., 133

Daiches, David, 39 n.10, 41

Dandelion Wine (Bradbury), 190

Daniel, Robert, 151

Dante, 44, 46; *Inferno*, 28

Das Hexameron von Rosenhain (Wieland), 19 n.4

Daudet, Alphonse, *Lettres de Mon Moulin*, 5

Davis, Joseph K., 39 n.6, 42

Davis, Thadious M., 133

Davis, William V., 36, 42

Dawson, William Forrest, 85

"The Dead" (Joyce, *Dubliners*), 19, 25, 26–27, 28, 29, 30, 31, 35, 36, 37, 38, 39 n.10, 40, 41, 42, 44, 45, 46, 47, 48, 49, 60, 114, 149

"Death" (Anderson, *Winesburg, Ohio*), 49, 50, 53, 55, 56

Death in the Woods (Anderson), 11, 187

De Beauvoir, Simone, *The Woman Destroyed*, 11, 193

The Decameron (Boccaccio), 2, 3, 21

De Chardin, Teilhard, 167, 168, 170, 171

DeFalco, Joseph, 10, 20 n.11, 75, 85

Delany, Paul, 42

Delia (Daniel), 3

"Delta Autumn" (Faulkner, *Go Down, Moses*), 121, 122, 123, 124, 125, 128, 129

Demmin, Julia L., 150 n.6, 151. *See also* Curley, Daniel

Denham, Robert D., 168

Denniston, Dorothy L., 133

"Departure" (Anderson, *Winesburg, Ohio*), 50, 54, 55, 60, 61, 68

Derounian, Kathryn, 73, 84 nn.4, 8, 85

Desmond, John F., 151, 168

Detweiler, Robert, 182

Devlin, Albert J., 133, 151

Dickerson, Mary Jane, 63 n.10, 65

Die schwarze Spinne (Gotthelf), 19 n.4

Die Serapionsbrüder (Hoffmann), 5

Dilworth, Thomas, 42

"Dissonant Symphony" (Steinbeck), 93, 94, 95, 104 n.4

Ditsky, John M., 104

"Divorcing: A Fragment" (Updike, *Too Far to Go*), 179

"The Doctor and the Doctor's Wife" (Hemingway, *In Our Time*), 17, 75, 80, 82

Doctor Martino (Faulkner), 137

Doctorow, E. L., *Lives of the Poets*, 13, 193

Domestic Particulars: A Family Chronicle (Busch), 9, 14, 190

Donaldson, Susan V., 133

Donnelly, Sheila Hurst, 133

Dorman-Smith, Captain, 77

Dos Passos, John, *U.S.A.*, 13, 193

Doyle, Sir Arthur Conan, *Adventures of Sherlock Holmes*, 5

Dream Children (Godwin), 20 n.13, 196

Driggers, Stephen G., 168

Drinnon, Richard, 79, 80, 86

Driskell, Leon, 168. *See also* Brittain, Joan T.

Dryden, John, *The Conquest of Granada*, 4

Dublin Diary (Joyce), 44

Dubliners (Joyce), ix, x, xi, xii, xiv n.2, 7, 10, 11, 15, 17, 18, 19, 21, 22, 25–48, 49, 60, 61, 65, 71–72, 76, 83, 83 n.1, 86, 88, 114, 116, 132–33, 149, 171, 181, 193, 198, 200; by character, 30–31; Christian imagery in, 34–35; composition and publication, 26–27; imagery in, 32–35; plot, 31–32; point of view in, 36–38; single external pattern in, 28–30; theme, 35–36; unity in, 27–38; works about, 39–48

Dubus, Andre, *Adultery and Other Choices*, 10, 63 n.9, 193–94

Duclos, Donald Philip, 116

Duffy, Edward, 42

Duffy, John J., 42

Dunleavy, Janet Egleson, 168

Dunn, Margaret M., 133

Dunn, Robert J., 168

Dupre, Roger, 86

Dussinger, Gloria R., 126, 133

Early, James, 122, 126, 133

Ebrecht, Ann, 168

The Education of H*y*m*a*n K*a*p*l*a*n (Rosten), 203–4

Eggenschwiler, David, 168
Egri, Peter, 86
Eliot, George, *Scenes from Clerical Life*, 4–5
The Elizabeth Stories (Huggan), 9, 197
Elkin, Stanley, *The Living End*, 194
Ellmann, Richard, 38 n.1, 39 n.10, 42
Emblems of Conduct (Windham), 9, 208
"An Encounter" (Joyce, *Dubliners*), 25, 26, 27, 28, 29, 30, 31, 32, 33, 36, 37, 41, 45, 47
"The End of Something" (Hemingway, *In Our Time*), 75
"The Enduring Chill" (O'Connor, *Everything That Rises Must Converge*), 156, 157, 158, 160, 161–62, 164–65
Engel, Monroe, 42
Enniss, Stephen C., 65
"L'Envoi" (Hemingway, *In Our Time*), 74, 78, 82
Epstein, Edmund L., 46. *See also* Cohn, Alan M.; Peterson, Richard F.
Erikson, Erik H., 67
"Eros Rampant" (Updike, *Too Far to Go*), 175, 177, 181, 182 n.1
Essays, Speeches and Public Letters (Faulkner), 116, 133
Etter, Kathryn, 151
Evanier, David, *The One-Star Jew*, 194
Evans, Elizabeth, 151
"Eveline" (Joyce, *Dubliners*), 15, 19, 25, 26, 28, 29, 32, 34, 35, 36, 49, 71–72
Evenings on a Farm near Dikanka (Gogol), 5
Everything That Rises Must Converge (Joyce), xi, xii, xv, 11, 14, 103, 155–71, 202; characters and their relationships in, 155–59; conflicts in, that lead to violence, 159–60; doubling in, 158–59; imagery in, 163–65; plot, 159–63; possibility of enlightenment in, 160–63; unity in, 155–66; works about, 167–71
"Everything That Rises Must Converge" (O'Connor, *Everything That Rises Must Converge*), 156, 157, 158, 159, 160, 161, 163, 165

Except for Me and Thee (West), 207
Exile and the Kingdom (Camus), 20 n.13, 191
The Exiles: And Other Stories (Quiroga), 203
The Eye of the Story: Selected Essays and Reviews (Welty), 153

Fairhall, James, 42
Falkner, Colonel William C., 116, 117, 119
Fant, Joseph L., III, 133. *See also* Ashley, Robert
Farewell to Folly (Greene), 3
Farnham, James F., 168
"Fathers and Sons" (Hemingway), 80
Faulkner, William, ix, xi, xv, 8, 13, 65, 91, 106, 119, 171; *Absalom, Absalom!* 108, 129, 130, 132; *As I Lay Dying*, 129, 130; *Collected Stories*, 20 n.17, 137; *Doctor Martino*, 137; *Essays, Speeches and Public Letters*, 116, 133; *Flags in the Dust*, 119; *Go Down, Moses*, x, xi, xii, xiv, 8, 10, 12, 14, 20 nn.14, 15, 21, 22, 27, 41, 76, 116, 117, 121–40, 181, 194; *The Hamlet*, 119, 133; *Knight's Gambit*, ix, xiv, 14, 194–95; *Selected Letters*, 20 n.15, 107–8, 116, 122, 123, 124, 131 n.3, 133; *The Snopes Trilogy*, xiv, 116, 119, 133; *The Sound and the Fury*, 129; *These 13*, 137; *The Unvanquished*, x, xi, xiv, 8, 9, 22, 31, 107–19, 121, 122, 123, 134, 137, 149, 194; *The Wild Palms*, 116, 134
Feeley, Kathleen, 166 n.5, 168
Feld, Bernard David, III, 151
Fenton, Charles A., 20 n.8, 77, 86
Ferguson, Suzanne, 42
Ferrell, Keith, 104
Ferres, John H., 62 n.2, 65
Fertig, Martin J., 65
Ficken, Carl, 86
Fielding, Henry: *Joseph Andrews*, 4; *Shamela*, 4
The Finer Grain (James), 7, 197–98
"The Fire and the Hearth" (Faulkner, *Go*

Down, Moses), 121, 122, 123, 124, 125, 126, 128, 129
Fischer, Therese, 42
Fisher, Richard E., 133–34
Fitzgerald, F. Scott, 7, 71; *The Basil and Josephine Stories*, 9, 195; *The Pat Hobby Stories*, 14, 195
Fitzgerald, Robert, 168
Flags in the Dust (Faulkner), 119
Flaubert, Gustave, 169
"Flight" (Updike, *Olinger Stories: A Selection*), 182 n.5
Flora, Joseph M., 86
Folks, Jeffrey J., 168
Fontenrose, Joseph, x, xiv, 96, 98, 100, 101, 104, 106
Ford, Daniel G., 134
Foster, Thomas C., 134
Fowler, Alastair, *Kinds of Literature: An Introduction to the Theory of Genres and Modes* and "The Life and Death of Literary Forms," 5–6, 7–8, 20 n.10, 21–22
Fox, Stephen D., 86
Framed stories or tales, 1–3, 5, 6–7, 8, 13, 51–52, 102, 204, 208
Frank, Waldo, 63 n.10, 65
Frazer, Sir James G., *The Golden Bough*, 86
Frazer, Winifred L., 116
French, Marilyn, 42
French, Warren, x, xiv, 97–98, 99, 104, 106
Freud, Sigmund, 40, 80; *The Interpretation of Dreams, Three Essays on the Theory of Sexuality*, and *Beyond the Pleasure Principle*, 86
Friedman, Alan, 21 n.21
Friedman, Alan Warren, 116, 134
Friedman, Melvin J., 168. *See also* Clark, Beverly Lyon; Lawson, Lewis A.
Friedrich, Gerhard, 34, 42
The Friendly Persuasion (West), 207
Fritz-Piggott, Jill, 151
Fuchs, Daniel, 86
Fuger, Wilhelm, 42

Fulkerson, Richard, 86
Fussell, Edwin, 54, 57–58, 63 n.6, 65

Gabler, Hans Walter, 38–39 n.1, 42
Gaines, Ernest, xv, 48, 171; *Bloodline*, 195; *A Gathering of Old Men*, 195
Gajdusek, Robert E., 42, 86
Gallant, Mavis, x; *Home Truths: Selected Canadian Stories*, 10, 20 n.13, 63 n.9, 195–96; *Overhead in a Balloon: Twelve Stories of Paris*, 16, 20 n.13, 196; *The Pegnitz Junction*, 13, 195
Gandolfo, Anita, xiv n.2, 42
Gardiner, John Rolfe, *Going on Like This*, 196
Garland, Hamlin, 7; *Main-Travelled Roads*, 7
Garrett, Peter, 27, 39 n.6, 42
Garrison, Joseph M., 43
Garson, Helen S., 168
Gass, William H., x; *In the Heart of the Heart of the Country*, 13, 196
Gautier, Theophile, 5
Geismar, Maxwell, 105
Gentry, Marshall Bruce, 168–69
Georgia Boy (Caldwell), 14, 190
"The Geranium" (O'Connor), 167 n.8
Gerogiannis, Nicholas, 73, 86
"Gesturing" (Updike, *Too Far to Go*), 174, 177, 178, 180
Getz, Lorine M., 166 n.5, 169
Ghiselin, Brewster, 28, 29–30, 31, 32, 33, 34, 39 nn.6, 10, 43
Gibaldi, Joseph, 2, 19 nn.2, 4, 21. *See also* Clements, Robert J.
Gibb, Robert, 86
Gifford, Don, 43
Gillespie, Gerald, x, xiv
Gillespie, Michael Patrick, 43
Givens, Seon, 43
"Giving Blood" (Updike, *Too Far to Go*), 175, 179, 180, 181 n.1
Gladstein, Mimi Reisel, 96, 105
"Go Down, Moses" (Faulkner, *Go Down, Moses*), 121, 123, 125, 126, 128, 129
Go Down, Moses (Faulkner), x, xi, xii, xiv, 8, 10, 12, 14, 20 nn.14, 15, 21,

22, 27, 41, 76, 116, 117, 121–40, 181, 194; characters, setting, and chronology, 124–25; composition and publication, 122–24; imagery in, 128–29; journey and hunting motifs, 121–22, 128–29; racial relations in, 122, 123, 125–26, 129; theme, myth, and point of view, 125–28; unity, 121–30; works about, 131–40

Gochberg, Donald, 63 n.7, 65

The Goddess and Other Women (Oates), 12, 201

"Godliness" (Anderson, *Winesburg, Ohio*), 49, 55, 61, 66, 67–68

Godwin, Gail, *Dream Children*, 20 n.13, 196

Goethe, Johann Wolfgang, *Unterhaltungen deutscher Ausgewanderten*, 19 n.4

Gogol, Nikolai, *Evenings on a Farm near Dikanka*, 5

Going on Like This (Gardiner), 196

Going to Meet the Man (Baldwin), 10, 14, 188

Gold, Herbert, 65

Goldberg, S. L., 43

The Golden Apples (Welty), xi, xii, 15, 19, 20 n.13, 38, 66, 76, 141–53, 176, 181, 207; characters in, 142–43; chronology and setting in, 143–45; imagery in, 148–49; theme and myth in, 141–42, 143, 145–48; unity in, 141–49; works about, 151–53

The Golden Bough (Frazer), 86

"Gold Is Not Always" (Faulkner, *Go Down, Moses*), 122

Goldman, Arnold, 43

Goldman, Morton, 107–8

A Good Man Is Hard to Find (O'Connor), 155, 202

Gordon, David, 79, 80, 86

Gordon, John, 43

Gorman, Herbert, 43

Gotthelf, Jeremias, *Die schwarze Spinne*, 19 n.4

"Grace" (Joyce, *Dubliners*), 25, 26, 29, 36

Gray, Paul Edward, 43

Grebstein, Sheldon, 39 n.5, 76, 86

Greene, Robert, *Farewell to Folly*, 3

"Greenleaf" (O'Connor, *Everything That Rises Must Converge*), 156, 158, 160, 161, 164, 165

Gregory, Horace, 65

Greiner, Donald J., 182

Gretlund, Jan Nordby, 171. *See also* Westarp, Karl-Heinz

Griffin, Peter, 86

Grimes, Larry E., 86

Grimshaw, James A., Jr., 169

Grimwood, Michael, 20 n.14, 122, 130–31 n.2, 134

Groseclose, Barbara S., 86

Gwynn, Frederick L., 107, 116–17, 134. *See also* Blotner, Joseph L.

Haas, Robert K., 122

Hagemann, E. R., 76, 84 nn.4, 9, 86–87

Halliday, E. M., 87

Halper, Nathan, 43

Hamilton, Alice, 182. *See also* Hamilton, Kenneth

Hamilton, Gary D., 131 n.7, 134

Hamilton, Kenneth, 182. *See also* Hamilton, Alice

The Hamlet (Faulkner), 119, 133

"Hands" (Anderson, *Winesburg, Ohio*), 11, 50, 51, 58, 64, 67

Hannum, Howard L., 87

Harbison, Sherrill, 117

Harris, Wendell V., 151

Harrison, James M., 87

Hart, Clive, 27, 43

Hart, John Raymond, xiv n.2, 43

Harter, Carol Clancey, 20 n.14, 131 n.7, 134

Hasbany, Richard, 83, 87

Hawkins, E. O., 117

Hawthorne, Nathaniel, 6, 7; "Legends of the Province House," 6; *Twice-Told Tales*, 6

Hayden, Mary H., 40. *See also* Brugaletta, John J.

Hayman, David, 34, 43

"The Heathen" (O'Connor), 158

Hedberg, Johannes, 43

Hedeen, Paul M., 87

Heffer, Linda, 39 nn.6, 7, 40. *See also* Bidwell, Bruce

Hemingway, Ernest, ix, xi, xv, 7, 106, 119, 139, 171; "Cross Roads," 83 n.3; *in our time* (1924), 73, 74, 77, 78, 82, 83 n.3, 84 nn.5, 6; *In Our Time*, ix, xi, xii, xiv, xv, 5, 7, 8, 10, 12, 16, 17, 20 nn.8, 11, 21, 22, 38, 42, 45, 64, 71–91, 103, 114, 121, 181, 196–97; *The Nick Adams Stories*, 87, 90; *Selected Letters*, 72–73, 74, 82, 84 n.6, 87; *Three Stories and Ten Poems*, xv, 74, 83 n.3, 84 nn.5, 6

Hendin, Josephine, 169

Hendricks, William, 48. *See also* West, Michael

Hendry, Irene, 43

Henke, Suzette A., 43–44. *See also* Unkeless, Elaine

Henry plays (Shakespeare), 3

"Here Come the Maples" (Updike, *Too Far to Go*), 180

A Hero of Our Time (Lermontov), xv, 5, 66

Herring, Phillip, xiii, 44

Herriot, James: *All Creatures Great and Small*, 197; *All Things Bright and Beautiful*, 197; *All Things Wise and Wonderful*, 197; *The Lord Made Them All*, 197

Higgins, Joanna, 39 n.10, 44

Hinkle, James, 117

Hinteregger, Gerald, 115 n.7, 117

Hoar, Victor, 117

Hochberg, Mark R., 134

Hodgart, Matthew, 44

Hoffman, A. C., 81, 87

Hoffman, Charles G., 81, 87

Hoffman, Daniel, 134

Hoffman, Frederick J., 65, 87, 117

Hoffmann, E. T. A., *Die Serapionsbrü-der*, 5

Holder, Alan, 117

Holladay, Sylvia A., 54, 62 n.4, 65

Holmes, Edward Morris, 111, 114 n.3, 117, 134

Homer: *Iliad*, 1; *Odyssey*, 1, 28–29

Home Truths: Selected Canadian Stories (Gallant), 10, 20 n.13, 63 n.9, 195–96

The House of Life (Rossetti), 4

Howard, Zelma Turner, 151

Howe, Irving, 55–56, 62 nn.4, 5, 65–66, 111, 117, 131 n.7, 134

Howell, Elmo, 117, 169

Huebsch, B. W., 50, 66

Huggan, Isabel, *The Elizabeth Stories*, 9, 197

Hughes, Langston: *Simple Speaks His Mind*, 197; *Simple Stakes a Claim*, 197; *Simple's Uncle Sam*, 197; *Simple Takes a Wife*, 197

Hughes, R. S., 105

Humma, John B., 39 n.10, 44

Humphries, Jefferson, 169

The Hunger Artist (Kafka), 198

The Hungry Ghosts: Seven Allusive Comedies (Oates), 201

Hunt, Anthony, 87

Hunter, Edwin R., 117, 134

Hyman, Stanley Edgar, 169

Idea (Orayton), 3

Idei, Yasuko, 134

Iliad (Homer), 1

In Constant Flight (Tallent), 205

"Indian Camp" (Hemingway, *In Our Time*), 72, 75, 76, 78, 79, 80, 84 n.5

Inferno (Dante), 28

Ingels, Beth, 94

Ingram, Forrest L., x, xi, xii, xiv n.1, xiv, xv, 8, 13, 18, 20 nn.18, 19, 21 n.22, 22, 39 n.6, 44, 52, 53, 58, 59, 60, 66, 87, 104, 108, 109, 110, 111, 114 n.2, 115 n.7, 117, 134, 156, 169, 191, 197, 198; *Representative Short Story Cycles of the Twentieth-Century: Studies in a Literary Genre*, x, xiv, xv, 22, 44, 66, 87, 104, 117, 134, 169, 191, 198

In Love and Trouble: Stories of Black Women (Walker), 207

in our time (Hemingway), 73, 74, 77, 78, 82, 83 n.3, 84 nn.5, 6

In Our Time (Hemingway), ix, xi, xii, xiv, xv, 5, 7, 8, 10, 12, 16, 17, 20

nn.8, 11, 21, 22, 38, 42, 45, 64, 71–
91, 103, 114, 121, 181, 196–97; composition and publication, 72–74; imagery in, 81–82; plot, 75–76; point of
view in, 80–81; protagonist of "composite personality" in, 71, 74–75, 80–
81; relation of story with vignette, 78–
80; reviewed, ix; setting and chronology, 76; theme, 77–78; unity in, 71–
84; *Winesburg* as pattern for, 7, 62,
71; works about, 84–91
The Interpretation of Dreams (Freud), 86
In the Heart of the Heart of the Country
(Gass), 13, 196
Irving, Washington, 6
Irwin, John T., 117
Isaacs, Neil D., 152
"Ivy Day in the Committee Room"
(Joyce, *Dubliners*), 25, 26, 28, 29, 36,
40
i zero (Calvino), 191

Jackson, Paul R., 87
Jain, Sunita, 105
James, Henry, *The Finer Grain*, 7, 197–
98
James, Stuart, 131 n.7, 134
Jedynak, Stanley L., 31, 44
Jenkins, Lee, 134
Jewett, Sarah Orne, *The Country of the
Pointed Firs*, 7, 198
Johnsen, William A., 44
Johnson, Edgar, 87
Johnson, Greg, 44
Johnston, Kenneth G., 87–88
Jones, David E., 39 n.1, 44
Jones, William M., 152
Jones, William Powell, 44
Joost, Nicholas, 88
Jordan, Richard D., 35, 44
Joseph Andrews (Fielding), 4
Joyce, James, ix, xi, xiv, 13, 19, 65, 72;
Chamber Music, 26, 43; *Dubliners*, ix,
x, xi, xii, xiv n.2, 7, 10, 11, 15, 17,
18, 19, 21, 22, 25–48, 49, 60, 61, 65,
71–72, 76, 83, 83 n.1, 86, 88, 114,
116, 132–33, 149, 171, 181, 193, 198,
200; *Letters*, 26, 27, 33, 39 n.2, 44; *A*

Portrait of the Artist as a Young Man,
40, 43, 48; *Stephen Hero*, 26, 47;
Ulysses, 28–29
Joyce, Stanislaus, 26; *Dublin Diary*, 44
"Judgement Day" (O'Connor, *Everything That Rises Must Converge*), 157,
158, 159, 160, 162, 163, 164, 165,
166 nn.1, 4, 5, 167 nn.6, 8
"June Recital" (Welty, *The Golden Apples*), 142, 143, 144, 145, 147, 148,
150 nn.1, 4
Jung, Carl G., 40; *Symbols of Transformation*, 86
The Jungle Books (Kipling), 17

Kafka, Franz, *The Hunger Artist* (*Ein
Hungerkunstler: Vier Geschichten*),
198
Kartiganer, Donald, 127–28, 131 n.7,
135
Keats, John, "Ode on a Grecian Urn,"
132, 135, 137, 138
Keen, William P., 35, 39 nn.6, 9, 44
Keller, Gottfried, xv, 66; *Das Sinnge-
dicht*, 19–20 n.4
Kennedy, Eileen, xiv n.2, 44
Kenner, Hugh, 39 n.10, 44
Kerr, Elizabeth M., 135, 152
Kessler, Edward, 169
Kiernan, Thomas, 104 nn.2, 4, 105
Killinger, John, 88
*Kinds of Literature: An Introduction to
the Theory of Genres and Modes*
(Fowler), 5–6, 7–8, 20 n.10, 21–22
King, Richard H., 135
Kinney, Arthur F., 20 n.14, 112, 117,
131 n.7, 135, 169
Kipling, Rudyard, *The Jungle Books*, 17
Klotman, Phyllis R., 197
Klotz, Marvin, 135
Knight's Gambit (Faulkner), ix, xiv, 14,
194–95
Knoll, Robert E., 117
Korenman, Joan S., 126, 135
Kreiswirth, Martin, 135
Kreyling, Michael, 152
Kronegger, Maria Elisabeth, 39 n.9, 45
Kruse, Horst H., 88

Künstlerroman, 9
Kuyk, Dirk, Jr., 135
Kyle, Frank B., 88

Lachtman, Howard, 34, 45
"The Lame Shall Enter First" (O'Connor, *Everything That Rises Must Converge*), 156–57, 159, 160, 162
Laroque, François, 45
Last Days (Oates), x, xiv n.2, 12, 63 n.9, 202
Latimer, Kathleen, 135
Laughlin, Rosemary M., 66
Lawrence, D. H., ix, xiv, 88
Lawson, Lewis A., 168. *See also* Friedman, Melvin J.
Lawson, Richard Alan, 135
Leahy, Sharon L., 135
Leatherwood, A. M., 45
Leaves of Grass (Whitman), 193
Lebowitz, Alan, 88
LeClair, Tom, 189
Lee, A. Robert, 88
Legacies (Potter), x, 20 n.13, 203
LeGuin, Ursula K., *Orsinian Tales*, 198–99
Leigh, David J., 78, 80, 88
Leigh, James, 45
Leiter, Louis H., 88
Lem, Stanislaw: *The Cyberiad: Fables for the Cybernetic Age*, 199; *A Perfect Vacuum*, 199; *Tales of Pirx the Pilot*, 199
Lemmon, Dallas Marion, Jr., xiv n.1, xv, 19–20 n.4, 60, 66
Le Morte D'Arthur (Malory), 2–3, 22
Lermontov, Mikhail, *A Hero of Our Time*, xv, 5, 66
Les Soirees de Medan (Zola), 20 n.18
Letters (Anderson), 20 n.12, 51, 63
Letters (Joyce), 26, 27, 33, 39 n.2, 44
Letters: The Habit of Being (O'Connor), 155, 166 n.7, 170
Letters de Mon Moulin (Daudet), 5
Levant, Howard, 105
Levi, Primo: *Moments of Reprieve*, 13, 199; *The Monkey's Wrench*, 13, 199; *The Periodic Table*, 13, 15, 199

Levin, Harry, 45
Levin, Richard, 28–29, 45. *See also* Shattuck, Charles
Levins, Lynn Gartrell, 128, 135
Lévi-Strauss, Claude, 127
Lewis, Robert W., Jr., 81, 88
"The Life and Death of Literary Forms" (Fowler), 5–6, 7–8, 20 n.10, 21–22
Limon, John, 135
Lindholdt, Paul J., 135
Lisca, Peter, 94, 97, 101, 105
"A Little Cloud" (Joyce, *Dubliners*), 15, 25, 26, 28, 29, 34, 35, 36, 46
The Little Regiment and Other Episodes of the American Civil War (Crane), 193
Litz, A. Walton, 27, 39 nn.3, 6, 45, 47, 131 n.5, 135. *See also* Scholes, Robert
Lives of Girls and Women (Munro), 9, 200
Lives of the Poets (Doctorow), 13, 193
The Living End (Elkin), 194
Lodge, David, 5
Logan, Jan H., 169
Lohafer, Susan, *Coming to Terms with the Short Story*, 17, 21 n.21, 22
Lohani, Shreedhar Prasad, 45, 88
London, Jack, *Tales of the Fish Patrol*, 199–200
"Loneliness" (Anderson, *Winesburg, Ohio*), 49, 68
Longley, John Lewis, Jr., 110, 115 n.7, 117, 135
The Long Valley (Steinbeck), 93
Loomis, C. C., Jr., 39 n.10, 45
Lorch, Thomas M., 53, 56, 62 n.4, 66, 169
The Lord Made Them All (Herriot), 197
Loss, Archie K., 45
Lost in the Funhouse (Barth), x, xiv, 13, 14, 189
Love, Glen Allen, 58, 63 n.6, 66
Love's Last Shift (Cibber), 4
Lowry, E. D., 81, 88
Lynn, Kenneth S., 88
Lyons, J. B., 45

McAleer, John J., 59, 63 n.6, 66
MacCabe, Colin, 45

McCarthy, Mary, *The Company She Keeps*, 200

McCarthy, Paul, 99, 105

McComas, Dix, 88

McDermott, John V., 169

McDonald, W. U., Jr., 152

McDonald, Walter R., 62 n.4, 66

McFarland, Dorothy Tuck, 169

McGee, Patrick, 135

McGuinnes, Arthur E., 45

McHaney, Thomas L., 117, 150 n.6, 152

MacKethan, Lucinda H., 152

Magalaner, Marvin, 34, 45

Magistrale, Tony, 169

Mahoney, John J., 59, 66

Maida, Patricia D., 169

Main-Travelled Roads (Garland), 7

Malamud, Bernard, x; *Pictures of Fidelman*, 15, 200

Malory, Sir Thomas, *Le Morte D'Arthur*, 2–3, 22

Manning, Carol S., 152

"Man of Ideas" (Anderson, *Winesburg, Ohio*), 68

Marching Men (Anderson), 51

"Marching Through Boston" (Updike, *Too Far to Go*), 175, 176, 180, 181, 182 n.1

Marcovaldo or the Seasons in the City (Calvino), 190

Marcus, Phillip L., xiv n.2, 45

Maresca, Carol J., 58, 66

Mark, Rebecca, 152

Marler, Robert F., 20 n.5

Marston, Jane, 169

The Martian Chronicles (Bradbury), 189–90

Martin, Augustine, 45

Martin, Carter W., 169–70

Martin, Jacky, 45–46

Martin, W. R., 197–98. *See also* Ober, Warren U.

Matthews, John T., 12, 20 n.14, 122, 130 n.1, 131 nn.7, 9, 135–36

Mawer, Randall R., 99, 105

May, John R., 166 n.5, 170

Meindl, Dieter, 46, 66, 88, 136

Mellard, James M., 66, 128, 136

Melville, Herman, 6, 7; *Piazza Tales*, 6

Memmott, Albert James, 110, 117

Memoirs (Anderson, 1942), 51, 64

Memoirs: Critical Edition (Anderson, 1969), 50, 51, 121, 164

Men and Their Women (Anderson), 11

Mérimée, Prosper, 5

Meriwether, James B., 114 nn.3, 4, 115 n.8, 117, 130, 136. *See also* Millgate, Michael

Messerli, Douglas, 152

Metamorphoses (Ovid), 2, 19 n.2

Meyers, Jeffrey, 72, 83 n.1, 88

Michener, James, *Tales of the South Pacific*, 13, 14, 200

Mickelsen, David, 136

A Midsummer Night's Dream (Shakespeare), 192

Millgate, Jane, 114 n.3, 117–18, 122, 128, 136

Millgate, Michael, 118, 129, 130, 136. *See also* Meriwether, James B.

Miner, Ward L., 118

Minter, David, 107, 118, 136

Modern Love (Meredith), 4

Momberger, Philip, 20 n.17

Moments of Reprieve (Levi), 13, 199

The Monkey's Wrench (Levi), 13, 199

Monteiro, George, 88

Montgomery, Constance Cappel, 84 n.9, 89

Montgomery, Judith, 46

Montgomery, Marion, 170

"Moon Lake" (Welty, *The Golden Apples*), 142, 144, 145, 147–49, 150 nn.4, 7

Moore, George, 42, 45, 48; *Untilled Field*, xiv n.2, 5, 7, 40, 41, 43, 44, 46, 200

Moore, Harry Thornton, 105

Moreland, Richard C., 152

Morris, Harry C., 150 n.6, 152

Morris, Wesley, 20 n.14, 127, 130, 131 n.7, 136

Morrissey, L. J., 37, 38, 46

Mortlock, Melanie, 97, 98, 105

"Mother" (Anderson, *Winesburg, Ohio*), 54

"A Mother" (Joyce, *Dubliners*), 26, 29, 33–34, 36, 43

Moynihan, William T., 27, 46

"Mr. and Mrs. Elliot" (Hemingway, *In Our Time*), 74, 78, 79

Mr. Bridge (Connell), 192

Mr. Palomar (Calvino), 15, 63 n.9, 191

Mrs. Bridge (Connell), 14, 192

Muller, Gerald H., 89

Muller, Gilbert H., 170

Munro, Alice: *The Beggar Maid* (or *Who Do You Think You Are?*), 9, 201; *Lives of Girls and Women*, 9, 200

Murphy, George D., 53, 66

Murphy, M. W., 33, 46

Museums and Women and Other Stories (Updike), 181, 182 nn.1, 6

"Music from Spain" (Welty, *The Golden Apples*), 142, 143, 144, 145, 147, 148, 149

The Music School (Updike), 182 n.1

Muste, John M., 136

My Name is Aram (Saroyan), 204

"My Old Man" (Hemingway, *In Our Time*), 75, 76, 78, 79, 84 nn.5, 6

Mystery and Manners (O'Connor), 161, 170

Nabokov, Vladimir, *Pnin*, 201

Nagel, James, 89

Nahal, Chaman, 39 n.5, 76, 89

Nakajima, Kenji, 89

Nakayama, Kiyoshi, 105

"Nakedness" (Updike, *Too Far to Go*), 174, 176

Napier, James J., 170

Neault, D. James, 152

The New Decameron (Zola), 20 n.18

The Nick Adams Stories (Hemingway), 87, 90

"Nick sat against the wall of the church" (Hemingway, *In Our Time*), 73, 84 n.8

A Night at the Movies (Coover), 13, 192

Nilon, Charles H., 136

Nilsen, Kenneth, 46

Noble, Donald R., 89

"Nobody Knows" (Anderson, *Winesburg, Ohio*), 55, 67

Nordanberg, Thomas, 118

Oates, Joyce Carol, x, 170; *By the North Gate*, 201; *The Goddess and Other Women*, 12, 201; *The Hungry Ghosts: Seven Allusive Comedies*, 201; *Last Days*, x, xiv n.2, 12, 63 n.9, 202; *The Poisoned Kiss and Other Stories from the Portuguese*, 13, 201; *Raven's Wing*, 202

Oates, Stephen B., 118, 136

Ober, Warren U., 197–98. *See also* Martin, W. R.

O'Brien, Edward J., 84 n.6

O'Brien, Matthew C., 118

O'Connor, Flannery, xi, xv, 48, 91, 106, 119, 139, 153; *Everything That Rises Must Converge*, xi, xii, xv, 11, 14, 103, 155–71, 202; "The Geranium," 167 n.8; *A Good Man Is Hard to Find*, 155, 202; "The Heathen," 158; *Letters: The Habit of Being*, 155, 166 n.1, 167 n.7, 170; *Mystery and Manners*, 161, 170; *The Presence of Grace and Other Book Reviews*, 170; *The Violent Bear It Away*, 155; *Wise Blood*, 155

O'Connor, Frank (Michael O'Donovan), 46

O'Connor, William Van, 126, 136

The October Country (Bradbury), 190

"The Odor of Verbena" (Faulkner, *The Unvanquished*), 108, 109, 113–14, 119, 121

Odyssey (Homer), 1, 28–29

Old New York (Wharton), 208

"The Old People" (Faulkner, *Go Down, Moses*), 121, 123, 125, 126, 127, 128–29

Oldsey, Bernard, 89

Olinger Stories (Updike), 10, 14, 173, 176, 182 n.5, 206

O'Neill, John, 66

The One–Star Jew (Evanier), 194

One Writer's Beginnings (Welty), 153

Ono, Kiyoyuki, 136

"On the Quai at Smyrna" (Hemingway, *In Our Time*), 74

Oresteia (Aeschylus), 110, 115

Organ, Dennis, 118

Orloff, Kossia, 136–37
Orsinian Tales (LeGuin), 198–99
Orvell, Miles, 170
Ostroff, Anthony, 32, 46
"Out of Season" (Hemingway, *In Our Time*), 73, 75, 78, 84 nn.5, 8
Overhead in a Balloon: Twelve Stories of Paris (Gallant), 16, 20 n.13, 196
Ovid, *Metamorphoses*, 2, 19 n.2
Owens, Louis, 105

"A Painful Case" (Joyce, *Dubliners*), 15, 25, 26, 28, 29, 34, 35, 36, 37, 41, 47, 48, 49
Pamela (Richardson), 4
Panchatantra, 2
"Pantaloon in Black" (Faulkner, *Go Down, Moses*), 121, 122, 123, 125, 126, 128, 129
"Paper Pills" (Anderson, *Winesburg, Ohio*), 54, 56
Papinchak, Robert Allan, 66
Parker, Alice, 89
"Parker's Back" (O'Connor, *Everything That Rises Must Converge*), 157, 158, 160, 162–63, 165, 166, 166 n.4, 167 n.7
Parrinder, Patrick, 46
Pascal, Richard, 137
Passions and Other Stories (Singer), 14
The Pastures of Heaven (Steinbeck), x, xi, xii, 11, 15, 17, 69, 93–106, 114, 149, 204; characters in, 95–96; chronology and plot, 96–97; composition and publication of, 94–95; imagery in, 101–2; irony in, 100–102; myth and religion in, 98–99, 100–101; point of view in, 100; theme, 97–100; unity in, 95–104; works about, 104–6
Paterson, Katherine, *Angels & Other Strangers: Family Christmas Stories*, 202–3
The Pat Hobby Stories (Fitzgerald), 14, 195
Pawlowski, Robert S., 66, 152
Peake, C. H., 31, 46
Pearsall, Robert Brainard, 89
Peavy, Charles D., 118

Pecora, Vincent P., 39 n.10, 46
The Pegnitz Junction (Gallant), 13, 195
Pei, Lowry, 152
Penner, Dick, 89
Penrod stories (Tarkington), 205
Peraile, Esteban and Lorenzo, 110, 118
A Perfect Vacuum (Lem), 199
The Periodic Table (Levi), 13, 15, 199
Permanent Errors (Price), 11, 63 n.9, 203
Peterson, Richard F., 46, 105. *See also* Cohn, Alan M.; Epstein, Edmund L.
Phillips, K. J., 137
Phillips, Robert L., Jr., 152
Phillips, William L., 50, 51, 66–67
"Philosopher" (Anderson, *Winesburg, Ohio*), 50, 69
Piazza Tales (Melville), 6
Picht, Douglas R., 62 n.4, 63 n.7, 67
Pickering, Samuel, 67
Pictures of Fidelman (Malamud), 15, 200
Pierce, Hazel, 190
Pigeon Feathers (Updike), 182 n.1
"Pigeon Feathers" (Updike, *Olinger Stories: A Selection*), 182 n.5
Pikoulis, John, 118, 137
The Pilgrim's Progress (Bunyan), 86
Pilkington, John, 114 n.3, 118, 137
Pitavy-Souques, Danièle, 150 n.6, 152–53
Pizer, Donald, 98, 104 n.6
Ploegstra, Henry Alden, 122, 137
"Plumbing" (Updike, *Too Far to Go*), 177–78, 181, 182 nn.1, 3, 6
Pnin (Nabokov), 201
Poe, Edgar Allan, 6, 7, 192; *Tales*, 6; *Tales of the Grotesque and Arabesque*, 6
Poems (Yeats), 150 n.2
"A Point of Law" (Faulkner, *Go Down, Moses*), 122
Poisoned Kiss and Other Stories from the Portugese (Oates), 13, 201
Polk, Noel, 153
Poor White (Anderson), 116
Porter, Katherine Anne, *Collected Stories*, 203

Portrait of the Artist as a Young Dog (Thomas), 205

A Portrait of the Artist as a Young Man (Joyce), 40, 43, 48

Potter, Nancy, *Legacies*, x, 20 n.13, 203

Powers, Lyall H., 118, 137

Prenshaw, Peggy Whitman, 153

The Presence of Grace and Other Book Reviews (O'Connor), 170

Price, Reynolds, *Permanent Errors*, 11, 63 n.9, 203

Princeton Encyclopedia of Poetry and Poetics, 19 n.1, 131 n.6

Propp, Vladimir, 48

Pryse, Marjorie, 118

Pugh, Elaine Upton, 147, 148, 149, 153

Pugh, Scott, 105

Pushkin, Alexander, *The Tales of Belkin*, 5

Quiroga, Horacio, *The Exiles: And Other Stories*, 203

Rabaté, Jean-Michel, 46

Ragan, David Paul, 137

Rahn, Walter, 105

"Raid" (Faulkner, *The Unvanquished*), 107, 108, 112, 115 n.8

Ramsey, William Currie, 112, 115 n.5, 118

Raven's Wing (Oates), 202

The Red Calvary (Babel), 13, 188

"The Red-Herring Theory" (Updike, *Too Far to Go*), 175

The Red Pony (Steinbeck), 9, 93, 204

Reed, Joseph W., Jr., 111, 118, 137

Reed, Pleasant Larus, III, xiv n.1, 6, 7, 20 n.6, 22, 46, 67, 82, 89, 118, 137

Reid, Ian, *The Short Story*, x, xv, 1, 5, 16, 20–21 n.20, 22

The Relapse (Vanbrugh), 4

Representative Short Story Cycles of the Twentieth-Century: Studies in a Literary Genre (Ingram), x, xiv, xv, 22, 44, 66, 87, 104, 117, 134, 169, 191, 198

"Retreat" (Faulkner, *The Unvanquished*), 107, 108, 112

Return of H*y*m*a*n K*a*p*l*a*n (Rosten), 203–4

"Revelation" (O'Connor, *Everything That Rises Must Converge*), 157, 159, 160, 162, 165, 166, 166 n.4

"The Revolutionist" (Hemingway, *In Our Time*), 16, 73, 74, 78, 79

Reynolds, Mary T., 28, 46

Reynolds, Michael S., 72, 83 n.3, 84 nn.4, 9, 89

Richards, Grant, 26, 27, 47

Richardson, Kenneth E., 126, 137

Richardson, Samuel, *Pamela*, 4

Ricketts, Edward F., 104 n.2, 104

Rideout, Walter B., 55, 58, 67

Rigsbee, Sally Adair, 67

The Ring and the Book (Browning), 4

"Riposte in Tertio" (Faulkner, *The Unvanquished*), 108, 113, 114, 114 n.1, 119

Riquelme, John Paul, 37–38, 47

Ristkok, Tuuli, 47

Roberts, George, 27

Roberts, John J., 89, 115 n.7, 119. *See also* Scott, R. Leon

Robinson, David W., 47

Rogers, Douglas G., 67

Rollyson, Carl E., Jr., 119, 137

Rosten, Leo: *The Education of H*y*m*a*n K*a*p*l*a*n*, 203–4; *Return of H*y*m*a*n K*a*p*l*a*n*, 203–4

Roth, Russell, 137

Rounds (Busch), 190

The Rover (Behn), 4

Rovit, Earl, 89. *See also* Brenner, Gerry

Rubin, Louis D., Jr., 153

Russell, George, 26

Ruzicka, William T., 119, 138

Ryan, Steven T., 170

Sadness (Barthelme), 189

The Salzburg Tales (Stead), 204

The Same Door (Updike), 182 n.1

Sams, Larry Marshall, 138

Sanderson, Stewart F., 89

San Juan, Epifanio, Jr., 47, 67

Saroyan, William, *My Name is Aram*, 204

Save Every Lamb (Stuart), 204–5

Scafella, Frank, 89

Scenes from Clerical Life (Eliot), 4–5

Scheherazade, *Thousand and One Nights*, 2

Schevill, James, 63 n.7, 67

Schleifer, Ronald, 138, 170

Schneider, Ulrich, 47

Scholes, Robert, 27, 34, 39 nn.2, 4, 47. *See also* Litz, A. Walton; Walzl, Florence

Schumann, Hildegard, 105

Scott, Bonnie Kime, 47

Scott, R. Leon, 115 n.7, 119. *See also* Roberts, John J.

Scouten, Kenneth, 170

Searching for Survivors (Banks), 14, 63 n.9, 188

The Seasons (Thomson), 4

Sederberg, Nancy B., 138, 170

Seed, David, 89–90

Selected Letters (Anderson), 63

Selected Letters (Faulkner), 20 n.15, 107–8, 116, 122, 123, 124, 131 n.3, 133

Selected Letters (Hemingway), 72–73, 74, 82, 84 n.6, 87

Selzer, John L., 138

Senn, Fritz, 31, 47

"Separating" (Updike, *Too Far to Go*), 175, 176, 177, 178

Shakespeare, William: *Henry* plays, 3; *A Midsummer Night's Dream*, 192. *See also* Sonnet cycles

Shamela (Fielding), 4

Shattuck, Charles, 28–29, 45. *See also* Levin, Richard

Shawver, Jurgen Michael, 67

Sherwood Anderson: The Writer at His Craft, 64

Shields, David, 47

Shields, John C., 170

Shilstone, Frederick W., 67

Shloss, Carol, 170

Short stories, first published in magazines, 5, 8, 26, 50, 83 n.3, 108, 111, 122, 123, 131 n.4, 137, 145, 173, 176, 182 n.2, 201

The Short Story (Reid), x, xv, 1, 5, 16, 20–21 n.20, 22

Short story cycles, 1–22; artist as protagonist, 13, 57, 200, 205; composite personality as protagonist, xii, 10; conventions, 14–19; development in twentieth century, 7–8; distinct from novel, x, xii, 8, 11; generic signals, 14–15; "integrated collection" defined, 22; interdependence of stories, 15–16; maturation of protagonist in, 8–10, 53, 58, 59, 71, 200, 201 (*see also Bildungsroman*; *Künstlerroman*); mythic patterns, 13, 98–99, 100–101, 109–10, 122, 127–28, 129, 141–42, 143, 145–48, 189, 191, 192; related forms before the twentieth century, 2–7 (*see also* Sonnet cycles); self-sufficiency of stories, 15, 16–18; "short story composite" defined, xv, 21, 22; "spectrum" of, xi; subgenres or types, 1–2, 8, 12–14; tension between parts, 12, 18–19, 61–62, 63 n.6; terminology, ix, x, 6, 17, 20 n.19; theme of isolation and fragmentation, 11–12, 56–58, 61, 187, 191, 196; unifying patterns, xii

"Shower of Gold" (Welty, *The Golden Apples*), 142, 143, 144, 150, 151 n.10

Shtogren, John Alexander, Jr., 90

Shurgot, Michael W., 47

Silverman, Raymond Joel, xiv n.1, 11, 22, 61, 67–68, 78, 81, 84 n.11, 90, 96, 97, 105–6

Simple Speaks His Mind (Hughes), 197

Simple Stakes a Claim (Hughes), 197

Simple's Uncle Sam (Hughes), 197

Simple Takes a Wife (Hughes), 197

"Simplicity" (Anderson, *Winesburg, Ohio*), 55

Singer, Issac Bashevis, *Passions and Other Stories*, 14

Das Sinngedicht (Keller), 19–20 n.4

"Sir Rabbit" (Welty, *The Golden Apples*), 142, 144–45

"The Sisters" (Joyce, *Dubliners*), 26,

28, 29, 30, 31, 34, 36, 37, 40, 41, 42, 44, 45, 46, 47, 48, 69
Skaggs, Merrill Maguire, 150 n.6, 153
Skei, Hans H., 138
"Skirmish at Sartoris" (Faulkner, *The Unvanquished*), 108, 113
Slabey, Robert M., 78–79, 90
Slatoff, Walter Jacob, 138
Smith, B. J., 90
Smith, Julian, 90
Smith, Meredith, 131 n.5, 138
Smith, Paul, 47, 73, 84 nn.4, 8, 90
Smith, Peter A., 90
The Smoking Mountain (Boyle), 13, 189
Snead, James A., 138
Snell, George, 106
Sniderman, Stephen Lee, xiv n.1, xv, 47, 62 n.4, 68, 90, 138, 195
The Snopes Trilogy (Faulkner), xiv, 116, 119, 133
"Snowing in Greenwich Village" (Updike, *Too Far to Go*), 173, 174, 176, 177, 180–81, 181 n.1, 183
Sojka, Gregory Stanley, 90
"Soldier's Home" (Hemingway, *In Our Time*), 10, 72, 75, 78
Somerville, Jane, 34, 47
"The Song of the Wandering Aengus" (Yeats), 145, 148, 207
Sonnet cycles, 3; *Amoretti* (Spenser), 3; *Astrophel and Stella* (Sidney), 3; *Delia* (Daniel), 3; *The House of Life* (D. G. Rossetti), 4; *Idea* (Drayton), 3; *Modern Love* (Meredith), 4; *Sonnets* (Shakespeare), 3; *Sonnets from the Portuguese* (E. B. Browning), 4
Sonnets (Shakespeare), 3
Sonnets from the Portuguese (Browning), 4
"Sophistication" (Anderson, *Winesburg, Ohio*), 50, 54, 55, 56, 60, 61, 68
The Sound and the Fury (Faulkner), 129
The Spectator (Addison), 4
The Spectator (Steele), 4
Speedboat (Adler), 187
A Sportsman's Sketches (or *Annals of a Sportsman*, Turgenev), 5, 7, 91

Staley, Thomas F., 27, 40, 47. *See also* Baker, James R.
Stead, Christina, *The Salzburg Tales*, 204
Steele, Richard, *The Spectator*, 4. *See also* Addison, Joseph
Stein, Gertrude, 83 n.1; *Three Lives*, 7, 20 n.13, 204
Stein, William Bysshe, 90
Steinbeck: A Life in Letters, 94, 104 n.4, 106
Steinbeck, John, x, xi, xiv, xv, 8, 13, 91, 119, 139, 171; "Dissonant Symphony," 93, 94, 95, 104 n.4; *The Long Valley*, 93; *The Pastures of Heaven*, x, xi, xii, 11, 15, 17, 69, 93–106, 114, 149, 204; *The Red Pony*, 9, 93, 204; *Steinbeck: A Life in Letters*, 94, 104 n.4, 106; *Tortilla Flat*, 93, 204
Steinke, Jim, 73, 90
Stephen Hero (Joyce), 26, 47
Stephens, Rosemary, 138
Stevens, Wallace, 15, 207
Stevick, Philip, 12, 18, 22
Stewart, J. I. M., 47
Stories from the Warm Zone and Sydney Stories (Anderson), x, 63 n.9, 187
Story and Discourse (Chatman), 62 n.1
A Story Teller's Story (Anderson), 62 n.1, 64
Stouck, David, 63 n.6, 68
"The Strength of God" (Anderson, *Winesburg, Ohio*), 55, 56
Stuart, Jesse, *Save Every Lamb*, 204–5
"Sublimating" (Updike, *Too Far to Go*), 174, 175, 178, 181, 182 n.1
Success Stories (Banks), 10, 14, 188–89
Sullivan, Walter, 170
Sultan, Stanley, 126, 138
Sundquist, Eric J., 138
Sutton, William A., 20 n.7, 51, 68
Symbols of Transformation (Jung), 86

Tales (Poe), 6
The Tales of Belkin (Pushkin), 5
Tales of Manhattan (Auchincloss), 188
Tales of Men and Ghosts (Wharton), 7, 207–8

Tales of Pirx the Pilot (Lem), 199
Tales of the Fish Patrol (London), 199–200
Tales of the Grotesque and Arabesque (Poe), 6
Tales of the South Pacific (Michener), 13, 14, 200
Tallent, Elizabeth: *In Constant Flight*, 205; *Time with Children*, x, 63 n.9, 205
"Tandy" (Anderson, *Winesburg, Ohio*), 64
Tangum, Marion Mast, 138
Tarkington, Booth, *Penrod* stories, 205
The Task (Cowper), 4
"The Taste of Metal" (Updike, *Too Far to Go*), 175, 181, 182 n.1
Tate, Allen, 39 n.10, 47
Taylor, Nancy Dew, 119
Taylor, Peter, *The Widows of Thornton*, 20 n.13, 205
Taylor, Walter F., Jr., 126, 138
Taylor, Welford Dunaway, 63 n.7, 68
"Teacher" (Anderson, *Winesburg, Ohio*), 55, 69
Tedford, Barbara Wilkie, 170
Theroux, Paul, 182
These 13 (Faulkner), 137
"The Thinker" (Anderson, *Winesburg, Ohio*), 53
Thomas, Dylan, *Portrait of the Artist as a Young Dog*, 205
Thomas, Maria, *Come to Africa and Save Your Marriage*, x, xiv n.2, 205–6
Thompson, Barbara, x
Thompson, Lawrance R., 138
Thomson, James, *The Seasons*, 4
Thorn, Eric P., 47
Thornton, Weldon, 139
Thousand and One Nights (Scheherazade), 2
"The Three-Day Blow" (Hemingway, *In Our Time*), 75, 80
Three Essays on the Theory of Sexuality (Freud), 86
Three Lives (Stein), 7, 20 n.13, 204
Three Stories and Ten Poems (Hemingway), xv, 74, 83 n.3, 84 nn.5, 6

Thurston, Jarvis A., 68
Tick, Stanley, 119, 139
Time With Children (Tallent), x, 63 n.9, 205
Timmerman, John H., 106
Tindall, William York, 29, 47
Tintner, Adeline R., 208
Tolomeo, Diane, 166 n.4, 170
Too Far to Go: The Maples Stories (Updike), xi, 11, 103, 173–83, 206; character and plot in, 174–76; chronology, 176; imagery in, 177–78; motifs in, 177–81; setting, 176; unity in, 173–81; works about, 182–83
Toolan, Michael, 139
Toomer, Jean, 7, 62, 63 n.10, 65; *Cane*, 7, 17, 62, 63 n.10, 206; uses *Winesburg* as model, 7, 62
Torchiana, Donald T., 31, 34, 39 n.10, 48
Tortilla Flat (Steinbeck), 93, 204
Townsend, Kim, 20 n.9, 63 n.10, 68
Trailer Park (Banks), 188
Trimmer, Joseph Francis, 115 n.5, 119
The Triumph of the Egg (Anderson), 62
The Troll Garden (Cather), 7, 192
Trust Me (Updike), 14, 20 n.16, 173, 206–7
Tuck, Dorothy, 119
Turgenev, Ivan, 7; *A Sportsman's Sketches* (or *Annals of a Sportsman*), 5, 7, 91
Twice Told Tales (Hawthorne), 6
"Twin Beds in Rome" (Updike, *Too Far to Go*), 174, 176, 179, 180, 182 n.1
"Two Gallants" (Joyce, *Dubliners*), 19, 25, 26, 27, 29, 32, 36, 40

Ulysses (Joyce), 28–29
Unkeless, Elaine, 43. *See also* Henke, Suzette
Uncle Tom's Children (Wright), 13, 208
Unterhaltungen deutscher Ausgewanderten (Goethe), 19 n.4
Untilled Field (Moore), xiv n.2, 5, 7, 40, 41, 43, 44, 46, 200
The Unvanquished (Faulkner), x, xi, xiv, 8, 9, 22, 31, 107–19, 121, 122, 123,

134, 137, 149, 194; characters, 108; composition and publication, 107–8; imagery in, 112–14; motifs and themes in, 110–11; mythology, comedy, and tragedy in, 109–10; point of view, 111–12; racial relations in, 110–11, 113; setting, time, and plot, 109; unity in, 108–14; works about, 115–19

Updike, John, x, xi; *Bech: A Book*, 13, 17, 173, 206; *Bech is Back*, 13, 173, 206; *Museums and Women and Other Stories*, 181, 182 nn.1, 6; *The Music School*, 182 n.1; *Olinger Stories*, 10, 14, 173, 176, 182 n.5, 206; *Pigeon Feathers*, 182 n.1; *The Same Door*, 182 n.1; *Too Far to Go: The Maples Stories*, xi, 11, 103, 173–83, 206; *Trust Me*, 14, 20 n.16, 173, 206–7

"Up in Michigan" (Hemingway, *In Our Time*), 73, 74, 84 n.5

U.S.A. (Dos Passos), 13, 193

Utley, Francis Lee, 139

Vanbrugh, Sir John, *The Relapse*, 4

Vande Kieft, Ruth, 146, 148, 150 n.6, 153, 171

Van Devender, George W., 119

Vashchenko, Alexandre, 139

"Vendée" (Faulkner, *The Unvanquished*), 108, 109, 112–13, 114

"A Very Short Story" (Hemingway, *In Our Time*), 16, 73, 74, 75, 78, 79

Vickery, Olga W., 119, 139

"A View of the Woods" (O'Connor, *Everything That Rises Must Converge*), 156, 157, 159, 160, 161, 163, 164, 165

Vinaver, Eugene, 3, 22

Vinson, Audrey L., 139

The Violent Bear It Away (O'Connor), 155

Voelker, Joseph C., 48

Volpe, Edmond L., 119, 126, 139

Waggoner, Hyatt H., 119, 139

Wagner, Linda Welshimer, 90, 139

"Waiting Up" (Updike, *Too Far to Go*), 179

Walcutt, Charles Child, 68

Waldhorn, Arthur, 90–91

Walker, Alice, *In Love and Trouble: Stories of Black Women*, 207

Walker, David, 139

Walker, William E., 119

Walsh, Ruth M., 34, 48

Walter, James, 131 n.7, 139

Walters, Dorothy, 171

Walzl, Florence, 28, 31, 34, 35, 36, 39 n.4, 47, 48. *See also* Scholes, Robert

"The Wanderers" (Welty, *The Golden Apples*), 19, 38, 142, 143, 144, 145, 146–47, 148, 149–50, 150 nn.4, 5, 7, 9, 151 n.10

"Was" (Faulkner, *Go Down, Moses*), 121, 122, 123, 124, 125, 126, 128, 129, 130

Watkins, Floyd C., 119, 126, 139

Watson, James G., 119, 139

Watt, F. W., 106

Watts, Emily Stipes, 91

"A Way You'll Never Be" (Hemingway), 80

Weaver, Gordon, *A World Quite Round*, 13, 15, 207

Weeks, Robert P., 91

Weinstein, Philip M., 139

Welty, Eudora, xi, 171; *Conversations with Eudora Welty*, 141, 144, 149, 150 n.8, 153; *The Eye of the Story: Selected Essays and Reviews*, 153; *The Golden Apples*, xi, xii, 15, 19, 20 n.13, 38, 66, 76, 141–53, 176, 181, 207; *One Writer's Beginnings*, 153

Weltz, Friedrich, 68, 91, 106

Werner, Craig Hansen, x, xv, 48, 171, 188

West, Jessamyn: *Except for Me and Thee*, 207; *The Friendly Persuasion*, 207

West, Michael, xiv n.2, 48. *See also* Hendricks, William

Westarp, Karl-Heinz, 166 n.1, 171. *See also* Gretlund, Jan Nordby

Westbrook, Max, 91

Westling, Louise, 153, 171

Wharton, Edith: *Old New York*, 208; *Tales of Men and Ghosts*, 7, 207–8
Wheeler, Otis B., 139
Whilomville Stories (Crane), 7, 193
White, Ray Lewis, 68–69
Whitlow, Roger, 91
Whitman, Walt, *Leaves of Grass*, 193
Whitt, Joseph, 91
"The Whole World Knows" (Welty, *The Golden Apples*), 142, 143, 144, 145, 147
The Widows of Thorton (Taylor), 20 n.13, 205
Wieland, Christoph Martin, *Das Hexameron von Rosenhain*, 19 n.4
"Wife-wooing" (Updike, *Too Far to Go*), 174, 175, 176, 181, 182 nn.1, 3
Wigginton, B. Eliot, 33, 48
Wight, Doris T., 39 n.6, 48
Wilder, Thornton, *The Bridge of San Luis Rey*, 7, 20 n.13, 208
The Wild Palms (Faulkner), 116, 134
Wilhelm, Albert E., 183
Wilkinson, Myler, 91
William Faulkner's Craft of Revision (Creighton), x, xiv, 21, 111, 116, 133
Williams, David, 119
Williams, Wirt, 91
Willis, Susan, 139
Wilson, Edmund, ix, xv, 73
Wilson, G. Jennifer, 115 n.7, 119
Wilson, Raymond, 69
Winchell, Mark Royden, 91
Windham, Donald, *Emblems of Conduct*, 9, 208
Windy McPherson's Son (Anderson), 51
Winesburg, Ohio (Anderson), ix, x, xi, xii, 5, 7, 8, 9, 11, 14, 15, 20 nn.7, 9, 12, 21, 22, 41, 49–69, 71, 74, 75, 76, 83, 85, 94, 103, 106, 114, 116, 121,
149, 152, 176, 187, 188; by chronology, 53; composition and publication of, 50–51; George Willard as protagonist of, 54–55; as Hemingway's pattern, 7, 62, 71; imagery in, 58–59; plot, 55–56; point of view, 59–60; prologue, 51–52; setting, 52–53; similar characters in, 53–54; theme, 56–58; unity in, 51–62; works about, 63–69
Winn, Harlan Harbour, III, xiv n.1, xv, 21 n.22, 91, 95, 100, 101–2, 106, 119, 139, 171
Wise Blood (O'Connor), 155
Wittenberg, Judith B., 114 n.3, 119, 139
Wood, Carl, 75, 81, 84 n.11, 91
Wood, Ralph C., 166 n.5, 171
Woodress, James, 192
A World Quite Round (Weaver), 13, 15, 207
Wray, Virginia Field, 171
Wright, David G., 48
Wright, Richard, *Uncle Tom's Children*, 13, 208

Yaeger, Patricia S., 153
Yancey, Anita V. R., 52, 57, 58–59, 62 n.4, 69, 100, 106
Yeats, William Butler, 15, 145, 148; *Poems*, 150 n.2; "The Song of the Wandering Aengus," 145, 148, 207
Young, Philip, 77, 79–80, 90, 91. *See also* Hemingway, Ernest, *The Nick Adams Stories*
"Your Lover Just Called" (Updike, *Too Far to Go*), 175, 179, 180–81, 182 n.1

Zender, Karl F., 140
Zlotnick, Joan, 69
Zola, Émile, *The New Decameron*, *Les Soirées de Medan*, 20 n.18

About the Author

SUSAN GARLAND MANN is Assistant Professor of English at Miami University of Ohio.